GENEALOGY OF NIHILISM

Nihilism is the logic of nothing as something, which claims that Nothing Is. Its unmaking of things, and its forming of formless things, strain the fundamental terms of existence: what it is to be, to know, to be known. But nihilism, the antithesis of God, is also like theology. Where nihilism creates nothingness, condenses it to substance, God also makes nothingness creative. Negotiating the borders of spirit and substance, theology can ask the questions of nihilism that other disciplines do not ask: Where is it? What is it made of? Why is it so destructive? How can it be made holy, or overcome?

Genealogy of Nihilism rereads Western history in the light of nihilistic logic, which pervades two millennia of Western thought and is coming to fruition in our present age in a virulently dangerous manner. From Parmenides to Alain Badiou, via Plotinus, Avicenna, Duns Scotus, Ockham, Descartes, Spinoza, Kant, Hegel, Heidegger, Sartre, Lacan, Deleuze and Derrida, a genealogy of nothingness can be witnessed in development, with devastating consequences for the way we live. As a dualistic logic, nihilism has come to ground existence not in life but in the absences beyond it. We who are, are no longer the living, but rather the living dead; in the death-wielding modern approach to knowledge, we are all reduced to cadavers.

The Trinitarian theology of *Genealogy of Nihilism* offers a counterargument that is sustained by nihilism even as it defeats it. In Christ's ontological synthesis of divine spirit and incarnation, and in the miraculous logic of the resurrection, theology reunites presence with absence, non-being with being. Seeing things in their actual complexity and incongruity, it allows for real difference. Conor Cunningham's elaborate and sophisticated theology, spanning the disciplines of philosophy, science and popular culture, permits us to see not simply how modernity has formulated its philosophies of nothing, but how these philosophies might be transfigured by the crucial difference theology makes, and so be reconcilable with life, and the living – with the very gift which being is.

Conor Cunningham is a doctor of theology and teacher of divinity at the University of Cambridge. His previous academic interests have included the study of Law, Social Science and Philosophy, and he was among the original contributors to *Radical Orthodoxy: A New Theology* (Routledge, 1999).

RADICAL ORTHODOXY SERIES
Edited by John Milbank, Catherine Pickstock
and Graham Ward

Radical orthodoxy combines a sophisticated understanding of contemporary thought, modern and postmodern, with a theological perspective that looks back to the origins of the Church. It is the most talked-about development in contemporary theology.

GENEALOGY OF NIHILISM

Philosophies of nothing and the difference of theology

Conor Cunningham

London and New York

First published 2002
by Routledge
11 New Fetter Lane, London EC4P 4EE

Simultaneously published in the USA and Canada
by Routledge
29 West 35th Street, New York, NY 10001

Routledge is an imprint of the Taylor & Francis Group

© 2002 Conor Cunningham

Typeset in Baskerville by
Rosemount Typing Services, Thornhill, Dumfriesshire
Printed and bound in Great Britain by
MPG Books Ltd, Bodmin

British Library Cataloguing in Publication Data
A catalogue record for this book is available
from the British Library

Library of Congress Cataloging in Publication Data
A catalogue record for this book has been requested

ISBN 0–415–27693–4 (hbk)
ISBN 0–415–27694–2 (pbk)

For my mother, Rachael,
who teaches me the logics of eternity

'It does not do to leave a live dragon out of your calculations, if you live near him.'

(Bilbo Baggins, from *The Hobbit*, as quoted by J. R. R. Tolkien)

CONTENTS

CONTENTS

ACKNOWLEDGEMENTS

The work presented here has been funded by the following: The British Academy; The Burney Fund (Faculty of Divinity); Rachael Cunningham; The Methodist Church – Belfast Central Mission; Martha McCormick; the estate of the late Revd Peter Good; E. O'Neill; Dr Robin Hutton; Louise Hutton (Snr); Graeme Paxton; M. Johnston; Murray Bell of 20:20 Architects.

I would also like to thank the following for the various ways in which each has contributed to my work: Phillip Blond; Anne Bottomley; Michael Devon; Dr Petà Dunstan (angel of the Divinity Faculty, whose messages were always lighter than they should have been); Dr Michael Hanby; Janet Hutton; Edwin Middleton-Weaver; Professor David McLellan; V. K. Millar; the Revd John Montag; Natasha Pearce; Professor Denys Turner; Dr James Williams; the Right Reverend Rowan Williams; and John Young.

Most of all I would like to thank: Crystal Cunningham; Sara Cunningham-Bell; Professor John Milbank; Dr Catherine Pickstock; the Revd Dr Michael Robson; and the Revd Professor Graham Ward. They have all given me the gift of their unfailing generosity and faith, intellectual and otherwise, and for that I am more than grateful.

PREFACE

This book does not seek to present a complete historical genealogy of nihilism, even though there is a loose chronology directing the progression of the chapters. What is rather offered is a genealogy which endeavours, first of all, to isolate certain crucial historical moments in the history of nihilism, moments which at time reveal clearly an intermittent development of prior influences. In the second place, I seek to isolate in all these moments a certain peculiar logic at work.

> What am I to do, what shall I do, what should I do, in my
> situation, how proceed? By *aporia* pure and simple.[1]
> (Samuel Beckett, *The Unnamable*)

There is, I suggest, an *aporia* involved in finitude. How do we know that to *think* is significant? Or rather, how do we know that *thought thinks*? It seems we require a 'thought of thinking'. However, if thought requires its own thought, then it can either be another thought or something other than thought. The former would initiate an infinite regress, for the supplementary thought would require its own thought, and so on, while the latter would ground thought in that which is not thought. But this means that all thinking would rest upon its own absence: thoughtlessness. This would, it seems, return us to the previous position. There, thought had presumed its own significance, which is not to think at all.

The aforementioned quandary can be seen throughout the history of philosophy. We pay witness to it in the dualisms employed to cope with this *aporia*. For example: Lacan and Deleuze ground sense in non-sense; Derrida grounds the Text in the Nothing, which is said to reside outside it; Heidegger grounds Being in *das Nicht*; Hegel, finitude in the infinite; Fichte, I in Non-I; Schopenhauer, representation in will; Kant, phenomenal in the noumenal; Spinoza, Nature in God, and God in Nature. The pervasiveness of such dualisms testifies to the importance of this *aporia*. What I suggest is that each of these philosophical dualisms rests within a monism that governs their generation. Part II argues that theology is able to avoid such dualisms and their concomitant hidden monisms, through a Trinitarian understanding of creation, which contends with the *aporia* of thought in a more beneficial manner. With regard to philosophy, it is suggested that despite the diversity already indicated, two basic 'traditions' are developed to deal with the *aporia*.

The first tradition is that which seeks to supplement thought only with another thought: *I think thought thinks*. This I equate with ontotheology. Ontotheology initiates an infinite regress; consequently, all its questions are asked by an answer: *the something*. (Plato addresses a similar problem in the *Meno*.) The second tradition is that which endeavours to contend with this *aporia* by supplementing thought with something other than thought. This I refer to as *meontotheology*. This is an appropriate name because it stems from what is termed *meontology*. *Meontology* is evident in the work of Plotinus when he places the One beyond being, which means that being is grounded in non-being (*meon*). When Deleuze grounds thought in what he calls 'nonthought' he appears to place his philosophy within a *meontotheological* legacy. The same goes for Heidegger when he speaks of Being by speaking of *das Nicht*. This tradition does not, therefore, evoke the notion of *the ultimate something* employed by ontotheology. Instead, *the ultimate nothing* governs its logic. In contrast to ontotheology, questions are not asked by one final answer: *the something*. Rather, there is but *one question* asked an infinity of times by *the nothing*. It is argued that both traditions are nihilistic. But I suggest that the first leads to nihilism, while the latter is the realised *logic* of nihilism.[2]

The Nothing as Something

Being is by nature what-is-not (*das Nichtseyende*).[3]
(F. Schelling)

[A]ll that exists lives only in the lack of being (*manque-à-être*).[4]
(Jacques Lacan)

It is possible to argue that the logic of nihilism is made manifest in the age-old metaphysical (ontotheological) question: *why something rather than nothing*? The logic of nihilism reads this question with a particular intonation. That is, why something? Why not nothing? Why can the nothing not do the job of the something? This leads me to define the logic of nihilism as a sundering of the something, rendering it nothing, and then having the nothing be after all *as* something.[5] Indeed, each of the philosophical dualisms involved above can embody this logic. For example, Spinoza, who is discussed in Part I, Chapter 3, has a dualism-within-monism of a single substance that is God or Nature. It is argued that this epitomises the logic of nihilism because each is never present except in the other: *God is made manifest in Nature, Nature manifests in God*. This allows Spinoza to have both in the absence of each. And this is to construe the nothing as something. Another example is that of Hegel, whose work is examined in Part I, Chapter 5. Hegel has a dualism within a monism of *Geist* that is both the finite in the infinite and the infinite in the finite. This is more easily understood if one uses the analogy of a *Gestalt* effect of aspect perception. Take the example of Jastrow's *duck-rabbit*.[6] One either sees the duck *or* the rabbit – never both at the same time. The mind oscillates between the two. But what must be remembered is that the appearance of two (God or Nature, duck or rabbit) disguises the *one* picture upon which they are made manifest. In this way there is only ever one, but this one picture is able to *provide* the appearance of two despite their actual alternating absences: nothing *as* something; the completely absent rabbit as duck, which is yet equally the completely absent duck as rabbit. Likewise, the finite or the infinite are but *Geist*, God and Nature are but *Substance*. Yet *Geist* only occurs as the insistent nothing of the infinite, which is also the insistent nothing of the finite; Substance only occurs as the insisting nothing of God, which is alternatively the insisting nothing of Nature.

An important word in this book is *provide*. 'Provide' etymologically stems from the word *videre*, meaning to see, and *pro*, meaning before. This word is employed in relation to nihilism so as to bring out the logic of the nothing *as* something. It performs this task because it can be made to suggest that nihilism 'provides' what it does not itself have – namely being. In this way for Spinoza, God 'provides' Nature and vice versa. This provision is referred to as the *provenance* of nihilism.

Nihilism, therefore, endeavours to have the nothing *as* something; it provides something out of nowhere. Such notions sound abstruse, and yet are characteristically exemplified in modern fields of learning. An example would be in the philosophy of mind, where an almost fanatical effort is made by some to reduce consciousness to nothing, at least nothing significant – yet still maintain that this pre-conscious essence of consciousness *provides* consciousness. Certain forms of evolutionary biology do the same in so far as they articulate the person purely in terms of genetic makeup, natural selection and so on. A notion such as the *genome* can act as a mechanism that allows phenomena to be reduced to their parts, while permitting the whole to remain as an epiphenomenon. Thus from one perspective the genome is an invisible abstract 'nothing', but from another the epiphenomenon of the biological body is itself the nothing; again we have two mutually exclusive aspects: genetic duck or actual rabbit. This is what one commentator calls the univocal Esperanto of the molecule.[7] Even the search for life elsewhere in the universe embodies the logic of the nothing *as* something. It does so because such efforts are, in some sense, guided by a wish to relativise life here: if we find life elsewhere life is no longer as significant. Cosmology often repeats such sentiments in a different form, because the pursuit to understand the beginning of life does in a sense eradicate that beginning; the before the universe is before 'before', just as we now have the living without life, and consciousness without consciousness. As one Nobel Prize-winning biologist puts it: 'Biologists no longer study life'[8] – which is another way of paraphrasing Michel Foucault's observation: 'Western man could constitute himself within his language . . . only in the opening created by his own elimination.'[9] Indeed, life has become a 'sovereign vanishing point' within every organism.[10] Are we not become, as Doyle says, '[A] meat puppet run by molecular machines'?[11] Is this what Blanchot means when he says that 'our suicides precede us'?[12] Discourses, such as Biology, appear now to be dealing with cadavers.[13] This is the nothing *as* something.

Part I traces a somewhat loose genealogy of the logic of nihilism as it has been defined above. Chapter 1 begins with Plotinus, for it is he who takes the One beyond being. It could be suggested that Plato is also guilty of this, but as Gadamer has pointed out: 'Plato's one is not at all a Neoplatonic *hen* (One).'[14] This is true because Plotinus' One is *epekeina noeseos*, which involves a 'double beyond';[15] the Plotinian One is beyond being (*ousia*) and also beyond thought (*noesis*).[16] By contrast, for Plato the Good is the unifying one of the many,[17] which grounds the Logos. Consequently, I place the 'beginning' of the genealogy developed below with him. It is Plotinus' *meontology* which spells the 'beginning' of the logic of nihilism. Yet this is true only when Plotinus' *meontology* is combined with the Neoplatonic understanding of causality, whereby *one comes from one*, and the element of causal necessity that this involves.

From Plotinus I turn to Avicenna, Henry of Ghent, Duns Scotus and William of Ockham, each of whom, it is argued, develops the logic of the nothing *as* something. What is important in this chapter is the introduction of the idea of a *univocity of non-being*. The univocity of non-being embodies the indifference being comes to display in relation to both God and actuality. That is to say, Avicenna develops the notion that metaphysics is about being, and that being prescinds from a consideration of both God and creatures, as it is indifferent to both. It is suggested that this notion, which is carried further by Ghent, Scotus and Ockham, is secretly a corollary of the Neoplatonist understanding of causality, its *meontology* and its necessitarianism. It is really because being, taken in mainly conceptual terms as univocal, does not concern itself more with existence than with nonexistence, that it does not concern itself more with God than with creatures, and is thereby unable truly to think their difference. Bearing in mind the *meontological* impulse which governs the birth of this logic, it seems fair – conceptually if not historically – to characterise this univocity as one of non-being rather than being.

Part I, Chapter 2 examines the notion of intuitive cognition as found in Scotus and Ockham, doing so in the hope of demonstrating the logic of the nothing *as* something at work in this Scotist–Ockhamist doctrine. Chapter 3 turns to the work of Spinoza, and substantiates the points made above in relation to Spinoza's monism. Chapter 4 discusses Kant, arguing that his philosophy embodies the logic of the nothing *as* something, in so far as each of the *Critiques* 'provides' something in the distinct absence of that which is purportedly given. For example, the first *Critique* endeavours to 'say' something about 'truth', in such a way that truth is made to apply only to a world of appearance. In a way, then, the 'nothing' that does not appear 'provides' appearances, which yet as only appearances are themselves 'nothing'. Chapter 5 examines the work of Hegel. Just as Kant causes everything to *disappear*, Hegel causes everything to *vanish* within a univocity of *Geist*, which has two alternating modes: the finite and the infinite. Chapter 6 discusses Heidegger's understanding of Being. Since Heidegger's Being rests on *das Nicht* it is argued that his philosophy falls within a Plotinian legacy. The last chapter of Part I offers an interpretation of Derrida, one that suggests that his philosophy combines both Plotinus and Spinoza. In so doing, he too develops the logic of the nothing *as* something, which he fails to deconstruct; Derrida has a dualism of Text and Nothing, which is akin to Spinoza's Nature and God, and this dualism likewise remains within a monism – now of *différance*, the new substance.

It is hoped that by the end of this section what will be apparent is the meontological (*meontotheological*) impulse involved in nihilism. For each thinker will, to some degree, have been shown to have a constitutive 'Nothing' that resides outside the 'Text' it enables. When Derrida comes to state that there is 'nothing outside the text', what may well seem now obvious is the 'traditional' nature of such a tactical pronouncement. Here are a number of examples. Plotinus has the One, as non-being, outside the 'Text' of *nous*; the same goes for Avicenna, whose essenceless God resides outside or before the generation of intelligence. Ghent, Scotus and Ockham develop and employ, to a greater or lesser extent, an intensional modality, one that places possibility outside the domain of the real, including God. Descartes, somewhat under the influence of Scotus' and Ockham's conception of divine omnipotence, constructs the 'Text' of the *cogito* by his 'method of doubt' which enables him to suspend (or bracket) existence. Spinoza has Substance reside outside the aspectual 'Text' of God or Nature, and it is this Substance which forces God to appear only in Nature, and Nature to appear only in God. Kant constructs the 'Text' of the phenomenal only by the no-thingness of the noumenal which lies beyond it. Hegel has the 'Text' of the finite by placing the infinite 'outside' it, to the degree that every finite manifestation is both enabled and negated by this infinitude. Husserl generates the 'Text' of the phenomenal only by bracketing (*epoché*) the question of existence; Heidegger has the 'Text' of Being only by invoking *das Nicht*; Deleuze has the 'Text' of sense only by having a non-sense outside it; both Sartre and Lacan have existence only within the lack of being. Levinas can only exist in a manner which is *otherwise* than being, which means that he too must have something constitutive outside the 'Text' of being; Badiou has the 'Text' of what he calls the event, by way of the *void* which resides outside it. Consequently, we can understand why Badiou asserts that man is 'sustained by non-being (*non-étant*)'.[18] From the above it seems fair to suggest that Derrida's position is not atypical: what Part II of this book will have to cope with is a possible riposte, one that argues that theology's doctrine of creation *ex nihilo* places it, too, within a similar predicament. Another important point is that the Plotinian notion of causality, in which only one comes from one, plagues most of the thinkers who appear below. For example, Derrida's nothing can only allow for *one* text; this univocity appears again and again throughout the following chapters.

Part II, Chapter 8 offers a preliminary critique of nihilism, one which is heuristically useful but less than conclusive. I then begin to develop an alternative logic ungovernable by the logic of alternating absence, and irrefutable by it. This is a theological logic. It takes the form of a discourse that articulates itself in terms of analogy, participation, the transcendentals, and divine ideas. Chapter 9 takes up many of the themes of Chapter 8 and seeks to deepen their validity. It examines what it means to have knowledge of something, arguing that knowledge relates to difference. Consequently, paradigmatic knowledge is God's knowledge of creation, as this knowledge knows difference to the extent that it is able to create difference, and other knowledge is only possible as an approximation to this: so as participation in divine and angelic knowledge and as anticipation of the *beatific vision*. Chapter 10 re-examines the logic of nihilism, arguing that its logic of nothing *as* something can be construed in a somewhat positive light, in so far as this logic can point to the idea of creation *ex nihilo*: nihilism's notion of creation *ex nihilo* is presented with particular reference to Deleuze and Badiou, and then to Sartre, Lacan and Žižek. In this way, there is a certain place for a *meontotheological* logic, which, however, cannot stand on its own, for on its own it too becomes monistic. It must be supplemented by 'theo-ontology' – yet the non-dominance of God by being retains a certain meontological moment; but this moment does not simply take us *beyond* being, rather, being is itself beyond.[19] In other words, being *qua* being *is* beyond. This is what Blondel called the 'beyond *of* thought'; not something beyond thought, but the beyond *of* thought, which being is.[20]

The 'discovery' that nihilism offers the possibility of a doctrine of creation should not wholly surprise us, for was it not Newman who spoke of the 'dispensation of Paganism'? Consequently, Paganism was an ore to be mined for the truth it contained. Indeed, this caused Newman to move away from an approach that was 'either/or', to one of 'both/and'. This is certainly to be encouraged. Yet it may be fair to suggest that Radical Orthodoxy deepens this principle. For it too calls us to move from 'either/or' to 'both/and'. Yet this move is somewhat radicalised, to the degree that it becomes an approach of 'both/and – either/or'. For is it not true, that if God is said to be anywhere, God is nowhere; but if God is somewhere, God is everywhere?

Notes

1 Beckett (1955), p. 291.
2 The word nihilism was first used by Jacobi; see Gillespie (1995), pp. 275–276, fn. 5.
3 Schelling (1997), p. 141.
4 Lacan (1992), p. 294. See Part II, Chapter 10 for a discussion of Lacan.
5 Although I did not derive my usage of this phrase from Schelling, he too speaks of the nothing *as* something. There is a similarity in meaning, in that the word 'as', in nothing as something, is meant to signify that the nothing is not actually something but is *as if it were*; see Schelling (1994), pp. 114–118.
6 See Jastrow (1900).
7 Doyle (1997), p. 42.
8 Jacob (1973), p. 306.
9 Foucault (1973), p. 197.
10 Foucault (1971), p. 277.
11 Doyle (1997), p. 36.
12 Blanchot (1986), p. 5.
13 For the idea that living beings are approached in modern discourse as if they were cadavers, see Part II, Chapters 8 and 10.
14 Gadamer (1986b), p. 137.
15 *Ibid.*, p. 28.
16 *Ibid.*
17 *Ibid.*
18 Badiou (2001), p. 14. For Badiou on the nature of the event see Badiou (1988).
19 On theo-ontology see Marion (1995) and Milbank and Pickstock (2001), p. 35.
20 *L'Action* (1936), pp. 308–309; quoted in Schmutz (1999), p. 182; italics mine.

Part I

PHILOSOPHIES OF NOTHING

It is fitting to say and to think this: that what is is. For it can be, whereas nothing cannot.

(Parmenides, Fragment Six)

The sophist runs off into the darkness of that which is not.
(Eleatic stranger, in Plato's *Sophist*)

One sticks one's finger into the soil to tell by the smell in what land one is. I stick my finger into existence – it smells of nothing.

(Kierkegaard, *Repetition*)

1

TOWARDS NOTHING

Plotinus, Avicenna, Ghent, Scotus and Ockham

This chapter examines some aspects of the work of Plotinus, Avicenna, Henry of Ghent, Duns Scotus and William of Ockham. My intention is to draw out the operation of the logic of nihilism. I do not for a moment argue that the thinkers discussed here are truly 'nihilists'. All that is being endeavoured here is to argue that there is an element in each of their work that does attempt to have nothing be *as* something.

Audacity: to be without being

> For both Plotinus and Heidegger, the Nothing is the impetus of our approach to what is most real in the world, although beyond essence and existence: the One, or Being. This is also an important point in Derrida's analysis.[1]
>
> (Eli Diamond)

In Hesiod's *Theogony* we are told the tale of a divine drama involving tolmatic patricide and mutilation, which is the very advent of the world. Ouranos, the highest god, fathers wild children whom he hates. Because of this hate, Ouranos buries these children in the bosom of the earth, where they lie like seeds. The earth sets out to free these children. She encourages Kronos, 'a most terrible child',[2] who is the first son, to attack his 'lecherous' father.[3] Kronos does so, castrating Ouranos in the process. In this way Kronos takes his father's place, and he in turn fathers sons with Rheia after forcing himself upon her.[4] These children are 'glorious', yet Kronos fears them for they might avenge Ouranos their grandfather. As a result Kronos swallows all the children, keeping them within himself. But Rheia hides one of these sons, who is called Zeus. Zeus is allowed to grow in strength and resolve, until the time when he attacks his father, binding Kronos with chains and emancipating his brothers.

Plotinus utilises this myth to explain the eternal procession of all from the One. For Plotinus Ouranos is the One, while Kronos is Intellect and

Zeus is Soul.[5] The myth encapsulates, in Plotinus' rather sanitised version, the movement of emanation, which arises *contra* the Gnostics by way of contemplation, and not discursive and agonistic activity. The One produces Kronos without need, but instead out of a plenitude which overflows. This mode of 'making' is external to the progenitor. When Kronos in turn gives birth to a 'beautiful progeny' he does so within himself, but for Plotinus this is not, as for Hesiod, a result of hate. For Kronos is said to love and adore his sons. Indeed, it is this love which causes Kronos to swallow them – thought remains inside the mind. But one 'stands apart': this is Zeus (Soul). And it is this standing forth which makes manifest the external world. Furthermore, this last child, who brings about the corporeal world, imitates his grandfather (Ouranos) since his generation is apparently external. For Plotinus the One would flow forever were it not for the castration carried out by Kronos. This castration restricts the flow of the One which in turn allows for the advent of the intelligible. It is this 'calling halt' that enables the dualism of subject–object, which is the basis of thought *per se*. If there was no cessation, then there would be no possible conceptualisation or *noesis*. But because this occurs within the belly of Kronos ('fullness'; Saturn) there would still fail to arise any visible world.[6] Plotinus has Zeus perform this task by 'standing forth' in the most audacious of manners. Yet here again there is no internecine strife. For Plotinus, Kronos hands over the governance of the world to Zeus in a most willing manner.[7] Nonetheless it will be argued that this myth epitomises the immanence involved in nihilism. For what proceeds from the One, which is beyond being and beyond preceding, must in a sense remain within its placeless providing.

Thus since Non-being is the father of all that *is*, there is a sense in which the *reditus* (to non-being) precedes the *exitus* (to being).[8] In other words, that which comes from the One 'follows' a (me)ontological return which ensures that its necessity does not infringe the simple, autarchical, supremacy of the One. This means that what emanates from the One, being, *is not*, in so far as to *be* is an inferior mode of *existence* compared to Non-being which is the only entity that really *is* (the really real). It is for this reason that Non-being can necessarily produce being without infringing simplicity, because to be is nothing. And as comparatively nothing, being does not actually escape the One, but remains immanent to it; being is in this sense an internal production. This is made possible by the protective negations which Plotinus employs at a methodological level throughout the *Enneads*.

To need: Nothing

The One *cannot* be alone (this is also the case with Avicenna's God, Henry of Ghent's, Duns Scotus', William of Ockham's, Suarez', Spinoza's, Kant's and Hegel's).[9] If this is true, how will Plotinus account for that which is 'produced' without reducing the status of the One? In other words, how can the One remain One? This ancient problematic here gives rise to certain philosophical moves which predispose the generation of the aforementioned nihilistic logic. Plotinus develops a *meontological* philosophy in which non-being is the highest principle. The One is beyond or *otherwise than being*.[10] This will, it is hoped, protect its simplicity. The consequence of such a move is a series of negations which will give rise to a fully immanentised realm, one that may accommodate the nihilistic logic of nothing *as* something.

We can identify at least four prophylactic negations. The first is that of 'tolmatic' language, which is to say, language that implies a fall from a state of grace: *to be is to be fallen*. Although Plotinus sets himself against the Gnostics on just this point he cannot, it seems, help but utilise their logic of creation as a fallen state. By so doing, he ensures that that which *is* becomes subordinate to that which is not, a consequence to be continually repeated. The second negation arises because in simply not being the One that which *is* is not: *to be is not to be*. So all that which emanates from the One is nothing, because it has being. The third negation is the 'negation of negation': the ineluctable return to the One. This return, as has been said, in a sense precedes every exit. The fourth negation concerns a series of repetitions of the original negation of the One itself. At some point each hypostasis imitates the One in its contemplative non-production of that which is.[11] Plotinus, *contra* the Gnostics, relies on contemplation to engender production. But the nature of this contemplation is, in a sense, non-production, since being consults nothing (the One) and repeats nothing in the innermost core of everything.

Thus that which proceeds from the One returns to the One – is always already returning. This desiring return is the contemplation of each emanation's nothingness. In this way the return precedes every departure, for every departure is but the 'embodiment' of a return. But this *provision* will be incomprehensible unless we remember Hesiod. For it was in recalling the *Theogony* that we learnt of Kronos giving birth to sons *within* himself. Now we have also learnt that it is characteristic of both the One and the Soul to produce externally. Yet I have argued that we can only understand the emanation from the One as that which, in a sense, takes place within its cavernous belly. How is this reconcilable with the idea of external generation?

The One's differentiation from all else cannot be spatial, for that would set something over and against it. So difference must, it seems, take place within and through the One: 'The One does not sever itself from it [all else], although it is not identical with it.'[12] (Hegel argues for a similar understanding in relation to the infinite and the finite.)[13] Plotinus is unable to posit an ontological difference: we see this to the degree that the One can produce only one effect, doing so necessarily. That is to say, the One re-produces itself in every emanation: the One is non-being and *being is not*. In this way the One produces nothing ontologically different from itself. For all difference, that is, being, fails to register a real distinction between itself and its cause. Why? Because any reality a being might be said to have would be its non-being, for only the One's non-being is truly real (or *really real*). Difference between the One and what falls beneath it is noticed only by an aspectual differentiation: like the aforementioned *Gestalt* effect of the *duck-rabbit*; but it must be remembered that both aspects manifest themselves on *one* picture.

Plotinus does hint strongly at the notion of a 'cavernous' – internal – *provision*, as he states that the universe is in the soul and that the soul is in the intelligible.[14] For each causes only one effect which must remain immanent to the cause as a result of causation's merely ontic logic. What is meant by this is that the One must look to an external logic, or rubric, which dictates and explains what difference is. In this way the One does not *create*, for the One cannot create difference, but must, instead, be protected from it. (It is argued in Part II that this is not the case for the Trinitarian God of Christian theology, for the Trinity creates difference from divine sameness.)[15] Furthermore, Plotinus asserts that the 'authentic [all] is contained within the nothing'.[16] Bréhier comments on this idea by speaking of the reabsorption of all into 'undifferentiated being'.[17] So too does Bouyer.[18] We know that for Plotinus the One is *otherwise than being*,[19] and that every addition is from non-being.[20] Indeed, we have only been as persons because of non-being.[21] This does suggest that the place of being is within the cavernous *belly* of non-being. Plotinus calls the world the soul's cave, and more pertinently he suggests that 'to depart does not consist in leaving in order to go elsewhere'.[22] It seems that the many which flows from the fecundity of the One does so only within the One. Indeed, as Gilson suggests, that which is *provided* 'loses itself in the darkness of some supreme non-being and of some supreme unintelligibility'.[23]

One: Audacity

Let us take a closer look at the idea of the One. We know that what is outside the One, in tolmatic terms, is by way of a certain audacity, a wish to be apart from all else: To 'desire to exist independently. It wearies of dwelling with another and withdraws into itself.'[24] These are, as Torchia points out, 'illegitimate acts of self assertion'.[25] This audacity is usually interpreted from the perspective of the One. But the positioning of the One as opposed to all else below is more ambiguous. The One (like Avicenna's God) cannot be alone. The One cannot be alone because that which proceeds from its plenitude does so necessarily. Furthermore, the One may well require that which emanates so that it can itself *be* the One. For Plotinus the One is self sufficient, yet this autarchical status may be achieved only by default. If there were no emanations there would be the nihilism of pure undifferentiated 'being' which may threaten the possibility of the One.[26] As Plotinus says, 'something besides unity (the One) there must be or all would be indiscernibly buried, shapeless within that unbroken whole'.[27] If there was only the One it might be unable to be the One, for we know for certain it must produce. But if the One requires company, that which accompanies it must be nothing because of this necessity, if simplicity is to be protected. In being nothing the One and the many are equivalent; this many is but the one that comes from the One. In this way the one that is produced is nothing. The One needs this one which is nothing. But in needing nothing it needs nothing but itself (for the One *is* non-being).

From this it may well be possible to consider the One as the first audacity. For the One endeavours to be apart from all else as the One. The One is this desire to be within itself and apart from all else. Furthermore, it is the desire to *be* without being. The One endeavours to be apart from all else but within the presence of a necessarily produced other from which it seeks to withdraw. If this is true, then the One may curiously be the idea of finitude: a finite immanent reality. The One is its unity, the *many* its difference (in the same way that Spinoza's God is the unity of Nature's many).

If the One is the first audacious unity, then we can think of this unity as the idea of a reality, a given, about and from which nihilism can speak. The One is, then, by way of a foundational circumscription that is definitive or absolute. As the finite leaves the One, standing apart from it, the One leaves the finite, standing apart from it. We must consider the One as the formation of the finite in an absolute sense. Finitude projects itself, becoming something it is not. What it becomes is indeed the finite, the idea of a stable place, fully present, *viz.*, immanent to itself. This finitude must be 'One' if it is to sustain its self-identity and so exclude appeals to a transcendent source.

To accomplish this, the 'finite' must become nothing, for only in becoming nothing will it avoid transcendence. If it is nothing, about what would transcendence speak? If finitude were something it would also be 'nothing' (as gift).[28] But in being nothing, being nothing in being at all,

7

it can speak itself utterly and completely. If this is the case, then the flight from the One is also the flight of the 'One'. The audacious standing apart of the finite from the One is the constitution of the finite as 'One'. We must remember that the Greeks used the term 'one' because they did not have a figure for zero.[29] Plotinus' One can be beneficially considered as zero.[30] For example, Plotinus argues that 'the One is not one of the units which make up the number two'; Avicenna will later follow this lead in saying that 'the smallest number is two'.[31] The One and the finite are both within the belly of the other, each generated by way of contemplative *provision*. The fall away from the One is a fall within the One. This fall is designed to recall that which is fallen before it falls. So it is always a fall within immanence.

If all that *is* comes by way of the One's non-being, then this One is possible only because of the world's 'non-being' (in this way the world, like Zeus, imitates the One). The One needs company, the world needs unicity. The nothingness of the world allows the Plotinian God to be accompanied, but to be accompanied by nothing, so protecting the supremacy and simplicity of this divinity. Likewise, the non-being of the One generates the world. There is a mutual constitution (*Deus sive natura*).[32]

There is, then, in Plotinus an inverted monism: what is other than the One is nothing, while the One is non-being. So there is in effect a univocity of non-being, one which is developed by Avicenna before being passed on to others.[33] It has been argued by a number of commentators that Plotinus is not monistic. For example, Gilson calls the accusation of monism an 'enormous mistake'.[34] But this is because Gilson fails to realise that what is other than the One, because of the nature of this alterity, cannot offer any ontological difference. The world slides towards the approaching God who is unable to be alone. Furthermore, the One can only produce one. In this way Plotinus' One remains very much within ontotheology's being. Plotinus replaces ontotheology's being (*the something*) with non-being (*the nothing*): different letters making the same word. This is his *meontotheology*, which is why we can agree with Cornelio Fabro when he asserts that the 'Neoplatonist idea of God . . . vanishes in the swamp of pantheistic monism'.[35] For monism is, it seems, the correct expression of pantheism. Likewise, Anton Pegis argues that 'God and the world so penetrate one another in the philosophy of Plotinus . . . that the famous flight of the One from being is the only way in which God can find freedom from the world'.[36] But in fleeing so, the world must inevitably follow. Indeed, it must be there waiting. For this return is its very beginning, its inception (*exitus*). In this sense, the pantheistic monism we can find in Plotinus is best thought of as a pan(a)theism. The *henological*, in this sense, leads to the *meontological*. It seems we are to have a god and a world within the foundational absence of both (dreams of which Spinoza is made).[37] The nothing *as* something has become everything.

The work of Plotinus is reconsidered in Part I, Chapter 7. The rest of this chapter will briefly trace similar Plotinian compulsions in the work of some other historical figures.

Avicenna needs nothing

Avicenna (*Ibn-Sina*) was directly influenced by Plotinus.[38] He took from the Neoplatonists the idea that being was equivalent to the intelligible (in this sense creating was thinking), and his emanation scheme closely echoes the Plotinian one. For Avicenna, as for Plotinus, from the One, in this case God, there could come only one effect (*ex unu simplici non fit nisi unum*).[39] This was thought to be necessary for the protection of divine simplicity. The one effect which did arise was that of the first intelligence. (For Avicenna this first intelligence was comparable to an archangel.) This first intelligence, in knowing God, created another intelligence. It was this duality that would allow the proliferation of subsequent intelligences (there are ten) and, indeed, of intelligence. The procession ceases at the level of the sensible as it is too impure to generate another heaven or intellect. The last of the intelligences was the 'Agent Intellect', or the *Dator Formarum* (*wahib al-suwar*). This Intellect emits all possible forms which are received by matter suitably disposed to receive it. For Avicenna, form is that which is created, not that whereby something is created. It is from this that the infamous accidentality of being (*wujud*) stems.[40] Nonetheless, the act of creation, or emanation, of the intelligence of the world is eternal and necessary. Contingency will not be ontologically recognised, it being but a matter of quiddity (*mahiyya*). The contingency we do witness is but the activity of matter.[41]

This emanation scheme is accompanied by an important historical dichotomy: '*tasawuur*' and '*tasdiq*'. These are *imaginatio* (*repraesentatio*, or *informatio*) and *credulitas*, respectively. The first is only predicative (what is it?), while the second is assertoric (is it?).[42] It is this division which both Gilson and Goichon argue engenders the Avicennian doctrine of being as an accident, for it is extrinsic to every essence.[43] We understand this notion better when we remember that for Avicenna there were three ways to consider an essence. The first was an essence considered in the mind. The second was an essence in a sensible thing. The third, and most controversial, was an essence considered in an absolute manner. That is, neither in a mind nor a thing but in itself. Furthermore, the essence, so considered, was allocated an appropriate, or proper, being (*esse proprium*).[44] As Owens says, 'The proper being is essential to it . . . something that of itself has being but not unity'.[45] Indeed, this being was given ascendancy in the world of Avicenna over being in reality, or even being in the mind.[46]

This third way of understanding an essence is easier to understand if we recall that for Avicenna an essence was possible through itself, considered in an absolute manner, but was necessary through another (*possibile a se necessarium ex alio*):[47] 'When we consider the essence of a thing itself quite apart from any condition, the thing itself is possible of itself' (Avicenna).[48] As Harm Goris says, 'Avicenna had claimed that the nonexistent about which we say something must at least have logical being in the mind.'[49] This logical being is the being of a possible essence. It is for this reason that Avicenna insists that *equinitas ergo in se est equinitas tantum.*[50] An essence comes before unity proffered by the mind or the sensible enracination. (Duns Scotus' common nature will operate like this.)

From this issues a certain univocity of being.[51] Back comments that Avicenna insists 'we have a particular non-sensible intuition of being'.[52] Avicenna articulates this idea through an allegory of the man born blindfolded who floats in the air yet still attains a knowledge of being.[53] Gilson argues that 'if the proper object of the intellect is being it must be able to comprehend it through a single act, and consequently to know it, in the same sense, whatever the species of being understood'.[54] This means, as Goichon says, that 'if the idea of being presents itself to the intellect before being separated in the idea of God or that of the idea of the creature, we shall surely find in the initial notion a certain irreducible content'.[55] As we will see below, existence has shifted from existentiality to an essential realm. For specificity resides only in the difference of the specific essence. This simply means that ontological difference is but a difference of essence; *this* essence rather than *that* essence. Gardet makes the point clearly, arguing that 'all [the] monistic postulates of *Ibn-sina's* thought converge beyond a certain metaphysical ontology towards univocity of being'.[56] This monism will be discussed below. For Avicenna it was the case that *ens prima impressione imprimitur in intellectu.* Consequently, being, not God, was to be considered the proper object of metaphysics. As a result commentators such as Jean Paulus find in Avicenna a precursor to Duns Scotus' univocity.[57]

The upshot of this univocity was a loss of the sensible realm. As creation emanates from the creator, being is only given to intelligence, to the extent that the creator does not give being directly to the sensible realm.[58] Indeed, as Goichon states, Avicenna is 'visibly embarrassed about passing from the intellectual relation with the thing known to the realization of the thing created'.[59] The problem is that God only knows things in so far as they are universal.[60] This causes Avicenna to insist that 'being has a relation with things in so far as they are intelligible, and not in so far as they exist in the concrete sense'.[61] For every possible essence to be known, and in this sense to-be, it must lose its particularity, its sensible embodiment and its contingency. (This is a consequence of Avicenna's Plotinian attitude to matter, which construes it as something negative, if not evil.) Each essence, as known, will be a deracinated, necessary, intelligible. This means that there cannot be modes of being, only a difference of essences and that these essences, which are forced to provide adequate ontological differentiation, are themselves *otherwise* than themselves. For these essences must become *necessary* in order to be at all. So the possible essence is only a possible essence in being necessary, and so is, in this sense, God. It is for this reason that Aquinas insisted that the *'conversio ad phantasmata'* is also a continual return to the sensible source. Goris makes the point that the 'expression *"conversio ad phantasmata"* is meant as a polemic contrast with Avicenna's (Neoplatonic) *"conversio animae ad principium in intellectum"'*.[62] Aquinas rejects Avicenna's approach as it seems to render the sensible unnecessary for actual understanding.[63] Because being is not given directly, nor necessarily, to the sensible, God only has a relation with the intelligent universal. Consequently, the sensible is somewhat superfluous. For this reason the world may only be by moving towards God to the point of absorption.

As Aquinas noted, Avicenna stated that everything except God had in itself a possibility for being and non-being.[64] The potential for non-being was prevalent to such an extent that every essence was said to have a positive orientation to non-being, or what Gardet called 'a non-postulation to being'.[65] For Avicenna, everything with a quiddity is caused.[66] It is for this reason that everything with the exception of the necessary Being has quiddity, and these quiddities are possible through themselves: 'To such quiddities being does not accrue except extrinsically'.[67] As a result, we can agree with Gilson that essences are measured by their lack of existence. Indeed, they are this lack of existence.[68] It is for this reason that God does not have an essence, but is instead pure existence (*Primus igitur non habet quidditatem*).[69] Every essence, it seems, presents us with a paradox. Let me elaborate. As an essence articulates itself it suffers dissolution, for there is a loss of the concrete, of particularity, existentiality and contingency. The positive orientation to non-being may be paradoxically its *'esse proprium'*. For each essence only *is*, it seems, in not being. This negation occurs at two levels. First of all, only God is being; consequently all essences are caused. In being caused we understand that they are nothing in themselves. Second, the intelligent expression of each essence is only had by its dissolving; every articulation is ontologically a disarticulation. Essences are possible in themselves to the degree that these possibles are 'God's data, given to, not by Him'.[70] In this sense, God gives each its to-be but not its to-be-able-to-be.[71] Yet an essence is nothing and its being cognised is its

11

undoing; the essence is only as it loses itself. Possibility becomes necessity (a necessity that seemed already to lie implicitly within that very 'self-given' possibility).

God: Without essence

We know that every essence (which is a nothing that is possible in itself, irrespective of God) is caused. God in not having an essence is uncaused, or is necessary. But this cause of Avicenna's begins to look more and more like that of Plotinus'. The essence is nothing in that it is only *'ab alio'*, or it is only by being another, *viz.*, God. Furthermore, it is nothing, in that its expression involves dissolution. This means that essence does not infringe divine simplicity. God, who has no essence, uses essences, essences which are nothing, to enable a world other than God. For the essentialised notion of being guarantees the *nothingness of being*, while God who necessarily causes essences ensures the *being of nothing*. Cronin says something similar: 'In the world of Avicenna an actualised essence or possibility is one to which it happens that it exists. But even as actual the possible *qua* possible is not. Just as *nothing happens* to the possible qua possible when it becomes singular or becomes universal, so *nothing happens to the possible when it happens to exist.*'[72] Avicenna's God causes nothing to be. This is the true meaning of being as an accident, or more accurately, being accidental.

For Avicenna it is understood that an essence is possible through itself while it is necessary through another. Yet if this is the case then it may be correct to argue that God is necessary through Himself but is possible through another. This becomes more tenable when we realise that the aforementioned univocity of being engenders a monism that renders the term God (and world) unstable. Avicenna states that 'God is called *Primus*; this term designates *only* the relation of his being to the universal'.[73] Consequently, there is no real creation apart from God in an absolutely ontological sense. As Zedler comments, God for Avicenna 'is first *only* in the sense that other beings must come after him'.[74] This may mean that the appellation 'First being' is but nominal, as nothing ontologically distinct comes after God. Goichon argues that Avicenna 'does not really escape the reproach of assuming, in this way, beings which are not truly distinct from the first being. The creation flows towards the same being which presents itself only with a difference of degree.'[75] This God cannot be separate from the world, as the essences which are the world are God's ideas stemming from his simplicity; therefore they are his possibilities and finally his own possibility. They are the only way God can create a being which does not offend simplicity. But because of this the nothingness of being (which essences are), and the being of nothingness (God's causation of essences), ineluctably link God and the world. Each slides towards the other as there is literally nothing to offer resistance. This is what Gardet calls Avicenna's 'impossibility'.[76] For Zedler this means that the 'world for all eternity dogs the footsteps of the Avicennian God; but more than that, it also tugs him in its direction'.[77] The possibility of the essences betrays their 'divinity', while the necessity of God illustrates the 'worldliness' of this (Neoplatonic) divinity. As with Plotinus each is the other, and both endeavour to make the something nothing and to make this nothing *as* something.

Henry of Ghent: the possibility of nothing

In Henry of Ghent we find a disciple of both Plotinus and Avicenna.[78] Indeed, Ghent's work can be characterised as an 'Avicennian attempt to salvage Neoplatonism', as Clarke puts it.[79] There are a number of important steps taken by Henry of Ghent that are essential to the shape of this story. The one that concerns us here is his treatment of divine ideas.[80] Henry was part of a group of scholastics who asserted that the divine ideas are relations of reason (*relationes rationis*) *vis à vis* the divine essence. In this way Ghent was similar to St Thomas Aquinas. (When Ockham comes to criticise those who advocate a *distinctio rationis* he selected Henry of Ghent as their representative.) For Ghent there are two moments or acts of knowing. The first is God's knowledge of his own essence; this knowledge is absolute and complete. The second act of knowing is God knowing what creatures are possible. But God in this moment also knows the possible being which creatures have in themselves. In this sense, God knows creatures both as identical to himself and as distinct from himself. As in the work of Aquinas, this possibility is articulated in terms of divine imitability: the creatures are so many ways that the divine essence can be imitated; in this their possibility lies. In actual fact this similarity with Aquinas is somewhat illusory, but this is only apparent when we consider subsequent moves made by Ghent.[81]

The most significant conceptual shift stems from the influence of Avicenna. Avicenna, as we know, had argued for a non-sensible intuition of being, and that this being was the proper object of metaphysics. Ghent incorporated this primacy. Indeed, his doctrine of analogy was constructed to cope with the Avicennian 'impression' of being (although 'being' is perhaps better characterised as *'res'*, as this was the highest transcendental for Ghent, as it had been for Avicenna).[82] Ghent realises that if being is prior to either God or creatures then being must be something common to both.[83] But this raises difficulties, as it appears to generate a *tertium quid*, one which may threaten the primacy of God in terms of truth and even ontology. To overcome any difficulties, Ghent produces a 'community of analogy'.[84] There is no real being apart from

God or creatures, yet being is a common concept under which both fall. And this common concept is not univocal but analogous, because the commonality actually stems from a cognitive lack. For the mind produces two concepts which are distinct. One of these is *privatively undetermined being*;[85] this notion of being *can* become determined. The other concept is *negatively undetermined being*; a negativity that is inherent and incurable, hence it is not merely privative. This means that the first concept of being is *undetermined* while the second is really *indeterminable*. The former applies to creatures, the latter to God. The commonality we witness at this level arises from a failure to distinguish these two concepts. So the commonality is a matter of *indistinct conception*. We prescind from determination, thus allowing the 'confusion' to remain. It is this confusion, or indistinct conception, that allows Ghent to develop an analogous concept of being.[86] Scotus will take this further, arguing for a univocal concept appropriate to both God and creature – although Jean Paulus questions whether Ghent's doctrine of analogy avoids univocity.[87]

The second and more relevant area of influence was Ghent's adoption of Avicenna's manner of conceiving essences absolutely. He does so in an effort to protect the objectivity of these essences; this is his Neoplatonic bias. Accordingly these essences are, *à la* Avicenna, allocated an *esse proprium,* which in the hands of Ghent becomes an *esse essentiae*. It is this move which will begin to alter radically the doctrine of divine ideas. To overcome the necessitarianism of Avicenna, Henry posits a realm of unactualised essences. By doing so the ineluctable realisation of a possible essence is removed; God freely chooses which of these essences is to be actualised. If an essence is actualised its *esse essentiae* becomes the being of existence (*esse existentiae*).[88] But this meant that Ghent had begun to separate the ideas from the divine essence. If they were different, then God, to be God, did not have to realise them. It also meant that these essences became more individual, as each distinct essence had its own distinct existence; this autonomy will be radicalised by Ockham. The possible essences, in possessing their own distinct existence and in being absolutely distinct, form part of an infinite pool of possibles.[89] They are without doubt formed by God's self-knowledge, but the nature of this self-knowledge has changed. For now self-knowledge conferred a new distinction upon the possible essences. The possibles are no longer the divine essence, but only what the divine essence knows as possible through its self-knowledge; the divine knowing does not know these possibles *as* the divine essence, because in being possible they are considered to have their own being, namely, the being of non-simple essences. For Aquinas, by contrast, the possible relations of imitability are identified with the divine essence, as essences do not have an *esse essentiae*.[90] Henry could not allow these essences to be exactly identified with the divine essence because he remained under the spell of

Avicenna.[91] If they were identified in this way they would become necessary. Separation was thereby the only road left open.[92]

Ghent divided the divine ideas into 'the essences of things in the divine knowledge as objects known . . . which are really other than (*secundum rem aliae*) the divine nature', and 'the *rationes* by which these are known, which are really identical with the divine nature'.[93] Pegis, commenting on this dichotomy, says that this is Ghent's 'true Avicennianism, distinguishing in the doctrine of divine ideas the *respectus imitabilitas in divina essentiae* and the *rerum essentiae in divine cognitione*'.[94] Ghent develops his own terminology to deal with this conundrum, that of an *idea* and its *ideatum*. As Ghent says,

> the ideas in God exercise causality in every way over the things of which they are forms, by constituting them in both their *esse essentiae* and their *esse existentiae*, and this according to the mode of the exemplary formal cause, therefore the relation of the divine idea to its *ideata* . . . is according to the first genus of relation, which is that between the producer and its product . . . so that it follows from the divine perfection that from the ideal ratio in God, the first essence of the creature flows forth in its *esse essentiae*, and second, through the mediation of the divine will, this same essence flows forth in its *esse existentiae*.[95]

The ideas are not *exactly* identifiable with the divine essence. As Sylwanowicz says, according to Ghent 'we can think of a created essence in itself apart from its dependence on the Creator first, before we ask the question whether its being (*esse*) is created or uncreated'.[96] This is obvious if we recall the indistinct conception of being. Ghent says that 'according to Avicenna being is imprinted in the mind by the first impression even before an understanding of either creatures or God is impressed in it'.[97] For Ghent, following Avicenna, this indistinct conception of being affords him the possibility of treating essences in themselves. He makes it clear whom he is following in such a consideration: 'Following the position excellently expressed by Avicenna in his *Metaphysics*, according to which the ideas signify the very essences of things'.[98] We can understand this better if we realise that for Ghent 'reality', as it were, comes in three 'levels'. First of all, there is what is actual; *res existens in actu*. Second, there is also what is merely imaginable, for example a chimera; *res a reor reris*. The third type of *res* was that which lay between the merely imaginable and the actual. This was the realm of the possible; *res a ratitudine*.[99] The realm of the possible 'possessed an ontological density'.[100] And this ontological density is the aforementioned *esse essentiae*. These possibles, with their appropriate being, become more understandable when we consider Ghent's conception of possibility.

Ghent offered three definitions of possibility. The first was that possibility (as something noble) depended on God's active power, while impossibility did not (as it was less than noble). The second found both dependent. The third definition, which seemed to go unnoticed by either Scotus or Ockham, was that a 'thing's ability or inability to be made is prior to any thing's ability or inability to make it'.[101] The ideas were then possible in themselves, at least on this interpretation. Even if they are not, they are necessary in terms of the divine intellect which *must* think them. But this residual separateness has to be resolved by Ghent on pain of offending divine simplicity. His solution is to make these ideas *nothing*. For Henry there are degrees of nothing. What is possible but not actual, is less of a nothing than impossibles. The former are *non-ens* while the latter are *purum non-est*. That which is impossible is always *maius nihil*. The divine essence gives both the *esse essentiae* and the *esse existentiae*. But the former is given, in some sense, necessarily. For this reason, the ideas are not wholly identifiable with the divine essence. Consequently, they must exhibit some degree of nullity. This, it seems, is the nothing *as* something which we have already encountered.

Duns Scotus and William of Ockham: univocity of Non-Being

Duns Scotus[102] was influenced by Henry of Ghent to such a degree that Gilson states that it is hardly possible to read Duns Scotus 'without having [Ghent's] writings at hand'.[103] The other great influence on Scotus was that of Avicenna.[104] From the latter Scotus inherited his notion of being,[105] his definition of essence,[106] and even of possibility with regard to these essences.[107] From the former Scotus was to inherit the view that the infinity of God was a positive perfection, that matter was also positive, and that the human being had a plurality of forms. Furthermore, the model of analogy Scotus criticised was Ghent's.[108] Scotus also conceived the divine knowledge in terms of moments, a conception that Ghent, following Avicenna's Neoplatonism, had also employed. As Marrone says, 'Duns adopted, nearly lock, stock and barrel, this vision of reality and ontological densities'.[109]

For Scotus of the *Lectura*, there were two atemporal moments (instants of nature) in the divine knowledge. For Scotus of the *Ordinatio*, which was written later, these two moments were each subdivided. For the *Lectura* the first moment consisted in God giving cognitive being to what the divine gaze knew as creatable. In the second moment God gives the creatable object *esse existentiae* by an act of will.[110] In the *Ordinatio* the first logical subdivision of the first moment is the divine production of intelligible being. God understands His own essence absolutely, or in itself. The second logical subdivision finds the intelligible object possible in itself. The order of these two is only logical, it is not temporal.[111] In the second moment, itself subdivided, God's intellect compares its own intellection to whatever intelligible is understood. This causes in itself a relation of reason. The second subdivision is the divine reflection on this relation of reason, which causes the relation to be known. And so all knowledge is virtually contained within God's knowledge of his own essence.[112]

These possible creatures do not, *contra* Henry of Ghent, possess *esse essentiae*, for the simple reason that for Scotus to have this type of being is to have a real being. An essence, for Scotus, was a great deal more than nothing. This was a result of the univocity of being, which itself stems from his formal distinction that simultaneously initiates a new logical modality of possibility (this is discussed below).[113] Were the possible creatures essences, then God would depend upon them as eternal objects for his knowledge. Instead Scotus insists that they are nothing: *'lapis ab aeterno intellectus non est aliquid, sed nihil'*.[114] They do, as nothing, retain a type of diminished being (*esse diminutum*), that of *esse objectivum*, which they have only in being known in the divine intellect.[115] This type of being cannot be thought of as positive. Yet we can agree with Cronin when he says that possible essences 'possess within divine intellection, as objects standing over against the divine knowing subject, the being which is proper to each's intelligible essence'.[116] Gilson appears to concur when he says that 'the divine ideas are God's *secundum quid*, that is, relatively and comparatively. In other words each of them is in God, but it is not God *qua* God . . . [for] there is an essence of ideas *qua* ideas . . . they cannot [then] purely and simply be God'.[117]

Ockham

Ockham comes to the question determined to remove even *esse objectivum* from these possible creatures.[118] Ockham criticised the traditional identification of the ideas with the divine essence. This criticism was fuelled by his overall concern to eradicate all metaphysical community and so enforce his ontology of indistinction, with its impervious singularity. It was this move that facilitated Ockham's particular conception of omnipotence, but it can be correctly expressed in the reverse: it was Ockham's novel version of omnipotence which gave rise to this ontology.[119]

The 'Venerable Inceptor' argues that the attempt to identify the ideas with the divine essence is incoherent.[120] His analysis employs the usual Ockhamian methodological presuppositions: principle of annihilation and numerical identity, enforced by the principle of non-contradiction. If the ideas are the divine essence they must either be that essence exactly or they can be relations of imitability. If they are the divine essence in a real and precise sense, then there can only be one idea as there is only one essence. If they are relations of divine imitability, which would allow for a plurality, they must be real relations. But the problem with this is that the Trinity is the only real relation in the divine essence. So they can be relations only of reason. If they are *relationes rationis* then they cannot be identical with an *ens reale* such as the divine essence.[121] A combination of real relation and a conceptual relation of imitability would fail because a composite cannot be identified with its parts.

For Ockham the ideas are exemplars or patterns that are known in the production of something. The word 'idea' is a connotative term. Consequently, it has only a nominal definition: principally signifying one thing directly (*in recto*) and signifying another obliquely (*in oblique*). It is this secondary signification that generates the illusion of a positive entity. This illusion is quickly dispelled when the term's primary signification is recalled, revealing its nominal quiddity (*quid nominas*). In this sense the word idea will only really signify a creature that is producible by God. The 'idea' is the thought of this creature which the divine intellect knows. This 'idea' functions as a pattern which is the exemplar of that creature. But this pattern is, in the Divine intellect, nothing other than the creature itself. We must remember that there can be no appeal to metaphysical concepts such as existence in the Thomist sense. The ideas are not means by which God knows something and the ideas are not likenesses of the creatures. Instead the ideas are the creatures themselves.[122] The word idea is employed to signify God's intelligent thought of them as creatable and so as other than himself. As God thinks of the creature that is creatable he thinks of that creature. So we understand an idea as God's knowledge of what is creatable by him, and that these ideas are in themselves nothing; they are nothing but themselves.[123]

The word idea directly signifies the creature and in a secondary sense signifies the realisation of that possible creature by God, and his knowledge of it. God knows through these ideas only in the sense that they terminate the act of knowing. That is, without them nothing would be thought. But this is simply a tautology: for something to be thought something must be thought and that which is thought is that which is thought. The full connotative nature of the word becomes apparent as the primary signification continually draws us back to the creature itself. In Ockham's world there could only be God or the individual creature, there can be no *tertium quid*. Thus when God creates the creature all he has thought of in that creation has been the creature. So the idea is only other from the creature as God's knowledge of what is possible for him to create. There is a distinct lack of any metaphysical community, for the creature does not *à la* Aquinas participate in God's act of to-be, nor is there a participation in any real universal community of essences.

What a creature *is* is itself. This is why we have the employment of a factual understanding of what 'is', because a fact is the conceptual tool needed to speak of what 'is' without relying upon other metaphysical concepts. Factuality allows a simple univocal mantra, as one only repeats the fact, so to speak. In this sense, an idea of a creature (that is only itself and as known by God) is nothing. The difference between the realised and an unrealised fact is only the fact.[124] The fact of its-self makes all the difference; but this difference, in being the individual fact, is no difference at all. What is meant by this is that the fact, as a possible creature, is its own possibility, and so when it is freely actualised by God it remains the same, and change is external to its own possibility. The only alteration is an act of God's will. This means that the something remains the *a priori* nothing it always was, even before or without God. This will be explained and elaborated on below. What we must accept at this stage is that for Ockham the ideas are nothing but the creatures themselves. Consequently, before the creatures are, the idea of them is at this point nothing. As McGrade points out, 'pure nothing plays as significant a role in Ockham's ontology as does the void for Democritus'.[125]

One consequence of Ockham's penchant for terminist logic is that there are three ways in which the word nothing can be employed: (a) syncategorematically, as a negative universal sign; (b) categorematically, in so far as it does not signify anything which actually exists; (c) lastly, as it depicts that for which existence is impossible.[126] Chimeras fall under the third use. When Ockham calls a creature a *purum nihil* it is meant in a categorematic sense. This indicates that, although a creature did not exist from all eternity, it could have existed from all eternity, and so it does exist as the nothing which the idea of its-self actually is. As Maurer points out, Ockham did not actually say that a divine idea is a nothing, 'but he implies this by a statement that a creature known from all eternity by the divine mind as something creatable is *unum nihil*, for a divine idea is precisely something creatable to which God can give real existence'.[127] As we know, Henry of Ghent and Duns Scotus both tried to render ideas nothing, but it was Ockham who managed to empty nothingness of all somethingness.[128] The nothingness of the divine idea is nothing but a pure and absolute possibility. The internal intelligibility of this possibility came from that very possibility alone. Ockham could utilise this notion to replace the need for an order of essences or even of being. As Maurer says, 'Ockham had to take the divine ideas more seriously than Scotus, because for Ockham the divine essence is not the exemplar of creatures.'[129] The implications of this are enormous and will be discussed below. The ideas are now only the creatures themselves, which are not anchored in the divine essence, but reside outside this essence as a possibility unto themselves, and yet, in being so, they are nothing. But the danger here is that if the negative implication of nothingness is weakened (if that can occur) then these ideas will possibly displace God, in that they will, in a Platonic sense, condition God's intelligibility and in the end his possibility.[130] At this stage it seems correct to invoke Anton Pegis' invective that Ockham represents 'Platonism minus the ideas'.[131] We will discover that this absence becomes more determinate than any Platonic idea ever did. Below we move from a discussion about divine ideas to one about Scotus' formalism, doing so in an effort to draw out some of the implications touched upon above. Following this we return to Ockham in an analysis concerning modal logic.

Possibly: Nothing

Duns Scotus initiated a new understanding of reality in terms of formality; a formality to become enshrined in the Scotist univocity of being.[132] Following Avicenna, Scotus argued that the first object of the intellect is *ens qua ens*. In making this move, existence was to become essentialised, as the difference between existence and essence came to be understood only as a formal distinction.[133] (Although it may be fairer to say that this is a pregnant implication in Scotus, which is later developed by Scotists.) Existence was itself an intrinsic mode of essence, becoming rather more conceptual than existential; being became what was thinkable.[134] This univocity of being could only be permitted if intrinsic modes of being could allow for internal differentiation without the mere addition of external difference – which would offend the status of being as the supreme transcendental. Thus according to modal distinctions, the difference appropriate to God and creature arises from the intensive degrees which an essence could attain. So God's being was qualified by the intrinsic mode of infinity – in which univocal being was 'virtually' included. This meant that God was rendered distinct without employing specific *differentiae* which would improperly suggest that being was a genus common to God and creatures. The concept of being which both God and creatures fall under is not, therefore, proper to God; it becomes so only under intrinsic qualification. Thus 'God is being' is a logical statement that nonetheless has some ontological purchase in that being is a formal reality in God: God as infinite being is lawfully a fully determinate metaphysical statement.

Scotus radically redefines the existent object and the balance between the universal and the singular. For him the object is composed of two aspects that exhibit a plurality of forms within every actuality – singularity of substantial form being denied (the common Franciscan view). An object consists of a common nature and a contracting difference, also known as an *haecceity*, that makes it singular.[135] The two aspects are formally distinct.[136] They can be conceived apart and are thus distinguishable. The phantasm presents to sensitive cognition the object's singularity: 'The phantasm represents with its entire function the object as something singular to the imagination.'[137] As this phantasm is sensory it can never bring about the reception of a thing's form, which is its universal aspect. Cognition of the thing's universality is achieved by the production of the intelligible species. The phantasm is sensory, so it cannot communicate to the intellectual faculty, while the intelligible species is a product of the agent intellect.

It is this formal element that prefigures modernity. As Alliez says, 'it is in his formalism that Duns Scotus would already singularly escape every form of the *via antiqua*'.[138] Scotus conceived the object in terms of multiple forms. Every object was composed of parts that had themselves a partial being, one which in terms of *potentia absoluta* was easily separated by the mind from its 'host' unity. These partial beings are formally distinct from the object, so the object becomes disembodied as it is forced to inhabit a world determined by the possible. As Alliez says, 'in the Scotist world everything that is conceivable apart possesses an objective reality, and in this respect has in God a distinct idea orientated toward a possible production'.[139] Each object loses its ontological unity, a unity only partially regained by practical representation. Linked with the formal distinction is the univocity of being, which asserts that the primary object of cognition is 'being' as ontologically drained, since indeterminate and neutral. Because each reality is mediated by a logical sameness of being, knowledge of being starts to usurp the primacy of theology. And since univocity thereby operates already as the possibility for all knowing, the measure of knowing begins to be a clear and distinct grasp of logically distinguishable items. In this way the primacy of adequation involving a real relation between knower and known starts to fade. Cognition is no longer necessarily about actual objects, but by way of the *potentia absoluta* is possible in principle without one (Scotus hints at this, and Ockham develops it much further). This means that veridicality will stem from successful representation, which can be mimicked by illusion, since a species is now thought of more as a mimesis of the known object. What is cognised becomes now literally the object of cognition, *viz.*, the object is terminated by the act of cognition rather than an intentional ecstasis. Alliez argues that this re-conception of the object of cognition is itself 'the birth of the object'.[140] And it is an object that 'negotiates its own modernity'.[141] Because it arrives within the act of cognition any fundamental notion of adequation is implicitly scuppered by the Scotist formalism. For how can one locate actuality if actuality itself is now defined in terms of 'real-possibles'? This is to some degree a precursor to the Cartesian reversal from '*ab esse ad nosse valet consequentia*' to '*a nosse ad esse valet consequentia*'. The poet Gerard Manley Hopkins described Scotus as the 'unraveller' and it seems, in a rather pejorative sense, that this is true.

To Be: Nowhere

> A new [modal] approach emerged from the idea of an omnipotent God.[142]
>
> (S. H. Knuuttila and L. Alanen)

> Being is fundamentally univocal for Ockham, i.e., actual being and possible being are not two kinds of being, but rather two aspects of the same kind of being.[143]
>
> (H. Lagerlund)

After the condemnations of 1277 there was a methodological application of the idea of an omnipotent God as a hypothetical counterpoint to that which was regarded as reality.[144] As Klocker says, 'what the world *de facto* is became entirely subordinated to what it could have been and what it might become'.[145] In this sense, every actuality became a limited expression of the possible. For Duns Scotus this meant that whatever existed was now to be considered in terms of alternative states of affairs. This, inevitably, was the secularisation of modalities.[146] What we witness at this time is a radical shift from an extensional (referential) modality to an intensional (sense-orientated) one, which is itself the advent of the concept in its modern form.[147] The starting point for Scotus was logical possibility (*possibilitas logica*);[148] interestingly it was Scotus who first introduced the term. That which existed had now to be considered not as actual but as factual for the univocity of being flattened the distinct sides of existentiality, essentialising being in the name of the possible: 'Realisation in the actual world is no longer the criterion of real possibility.'[149] Any particular entity contained within itself its own dissolution, for it was composed of a plurality of forms which possessed their own appropriate being. This new modality took these quasi-forms and realised them counterfactually, such that the object from which these possible forms were taken could not legitimate its own unity over these alternatives. In other words, the very possibility of an intensional modality forbade the provision of any legitimacy to the actual. (We see here the beginnings of the Nietzschean corollary, for that which 'is' will be forced to fight for its place in this world, as numerous alternatives struggle to disturb it.) The possible (including compossible states of affairs) possesses an intensional being given to it by God who bestows it by thinking its possibility, yet that which receives is always already

22

potentially intelligible.[150] Ockham wrote, 'If it is possible it is possible before it is produced in intelligible being.'[151] It is this which begins to complete the Scotist unravelling.

Scotus declared, 'I do not call something contingent because it is not always or necessarily the case, but because its opposite could be actual at the very moment it occurs.'[152] Yet to define contingency in terms of counter-factuality is to misplace it. For to do so introduces a contorted form of necessitarianism, since that which is is not necessary *here* but it is necessary in itself. The apriority generated by a conception of the possible as not anchored in the essence of God will perforce insist on the necessity of that which is thought. There is no longer any actual contingency but instead virtual necessity. As Scotus says, 'I do not say something is contingent but that something is caused contingently.'[153] This illusion of contingency stems from a notion not involving any particular entity but rather the *hic et nunc* in general. It is this which is rendered contingent, not *a* here and now but *the* here and now *in toto*, which is regarded as the instantiation of one possible order, not as a series of unique actualities which establish their possibility only with their actuality.[154]

It is this loss of the 'here and now' which produces what Alliez calls an 'order with no Sunday'.[155] This is because every would-be Sunday is displaced by the simultaneity of other possibles that do not simply struggle from outside the 'Sunday' but rise up from inside, as monstrous parts become wholes. This *mereological* (part-to-whole) nightmare means that 'identifiability is not bound to any single world'.[156] There can be no qualitative legitimacy invoked for the presence of one rather than another. As Burrell says, 'Scotus looks more at features of things than at things themselves.'[157] Consequently, Scotus looks at the world as a 'conceptual system'.[158]

This diremption of the here and now precipitates an *a priori* realm, articulated by the ruminations of an intensional modality. The possible, in being potentially intelligible (*esse intelligible*), is independent of God and does not receive this potential from God. Instead the creature is possible in itself. Ockham argues, in an Avicennian manner, that 'possible being is something a creature has of itself'.[159] Things are now intrinsically possible in an absolute sense.[160] However, this possibility is only of itself formally speaking. It remains *principatively* dependent on God, and yet this seems to mean very little:[161] 'A creature is possible, not because anything pertains to it, but because it can exist in reality.'[162] Scotus appears to argue that the possible becomes an *a priori* condition of intelligibility, one which would be untouched by the non-existence of God: 'This logical possibility could remain separately in power by its own nature even when there were, *per impossibile*, no omnipotence to which it could be an object.'[163] For Scotus and Ockham the proposition 'the world will be' is independent of the actual world.[164] The possibility of such a proposition is determined by the compossibility or incompossibility of *terms*. In other words, possibility is a matter of the non-repugnance of terms.[165] For this reason we can agree with Alanen when he says that for Ockham possibility is a 'predicate of propositions and not of things'.[166] These propositions, which epitomise this modern modality, are called neutral propositions.[167] God does not allocate a truth value to propositions until after the first instant of nature. (This is somewhat analogous to a notion of being which prescinds from determination, which is to say that both being and possibility occupy a place before existence and God.) Furthermore, God must think these propositions. As R. van der Lecq says, 'God produces things in their intelligibility, but the act of production is not an act of God's free will; it is an act of his intellect and therefore necessary, according to Scotus.'[168] Knuuttila argues that for Scotus 'God necessarily thinks about whatever can be thought about'.[169] We must remember that for Scotus the divine intellect 'is not an active power'.[170] If there was no world nor *per impossibile* no will . . . the ontologically relevant matrix of synchronic possible states of affairs would remain the same' (as Beck puts it).[171] Suarez later occupies a similar position when he says that eternal truths which are known by God 'are not true because they are known by God, but rather they are thus known because they are true . . . [T]hey are eternal, not only as they are in the divine intellect but also in themselves and prescinding from it.'[172]

Aquinas refuses such an option: 'Yet if one considered [the possibility] that both intellects [Man's and God's] might vanish (which is impossible), the concept of truth would in no fashion remain (*nullo modo veritatis ratio remaneret*).'[173] Knuuttila and Alanen state that 'until the early fourteenth century possibilities were treated as having a foundation in God; in the modern theory they were dissociated from this ontological backing'.[174] Not only are possibilities independent of God, but 'Divine actuality disappears behind the infinite variety of what is possible', as Klocker puts it.[175] Essences, conceived as the logical possibility of terms, are the foundation of this logico-epistemic modality.[176] As Klaus Jacobi argues, the 'semantics of possible worlds is expressly or implicitly bound up with a metaphysics of essence'.[177]

Because this intensional modality is a logical modality it does not require a cause (it is in a sense *causa sui*).[178] The possible is no longer defined by the actual, but is now more defined than the actual. This is the ascendancy of the law of non-contradiction.[179] The 'law' (what is possible) is prior to the 'law-giver' (God).[180] The consequence of this is the loss of language, matter, and time. Scotus, Ockham, and indeed Ghent,[181] advocate an Avicennian understanding of possibility. For each understands possibility as intrinsic to what is possible, *viz.*, what is possible is possible by definition, hence it is an intensional modality. What we see here is a loss of creation, causation, actuality, and contingency. Instead there is the elaboration of a merely 'diacritical' being. In other words, the 'world' appears only within the occult workings of terms which afford some nominal notion of cognitive representation.[182] Within this 'tradition' being is essentialised, in that what counts as being is less than existence – being becomes an *a priori* realm of possible essences. Further, this essentialised being becomes factualised. As Gilson says, 'Scotus forbears any attempt to characterise the actual existence of things, treating that *fact* as more like a presupposition'.[183] In a similar vein Burrell makes the point that a consequence of this modal shift is that 'possible worlds become as engaging as the actual world, since nothing distinguishes actual from possible except the mere fact that it happens to exist'.[184] Such an understanding is also prevalent in Ockham.

Ockham had two cognitive theories: that of the *fictum*, or objective-existence theory; and the *intellectio*, or mental act theory.[185] Each required the positing of unactualised possibles. By eventually moving to the second theory, Ockham endeavoured to reduce these entities to one act of cognition. But as he himself realised, this required that the Divine cognition be equally of all things. Yet Ockham thinks that God's act is more akin to the rational act than the nonrational. So the divine act cannot be equally of all. What Ockham must then do is transfer the onus onto the working of terms, so as to provide the requisite difference. Essences become 'beings', then these become merely logical phenomena. As Ockham says, 'logical potency represents a certain way in which terms can be combined by the mind'.[186] Alanen, commenting on this passage, argues that for Ockham 'possibility in the absolute sense is . . . a predicate of propositions and not of things'.[187] It is, as Adams says, 'just that God and creatures are eternally apt to be signified by the terms'.[188] Whatever is understood (and it seems this goes for God's self-understanding) is 'nothing although understood'.[189] Even for Scotus the 'relation of compossibility and incompossibility of the terms are and remain the same regardless of whether the things signified exist or whether there is my intellect to combine them'.[190] The operation of these terms in generating intelligibility depends, literally, on nothing (acting *as* something). As Scotus says, 'everything which is unqualifiedly nothing includes in itself the essence of many'.[191] For Ockham this nothing is just as operational. McGrade argues, 'Ockham has plenty of nothing, and nothing is plenty for him'.[192] As already said, this logical intelligibility, in being logical, does not require a cause. Furthermore, it relativises *this* world by engendering possible worlds. Ross argues that 'creation has no place at all because all possibilities are equally real and equally actual'.[193] Possible worlds deny actuality in terms of a view-pointed perspectivalism. In other words, being is now world-relative. Furthermore, logical modalities endeavour to remove all tensedness from propositions, rendering lived discourse atemporal. This endemic formalism (and its accomplice possibilism) fails to interpret terms in any first-order sense of understanding. So we can see that there is indeed a loss of actuality, contingency, and time: a lack of tenses is deemed veridically irrelevant because of view-pointed actualism and the self-causation of logic. Instead we must insist, with Ross (because these systems are not 'theologically neutral'[194]), that there are no empty possibles. Even if we entertained the notion of empty possibles we would be unable to name them, as there would not be enough transcendent determinacy to allow for indexical context. Consequently, they would remain logically inaccessible. Furthermore, it must be understood that being is not exhausted by kinds, nor kinds by cases.[195] As Ross insists, 'God settles what might have been in so far as it is a consequence of what exists'.[196] Consequently, an intensional logic is dependent on the actual nature of things which permit such modal abstractions. The intensional content 'parasitises' the real world.[197] The possible is understood in terms of actual knowledge *a posteriori*, because 'power is known through its acts'.[198] However, we must not define possibility *a posteriori* but only what is possible, otherwise we remain vulnerable to Lovejoy's 'principle of plenitude', which argues that what is possible is realised in actuality.[199] Furthermore, to do so would be to advocate merely a statistical understanding of possibility. This is a distinction clearly articulated by Klaus Jacobi.[200] It is this which most advocates of intensional modalities misunderstand. As a result they treat intensional logics like a big extensional logic, in that they make intensional names into 'things'[201] and so take us to places to which we should not go, indeed to the feet of nothingness, where formal 'Satanic notations whisper the ontologies'.[202] Instead the formal must serve the actual. Logic should be interpreted meta-linguistically, according to lived usage and first-order expressions.[203] Aquinas accepts a logical or intensional understanding of modal notions, but these are parasitic on the 'semantic richness of first-order language', as Goris puts it.[204] For this reason, the intensional meaningfulness of discourse rests on an understanding of the actual world.[205] As Schmidt puts it: 'Truth, and truth about real being, is the end and final cause of logic.'[206]

Ens infinitum: ens univocum[207]

Every other being distinct from the infinite being is called 'a being' by participation because it *captures a part* of that entity present there perfectly and totally.[208]

(Duns Scotus)

For Scotus there is a somewhat weaker distinction between essence and existence than there is for Aquinas. Two theses will be argued in this section. The first is that for Scotus there is no *real distinction* in a creature, nor in God. That much is incontrovertible, but this is extended to suggest that there is in effect, for Scotus, no real distinction *between* God and creatures. So the second thesis is that there is, then, effectively for Scotus, only a formal distinction between God and creatures. We can think a difference, so there is one, but this difference is but a formality.

The basis for the above is what has been referred to as the univocity of non-being. If Plotinus' *meontology* is combined with Avicenna's understanding of being as the subject of metaphysics, a univocity of non-being is approached; especially if it is remembered that Avicenna's being prescinds from both God and creature, universal and particular, actual (existent) and possible (non-existent). Furthermore, it was argued above that Henry of Ghent located the divine ideas somewhat outside the divine essence – a move which facilitated an embryonic espousal of an intensional modality. As we saw, this modality was taken up and developed by Scotus and Ockham. It can be witnessed in Scotus in his advocacy of a univocity of being and the formal distinction, along with the advent of *a priori* logical possibility. Ockham betrays the presence of this modality in his advocacy of a logical possibility, which does not depend on the existence of God. This possibilism manifests itself in his nominalism and in his subsequent dependence on the logic of terms and propositions.

Taking the above moves in conjunction with the notion of a univocity of non-being is not outrageous. Such a univocity is witnessed in so far as being is also that which is not, in an existential sense. For essences are eternal; or as Gilson puts it: 'Essences always exist.'[209] Richard Cross, an extremely sympathetic reader of Scotus, argues that possibilities 'have their properties without their needing to exist in any sense, whether as thought objects or as extra mental reality'.[210] This echoes Scotus' understanding of contingency. For Scotus, as we have seen, does not say that there *are* contingent things, but merely that things are *caused* contingently.[211] This causation has more to do with synchronic contingency than that of actuality. That is to say, contingency is not a circumstance of something existing after not existing, but that *this* configuration is contingent; for in a sense every possibility is eternal. Consequently, a possible always exists. In this way contingency cannot rest on actual objects being contingent, for all beings are, in terms of their possibility, necessary, that is, *a priori*; necessary in their pure possibility without reference to the actual. As a result it is the *configuration* of possibilities caused by God's will that allows for contingency. Such a configuration remains immanent to its being represented thus and so. This will be explained below.

Scotus' formalism, along with the axiomatic absolute power of God, causes all beings to lose their substantial form. Each entity is always other than itself, or it has an other *in* itself. For each being has a legion of forms which exist. They may not actually exist in an existential sense – nonetheless they still exist as eternal essences. What, then, enables the cognitive presentation of a singular entity that has within itself many other existents is re-presentation. By this I mean that cognition is a matter of construction, that is, re-arrangement. For this reason Alliez says that 'everything that does not imply contradiction is in a certain fashion *res* because every reality, even empirical, not only experiences a composition, but also depends on a constitution of a point of view'.[212] Scotus tells us that as a finite being is less than the infinite, it represents a part of that infinitude. It is for this reason that Gilson is correct to call Scotus' metaphysics 'practical'.[213] Cognition is practical in that it must 'make' that which is cognised, to the degree that any cognised object has a number of unrealised synchronic possibilities which could have been configured by a different re-presentation. Alliez argues that not only has re-presentation become absolute, but the subjective and objective realms have in Scotus become the same: 'Because the Scotist doctrine of the plurality of distinct forms *a parte rei* applies indifferently to the domain of being and to the soul, those two aspects, objective and subjective, say the same.'[214] Why is this the case? Because reality does not logically exclude cognition in the absence of an object, a state of affairs reflected in the virtuality of every being. What is meant by this is that every being is virtually more, less, or different because it lacks a single substantial form. Consequently, every entity is composed of a plethora of forms that are realised formally, which means that they possess a certain type of being. The formal thought of an essence, which is a logical possibility, exists; but we do not always cognise it; though this essence is there only formally it is nonetheless real. In this way, every cognition, that is, representation, involves an absent concrete object. The object which we represent is not there to the degree that it is only within our representation, in so far as it is also other than how we do represent it. This is a consequence of the object's aforementioned virtuality.

We now turn to the notion of infinity, so as to elaborate the notion of the univocity of being, and to further explicate the virtual nature of every entity.

Infinity

From the plenitude of its 'virtual quality' *the infinite is measuring everything* else as greater or lesser to the degree that it approaches *the whole* or recedes from it.[215]

(Duns Scotus)

28

> The real goal of the tendency which is dragging men and things toward *pure quantity* can only be the final dissolution of the present world.[216]
>
> (René Guénon)

Following Henry of Ghent, Duns Scotus treats infinity as a positive perfection.[217] Ghent had thought that it was a negative term but a positive affirmation.[218] As Davenport puts it: 'In an absolute sense, Henry argues, the word "infinite" negates a negation, and is therefore strictly equivalent to an affirmation.'[219] A more positive understanding of infinity was bequeathed to Ghent, Scotus and Ockham by Augustine's two conceptions of quantity: *quantitas molis* (quantity of bulk), and *quantitas virtutis sive perfectionis* (quantity of perfection). The first was augmented by the application of a standard unit. The latter was the rationalisation of intensive phenomena, for example, colour.[220] Aquinas only allowed this second type of infinite to apply to spiritual perfection.[221] Furthermore, this application was negative. In Aquinas, as Davenport says, 'There is no single continuously increasing quantity . . . [I]n place of the "smooth" *scala perfectionis* envisaged by Augustine, proceeding by degrees . . . Thomas presents a discontinuous system.'[222] Davenport may not be correct about Augustine, but it is true that Scotus makes the notion of an intensive infinite fundamental to his system.[223] For Scotus, infinity is not only a perfection but is the simplest of concepts we have of God.[224] It is for this reason that we should understand that Scotus' infinity is an intrinsic mode. That is, it does not come by addition; instead it is intensive and actual.[225] For Aquinas, infinity is understood as a negatively relational property, which is to say that God is infinite because God lacks any relation to a limiting entity, such as matter; consequently, infinity is a negative perfection.[226] But for Scotus it is actual, that is, it is all at once, which means that this infinity is not constituted by the relativity of a non-relation. What is important for us here is how we read this Scotist infinity.

A small infinity[227]

> It is only inasmuch as I am infinite that I am limited.[228]
>
> (Maurice Blanchot)

Richard Cross suggests that 'an uncharitable account would be that Scotus' God is just a human person writ large'.[229] Yet this is exactly the reading offered by Louis Bouyer: 'The thrust [of Scotus'] thought inevitably makes this infinity nothing but an infinite magnification of what we are.'[230] Thus it in effect rests upon an understanding of infinity which suggests that its quantitative logic requires that the infinite share a sliding scale with the finite. When one reads what Cross has to say on the matter of infinity he appears to concede, whether knowingly or not, such a conception: 'It is ultimately one of Degree' – even if, to be sure, for Scotus an infinite degree is not comparable with any finite degree.[231] This notion of infinity will be explored below in an effort to draw out the difficulties involved in its conception and in its application to God. Part II, Chapter 10 returns to the matter. This should be kept in mind so that what is written here is not simply taken as conclusive. (For example, it is argued in Part II, Chapter 10 that Gregory of Nyssa's use of infinity is important.)

What is suggested here is that if infinity is a quantitative matter of degree then it cannot allow for a real ontological difference. For we can certainly say x is more than y, but we cannot say that to be more is 'more' in a qualitative sense. If it is said 'I love my wife *more* than I love you', does it mean that this is a better love by reason of its quantity? Maybe not, because one does not love one's wife more, rather one loves her differently. The word *more* merely distracts; one could love obsessively, pathologically, and that would not be necessarily good; indeed, it may be an inferior form of loving. Can Scotus not argue that his *more* is qualitative? Maybe, but a sympathetic and, with regard to this topic, his most sophisticated interpreter, argues decisively that Scotus' conception of infinity is purely quantitative.[232] What is important is that the problem of a shared scale, or frame of reference, reappears. In an earlier quotation we saw Scotus define the infinite as the measuring in degrees of what approaches or recedes from *the whole* which is the infinite. The problem with infinity is that it always seems to be *ordinal* (if so it is subordinate to the series of which it is the nth value). But according to Scotus, infinite being 'exceeds any finite being whatsoever, not by some assigned proportion, but beyond every assigned, or assignable proportion'.[233] Nevertheless, Davenport, commenting on infinite being, says that although the infinite 'cannot be reached by finite steps, it belongs conceptually to the same univocal "measure" of excellence to which the finite belongs'.[234] A consequence of this is, as Scotus argues, that 'everything finite, since it is less than the infinite, represents a *part*'.[235] This appears after all to confirm the implication that the difference of the infinite relies on the limitations of the finite. So, when Scotus says that the infinite is above every assignable proportion, this may not mean that the infinite is beyond every proportion, for it is only beyond every *assignable* proportion. It can only be conceived, and indeed only exists in its essence, in contrast to the finite; in this way it is dependent in its distinct reality on the limitations of the finite. It is logically possible that a proportion could exist yet remain unassigned, for there is indeed a proportion, it is simply not available. There is therefore a 'measure' that lies outside the infinite and the finite and the measure is, of course, being.

But Scotus explicitly asserts that 'God and creature share in no reality'.[236] He also declares that 'Every created essence [is] nothing other than its dependence with regard to God.'[237] How do we reconcile this with the possibilism mentioned earlier according to which essences always exist, for there would be the same logical possibilities even if God did not exist? Yet the two aspects do not conflict, for indeterminate being is itself the 'arch possibility' whose insistence engenders the real according to an outlook that is at bottom both essentialist and logicist. Hence God and creatures do share in a certain 'non-reality', whose nullity is nonetheless fundamental.

Rudi Te Velde has written an interesting article comparing Scotus and Aquinas in relation to nature and will.[238] What is of relevance for us is the fact that Te Velde argues that for Aquinas nature includes a natural inclination to transcend itself. For nature depends on God, and in this way is like part to whole. Consequently, in seeking its own good, nature will seek the universal good. The creature *is* by way of participation, the consequence of which is that the creature is more directed to God than it is to itself. For Scotus there is no such inclination and no notion of self-transcendency; nature is for him more immanent. It is possible to suggest that the reason that nature does not move *towards* God in Scotus is because nature or 'reality', with all its essences, is in a certain sense not dependent on God, because it is, as a 'part' of the infinite, 'self-possessed'; a slice of being in its own right. (In this way an echo of Avicennian Neoplatonism is sustained; nature is, in this sense, a piece of divinity.)

It may be for such reasons that Alliez speaks of Scotus in terms of a 'constructive monism',[239] while Goodchild simply calls Scotus' monism a 'strange monism'.[240] Goodchild makes the point that some Scotist scholarship makes the mistake of conceiving the univocity of being in a Neoplatonic manner. He correctly argues against this, for the simple reason that in Scotus one and being are diverse, and must remain so;[241] these transcendentals are separate. Is the interpretation of Scotus offered here guilty of the same mistake? Maybe not, in so far as it is being argued that the univocity of being logically implies a univocity of non-being. Consequently, I am arguing that for Scotus *being is not* (since it is a partially determined essence), and that *there is but one being*, which in its unity is formally distinct from itself, such that univocity of being again for this reason 'is not' being; already as one being it departs from pure existence. This is the *meontotheology* of nihilism's logic: nothing *as* something. It is this which finite and infinite share. Certainly it was not Scotus' intention to develop a metaphysical system that permits such an interpretation, but this does not mean that such an interpretation is illegitimate. We have eternal essences, a nature not inclined towards its maker, and a univocity of being which is there to rid us of being, by making it indifferent. This points us in the direction of Descartes in terms of the practical representation of cognition, and Spinoza and Hegel in so far as God and Nature, infinite and finite, are seen as an aspectual dialectic of a monistic whole in the fashion of Jastrow's *duck-rabbit*. One 'picture' gives two aspects, distracting us forever from the one that moves, and moves us, between these aspectual perceptions. This will become more cogent as this book proceeds, especially in Part II, Chapter 10.

The next chapter discusses Scotus' and Ockham's doctrine of intuitive cognition, in an effort to corroborate this chapter's idea that there is a latent univocity of non-being, in so far as intuitive cognition provides a further example of the logic of nihilism: nothing *as* something.

Notes

1   Diamond (2000), p. 201.
2   Hesiod (1993), line 136.
3   *Ibid.*, line 138.
4   *Ibid.*, line 457.
5   Plotinus, *Enneads*, trans. S. Mackenna (1991), III. 5, 2. and V. 8, 12 (hereafter Enn.).
6   One is here reminded of the painting by Rubens entitled *Saturn*.
7   Enn. V. 8, 13.
8   As Pegis (1942) says, 'The whole of being must be considered not only as being but also as non-being, for non-being is the mysterious co-principle of its interior intelligibility', p. 157.
9   See Part I, Chapters 2, 3, 4 and 5.
10 By employing such a phrase I am endeavouring to implicate the work of Levinas within this tradition. See Levinas (1991). I would also be keen to include Jean-Luc Marion within the same; see Marion (1991). See Part II, Chapter 10 where Levinas is briefly discussed.
11 This idea of non-production is important because it embodies the notion of the nothing *as* something. Throughout this book I refer to this non-production as provision. I employ this word because of its suggestive etymology. For the word provide stems from the word *pro*, which means before, and the word *videre*, which means to see. In this way I intend to suggest that the *provenance* of nihilism is to provide before provision. For example, the provenance of nihilism enables us to *be without being*, say without saying something and so on. One need only think of Saussure, for whom language was bereft of positive terms. This provision is, then, the nothing *as* something. See Part II, Chapter 10.
12 Enn. V. 3, 12.
13 The reason why the One (or Hegel's infinite) is not apart from all that falls beneath it, yet is not identical to it, is because of their proximity. That is to say, the One is *so close to the many*, ontologically speaking, that the many

cannot form a wholly separate identity from which the One could be completely apart or with which the One could be equated. The same goes for the finite in Hegel. For Hegel does not simply equate the infinite with the finite, nor does he argue that they are separate. This is because the finite is too ontologically close to the infinite to be able to develop a separate identity (an ontological difference) that could accommodate either severing or joining. See Part I, Chapter 5.

14 Enn., V. 5, 9.
15 See Part II, Chapter 9.
16 Enn., VI. 4, 2.
17 Brehier (1953), pp. 101 and 106.
18 See Bouyer (1999), p. 210.
19 Enn. V. 2, 1.
20 *Ibid.*, VI. 5, 12.
21 *Ibid.*
22 *Ibid.*, IV. 8, 3; VI. 5, 12.
23 Gilson (1952a), p. 20.
24 Enn. IV. 8, 4.
25 Torchia (1993), p. 11.
26 This is the problem facing the omnipotent God of Ockham and Descartes.
27 Enn. IV. 8, 6.
28 In Part II, Chapter 10 the possibility of nihilism being read in terms of givenness is considered. In this way the nothing *as* something could be interpreted as a sign of creation.
29 See Kaplan (1999).
30 I agree with Gadamer when he argues that Plato's one is not Plotinus' *hen* (One). For Plato's one and indeed the Good are the dialectical unity involved in the many. In this way the one is more about the dialectic between *peras* (limit), and *aperion* (unlimited, indefinite); see Gadamer (1986b), pp. 28–29, and p. 137. More generally see Klein (1968).
31 Avicenna, *Nadjat*, p. 365; Plotinus *Enneads* V, quoted in Afnan (1958), p. 114.
32 Such mutual constitution continually reappears throughout this book. For example, in Spinoza God is Nature, while Nature is God; in Hegel the finite is the infinite, the infinite is the finite; in Derrida the Text is defined by the Nothing outside it, while the Nothing is defined by the Text to which it is 'exterior'.
33 As Pegis (1942) argues, 'From Platonic realism to nominalism the line of descent is both direct and inevitable', p. 172. I would argue that it is Neoplatonism which leads us to nominalism. Plato leaves open other possibilities, and such interpretations are beginning to be explored by John Milbank and Catherine Pickstock.
34 Gilson (1952a), p. 23.
35 Fabro (1970), p. 100. In this article Fabro argues that Neoplatonism leads to 'Death of God' theology.
36 Pegis (1942), p. 174. See also Azcoul (1995), pp. 86–101, who also argues that Plotinus is both a pantheist and a monist.
37 Gerson argues that to read Plotinus as espousing a *henology* is to ignore the specific causation of finite being, as opposed to being in general; see Gerson (1994), pp. 236–237, fn. 44. On *henology* see Aertsen (1992b).

38 For a translation of Avicenna's *Metaphysica*, taken from the *Al-Shifa* (the *Healing*), see Avicenna (1973b); for a French translation see Anawati (1978). For a translation of the *Logica*, see Avicenna (1974). There are also two other translations of works on logic: see Avicenna (1973a) and (1984). Translations from the *Metaphysics Compendium*, which is a summary of the *Shifa*, are from secondary literature. For a general biography, with an introduction to Avicenna's works on theology and accompanying translations, see Avicenna (1951).

39 This principle embodies a notion of creation involving a double necessity. First, that of mediated creation, and second, necessary emanation, because the Necessary Being creates only by nature.

40 See Zedler (1948), p. 149; see also *idem* (1976); more generally see *idem* (1981).

41 'Avicenna does not recognise contingency as an ontological modality, but only as a condition in the nature of things', Goichon (1948), pp. 58–59. For Avicenna 'modality is determined on the level of quiddities in themselves', Back (1992), p. 237.

42 These questions come from Aristotle's four questions in the *Posterior Analytics: an sit, quid sit, quia est* or *quiale est*, and *propter quid sit.*

43 'To those things which have quiddities that are possible *per se*, being, does not accrue except extrinsically but the first principle does not have any quiddity', Avicenna, *Metaphysica*, tract. viii, cap. 4, fol. 99r. *Esse* is 'something that happens to an essence, or something that happens to its nature', *Metaphysica*, tract. v, fol. 87, quoted by Zedler (1976), p. 509. For Averroes' critique of Avicenna on being as an accident, see the eighth discussion in *Tahafut al-Tahafut*, in Averroes (1954), p. 235. For the place that Gundissalinus, Avicenna's Latin translator, played in Aquinas' interpretation of Avicenna's understanding of being as an accident see O'Shaughnessy (1960).

44 *Metaphysica*, tract. i,. cap. 66, fol. 72, vi. See Owens (1970), p. 4.

45 Owens (1970), p. 4.

46 'In Avicenna the *esse proprium* of the essence enjoyed a priority over being in reality and its being in the mind', Owens (1970), p. 11.

47 An essence was 'in itself possibly existent. For if it had not been possibly existent in itself it never would exist at all', *Metaphysics Compendium*, bk. I, pt. 2, tract. 6, 54–56; quoted by Adams (1987), p. 1068; 'Every being which is necessary through another not itself, is possible in itself', *ibid.*, cap. III, p. 69; quoted by Owens (1970), p. 4.

48 *Metaphysics Compendium*, cap. II, 69; quoted by Smith (1943), p. 342.

49 Goris (1996), p. 153.

50 *Metaphysica*, tract. v, cap. 1. This horse is the animal found in Avicenna's *Logica*: 'Animal is in itself a certain something, and it is the same whether it is sensible or understood in the soul. But in itself its being is neither universal nor singular . . . animal in itself is whatever animal is understood in the mind to be, and according to what animal is understood to be, it is animal only. But if in addition to this it be understood to be universal or singular or something else, then in addition to what animal is, there is understood something that happens to animality', *Logica*, 1, fol. 2rb; 'Equinity in itself is nothing but equinity, for in itself it is neither one nor many, nor existing in concrete

34

individuals nor in the mind', *Metaphysica*, tract. v, cap. 1. For this reason, being is something 'that happens to essence or something that accompanies its nature', *Logica*, 1, fol. 87ra. This beast reappears in Henry of Ghent and Duns Scotus.

51 This univocity is more apparent if we understand that the extrinsic nature of being cannot but make everything be in a univocal manner, but, more importantly, for Avicenna the intellect receives a primary impression of being which naturally prescinds from divine or creaturely consideration. Being is a flat eternal plane without beginning or end (see *Metaphysics Compendium*, I, 1, tract. 7). Being only leads us to the essences, which are eternal yet deserving of non-being.

52 Back (1992), p. 243.

53 See Goichon (1956), pp. 109–110 for a translation of the text: *Shifa*, I, 281.

54 Gilson (1927), p. 104; *idem* (1929–1930).

55 Goichon (1969), p. 13.

56 Gardet (1951), p. 555; quoted by Goichon (1969), p. 13.

57 See Paulus (1938), p. 55.

58 See Goichon (1969), p. 21.

59 *Ibid.*

60 God 'comprehends the particular things in so far as they are universals', *Nadjat*, 404, quoted by Goichon (1969), p. 22. In contrast see Aquinas *De Veritate*, q. 2, a. 5 and a. 6.

61 *Shifa*, 593, quoted by Goichon (1969), p. 21.

62 Goris (1996), p. 200, fn. 136.

63 See Goris (1996), p. 201, fn. 137.

64 Aquinas, *De Potentia*, q. 5, a. 3.

65 Gardet (1951), p. 549. Quoted by Goichon (1969), pp. 31–32, fn. 1. Avicenna argues that essences 'do not deserve to be . . . they deserve privation', *Metaphysica*, tract. viii, cap. 6. See Gilson (1952a), p. 78.

66 'Everything having a quiddity is caused', *Metaphysica*, tract. viii, cap. 4, fol. 99r.

67 *Metaphysica*, tract. viii, cap. 4; quoted in Zedler (1976), p. 510.

68 See Gilson (1952a), p. 81.

69 See *Metaphysica*, tract. vii, cap. 4, fol. 99r. See also Aquinas, *De Ente et Essentia*, ch. 5; Gilson (1952a), p. 80; (1978), p. 127; (1994), p. 456, fn. 26; Burrell (1986), p. 26. What the necessary existent does have is *anniyya*; see Frank (1956) for the history and meaning of this term. *Anniyya* appears to mean existence. There is little doubt that Avicenna did allow for an understanding of being which considered it an accident, but in fairness to Avicenna it may be better to consider such a 'doctrine' a blunder; see Burrell (1986), p. 26. This blunder seems to have been a sure sign of the limitations of Avicenna's metaphysical system. Anawati (1978) blames the development on Avicenna starting 'with essence in such a way as to arrive at the existing (*esse*) which effects it as though it were an accident', p. 78. Macierowski (1988) challenges this interpretation of Avicenna, arguing that Avicenna did not mean to assert that the first necessary being did not have an essence; this article contains a collection of translated texts relevant to the issue. But, as O'Shaughnessy (1960) argues, 'even the most favourable construction put on Avicenna,

however, cannot obscure the fact that in his metaphysical system the real order tends often to appear as a projection of the logical', p. 679. The absolute consideration of an essence, for example the animal in the *Logica*, which becomes the horse in the *Metaphysica*, and the *Metaphysics Compendium*, generates a realm apart from God. These essences considered in an absolute manner, along with the first impression of being, engender a realm before a consideration of God. We are able to consider essences as the truth of things. But these essences are possible in themselves, and so are independent of God. Furthermore, being, in its first impression, does not involve a consideration of God. For this reason, being, not God, is the subject of metaphysics. What this seems to mean is that essences, as eternal possibilities, independent of God, and being as a first impression on the soul, allow for an understanding of truth and being apart from God, even though these essences have no truth or being, as such; see Cronin (1966), p. 177. All that which is, accrues being extrinsically. Yet in so doing they are in no need of being, or rather being is of no concern. This is especially pertinent when we consider that being, which is accidental to all that is, is God yet can be rightly considered apart from God. Here we have the nothing *as* something. Metaphysics is about being, but being, because it is considered apart from God, leads us to the essences which are eternal; eternally nothing, even when they are. As a result we can agree with Paulus (1938), when he says that in Avicenna, 'Epistemology commands and subsumes ontology', p. 12. Metaphysics becomes, in a sense, the science of non-being *qua* non-being.

70 Smith (1943), p. 347. Cronin (1966) concurs, saying, 'In the doctrine of Avicenna the possible in itself is set over and against God . . . for God the possible is a datum given to, not by, Him', p. 175. Francis Cunningham finds the idea of a realm of independent possibles in Avicenna 'libelous': see F. A. Cunningham (1974), p. 197.

71 Smith (1943), p. 357.

72 As Cronin (1966), pp. 176–177; italics mine. See *Metaphysica*, tract. viii, cap. 6, fol. 100ra.

73 *Metaphysica*, tract. i, cap. 2, 5; quoted by Zedler (1948), p. 134; italics mine.

74 *Ibid.*, italics mine.

75 Goichon (1969), p. 26

76 Gardet (1951), p. 557; quoted by Goichon (1969), pp. 27–28.

77 Zedler (1948), p. 139.

78 'Henry drew his inspiration both from Avicenna and Neoplatonism', Clarke (1982), p. 124. Pegis (1968) speaks of Ghent's 'preference for Avicenna', p. 246; see also Pegis (1942), where he speaks of 'the Avicennian persuasions of Henry of Ghent', p. 170. Marrone (1985) argues that 'the origin of [Ghent's] ideas went back to Avicenna', and, 'Henry's thought seems to have been particularly sympathetic to Neoplatonism', pp. 105, 141; Paulus (1938), suggests that Ghent paid 'a greater attention to Neoplatonic theories', p. 148, and Ch. 2 generally.

79 Clarke (1982), p. 124.

80 See Paulus (1938), pp. 87–103 for a discussion of Ghent on ideas.

81 See Part II for a discussion of Aquinas.

82 See Paulus (1938), pp. 52–60.

83   See *Summa Theologiae*, q. 2, a. 21; cited in Dumont (1998), p. 300.

84   *Ibid.*, p. 301.

85   On this see Davenport (1999), pp. 98–99.

86   Ghent develops his notion of indistinct conception in *Summa Theologiae*, q. 2, a. 21–24. See also Marrone (1988), p. 33.

87   See Paulus (1938), p. 65.

88   On Ghent's *esse essentiae*, see Cronin (1966), pp. 178–186; Marrone (1985), pp. 105–113.

89   Maurer (1990), p. 370.

90   Paulus (1938) argues that Aquinas, unlike Ghent, knows only the divine essence as the source of divine ideas, see p. 101; see Pegis (1942), p. 176.

91   As Pegis (1942) says, concerning Ghent's doctrine of divine ideas, 'Avicenna has the ascendancy over St Augustine. And this Ascendancy means . . . an introduction of the Platonic forms into the divine intellect as an order of essences, really distinct from the divine essence and really distinct in their essential being', p. 175. See Maurer (1990), p. 370; Pegis (1969) and (1971).

92   This is why Clarke (1982) accuses Ghent of deontologizing the divine ideas; see p. 124.

93   *Summa Theologiae* (hereafter Summa), q. 68, a. 5, 7–14; quoted by Clarke (1982), p. 124.

94   Pegis (1942), p. 175.

95   Summa, q. 68, a. 5, 7–14. This passage is quoted by Pegis (1942), pp. 176–177; and Clarke (1982), p. 124.

96   Sylwanowicz (1996), p. 188.

97   Summa, q. 2, a. 21; quoted in Brown (1965), p. 121.

98   *Quodlibetal Questions*, q. IX, 2; quoted in Paulus (1938), p. 91, n. 1; Pegis (1942), pp. 175–176; Clarke (1982), p. 124.

99   As Marrone (1988) says, Ghent 'wanted to create some sort of ontological category half-way between fiction and actuality', p. 38.

100 Marrone (1996), p. 177.

101 *Quodlibetal Questions*, V, q. 3; see Adams (1987), ch. 25.

102 For Scotus' texts see Scotus (1950). Relevant translations are *A Treatise on God as First Principle* (1966); *God and Creatures* (1975); *Philosophical Writings* (1987); *Contingency and Freedom, Lectura*, 1, 39, see Vos (1994); *Duns Scotus Metaphysician* (1995).

103 Gilson (1955a), p. 447.

104 As Gilson (1927) says: 'The doctrine of the univocity of Being is represented in Duns Scotus' eyes by Avicenna's Philosophy', p. 147; but Gilson does make the point that the two philosophies must not be confused. The true difference resides in Scotus' formalism, see *ibid.*, p. 187; see also Gilson (1952b), pp. 84–94 for a comparison of Duns Scotus and Avicenna. See also Marrone (2001), vol. 2, pp. 493–494.

105 'Duns Scotus has not radically altered the Avicennian notion of being', Gilson (1952a), p. 89.

106 *Ibid.*, p. 84. 'Duns Scotus adopts the whole metaphysics of essence from Avicenna', Klaus Jacobi (1983), p. 107. The term 'metaphysics of essence' comes from Gilson (1952b), p. 109.

107 See Adams (1987), p. 1075.

108 See Burrell (1973), pp. 96–101.

109 Marrone (1996), p. 178.

110 *Lectura*, I, d. 43, q. un, n. 22; see Marrone (1996), p. 181.

111 See Knuuttila (1996), who puts it like this: 'Scotus thought that God first knows His essence in itself and then thinks about whatever else could be (the distinction is logical not temporal). It is only "after" this act of thinking about possible beings in themselves that God thinks about the relation of ideas to His essence', pp. 135–136. Cronin (1966) makes a similar point when he argues that for Scotus an *esse intelligible*, for example a stone, has a relation to the 'divine intellection, whereas yet there is no relation of the divine intellection to the stone', p. 191. Knuuttila (1996) concurs, stressing that 'it is important to notice that the objects of knowledge in the second instant of nature [that is, second subdivision of the first moment], are introduced in *esse intelligible* and known in themselves directly, without recurrence to what took place in the first instant of nature', p. 136. Normore (1996) argues that for Scotus God creates the basis for logical possibilities, but that the repugnance and non-repugnance of these possibilities are independent of God.

112 See *Ordinatio*, I, d. 35, q. u, n. 32.

113 For a discussion of divine ideas in Scotus see Gilson (1952b), pp. 279–306.

114 *Reportata Parisiensia*, I, d. 36, q. 2, n. 29.

115 This *esse objectivum* is *esse intelligible*.

116 Cronin (1966), pp. 198–199.

117 Gilson (1952a), p. 86. Elsewhere Gilson makes the point that God's ideas of creatures 'are not views of His essence nor even of His imitability', Gilson (1991), p. 160.

118 For Ockham's texts see (1967). For relevant translations see *Summa Logicae*, 2 vols., (1974), (1980); *Philosophical Writings* (1990); *Quodlibetal Questions* (1991); *Five Texts on the Mediaeval Problem of Universals* (1994). This last contains a translation of part of Ockham's *Ordinatio*.

119 The exact nature of Ockham's idea of divine Omnipotence is controversial. People such as Courtenay argue that it was a traditional version, in that it did not, in articulating the dichotomy of *potentia ordinata/potentia absoluta*, employ the latter as a form of action. But it appears that, for Ockham, this capacity is itself active, as everything in the Ockhamian world comes under its constant activity. In this sense *potentia absoluta* is an axiomatic *active capacity*. As Ozment (1980) says of the distinction, it is 'the most basic of Ockham's theological tools', p. 38. See Courtenay (1984a) and (1990); Pernoud (1970) and (1972); Adams (1987), pp. 1186–1207; for criticisms of Adams' view see Gelber (1990). Those who argue that the use of the distinction leads to sceptical ends include the following: Kennedy (1983), (1985), (1988) and (1989); Oakley (1961), (1963), (1968) and (1979); Randi (1986) and (1987); Funkenstein (1975a), (1975b), (1986) and (1994); van den Brink (1993). See also Dupré (1993); Gillespie (1995).

120 'Venerable Inceptor' is a name by which William of Ockham goes in the medieval textbooks.

121 See Maurer (1990), p. 370. See also Adams (1987), ch. 24.

122 *Ordinatio*, I, d. 35, q. 5.

123 *Ordinatio*, I, d. 43, q. 2.

124 *Ibid*.
125 McGrade (1985), p. 154.
126 *Ordinatio*, I, d. 36, q. 1.
127 Maurer (1990), p. 376.
128 See Pegis (1942).
129 Maurer (1990), p. 377.
130 When Platonism is referred to, its most pejorative interpretation is implied.
131 Pegis (1942).
132 'There is a science which investigates being, and one science studies a univocal subject', *Metaphysics*, IV, q. 1, n. 2; 'Scotus works with a notion of being which is common and univocal', Gilson (1952b), p. 454; 'Scotistic metaphysics is constructed on the concept of being because there is no other idea which will permit us to attain God', Gilson (1927), p. 100. See also Shircel (1942); Barth (1965); Hoeres (1965); Marrone (2001), vol. 2, ch. 15.
133 For a discussion of the Scotist essentialising of existence see Gilson (1952a) and (1952b).
134 The lineage of such a notion may well run from Plotinus, when in the *Enneads*, he equates being and intelligence; of course the equation of being and thought had been made by Parmenides. This move was taken up by Avicenna who sought to consider essences in an absolute manner. Simultaneously he conceived being as somewhat univocal and accidental; univocal in terms of an irreducible intuition of being, and accidental in that knowledge was not affected by any existential notion of being, as it remained epistemically indifferent to being. Ghent follows Avicenna's lead, for he too considers being in an almost univocal manner, as his analogous concept of being arises from the first impression of the intellect, *à la* Avicenna, prescinding from determination. Scotus adopts this and extends it. It is not outlandish to see Descartes and Kant on the horizon, although this is not exactly the trajectory of this thesis. This legacy passes easily to the likes of Bertrand Russell: 'Being as that which belongs to every conceivable object of thought . . . Whatever can be thought of has being', Russell (1903), pp. 449, 451.
135 As Ross (1986) argues, this mode of individuation will fail because it requires 'deeper individuals', p. 328.
136 On Scotus' notion of formal distinction see Grajewski (1944), Wolter (1965).
137 *Ordinatio*, I, d. 3, q. 1, n. 357.
138 Alliez (1996), p. 201.
139 *Ibid*., p. 209.
140 *Ibid*., p. 209.
141 *Ibid*., p. 208.
142 Knuuttila and Alanen (1988), p. 2.
143 Lagerlund (2000), p. 110.
144 Pierre Duhem is traditionally seen as offering a strong interpretation of the Parisian condemnations, while Koyré offers a weaker reading, limiting the extent of their subsequent influence. Grant has recently restated the stronger reading: Duhem (1985); Koyré (1957), (1949), (1956); Grant (1979), (1982), (1985). Murdoch (1974) says the condemnations led to the push of 'questions beyond the confines of the physical possibilities licit within Aristotelian

natural philosophy into the broader field of what was logically possible', p. 72. McColley (1936) states that 'There occurred in 1277 one of the most important events recorded in history', p. 399. See also Wippel (1977); Hissette (1977); for an English translation of the Parisian text see Hyman (1983).

145 Klocker (1992), p. 108.

146 Knuuttila and Alanen (1988), p. 2.

147 This is the interpretation proffered by the 'Helsinki School', under Hintikka and Knuuttila, his pupil. See Knuuttila (1978), (1981a), (1981b), (1982), (1993), (1995) and (1996); see also Alanen (1985) and (1988); Hintikka (1981). Knuuttila is of the opinion that medieval thinkers employed a statistical understanding of modality, hence a merely extensional one. Klaus Jacobi argues that Aquinas *et al.* did not hold a merely statistical understanding of modality; see Jacobi (1983), p. 94. Goris (1996) concurs with Jacobi, pp. 257–275. Sylwanowicz (1996) argues that Scotus did not hold an intensional modality as Knuuttila *et al.* conceive it.

148 *Ordinatio*, I, d. 2, p. 2, q. 1–4, n. 262; *Ordinatio*, I, d. 43, q. un, n. 16 (hereafter Ord.).

149 Knuuttila (1982), p. 354.

150 As Vos (1994a) says, '*Possibilitas logica* is an irreducible ontological quality of things themselves. Only in so far as the aspect of factuality is concerned is God's will the cause of contingent things . . . The *potentialis realis* of God is the cause of the factual existence of contingent beings, and is not the cause of their *possibilitas logica*', p. 30.

151 Ord. I, d. 43, q. 2. See Lagerlund (2000), p. 94.

152 Ord. I, d. 2, p. 1, q. 1–2, n. 86; cited by Knuuttila and Alanen (1988), p. 35.

153 Ord. I, d. 2, q. 1, a. 2, n. ad. 2. This encourages Burrell to call this view of contingency 'voluntarist': (1990), p. 252. For a different view of Scotus' understanding of contingent causality see Sylwanowicz (1996).

154 Vos (1994) insists that 'Discovery of synchronic contingency marks the start of Scotus' career as a scholar', and it was this 'synchronic contingency that can be regarded as the cornerstone of so-called possible worlds semantics', pp. 6, 30. On synchronic contingency in Scotus see Vos (1985), (1998a), (1998b); Dumont (1995).

155 Alliez (1996), p. 225.

156 Knuuttila (1986), p. 210.

157 Burrell (1990), p. 111.

158 *Ibid.*, p. 115.

159 Ockham, Sent. I, d. 43, q. 2; cited by Knuuttila and Alanen (1988), p. 38. As Lagerlund puts it: 'For [Ockham] possibility does not depend on the existence of the world or on the existence of God's mind or any other mind'; Lagerlund (2000), p. 92.

160 See Alanen (1985), p. 175.

161 Ord. I, d. 43, n. 5–7.

162 Ord. I, d. 43, q. 2; cited by Alanen (1985), p. 182.

163 Scotus, Ord. I, d. 36, q. 60–61.

164 See *Lectura*, I, d. 39, q. 1–5 n. 69.

165 See Scotus, Ord. I, d. 7, q. 1, 27; see Alanen (1985), p. 178.

166 Alanen (1985), p. 175.

167 See Vos (1994), pp. 28–33; Beck (1998).

168 van der Lecq (1998), p. 92.

169 Knuuttila (1996), p. 137. See Ord. I, d. q. 4, n. 262, 268.

170 Ord. I, d. 43, q. u, 6.

171 Beck (1998), p. 128.

172 Suarez (1983), pp. 200–201. On Suarez see Marion (1981). Descartes seems to oppose Suarez on just this point, for it is said by him that God forms truth like a king who lays down rules in his kingdom. Yet, as Marion makes clear, Descartes has not challenged Suarez' basic presupposition, namely, that these ideas are exterior to God; (1981), pp. 134–139. Furthermore, Descartes' protection of the divine transcendence does not stop the Cartesian God from being subjected to other 'laws'. Gillespie (1995) makes the point well: 'Deception . . . is the consequence of imperfection and no such imperfection is found in God. That is to say, deception requires self-consciousness, which is the basis for distinguishing oneself from others. God, however, is not self-conscious. God thus is no deceiver . . . [Descartes'] God is an impotent God, not an omnipotent God, a God who has lost his independence and become a mere representation within human thinking', pp. 61–62. See also Marion (1998).

173 *De Veritate*, q. 1, art. 2.

174 Knuuttila and Alanen (1988), p. 41.

175 Klocker (1992), p. 114.

176 As Cronin (1966) says about Scotus: 'He inherits from and maintains the essentially platonic thesis of Avicenna and of Henry of Ghent, namely, that for whatever is conceivably intelligible there is given that conceivably intelligible essence', p. 199. Van der Lecq (1998) concludes that 'Scotus commits himself to a certain kind of reality of the possibles', p. 97. These possibles are, as McGrade (1985) argues, 'really nothing. They are beyond being', p. 154. For the Platonic legacy of Avicenna, Ghent, Scotus and Ockham, see Paulus (1938), p. 135; Pegis (1942); Gilson (1952b), p. 111. (It may be more accurate to describe this legacy as Neoplatonic.)

177 Klaus Jacobi (1983), p. 107.

178 See Alanen (1985), p. 175; see also Karger (1980), pp. 250, 256.

179 If Henry of Ghent had intended to overcome the necessitarianism of Avicennian essences, which must in being possible become realised, he did so (as did Scotus and Ockham) by letting them exist necessarily in the *a priori* realm of logical possibility. Avicenna's essences do in the end retain their necessity, doing so in being a nothing *as* something.

180 In a sense we can begin to read Kafka's tale 'Before the Law', as an allegory depicting modernity's death of God.

181 'Henry was but a hair's breadth from the strictly logical definition Duns would later provide', Marrone (1996), p. 184; see also Marrone (1988).

182 As Blumenberg (1983) says, reality 'became an amorphous sea of particulars, on which the concept creating understanding had to set up orientation marks', p. 519. This is what Blumenberg calls Ockham's 'phenomenalism', *ibid.*, p. 189.

183 Gilson (1952b), p. 248; italics mine.

184 Burrell (1990), p. 118. Blumenberg (1983) refers to the notion of a plurality of worlds as: 'The idea [which] was to become one of the essential factors in the disintegration of the metaphysical idea of the cosmos, preparatory to the modern age', p. 156.

185 See Boehner (1958), pp. 96–110; see also Adams (1977), pp. 144–176.

186 Quoted by Alanen (1985), p. 178.

187 *Ibid*.

188 Adams (1987), p. 1051.

189 Ord. I, d. 36, q. 1.

190 Alanen (1985), p. 180.

191 Ord. I, d. 43, q. un, n. 18.

192 McGrade (1985), p. 154. McGrade is here playing on Gershwin's *Porgy and Bess*.

193 Ross (1989), p. 268.

194 *Ibid*., p. 256.

195 See Ross (1990), p. 189.

196 Ross (1986), p. 319.

197 See Goris (1996), p. 188, fn. 10.

198 *Ibid*., p. 274.

199 See Lovejoy (1960).

200 See Klaus Jacobi (1983), p. 193.

201 See Ross (1986), p. 317.

202 Ross (1989), p. 271.

203 See Moody (1975), pp. 371–392.

204 Goris (1996), p. 275.

205 *Ibid*., p. 274.

206 Schmidt (1966), p. 318. According to Schmidt, Aquinas does understand logic as intensional, but only on a 'secondary plane', *ibid*.

207 On *ens infinitum* see Catania (1993).

208 *Quodlibetal Questions*, q. 5.57; italics mine. The language of 'capture' resonates with Plotinian audacity.

209 Gilson (1952a), p. 86.

210 Cross (1999), p. 176, fn. 36.

211 See Ord. I, d. 2, q. 1, a. 2, ad. 2.

212 Alliez (1996), p. 210.

213 Gilson (1952b), p. 303.

214 Alliez (1996), p. 210.

215 *Quodlibetal Questions*, q. 5.57; italics mine.

216 Guénon (1953), p. 139.

217 As Caffarena puts it: 'Entire la téologia natural de San Tomas, centrada alrededor del Ser Subsistente, en que la Infinitud como nota expresa no juega papel preponderante, y la de Duns Escoto, toda centrada en al Ens Infinitum, puede ocupar un puesto intermedio, que explique en parte la evolucion, Enrique De Gante'; quoted by Davenport (1999), p. 99, fn. 39; see also Caffarena (1958).

218 See Gilson (1955a), p. 449.

219 Davenport (1999), p. 152. For Ghent's understanding of infinity see Gilson (1952b), p. 208.

220 See Davenport (1999), which is an examination of the idea of this intensive infinite.

221 See *Summa Contra Gentile*, 1, 43.

222 Davenport (1999), pp. 65–66.

223 See Vignaux (1976), pp. 264, 497; Bonansea (1983), pp. 135–138.

224 Ord. 1.3.1.1–2, n. 58.

225 See *Quodlibetal Questions*, q. 5; *Tractatus de Primo Principio*, chapter 3.

226 *Summa Theologiae*, 1, q. 7, a. 1.

227 For an excellent analysis of quantitative logic see Guénon (1953), (2002).

228 Blanchot (1986), p. 64.

229 Cross (1999), p. 45.

230 Bouyer (1999), p. 260.

231 Cross (1999), p. 39.

232 See Davenport (1999), ch. 5.

233 *Quodlibetal Questions*, V.

234 Davenport (1999), p. 280.

235 *Quodlibetal Questions*, V; italics mine.

236 Ord. 1.8.1.3, n. 82.

237 *Opus Oxoniense* II, d. 17, q. 2, n. 5.

238 Te Velde (1998).

239 Alliez (1996), p. 212.

240 Goodchild (2001), p. 164; see also Smith (2001).

241 *Ibid.*, p. 165.

2

SCOTUS AND OCKHAM

Intuitive cognition – to cognise nothing

Intuitive cognition did not originate with William of Ockham, although it did receive what can only be described as a revolutionary treatment at the hands of the *inceptor*. However, Duns Scotus had already given intuitive cognition an unprecedented importance and even before Scotus the doctrine of *notitia intuitiva* was inchoately present.[1] The motives for developing the notion stemmed from the problems generated by the Franciscan belief in direct knowledge of individuals, a belief that became officially sponsored in 1282.[2] This created a problem, as Scotus advocated a form of species theory which seemed to provide little, if any, direct cognition of actual substances, since species only communicated accidents and these were only 'represented'. The fact of mediation, it seemed, introduced an epistemic gulf between the species and the objects which generated them. As Tachau says, 'it introduced the probability that perceptions of extramental reality were not only sometimes, as in the case of sensory illusion, but inevitably inaccurate or approximate'.[3] Scotus sought to resolve this by utilising the idea of intuitive cognition.[4]

Along with abstract cognition there was concurrent intuition that provided the knower with direct existential knowledge. This form of cognition was immediate, and it occurred both in the intellect and in the senses. Aristotle had insisted that the intellect knew universals while the senses dealt with individuals. Both Duns Scotus and Ockham thought to interpret this inclusively, *viz.*, the intellect did indeed know the universal but it also knew the individual. This interpretation was given some weight by another Aristotelian doctrine that superior powers could always do what inferior powers did. To Scotus and Ockham it would be a breach of this principle not to allow the superior power, that is, the intellect, to enjoy the abilities of the inferior power, the senses. However, this *cognitio singularis* was for the *viator (pro statu isto)* a knowledge of existence, not of singularity *per se*. For a knowledge of singularity one would have to wait for heaven (*in patria*). As Scotus says, 'there can be such an intellectual cognition, which is called "intuitive"; otherwise the intellect would not be certain concerning the existence of any object. Nor

44

can this intellectual intuition (or intuitive intellection) be had by means of a species present, because the species represents indifferently an existent or non-existent thing'.[5]

For Scotus the two modes of cognition differ according to their 'object'. For abstract cognition this object is the species, which is similar to the extramental object that is itself the cause of intuitive cognition. The latter type of cognition is rather conditional upon the presence and existence of the object (*praesentialiter existens*). It is this prerequisite which enables Scotus to introduce a further distinction, namely, that of perfect and imperfect intuitive cognition. Perfect intuitive cognition is the aforementioned cognition of a present and existing object, and imperfect intuitive cognition is a cognition that involves intuitions of objects that were once present and existing, but are no longer so. It is this type of cognition that enables memory. But this was bound to generate problems. As Tachau says, even 'a sympathetic reader may find that the notion of imperfect intuitive cognition retains aspects of the notion of abstractive cognition'.[6] The problem was the possibility of discernible difference, a problem to be resolved by Ockham's use of *habitus*.[7]

William of Ockham accepted Scotus' doctrine of intuitive cognition, but only did so by radically transforming it. Furthermore, according to Paul Vignaux the distinction between abstract and intuitive cognition may be '*le point de départ de la théorie de la connaissance, peut-être de toute la philosophie de Guillaume d'Ockham*'.[8] As was generally the case, Ockham employed the dichotomy between sensation and intellect. Each of these has corresponding abilities, but generally everything the sense can cognitively do so also can the intellect; the converse is not held to be true. Cognitive powers are divided into acts that are apprehensive (*apprehensivus*) and acts that are adjudicative (*iudicativus*). This distinction is, for Ockham, primary and will shape his whole understanding of cognition. Adjudicative acts only occur in the intellect, because they are complex, while apprehensive acts occur both in the intellectual and in the sensitive faculties, as they are incomplex or complex.[9]

With regard to the intellect Ockham says there are two acts. The first of the two possible intellective acts is that of apprehension. This relates to anything that can be a term for either an incomplex or complex intellective act. Both incomplexes and propositions can act as a terminus for apprehension. One can apprehend a thing but one can also apprehend a demonstration or a proposition. The second act is that of adjudication, but this is only of complex objects as it will always involve either dissent from or assent to that complex object. If you do not have the assent or dissent you quite obviously do not adjudicate, but only apprehend. Because this act involves this definitive element it perforce excludes incomplexes because one cannot assent or dissent to an incomplex; one can only use an incomplex to construct a complex which can then enable judgement. For example, if I apprehend a ball I cannot assent or dissent to that ball until it is used in a complex, such as 'this ball does not exist'. It is for this reason that Ockham insists that our 'intellects do not assent to anything unless we believe it to be true, nor do we dissent from anything unless we believe it to be false'.[10]

This is why 'every act of judgement presupposes in the same faculty a non-complex cognition of the terms; for it presupposes an act of apprehension and the act of apprehending a proposition presupposes non-complex cognition of the terms'.[11] It is this intellective act that enables scientific knowledge (*scientia*). What is essential for an understanding of Ockham's doctrine of *notitia intuitiva* is that the act of apprehension is absolutely separate from judgement. This is because 'ontologically' speaking, for Ockham, that which it is not a contradiction to conceive apart is actually apart. In this sense every non-relative reality is a *res absoluta*. It is, as Ockham argues, possible to imagine the apprehension of a proposition and yet the withholding of assent or dissent. It is for this reason that the two acts are indeed absolutely distinct, and it is this distinction that will give rise to the accusation of scepticism.

The intellect can have two distinct non-complex apprehensive cognitions of things. One of these cognitions causes evident knowledge; the other cannot, no matter as Ockham puts it, 'how intense'.[12] These cognitions do not necessarily differ in terms of the object cognised. In fact, for Ockham, they have the same object. He states clearly that 'the same thing is known fully under the same aspect by either cognition'.[13] The reason that Ockham insists on this point is to unify the cognitive process with regard to its object, disabling the requirement of extra metaphysical entities which he is at pains to eradicate. The mention of 'aspects' is explicitly to counter Duns Scotus' demand for the formal distinction, which is employed to consider individuals under the aspect of universality. By arguing that both cognitions afford the same object there is little need for the generation of (hypostasised) metaphysical entities.

These two cognitions, one of which can cause evident knowledge while the other, although being the same in 'appearance', cannot, are intuitive and abstract respectfully. Abstract cognition is defined by Ockham as a cognition which is 'indifferent to existence', as that cognition which 'abstracts from existence and non-existence and from all other conditions which contingently belong to or are predicated of a thing'.[14] But this will have to be qualified when it becomes apparent that, in one sense, intuitive cognition is also indifferent to existence in so far as it can cognise non-existents. What will start to become obvious is that there is a conceptual, rather than perceptual, difference at work in the distinction between the two cognitions. For Scotus, abstract cognition had been perceptually different from intuitive cognition as its object was different

– one cognised species and universal concepts, while the other cognised the actual existence of these. But, as already mentioned, this distinction – as far as Ockham was concerned – generated unwanted metaphysical entities. Because of this he shifted the distinction from a perceptual to a conceptual plane. Abstraction is, in this sense, perceptually identical to intuitive cognition, the difference residing in the conceptual approach each took to 'objects'.[15]

Ockham defines intuitive cognition as cognition 'that enables us to know whether the thing exists or does not exist'.[16] So even here it 'looks' the same as abstract cognition for it considers both existence and non-existence. Ockham argues that

> intuitive cognition, necessarily, and in- and of itself, is neither more of existence than of non-existence, nor does it more consider the existence than the non-existence of a thing. Instead it considers the existence as much as the non-existence of a thing. . . . Abstractive [cognition] however considers neither the existence nor the non-existence of a thing, since the judgement either that a thing exists or that it does not exist, cannot be had by means of abstraction.[17]

It is the possibility of adjudicative acts that distinguishes the two, not abstract cognition's indifference to existence or non-existence because this, in a sense, would 'look' the same as an intuitive knowledge's cognition of either an existent or a non-existent. It seems to have been Ockham's intention to make the two types of cognition 'look' the same so that no positive metaphysical entities are generated. These would allow for the possibility of reality which is otherwise than individual, and for Ockham everything outside the mind is by definition individual.[18] It would be because of a perceptual difference that metaphysical entities would be generated as they would be employed to both describe and unify the cognised object.

Ockham articulates five reasons upon which the distinction between abstract and intuitive cognition cannot be based, these being mistakenly employed by Duns Scotus. The first is the assertion that the two differ according to the presence or existence of the object (*res praesens et existens in se*). This cannot be the case because, as will be discussed below, God can conserve the intuition of an object in both its absence and non-existence: 'whatever God produces by means of secondary cause, God can produce and conserve immediately and without their aid'.[19] From this we know that the act of intuition itself can be the terminus of an intuitive cognition. The second reason is that the two cognitions are supposed to cognise the object in different degrees, abstract cognition only presenting the object in a diminished likeness. This is not the case. Instead, they attain the same object under the same aspect (*sub eadem ratione*). The third reason was that they differed according to formal cause. Scotus had argued that there were two '*rationes formales motivae*', one which moved the intellect to intuitive cognition, the other to abstract, the object and the intelligible species respectively. But because for Scotus they can both be caused by God without an object, they do not have 'ontologically' distinct formal causes. The fourth reason is that intuitive cognition has an annexed real and actual relation with the object, while abstract cognition has only a potential relation. But the argument against this again stems from divine omnipotence. A real relation, as Scotus agrees, cannot have non-being for an object, but as an intuitive cognition is possible *de potentia absoluta* every supposed real relation is separable (or reducible, as it is only a connotative term). Consequently, real relations are inessential and so unable to function as a distinction. The fifth reason is that the presence of the object known distinguishes the two cognitions, it being perfectly represented in an intuitive cognition. For Ockham, this is incoherent, as God can provide us with intuitive cognition of what is not present.[20] Instead of these five reasons, abstract and intuitive cognition differ in themselves (*seipsis*): hence, as already said, it is not a perceptual difference. (Not only is there no perceptual difference between these two different types of cognition, there is also no perceptual difference within those cognitions, as will be argued below.)

Just as Ockham adopted and adapted the Scotist dichotomy of intuitive and abstractive cognition, he also utilised and adjusted the distinction between perfect and imperfect intuitive cognition. Natural perfect intuitive cognition is cognition of what is now present; *hic et nunc*, while imperfect, or *recordative*, cognition is that 'through which we judge a thing to have been or not to have been'.[21] This differs from abstract cognition in being temporal, as it involves what does or does not exist. Imperfect knowledge is the result of a habit, which results from a sequence beginning with perfect knowledge. There is an exegetical debate that does not concern us here except to say that it involves the role of abstract cognition. There appear to be two incompatible positions put forward by Ockham. The first interpretation ascribes to abstract cognition the role of partial cause of the cognitive habit. The second attributes causation to perfect knowledge alone. Boehner argues that the first version was actually developed after the second.[22] Gordon Leff finds Boehner's arguments confusing but agrees that the first version was the one adopted by Ockham.[23] It seems that at the same time as one has a perfect intuitive cognition, one simultaneously has an abstract cognition. This abstract cognition, along with the intellect, is partial cause of a habit that allows imperfect intuitive cognition. The temporality of the cognition stems from the coincidence of the abstract cognition, as partial cause of it, with perfect intuitive cognition. Yet it remains purely abstract because it is caused by abstraction and not intuitive knowledge, and it is an Aristotelian axiom that like acts produce like habits.[24]

This brings us to William of Ockham's notorious doctrine; the *notitia intuitiva* of non-existents. For Ockham there are a number of fundamental principles which shape his work. One of these is, 'God is able to produce the proper effects of secondary causes in the absence of those secondary causes';[25] another, 'anything is to be attributed to the divine power, when it does not contain a manifest contradiction'.[26] These enable the principle of annihilation, which states that every non-relative reality can, without contradiction, exist without any other non-relative reality by virtue of divine power. This is Ockham's 'ontological' isolationism, which is governed by the principle of non-contradiction. Consequently, identity is based on numerical unity. Because of this one can have intuitive cognition of a non-existent, as the act of cognition is itself the terminus for the cognition. It must be, for we know *de potentia absoluta* that God can offer us intuitive cognitions in the absence of the cognised objects. If this were not the case then God would not be able to dispense with secondary causes, in the way already suggested, and this would seriously threaten God's omnipotence as conceived by Ockham.[27]

An act of cognition is itself a non-relative reality. It is certainly caused by extra-mental objects, but these are secondary influences in that they are only partial causes of any cognition. If Ockham could not assert the possibility of an intuitive cognition of non-existents then he would have to allow for a perceptual difference between abstract and intuitive cognition, and, as said above, this would give licence to the likes of Duns Scotus to posit the existence of metaphysical entities, other than individuals, which possess some form of reality outside the mind (in terms of not being mind dependent). Consequently, Ockham deems intuitive cognition to be distinct in terms of its ability to cause evident knowledge, which is the basis of all contingent facts.

Ockham's concern for metaphysical parsimony is enforced by the principle of non-contradiction, a principle elevated to a position which it had never before occupied. Combining this principle, which is now taken to define identity in terms of numerical unity, with the principle of annihilation, metaphysical 'stalwarts' such as essence and, in a sense, existence, are dissolved. They become nominal, or more accurately connotative terms, and so are reducible to an individual. For example, if there is such a thing as an essence that is not connotative, then, Ockham argues, God would be unable to destroy one man without destroying all that which participates in the essence of man. It is important to realise that the belief in intuitive cognition of non-existents provided Ockham with a conceptual arsenal to use against his more metaphysically prolix predecessors.

49

If indeed the defining characteristic of intuitive cognition is the ability to cause evident knowledge, that is, contingent propositions, then we can see how non-existents do not disturb this criterion. If a cognition can supernaturally exist in the absence of a cognised reality then it will, being intuitive, still be able to cause evident knowledge; the knowledge, in this case, being negative. This is why Leff calls intuitive cognition 'existential in the full sense'.[28] Ockham's only guiding principle as to what can actually be cognised is that it not be repugnant to existence. This is the development of the modality discussed above. Such an expanded existentiality generates a number of significant shifts in our understanding of what it means to exist.

As Boler comments, 'Ockham was not fully in control of the implications of his having defined intuitive cognition in terms of true propositions.'[29] It seems that intuitive knowledge comes to be less existential and more about evidential propositions. Leff, who was quoted above extolling the full existentiality of *notitia intuitiva* in his book on Ockham, in an essay published a year later says that it is only 'secondarily and contingently existential' – its primary concern being that it is evidential.[30] This, it seems, is what he means by a conception of truth as logical and conceptual, a notion he attributes to Scotus and Ockham.[31] This re-orientation, according to Leff, was taken by Ockham to its 'literal' and logical conclusion, in substituting a conceptual and logical order for a metaphysical one.[32] Intuitive cognition appears to reside less and less in actuality and more and more in factuality.[33]

Ockham is *factualising actuality*, an event that gives credence to Gilson's contention 'that human knowledge would be practically indistinguishable from what it is, even though all its objects were destroyed; nothing is necessarily required to make knowledge possible, but the mind and God'.[34] Existence matters little in the Ockhamite world, where facts are the units of knowledge, and these are logical, not metaphysical, 'entities'. Below, however, I will examine this accusation that Ockham's work leads to scepticism.

After the publication of Étienne Gilson's Harvard lectures in the 1930s a controversy ensued.[35] In that publication Gilson had a chapter entitled 'The road to skepticism', the contents of which argued that William of Ockham's work led to a particular form of scepsis. This was vigorously denied by a number of academics, the most notable being Fr Boehner and E. Moody.[36] Boehner published an article on Ockham's doctrine of *notitia intuitiva*, concentrating on intuitive cognition of non-existents, as this had been the source of most of the claims for Ockhamian scepticism.[37] In this article Boehner had defended Ockham, vigorously contesting Gilson's interpretation of the 'Venerable Inceptor'. This article prompted Anton Pegis to write a reply defending the accusation of scepticism levelled at Ockham by Gilson.[38] Fr Boehner returned the compliment by attacking Pegis' stance on the subject.[39] Pegis did not reply for a number of years, but was finally encouraged to do so by the publication of Fr Sebastian Day's book on intuitive cognition in Scotus and Ockham, a book written under the supervision of Fr Boehner.[40] This book criticised Gilson's interpretation and asserted that Pegis' failure to respond to Boehner's second paper indicated defeat. Consequently, Pegis did respond by publishing another paper. The legacy of this debate can still be witnessed in the work of revisionist writers who side with Moody, Boehner, Day *et al.*, while the likes of Maurer write under the influence of both Gilson and Pegis. Below I briefly examine the main tenets of Anton Pegis' interpretation, before moving on to more contemporary versions of the debate.

It was argued that intuitive cognition of non-existents allowed for false existential judgements, because one could never be sure if the object intuitively cognised was actually there or not. This possibility for error lay in Ockham's definition of intuitive cognition, as found in his commentary on the *Sentences*.[41] Pegis correctly divides this definition up into two parts. The first speaks about judgements of existence, the second about judgements of non-existence. Ockham says, 'Through intuitive knowledge we judge a thing to exist, and this in general, whether the intuitive knowledge is caused naturally or by God alone supernaturally.'[42] If this cognition is caused naturally a suitable degree of nearness is required. But if it is caused supernaturally this proximity is superfluous. God is able to cause an intuitive cognition of an object in Rome – in doing so we will judge that it exists thus and so. Here already, Pegis contends, Ockham has crossed his Rubicon.[43] It is the redundancy of presence and existence as a prerequisite for intuitive cognition that Ockham utilises to differentiate his doctrine from that of Duns Scotus'. As we already know, Scotus requires both presence and existence for intuitive cognition. Pegis' point is that this reconception of *notitia intuitiva* is the moment of scepticism.

Ockham states, 'it is compatible that the object be nothing, or that it be at a very great distance; and however far away be the intuitively known object, I can immediately judge through it that the object exists, if it exists in the above way'. Pegis' argument, at this point, rests upon the contention that there are two parts to the definition of *notitia intuitiva* at work here. The first is '*per cognitionem intuitivam judicamus rem esse quando est*'. The second is '*eodem modo per cognitionem intuivam possum iudicare rem non esse, quando non est*'.[44] The first allows one to have a supernaturally caused intuitive cognition yet still judge that the object or the cognition exists, because at this point the second part of the definition has not been introduced. An intuition caused *a solo Deo* still gives rise to positive judgements, but as this is supernaturally caused, the 'object' is a '*purum nihil'*. The only condition this *purum nihil* will have to meet is that it is possible, *viz.*, that it is not repugnant to being.

Is the supernatural causation of the intuitive cognition, in the first part of the definition, only referring to proximity and not to non-existence? If so there is never actually a false judgement, only a miraculous one. The example given in this section is of an object beyond a suitable nearness. But when differentiating his position from Scotus, Ockham says that neither 'presence nor being suitably near' is required. As this is still dealing with the first part of the definition, one could interpret it in Pegis' favour. For presence is not the same as proximity so it may well refer to existence. But immediately below this Ockham distinguishes, whether deliberately or not, between existence and presence. He speaks of a thing 'present and existing'. This does not scupper Pegis' interpretation because even if there is this differentiation, what is thus differentiated can still accommodate his view. Ockham explicitly states that neither existence nor presence is required for an intuitive cognition, and it does appear that at this point we are still only defining *notitia intuitiva* as that by 'which we judge a thing to exist when it exists'.

There may well be a confusion here, one which resides in conflicting understandings of what it means to exist. For Pegis it is a presently existing metaphysical subject; for Ockham it is to be a fact, to employ an anachronistic term. So if there is a supernaturally caused intuitive cognition of something which does not exist and a judgement of existence, according to the first part of the definition, this judgement will be the existence of an act of cognition. In this case it will be an abstract cognition which is still conditioned by the possible. If we assent to the existence of a non-existent we do so only in terms of how it exists. As Ockham says, we will judge it to exist 'if it exists in the above way'. This way to exist is as a non-existent, which is a pure nothing. Pegis would be happy with this, as it appears to confirm his accusation of scepticism. But, for Ockham, this would not be sceptical because, as Pegis observes, Ockham has rendered the distinction between the possible and the actual useless.[45] So to be thinkable is to exist in the manner of a possible; this is why Alanen says that for Ockham things are 'possible absolutely'.[46] So, as McGrade says, the *purum nihil* 'turns out to be a very rich and plentiful nothing'.[47]

Gilson's charge that, according to Ockham, it does not matter for human knowledge whether the extra mental world exists or not, is correct. But Pegis, when delivering Gilson's charge, must take into consideration the modality employed by Ockham. When Pegis insists that Ockham does at least in one place allow for a judgement of existence to be assented to, he must be aware that the possible does 'exist'. And Ockham will insist that he is able to discern the difference between an intuitive cognition of a possible (with a judgement of existence in terms of how a possible exists), and an intuitive cognition of an object that presently exists, not in the manner of a possible but in the manner of a realised possible; in this sense both are evident cognitions, but they are two different evident cognitions. This difference is not a difference of perception, but the difference of an event. The two cognitions are two different events. But are they generically different? The first is a type of cognition that lacks any secondary causation, *viz.*, an object, and so it is unable to give rise to the cognitive *event* that is the second cognition. The first cognition is intuitive because it is of what is possible – one can never intuitively cognise a chimera;[48] it is able to tell us that this possible exists, but does not exist in a realised sense. The second cognition tells us that the intentional object exists both as a possible and as a realised possible.

In the *Quodlibetal Questions* Ockham asserts that God cannot cause in us an evident cognition of that which does not exist, as that would be a contradiction.[49] Furthermore, Ockham clearly spells out why we have different judgements:

> It is not absurd that some cause with another partial cause will cause some effect, and nevertheless that the former cause alone without the latter partial will cause the opposite effect. And hence intuitive cognition of a thing with the thing itself causes the judgement that the thing is; when however, the thing itself is not, then the same intuitive cognition without the thing will cause the opposite judgement.[50]

This passage concerns the second part of the definition of intuitive cognition where it is defined as that which enables both the judgement of that which is and of that which is not. This would seem to contradict the first part which, as Pegis rightly argues, does seem to allow for a positive judgement of existence even though one is dealing with an unrealised possibility. However, the judgement of non-existence means the judgement that it does not exist in actuality. Here Pegis concedes to Boehner that God does not in this instance trick us like a conjuror with an illusion: however, Pegis rightly points out that Ockham does describe the fully intuited possible at times as 'non existent'. With Gilson, in the Thomist tradition, Pegis rightly asks whether one can reduce contingent actuality to a kind of simulacrum within possibility in this fashion, without thereby covertly invoking actuality.

Another criticism levelled at Ockham with regard to scepticism is that his doctrine of intuitive cognition is circular. The point at issue is whether it is a vicious circularity or not. As Wengert says, 'Ockham holds that the reliability of intuitive cognition is established by the relation of intuitive cognition to evident cognition.'[51] But this means that the veridicality of this mode of cognition is *retrospective*. We are able to know that we have an intuitive cognition when evident cognition occurs. The problem with this is that we only know that what we have is evident when we know that it is caused by intuitive cognition. It would be reasonable to expect that intuitive cognition determines evident cognition, as it is this form of cognition which is supposed to cause evident knowledge. But Ockham, as we see, has reversed the order. This forces Ockham to anchor the process in the security of formal definitions. As Wengert says, 'evident cognitions as [Ockham] defines them are by definition true'.[52] But this simply shifts the problem. If the only distinction is one of definition, then intuitive cognition cannot but be retrospective, and indeed rather occult. Streveler points to this retrospective element when he says that 'when an existential judgement turns out to be false, it is *then* based upon abstract cognition'.[53] Richards makes exactly the same point, namely that 'any kind of cognition which leads to deception would *by definition* not be an intuitive cognition'.[54] This circularity makes distinction impossible or, as Scott puts it, it is a distinction without determinable difference.[55] Ockham appears to reconceive cognition in only logical terms; in a sense, it only occurs within terms. Streveler declares that this was Ockham's crucial insight: reconceiving epistemology as a logical problem.[56] Likewise, Boler argues that Ockham's 'analysis . . . is controlled directly not by any observation of the parade of cognitive activity but rather by the demands of the analysis of propositions'.[57] Finally, Vossenkuhl explicitly states that 'to know the meaning of a thing is equivalent to the intuitive knowledge of it . . . to posit the intuitive cognition of a non-existent thing is therefore equivalent to stating the meaning of a term or name which stands for that thing'.[58]

Cognition is, then, retrospective because we must look at that which comes after it to determine which type of cognition it 'was'. But even such a retrospective recognition exists only formally. This becomes more obvious when we hear Ockham in the *Quodlibetal Questions* saying that 'God can cause assent which is of the same kind as evident assent. But this assent is not evident because what is assented to is not as it is in fact'.[59] Ockham's reassurance rests purely on a matter of definition. And we must ask, with Richards, 'how effective a definitional procedure is at avoiding skepticism'.[60] These assents, which are *eiusdem speciei* as evident cognition, disable any notion of introspective discernment, because as creditative act (*actum creditivum*) they will appear at every level, apart from a strictly formal one, indistinguishable from an evident cognition. So not only is intuitive cognition dependent on retrospective recognition, this belated identification is impossible *a priori*. For what it identifies as evident could just as easily be merely creditive, especially when we remember they are of the same 'kind' as each other. In this sense intuitive cognition is only 'nominal', as it only occurs within the formalism of logical terms and functional definitions. As Woznicki says, 'Ockham's metaphysics became a pure logic'.[61] It may be recalled that intuitive cognition is called by both Scotus and Ockham 'perfect', but it seems that its only perfection is that of tense. If this is indeed the case then we can see that it is more similar to the cognition of an existent possibility, which we can think of as having an imperfection also only in terms of tense.

The above is exacerbated when we consider that in the Ockhamian world we cannot rely upon the omnipotent God not to deceive us. Adams makes just this point when discussing Fr Boehner's defence of Ockham.[62] She argues that Boehner 'fails to show that Ockham's admission of the logical possibility that God could deceive us, does not really lead to skepticism'.[63] Furthermore, Adams continues, 'Ockham's assertion of the divine omnipotence, together with his grounding of ethical distinction in the concept of obligation, rule out an *a priori* demonstration that God is no deceiver'.[64] This is especially problematic when you consider that, for Ockham, goodness is by *definition* that which God does, so that if God were to deceive he would not fall short of perfect goodness.[65]

It has already been noted that a fundamental distinction for Ockham is that between apprehension and judgement. Because each of these acts is a non-relative reality they can, as we already know, exist without the other. This means that we can have intuitive apprehension and still a judgement need not logically follow. Consequently, we are returned to the problems of retrospective recognition and merely definitional intelligibility.[66] In actuality, or in factuality as it is here becoming, this means that cognition is indeterminable. An apprehensive intuitive cognition of an existent 'looks' exactly the same as that of a possible existent. What is required to introduce distinction is judgement, but it must rely on this intuitive cognition to provide it with that which it judges. In this sense apprehensive intuitive cognition sees, but sees darkly, because what one sees may not have been seen, while judgement without apprehension sees only in the dark. And even when the two are combined there is still obfuscation (from *fuscus* meaning dark), as judgement must rely upon indistinct apprehension. For there is never any perceptual difference; it must be remembered that cognition is an act without appearance. Ockham asserts 'that we have a cognition proper to one singular thing, not on account of a greater likeness to one than to another'.[67] So the two modes of cognition presuppose each other. This circularity will again take us to seek veridicality in the logic of formal definitions. It seems that we cognise in the dark; that which we cognise is always dark matter, or a matter only for the dark. Science becomes a 'noctuary'.

We have just observed that existence and non-existence 'look' the same to apprehensive intuitive cognition. It seems that this may be the case because, as intimated earlier, Ockham has factualised actuality. What it means to exist has radically altered. Existence now means to be either possible or to be a realised possibility. Ockham wishes to dismantle any metaphysical community, and this is why actuality becomes factualised; a fact is ontologically isolatable, and it does not require metaphysically sophisticated ideas, such as being and essence (which require an identity other than a purely numerical one). Were being and essence admitted then both the principle of annihilation, with its 'ontology' of singulars, and Ockham's notion of omnipotence would be impossible. Ockham must, therefore, dilute the difference between existence and non-existence. He does this by making the abstract and intuitive perceptually indistinct, in allowing an extension of intuitive cognition's remit to include non-existence. This means that existence is a matter of fact, *viz.*, it is a singular cognitive event which is without appearance. In this sense, a fact will remain the same as it did before it existed. That is, it will remain as nothing. (Again we see that univocity really is one of *non-being*.)

An Ockhamian individual must not allow '*nothing*' to become a positive privation, otherwise a metaphysical existentiality will arise, along with its requisite metaphysical community, which resides within and beyond numerical unity. If *nothing* becomes a positive privation, the individual will no longer be 'simple' in the manner Ockham requires it to be. For the individual to be an absolute thing it must not be externally determined. Instead it must, as itself, contain or be its own factual intelligibility (this is to be found in its formal definition). The only difference between this fact as a real-possible and as a realised-possibility can be the will of Ockham's omnipotent God. This means that the nothingness which resides outside every absolute thing must become part of that thing. Of course it would be a contradiction, even for Ockham, to make the nothing something, but it is not contradictory to make the nothing part of the something as the something. In this sense nothing becomes a connotative term, signifying the something primarily and the absence of all else secondarily. This *nothing* is all important for Ockham's ontology because it is the nothing that surrounds the factuality of the absolute thing which defines it, if not constitutes it. Only through the possibility of this nothing outside the individual do we have the individual. Ockham would, of course, complain that this interpretation forces him to hypostasise the nothing, but this is exactly what Ockham does. Nominalism requires, contradictorily, just this one (non-)universal. But this hypostasised nothing is, I suggest, in effect none other than Ockham's omnipotent God, who is ripe for development into the immanent nullity of Baruch Spinoza's Substance.

The next chapter examines Spinoza's book *The Ethics*, in an effort to locate the nothing operating more openly *as* something. Hegel accuses Spinoza of *acosmism*, but the chapter below argues that it is wiser to think of Spinoza as an advocate of *pan(a)theistic acosmism*. Spinoza's God may absorb the cosmos, but Nature also absorbs God.

Notes

1 Tachau (1988), p. 70.
2 See Boler (1982), p. 461.
3 Tachau (1988), p. 69.
4 See Wolter (1982) for a history of the development of this doctrine in Duns Scotus.
5 Ord. IV, d. 45, q. 2.
6 Tachau (1988), p. 72.
7 See Fuchs (1952).
8 Vignaux (1948), p. 11.
9 The term 'complex' stems from Aristotle's use of the word *symploke*, in the *Categories* 1a 16. This term means to combine, or bring together. See Aristotle (1984).
10 Prologue to the *Ordinatio*, q. i, N sqq.; see Ockham (1990), p. 18.
11 *Ibid.*, p. 19.
12 *Ibid.*, p. 20.
13 *Ibid.*, p. 23.
14 *Ibid.*, pp. 22–23.
15 This will give rise to Ockham's development, and axiomatic use of, supposition theory which will be his non-metaphysical version of the Scotist formal distinction. See Ockham (1974) and (1980), *Summa Logicae*, 2 vols.
16 *Ibid.*
17 See I Ord. prol. q. 1; cited by Tachau (1988), p. 119.
18 *Sed omnis res extra animam est singularis.*
19 *Quodlibetal Questions*, IV, q. 22 and VI, q. 6.
20 See Ord. Prol. q. 1, 35–37.
21 *Reportatio* II, q. 12–13; cited by Tachau (1988), p. 123.
22 It is second in terms of where it appears in the text. See *Reportatio* II, q. 14–15 g. See also '*Notitia intuitiva* of non-existents', in Boehner (1958).
23 Leff (1975), p. 30.
24 See Leff (1975), pp. 30–34; more generally see Fuchs (1952).
25 *Quodlibetal Questions*, VI, q. 6; see also IV, q. 22.
26 *Ibid.*
27 It has already been suggested above that Ockham's notion of *de potentia absoluta* is an axiomatic *active-capacity*.
28 Leff (1975), p. 10.
29 Boler (1982), p. 469.
30 Leff (1976), p. 62.
31 *Ibid.*, p. 48.
32 *Ibid.*, p. 58.
33 Blumenberg (1983) speaks of the 'groundlessness of the factual world', p. 163.

34 Gilson (1937), p. 82.
35 *Ibid.*
36 See Moody (1935) and Pegis (1937), which is a review of Moody's book.
37 Boehner (1943).
38 Pegis (1944).
39 Boehner (1945).
40 Pegis (1948); Day (1947). See also Pegis (1942).
41 Boehner (1943) published an extensive article, which included an edited version of the relevant text. The text was an excerpt from Ockham's commentary on Peter Lombard's *Sentences* (Sent. II, qq. 14–15). Karger (1999) contends that Boehner misreads Ockham's doctrine of intuitive cognition. As a result he bequeathed to commentators a somewhat mistaken approach.
42 Cited in Pegis (1944), p. 473.
43 *Ibid.*
44 Sent. II, q. 15e; see Boehner (1943), pp. 248–250.
45 Pegis (1944), p. 478.
46 Alanen (1985), pp. 157–187.
47 McGrade (1985), p. 154; see also Adams (1977).
48 See *Quodlibetal Questions,* VI, q. 6.
49 *Ibid.,* V, q. 5.
50 Ord. I, prol. q. 1.
51 Wengert (1981), p. 427.
52 *Ibid.,* p. 427.
53 Streveler (1975), p. 228; italics mine.
54 Richards (1968), p. 353; italics mine.
55 Scott (1969), pp. 45–46; see also Brampton (1965); Davis (1974).
56 Streveler (1975), p. 235.
57 Boler (1976), p. 86.
58 Vossenkuhl (1985), p. 39.
59 *Quodlibetal Questions,* V, q. 5.
60 Richards (1968), p. 362.
61 Woznicki (1990), p. 172. Aquinas treated the truths of logic as secondary intentions. First intentions are concepts of reality, the semantic richness of meta-linguistically conceived thought; see Schmidt (1966), and Moody (1975).
62 Adams (1970).
63 *Ibid.,* p. 397.
64 *Ibid.*
65 *Ibid.,* p. 398.
66 *Ibid.,* p. 393. 'True by definition.'
67 *Quodlibetal Questions,* I, q. 8.

3

SPINOZA

Pan(a)theistic acosmism

Spinoza is the Christ of philosophers.[1]
   (Gilles Deleuze and Felix Guattari)

Let us say of this Christ [that he offers] a salvation that promises *nothing*.[2]

                                      (Alain Badiou)

Introduction

A Marrano was a Jew who converted to Christianity in order to avoid the Inquisition.[3] It was thought that such people only adhered to the outward displays of the Christian religion so that they were able to continue their Judaism secretly within that public display. If we use this image of a double move we can perhaps learn to give a better reading of Spinoza's words as found in the *Ethics*.[4] I argue here that Spinoza was implicitly involved (whatever his conscious intent) in a radical project of rewriting the words of common philosophical parlance, because he collapses their 'original' meaning and uses them as Trojan vehicles to traffic nothing less (or nothing more) than nihilism. In terms of the *aporia* articulated in the Preface to this book, Spinoza copes with it by generating the dualism God or Nature; God supplements Nature, while Nature supplements God. But the simultaneous movement between each betrays a monism, in terms of a single substance.[5] Below I briefly outline the thought of Spinoza as found in the *Ethics*, sticking closely to the text, and employing the terms and arguments to be found there. I then look a little closer at the components of that philosophy before articulating the consequences or the 'reality' of Spinoza's words.

There is only One of us

Spinoza begins the *Ethics* with a methodological definition of *causa sui* and an explication of a tripartite scheme: substance, attribute and mode. (This is similar to the Plotinian triad: One, intellect and soul.) *Causa sui* is that whose essence involves existence. This formulation will hold great importance for Spinoza, leading some such as Lermond to declare that the *Ethics* is nothing but the ontological argument (an immanent one).[6] The first four definitions will later be identified with God, a move which allows Spinoza to simultaneously use each 'under erasure'. This will be explained below. For Spinoza, substance (*substantia*) is that which can be conceived through itself or whose conception does not involve another.[7] An attribute (*attributum*) is that which expresses the essence of substance.[8] Finally, mode (*modus*) is the modification of a substance.[9] Any modification will only be articulated in terms of an attribute and an attribute is nothing but an essential expression of substance. This schematic is articulated within the shadow of *causa sui* and the understanding that 'all things exist either in themselves or in something else'.[10]

Substance: None

At this point Spinoza is developing his geometric philosophy on the understanding that there can in theory be more than one substance. For example, he further defines *substantia* as that which is 'necessarily infinite' and that to which 'existence appertains'.[11] But from the idea that something exists either through self-conception or through that of another, it follows that 'there cannot exist in the universe two or more substances of the same nature or attribute'.[12] If this were not the case then the conception of one substance would *per accidens* involve the conception of another substance. Consequently, neither would be conceptually autarchical. As a result they would fail to attain the appellation *substantia*. But as soon as we identify God, an absolutely infinite being,[13] as *causa sui* we will begin to realise that the category of substance is somewhat 'apophatic' in that its invocation will simultaneously announce its dissolution.

Spinoza says that 'the more reality or Being a thing has, the more attributes belong to it'.[14] But as God is infinite being, or an infinite being, God must include in his self-conception an infinite number of attributes. This means that there cannot be an attribute which God's self-conception does not include. If this is the case, then, there can be no substance other than God. Spinoza declares this to be the case: 'Except God no substance can exist or be conceived.'[15] This use of the concept 'God' has therefore enabled Spinoza to rid the world of all substances (and eventually of all substance).[16] Furthermore, the concept '*Deus*' disables all alternative conceptions, for any conception, by definition, would have to be conceived in terms of an attribute. But this necessarily involves God: 'If any other substance than God exists it must be explained by means of some attribute of God and thus two substances would exist possessing the same attribute.'[17] From the very fact that every substance is necessarily infinite there can be only one substance.[18]

Attributes: None

We already know that an attribute expresses the essence of a substance as perceived by the intellect.[19] There are an infinity of attributes, although we only know two: *cogitatio* and *extensio*.[20] As Spinoza says, thought is one of the infinite attributes of God which expresses the eternal and infinite essence of God: God is a thinking thing.[21] The attribute of extension is formulated in a similar fashion: 'Extension is an attribute of God, or God is an extended thing.'[22] The understanding of attribution follows from the definition Spinoza gives to an idea: 'By idea I understand a conception of the mind which the mind forms by reason of its being a thinking thing.'[23] He uses the word conception to communicate the active element involved in every idea. In a sense, an idea is but an 'act'. Spinoza develops his notion of idea by introducing the term *idea adaequata*. We have an adequate idea when its conception includes all intrinsic denominations of a true idea.[24] What this means is that an adequate idea expresses that which it is without recourse to an unknown cause. Spinoza wants an idea to be adequate in the sense that its conception is literally self-explanatory. It must correspond exactly to its *ideatum* although it need only refer to itself: 'The order and connection of ideas is the same as the order and connection of things.'[25] So if we have an adequate idea and we order these ideas adequately we will leave *no space* within our account: it will be causally *full*.

An attribute, in expressing the essence of a substance, expresses the essence of God. But God's essence is one. This is why Spinoza will continually use the phrase 'in so far as'.[26] Thus we have the attribute of extension only *in so far as* God is considered as an extended thing. So every articulation of the one substance continually returns to that *sole* source. For Spinoza, a particular thing or thought is only to be considered in terms of its being a particular modification of God's essence.[27] A particular thing is a mode, a mode in which God can be *expressed*. The notion that everything is but a modification enables Spinoza to retain his monism. For all that *is* resides only as an expression of the *one*, and it will remain so only as it returns to the *one*. Any attribute is only conceivable if we consider God to be existing in *this* way. An example of this conception will be a mode. The mode reduces to the attribute while an attribute reduces to the one substance. This substance is referred to as *'Deus sive natura'*. Spinoza also formulates this dichotomy in terms of passivity or activity, so that we can think of it as *natura naturata* or else as *natura naturans*. Any particular thing or thought, is only *in so far*

61

as we consider it in passive terms. As soon as it is considered active it returns to the One of which it is but a modification. Consequently, the particular thing is nothing but 'God'.

As expressions of the essence of God, attributes obviously play an extremely important role in the world of Spinoza. For they, like the term substance, prevent alternative conceptions that could re-introduce a metaphysical plurality. An attribute expresses the essence of a 'God' who is immutable.[28] Because of this an attribute must, in a sense, express *all* of 'God'. God's essence has an infinity of attributes, but each of these is itself infinite: 'The idea of God from which infinite things in infinite ways follow can only be one.'[29] Infinitude must be balanced with monistic simplicity: 'Under the attribute of thought or under any other attribute we shall find the same order and one and the same connection of causes.'[30] So any one attribute expresses the same essence, but unless it expresses *all* of that essence, Spinoza will be in danger of introducing a *noumenal* element which will happily accommodate the possibility of an essence or substance more original or more essential. In a sense, such an element would reside *below* the attributes. This would be the case if attributes expressed only a part of the divine essence, only covering part of the whole. This would mean that substance was something other than these attributes – that, ontologically speaking, it comes 'behind' them, even though they are expressing it. If this were the case then a 'space' for transcendence would be left open, as the world, in terms of God's essence, would not be completely immanent.[31] Spinoza tries to avoid this problem by intimating that attributes express 'all' of the divine essence, *in so far as* the divine essence is considered in the manner of *this* attribute.

Nothing: Much

Such are the basic elements of Spinoza's philosophy. Two consequences appear immediately to arise. First, the divine essence is in fact better understood, metaphysically speaking, as nothing. Second, attributes, which are a complete expression of the divine essence *in so far as* they are aspects of it, are also nothing. Spinoza forces the attributes to collapse and likewise the divine essence. There really are two infinities at work. The first of these is the *external* infinity, in that every attribute is only one from an infinity of divine attributes. The second infinity is the *internal* one, because as an expression of the divine essence each attribute must be itself infinite.[32] This means that each attribute is *all* of the divine essence. Spinoza could argue that the single attribute does express *all* of the divine essence considered in its own particular expression of God, for example extension. But it will not make sense for extension to consider thought. It is in this sense that, for Spinoza, truth will always be the 'criterion of itself'.[33]

One attribute cannot lead to another, for each is its own complete world and there could, in a sense, be no bigger world. However, if every attribute carries within itself the mark of its own infinitude then it bears its own dissolution. For the attribute to be able to express the divine essence in terms of the attribute's *own* infinity the divine essence must be nothing. Only in this way can Spinoza avoid precipitating an unwanted noumenality. Conversely, the divine essence, in being expressed by an attribute which, as merely partial, is ontologically nothing, must itself be, again, ontologically nothing. Spinoza will, of course, endeavour to avoid the negative implications of this by negating the nothingness of the nothing (as later, Hegel).[34] He will take away the negativity of nothingness and appears to render it as divine plenitude. This move seems to accord with what I argued to be the very logic of nihilism, *viz.*, to render the something metaphysically nothing and to attempt to have the nothing perform *as* something. Nonetheless, Spinoza does not allow for any notion of metaphysical nothingness. He does not permit non-being in any way to *be* (Bergson later follows his lead).[35] As Lermond comments, for Spinoza 'beyond being non-being is not'.[36] At first glance we may be inclined to agree, but this non-being, which is *not* in reality, occurs within the text of Spinoza as that which is, *viz.*, as being. For Spinoza, on the reading offered here, being is nothing, since it is the one Substance exhausted in its expression as attributes and modes, whose partiality is itself a limitation and negation of the one Substance.

We have begun to see that, for Spinoza, Substance is there to ensure there are no substances and attribute and mode are there to ensure there are no particular things, in any ontological sense – so reinforcing the ontological monism. This may mean that each concept or category used accommodates a self-dissolution; Substance removes all substances and so on. In this sense Spinoza's categories and concepts only begin to speak within the disappearance of that about which they speak.

For the Love of God

For Spinoza there is an epistemic hierarchy accompanying his tripartite schematic and there are three levels to this hierarchy. The first level perpetuates the greatest degree of ignorance. This ignorance is dispelled as we move through the levels. *Cognitio primi generis* consists of *opinio* that functions on the back of *imaginatio*. *Cognitio secundi generis* consists of *notiones communes* which register ontologically valid sameness (universals). This level is that of reason for it is the *ordo-intellectus*, and consequently it seeks necessity.[37] The last level is *scientia intuitiva* which is the epistemic provision of this desired necessity. (This level results from a 'proper love of God'.) When we reach the third level we are aware that nothing occurs without necessity. We know this because we have developed *idea adaequata*. These enable us to realise the causation involved in every event and in everything. The type of causation involved at this level of knowledge is called *causa adaequata*.[38] This causation carries all its effects within its own self-perception. This means that nothing happens without a full causative explanation. To view things from this level is to do so according to eternity (*sub specie aeternitatis*).

I did it: Because

For Spinoza, there must be a reason for everything that is, and for that which is not.[39] It is only the vulgar work of the imagination that generates fictitious notions such as free will and contingency.[40] Echoing Plotinus and Avicenna, Spinoza argues that 'there exists nothing in the universe contingent but all things are determined by the necessity of the divine nature'.[41] Because of this 'things could not have been produced by God in any other way or order than that in which they were produced'.[42] The obvious reason for this is that a change in the 'created order' would necessarily involve a change in the will of God and God is, of course, immutable. The *underlying* reason for this resides in the fact that there is a univocal modality employed by Spinoza to secure his fully immanentised existence. We naturally perceive things to be contingent, but this is only the result of an imperfect knowledge; as a result it fails to bear any ontological weight. Consequently, 'contingency' is unable to suggest other metaphysical notions such as creation *ex nihilo*.[43] However, Spinoza does allow for two versions of contingency. The first is merely the 'liability to corruption' that things exhibit. Because all things have an indefinite duration we are unable to ascertain when they will indeed change or pass away.[44] The duration of any body depends upon 'the common order of nature and the constitution of things'.[45] But God has an adequate knowledge of more than one body. Consequently, God has an adequate knowledge of all bodies. And so for God, or according to eternity, there is no contingency, because in a metaphysical sense there is no change at all. The second notion of contingency is that which we come across when we consider the essence of something and regard the fact that existence is not its essence.[46]

For Spinoza, epistemic lack is the source of our fictions, as there is nothing in reality that could afford any ontological falsity. Falsity (e.g. contingency) is but a consequence of this epistemic privation.[47] Indeed, there is 'nothing positive' in ideas that would enable ontological falsity.[48] This is very interesting because it allows us to notice the strategy that Spinoza has adopted in his nihilistic monism. No idea has anything positive about it, even the idea of God, though Spinoza does not cite this example. This means that at a metaphysical level philosophical discourse actually speaks about nothing.

Through his particular notion of divine plenitude Spinoza transforms causation. 'There is no cause except the perfection of God's nature.'[49] For this reason, 'God is the immanent and not the transitive cause of all things'.[50] Spinoza is rendering efficient causality the same as *causa sui*, but at the same time he will only allow *causa sui* to be spoken of as if it were efficient causality.[51] God causes himself efficiently. In so doing, any notion of final causality is problematised, since everything is perfect as it is. Everything is always already. As Lermond says, 'divine fullness of being grounds Spinoza's critique of final causes'.[52] God's *why* is existence itself: 'the reason or cause why God or nature acts and why it exists is one and the same; therefore, as God exists with no end in view, he does not act with any end in view, but has no principle or purpose in existing or acting'.[53] There is literally no place or space for purpose to occur in the world of Spinoza. *This* way is *that* way. All that *is* has always been and, in another sense, is nothing at all; except, for the moment, the Spinozist God. The existential understanding of being needed to accommodate purposive finality is lacking in a completely immanentised totality. It is for this reason that Spinoza calls all notions of final causes 'fabrications'.[54]

I Am: Not

Spinoza's understanding of the subject is interesting as it illustrates the general direction of the *Ethics*. There is no Cartesian dualism between mind and body, but instead what is sometimes referred to as ontological parallelism. The mind is nothing but the idea of the body and the body is the *ideatum* of the mind.[55] We never move from the mind to the body, but rather everything that modifies the body modifies the mind: 'nothing can happen in the body which is not perceived by the mind'.[56] It must be remembered that the attribute of thought is not different from that of extension but is, in a sense, the same thing looked at in different terms. The mind and the body are, in this way, the same; although the mind never knows the body and the body never 'knows' the mind.[57] While one speaks the other is not, at least in terms of that attribute's infinitude. Each attribute can only speak what the other says in speaking what it itself says as a particular attribute; hence it is only able to register self-modifications. If there is a modification to the body there is also a cognitive modification, in that there is an idea of that bodily modification. The reason for this is that the subject is not first and foremost bodily and then secondarily a mind, while the converse is just as inaccurate. Thought is extension, or is that which is extended but conceived in a completely different manner; for it too represents the same divine plenitude. To understand this we must continually recall that an attribute is 'internally' infinite and so is a totality.

The subject is a configuration of bodies, or in terms of the mind (which is the idea of the body) it is a configuration of ideas. In the *Ethics* we have *corpora simplicissima*. These are single parts or ideas which will reciprocally form *corpora composita*. Every body is formed from many parts which are, in a sense, bodies; these can conspire to constitute an 'individual'. They do so through a certain reciprocal *ratio* of motion and rest. It is this *ratio* that precipitates a union. Parts acting in unison are called *corpora invicem unita*.[58] The parts that form an individual can change over time, growing and shrinking; this will not destroy the individual as long as the proportional *ratio* is maintained.[59] The human body (*corpus humanum*) is constituted by many parts and, in a sense, by many bodies; these bodies are themselves composite.[60] The same goes for the ideas that form the mind.[61] It is only this *ratio* that prefers *this* individual.

Desiring: Nothing

It is when we look at emotions that some sort of ontological qualification appears. According to Spinoza an emotion (*affectus*) is the modification that pertains to a body which either increases or diminishes the power of that body.[62] The *Ethics* treats emotions as if they were planes or lines, doing so in order to ensure that there are no explanatory lacuna. If the modification diminishes the power of the body, it is a *passio*. On the other hand, if we are able to be the adequate cause of those modifications we transform an altercation into an alteration, bringing something exterior 'within the sides' of our body; consequently, it is no longer an infringement. Being the adequate cause of the modification extends the body: it will, through the third level of knowledge, extend as far as eternity, in terms of an intellectual love of God. We call this adequately caused modification an *actio*. By contrast passivity leaves epistemic spaces of vulgarity which are the source of our misery. The 'ontological' element is introduced to explain the impulse of the perpetuated *ratio*. Spinoza calls it *conatus*: 'Each thing in so far as it is in itself endeavours to persist.'[63] And it is this endeavour to persist that defines the individual. The individual is *this* and nothing but *this*.[64] 'The force with which man persists in existing is limited and is far surpassed by the power of external causes.'[65] But it is the principal endeavour of our mind to affirm the existence of the body; any thing which does not affirm the body is not of the mind but is opposed to the mind.[66]

The important point is that although the force of persistence is limited, the duration is indefinite.[67] This is interesting for us because it helps us understand the Spinozist individual. This individual is not a substance. Furthermore, it is not distinguished from other beings because of a substantial difference.[68] Consequently, this individual does not have free will nor does it have a faculty of willing; the will and intellect are one. In reality there are only particular volitions which are caused,[69] and as a result the individual never really perceives anything. So, for Spinoza, 'when we say that the human mind perceives this or that, we say nothing else than that God . . . has this or that idea'.[70] It is for this reason that Spinoza refers to the indefinite duration of the individual. Spinoza must ensure that the individual is indefinite so that, ontologically speaking, the individual can be capable of identity with God. This is so, especially, when we consider it from the divine perspective. The individual must be able to be God so that there is no individual; and God must be that individual to ensure that there is no (transcendent) God. This is the ultimate outcome of Spinoza's univocity of being (or of non-being): everything is in the same way because nothing *is*.

To Not Be: Saved

The *Ethics* expounds a soteriology, a salvific plan based on epistemic progression. The three levels of knowledge have already been articulated above. As one moves from the first to the third level one attains and practises an intellectual love of God (*amor intellectualis Dei*). In this progression we move from pain (*tristitia*) to pleasure (*laetitia*).[71] The former is a passion that leads to less perfection while the latter does just the opposite. Perfection is a matter of virtue which is itself a matter of power.[72] The Good (*bonum*) is that which is useful in terms of an increase in virtue which is an increase in power.[73] Spinoza is here going beyond 'Good and Evil', but is not going beyond the 'good and the bad'; as Nietzsche said, 'Beyond good and evil, at least this does not mean beyond good and bad.'[74] The *Ethics* is developing a non-metaphysical understanding of values which even contains a soteriological element. Salvation lies in viewing the world *sub specie aeternitatis*, as this will provide the adequate causation needed for complete determination. We are saved in that our bodies are extended to eternity, for they are extended by the idea of the one substance of which we are a determinate part. The idea which accompanies this bodily expansion is the idea of God. Or rather, it is the idea of God which expands our body. The idea of God has all 'creation' as its *ideatum*, 'creation' is God's body and this body is *not not* creation's or a creature's. At least this is the case for the saved. The unsaved will continue to inhabit vulgar fictions such as ontological individuality and so the possibility of death remains. But for the saved there is no death because there is a proper understanding that there is no life.

Virtue, which is increased power and so a more persistent *ratio*, is its own reward.[75] Eternity for the saved is not related to time. Instead, it is a practical perspective inhabited knowingly by the enlightened: 'The more the mind understands things by the second and third kinds of knowledge, the less it is acted on by emotions which are bad and the less it fears death.'[76] This fear dwindles further the more we experience our eternity: 'The human mind cannot be absolutely destroyed with the human body, but something of it remains which is eternal . . . eternity cannot be defined by time nor have any relation to time. But nevertheless we sense and experience that we are eternal.'[77] Death is defined by Spinoza as that condition in which the parts of a body 'are disposed that they acquire a different relation of motion and rest'.[78] But death has no reality, just as there is nothing actually bad in the world. Spinoza is adamant about this last point because it prevents any notion of comparison that might again open up a space for a metaphysics of purpose.

Everything is perfect as it is, for it is absolutely necessary, being a determined expression of God's essence: 'Nothing happens in nature which can be attributed to a defect of it: for nature is always the same.'[79] For example, Spinoza recommends a life of crime if that is indeed your 'nature': 'If anyone sees that he can live better on the gallows than at his table he would act very foolishly if he did not go hang himself.'[80] This allows us to realise that in the world of Spinoza there can be no difference between a Holocaust and an ice-cream.[81] Any qualitative discrimination can only stem from the function of our perspective, as a *ratio* seeking to persist. The individual is, then, to realise that it is but a modification of God, while God will be but those modifications, those individuals which are, as stipulated, nothing (since they are not, ultimately, individuals).

Every concept or category Spinoza utilises is used to its own destruction. He radically alters the meaning of a theory, not by arguing openly against it or proposing some change, but through a use of the word which initiates a transmogrification that quickly forgets itself. The strategy adopted by Spinoza I call 'epistemic-anaplerosis', since he fills each concept to such a degree that it implodes; it is implosion rather than explosion because that with which it is filled is literally nothing. This is a result of Spinoza's doublespeak. As Funkenstein comments, 'Spinoza uses terms and notions entrenched in the philosophical and exegetical tradition of the Middle Ages, seemingly accepting their validity while inverting their meaning.'[82] He translates each of these notions or terms into what Yovel calls 'systematic equivalents'.[83] It is for this reason that Deleuze says that 'the *Ethics* is a book written twice simultaneously'.[84] The categorical implosion is managed because Spinoza employs an extreme form of univocity and naturalism.[85]

One voice: Naturally

In the *Ethics* there is a *univocity of cause*, because efficient causality and *causa sui* become equivalent. Consequently, any notion of final causality is explained away. There is also a *univocity of attributes*. I have already commented on the internal/external infinity involved in an attribute. This univocity is a consequence of that infinity. For each attribute is a 'total' expression of God *in so far as* its world is concerned, and all attributional worlds say the same, for they say the same totality, *viz.*, God. This must be the case, as already argued, if there is not to be a noumenal space behind any attribute or collection of attributes. If there were, Spinoza would be unable to collapse the individual into God and God into the individual. Hence the formulation *Deus sive natura*. There is a third univocity, and it is the *univocity of modality*. All that exists exists perfectly and there is no place for metaphysical notions such as contingency or possibility; everything exists necessarily. What these three univocal elements allow is the assertion that nothing metaphysical occurs in the world.[86]

The naturalism which Spinoza employs is, as Mason says, 'startling'.[87] But it is even more so than Mason suspects. Spinoza reduces all that is to naturalistic explanation, leaving no space for metaphysical mischief. Yet he goes further, and reduces Nature itself to 'naturalistic' explanation. Nature itself does not, as it were, exist. Spinoza manages this undeclared mental gymnastics by playing Nature against the idea of God, i.e., by reducing God to Nature he must perforce also reduce Nature to God. Thereby he ensures Nature does not exist in any metaphysical sense. This Nature does not exist – its diversities, separations, finalities and pathos are all illusions. In this way, Spinoza manages to do away with God and Nature by simultaneous evocation, for each carries within it an infinitude that ensures its metaphysical dissolution. The category Substance is lost, because there is only one, and it exists purely in attributional modifications which are themselves nothing. So Substance has no more content than attribute and mode; the same goes for God and Nature.

Lloyd makes the obvious point that 'the inadequacies of self-knowledge could be transcended only by self-destruction'.[88] A self is but an epiphenomenal parochial configuration, articulated only by an ontologically fictitious perspective. This is not necessarily negative, as it is our salvation to realise its fictional status.[89] To realise our own dissolution is to disown it. The individual is to lose its life because that might allow for a metaphysical understanding of being. But this individual is also to lose its death.[90] For while persisting it cannot be said to be alive; nor, when this persistence is overcome by an external force, is it exactly dead. For in that case there would have to be a metaphysical space from which the notion of loss could be constructed, but there is only 'plenitude'. This individual is highly Scotist, for it appears to be composed of equally legitimate 'forms' or parts, which are all potential individuals. It is this Scotism that allows Spinoza to avoid loss. The fiction of a loss in his philosophy could only come from the perspective of that which is no more, whereas the persistence of a *ratio* is from the perspective of God. It is this which disables death. Here we begin to realise that nothing or no-one happens in this world.

The *facies totius universi* fails to register any actuality. This is why Spinoza will say 'nature is always the same', or that 'we can easily conceive that all nature is one individual whose parts, that is bodies, vary in infinite ways without any change of the individual'.[91] The methodological use of God ensures that the world is nothing or that all specificity is lost (hence Hegel's accusation of *acosmism*). The eternity which we are to seek is the very absence of actuality: that which declares this world to be nothing. This eternity endeavours to have this nothing perform *as* something, while simultaneously remaining in itself nothing so as to prevent there being anything. Every space must be filled to exclude that which it pretends to be: God, Nature, Substance, individuals, emotions, virtue, life, death, belief. As Lermond says, 'The truth of eternity is an absolute realisation of being for which there can be no this or that, no one or the other, eternity is everything.'[92] Spinoza makes God this everything. But, as Baudrillard says, 'there have always been churches to hide the death of God and to hide the fact that God is everything which is the same thing'.[93]

What Spinoza does is to collapse every term he uses, employing it so as to exclude its previous meaning, and any possibility of a meaningful return. This is never more so than with his use of the word 'God'. The consequence of the *Ethics* is that the world is nothing. But it still acts as if it were something, an act which occupies every space within which something (metaphysical) could be. This ab-use of words even goes to the extreme of using the word 'being', which he tellingly likens to an expletive: 'It is to the existence of modes alone that we can apply the term Duration; the corresponding term for existence of Substance is Eternity, that is infinite enjoyment of existence or – pardon my Latin – of being.'[94] For Spinoza every space must be filled. To be so, everything must be its opposite. Only in this way will everything that *is* be full to the brim with nothing.[95] 'The one must be many, the many must be one.'[96] If the one were not many then it would lack and so a space would open up. Likewise with the many: if it were not one then there would be the conceptual space for an other. If the one were one it would be so in the conceptual presence of others, and the same goes for the many. (*Hen estin kai pan.*) This pathological epistemic *anaplerosis* is nowhere better illustrated than in Spinoza's explanation of Adam's ordeal with the forbidden apple. According to Spinoza, God's telling Adam not to eat the apple was purely informative, not prohibitive. Empirically the apple happened to be poisonous for Adam and would initiate a de-compossible relationship. This account of the myth manages to exclude the possibility of metaphysical values or worth, and it again represents the impulse to explain everything, or to explain everything away. It will be these explanations that will occupy the place of that which they explain away.

This is the nihilistic logic that has the nothing be *as* something. Spinoza's God is vitalistic, and voluntarist, while Nature is transcendental (each being in the absence of the other), so allowing for a plenitudinal nihilism. Hegel said 'when beginning to philosophize one must first be a Spinozist'.[97] It seems that philosophy not only begins with Spinoza but remains with Spinoza. (This was certainly Jacobi's contention.) Furthermore, Heine is correct in saying that 'all contemporary philosophies, perhaps without knowing it, are looking through eyeglasses that Baruch Spinoza polishes'.[98] Badiou appears to be correct about this Christ of philosophy. For Spinoza does indeed promise *nothing*.

The next chapter examines the work of Kant, in an endeavour to construct an interpretation which argues that Kant causes all to disappear. In this way, Kant's philosophy is also shown to display the workings of nihilism's logic: nothing *as* something.

Notes

1 Deleuze and Guattari (1994), p. 60.
2 Badiou (2000a), p. 101; italics mine.
3 See Yovel (1989).
4 Spinoza (1993), *Ethics*.
5 See Part II, Chapter 10 for a development of this idea.
6 Lermond (1988), p. 14.
7 *Ethics*, Pt. 1, Def. 3. In this chapter all quotes will be from the *Ethics*, unless otherwise indicated.
8 Pt. 1, Def. 4.
9 Pt. 1, Def. 5.
10 Pt. 1, Prop. 4.
11 Pt. 1, Props. 8 and 7.
12 Pt. 1, Prop. 5.
13 Pt. 1, Def. 6.
14 Pt. 1, Prop. 9.
15 Pt. 1, Prop. 14.
16 Yet this God is set against a Nature with which it is equivalent. As a result the substance which this God has got rid of comes back to haunt both God and Nature. For it is, I suggest, the *name* in Spinoza's philosophy for the absence of both.
17 Pt. 1, Prop. 14.
18 Pt. 1, Prop. 7.
19 Pt. 1, Def. 4.
20 See Pt. 2, Props. 1 and 2.
21 Pt. 2, Prop. 1, proof.
22 Pt. 2, Prop. 2.

23 Pt. 2, Def. 3.
24 Pt. 2, Def. 4.
25 Pt. 2, Prop. 9, proof.
26 See Scruton (1986), pp. 69–70.
27 See Pt. 2, Prop. 1, proof.
28 'God, or all his attributes are immutable', Pt. 1, Prop. 20, Corollary 2.
29 Pt. 2, Prop. 4.
30 Pt. 2, Prop. 7, note.
31 Theologically speaking this would not be a very satisfactory 'place' for transcendence as it would remain definitively indebted to secular logics.
32 It will argued below that Heidegger has something similar, in that he has an external infinity of death and an internal one which is time. Each of which leads Dasein to nothingness; see Part I, Chapter 6.
33 Pt. 2, XLIII, note.
34 See Part I, Chapter 5.
35 See Bergson (1983), pp. 272–297.
36 Lermond (1988), p. 26.
37 'It is the nature of reason not to regard things as contingent but as necessary', Pt. 2, Prop. 44.
38 See Pt. 3, Def. 1.
39 See Pt. 1, Prop. 11, second proof.
40 See Pt. I, Appendix
41 Pt. 1, Prop. 29.
42 Pt. 1, Prop. 33.
43 Part I, Chapter 5 argues that for Hegel contingency is 'contingent'.
44 See Pt. 2, Prop. 31, Corollary.
45 Pt. 2, Prop. 30.
46 See Pt. 3, Def. 3.
47 Pt. 2, Prop. 35.
48 Pt. 2, Prop. 33.
49 Pt. 1, Prop. 17, Corollary 1.
50 Pt. 1, Prop. 18.
51 See Deleuze (1988), pp. 53–54.
52 Lermond (1988), p. 17.
53 Pt. 4, Preface.
54 Pt. 1, Appendix.
55 Pt. 2, Prop. 13.
56 Pt. 2, Prop. 12.
57 Pt. 2, Prop. 19.
58 Pt. 2, Axiom 2, Def.
59 Pt. 2, Lemma 5.
60 Pt. 2, Postulate 1.
61 Pt. 2, Prop. 15.
62 Pt. 3, Def. 3.
63 Pt. 3, Prop. 6.
64 Pt. 3, Prop. 70.
65 Pt. 4, Prop. 3.
66 Pt. 3, Prop. 10, proof.

67 Pt. 3, Prop. 7.
68 Pt. 2, Prop. 13, Lemma 1.
69 Pt. 2, Props. 48, 49, and Corollary.
70 Pt. 2, Prop. 11, Corollary.
71 Pt. 3, Prop. 11, note; Defs. 2 and 3.
72 Pt. 4, Def. 7.
73 Pt. 4, Def. 1.
74 Nietzsche (1994), first essay, sec. 17.
75 Pt. 5, Prop. 42.
76 Pt. 5, Prop. 38.
77 Pt. 5, Prop. 22.
78 Pt. 4, Prop. 39.
79 Pt. 3, Introduction.
80 Quoted by Deleuze (1988), p. 37, fn. 11.
81 See Part I, Chapter 8.
82 Funkenstein (1994), p. 21.
83 Yovel (1989), p. 146.
84 Deleuze (1988), p. 28.
85 Deleuze (1992) links Spinoza's univocity with Duns Scotus', pp. 48–49, and 63–65.
86 See Deleuze (1992), pp. 332–333.
87 Mason (1997), p. 117.
88 Lloyd (1994), p. 25.
89 Thinkers such as D. Z. Phillips advocate much the same today in similar religious language.
90 Part II, Chapter 8 argues that discourse which causes a loss of life and a loss of death is analogous to a 'holocaust'.
91 Pt. 3, Introduction; Pt. 2, Lemma 4.
92 Lermond (1988), p. 42.
93 Baudrillard (1976), p. 35.
94 Quoted by Mason (1997), p. 236, fn. 31.
95 We will see in Part I, Chapter 5 that this holds also for Hegel.
96 Lermond (1988), p. 8.
97 Hegel (1955), 3: 257.
98 Quoted by Yovel (1989), p. 52.

4

KANT

Causing all to disappear

Introduction

It is possible to suggest that each of Kant's three critiques embodies a particular disappearance. The first *Critique* endeavours to 'say' something about 'truth'; in so doing the world must be reduced to the status of mere appearance. This reduction enables Kant to speak, in that he is no longer plagued by the scepticisms of the empiricists. Kantian philosophical discourse is, then, predicated on the disappearance of the world. The second *Critique*, which concerns practical reason, attempts to tackle the issue of moral practice, the good as such. But here again it is possible to suggest that Kant is only able to have his morality, that is to 'do' good acts, if nature is usurped to some degree by a noumenal realm that allows for freedom from the hegemony of mechanistic laws. In the third *Critique*, Kant discusses beauty and the sublime. This involves the possibility of sight, a 'seeing' of the beautiful. But again this is only possible if beauty is merely subjective (yet universal), not involving the existence or perfection of any object. Furthermore, beauty does not involve knowledge. This aesthetic involves, *contra* Aquinas, no cognition in any manner.[1] So in the first *Critique* the world becomes mere appearance, and upon this rests our ability to 'say'. In the second *Critique* we lose nature, and upon this rests our ability to 'do'. In the third *Critique* we lose the visible object and upon this rests our ability to 'see'. These disappearing acts will be carried out in a privileged manner by 'man', the subject. Like Spinoza's epistemically informed philosopher (and, as we shall see, Hegel's universal thinker and Heidegger's Dasein), we have the Kantian subject, with its Copernican revolution, who will be the site of this triple vanishing.

After outlining these three distinct conjurations, I shall then go on to show how they are all really aspects of a single monistic feat of dissolution.

To Say: Nothing

Knowledge begins with experience, it does not follow that it
all arises out of experience.[2]

We have already, in this quotation, the approach that Kant will take to
the problem of knowledge. For here we see a concession to the
empiricists, namely that experience is fundamental; at the same time
Kant nods to the rationalists in assenting to some form of deductive
procedure. Leibniz, the great representative of the rationalists, divided
our knowledge into truths of reason and truths of fact. The former are
analysed into statements of identity, or statements the opposite of which
are contradictory; the truths of reason are based on the law of non-
contradiction. Hume, as an empiricist, has a somewhat similar contrast
between relations of ideas and matters of fact. The former are provable
by the mere operation of the mind, for these do not incorporate a
reference to existence as such; Hume thinks of mathematics and
geometry as being based on this type of reason. Matters of fact which are
inherently experiential allow for an opposite conception, *viz.*, it is never
contradictory to think of the opposite of what is experienced as being
possible. Experience seems to contain this epistemic flexibility because
the temporality of existence incorporates a 'wait and see' policy.

Within this shared conceptuality, the emphasis diverges. To Hume the
fundamental centrality of experience for knowledge is accepted, while
with the rationalists it is insisted that not all we use to construct our
experience itself comes from experience. Kant's delicate balance of
rationalist deduction and empiricist induction is only possible because of
the new reference to transcendental subjectivity. Experience, for Kant, is
experience 'for me'. This reformulates the problem, because already
within experience we will 'find' something necessary, namely 'me', the
subject. Kant asks, what do we require to enable experience 'for me'? He
does not ask about some neutral experience, of whatever kind. To
articulate such an experience, permanent notions will begin to force
themselves upon us. Experience *qua* experience needs to be experienced;
this includes a requisite duration.[3] In other words, we cannot derive
knowledge from pure experience, nor can experience be devoid of
conceptualisation. Deduction from concepts is also rejected. For Kant,
'experience is itself a species of knowledge that involves understanding'.[4]
This is Kant's 'Copernican revolution': 'Hitherto it has been assumed that
all our knowledge must conform to objects . . . we may have more success
in the task of metaphysics, if we suppose that objects have to conform to
our knowledge.'[5] This is the 'true path' which philosophy is to take.
Experience is experience only as experience for us. For this reason, 'the
object (as object of sense) must conform to the constitution of our faculty

of intuition'.[6] We are to concern ourselves with appearances, not with what Kant calls 'things-in-themselves'.

Kant reformulates both the rationalist and empiricist bifurcation of our knowledge. First of all he argues that empirical knowledge does not afford us 'strict universality',[7] only *a priori* knowledge will do that. We are to discover such *a priori* knowledge by stripping away from our empirical concepts every empirical feature. Kant gives the example of a body.[8] If we remove the colour, hardness, softness, weight, impenetrability and so on, there still, according to Kant, remains the space which the body 'now entirely vanished' occupied. It is this space which is *a priori*; we cannot be rid of it. In this sense, every experience will 'force concepts of permanence upon us'.[9] This first division of knowledge into *a priori* and empirical (*a posteriori*) is extended as Kant introduces the dichotomy of analytic and synthetic judgements. Analytic judgements approximately correspond to Leibniz's truths of reason, while synthetic judgements concern matters of fact. For Kant, analytic judgements are merely explicative, adding nothing to the content of cognition.[10] In contrast, synthetic judgements are ampliative, for they augment our cognition.[11] An analytical judgement is one in which the predicate A belongs to the concept B. In a synthetic judgement the predicate does not belong to the concept, but it does 'stand in connection with it'. An example of the former would be 'all bachelors are unmarried', because analytic judgements are based solely on the principle of contradiction.[12] An example of a synthetic judgement would be 'some bodies are heavy'. This contains something in the predicate which is not actually in the concept of body, while the judgement that 'all bodies are extended' would be merely analytical. As experience is ampliative, Kant asserts that all judgements of experience are synthetic. It would indeed be absurd to argue that analytic judgements were ampliative, for they are atemporal, consequently foregoing of addition. This distinction is not new, but it is radical.

However, the Copernican revolution, so promised, arrives when Kant argues that synthetic judgements can actually be *a priori*. This seems to be a contradiction. For how can something ampliative be *a priori*? That is, how can experience arise apart from experience? Kant is able to accomplish this move because he has already redefined experience. In Kantian terms, it would not be possible at all without these synthetic *a priori* judgements, because experience to be experience must be experienced; to be experienced, *someone* must be there to have the experience. There is no such thing as experience devoid of 'subjective' constitution. This allows Kant to deduce certain synthetic *a priori* judgements, for without these there could not be any experience, no experience 'for me'. Kant's most famous example of an *a priori* synthetic judgement is that of the arithmetical sum 7+5. It is Kant's contention that the concept of such a sum does not include the number 12. The concept does include a number which is the sum of the two, but it does not tell us what this number is. There must be an act of synthesis if we are to discover the number 12. Another example is that of the proposition that the straight line between two points is shortest. According to Kant, our concept of a straight line does not include quantity, hence the judgement must include intuition which enables synthesis.

For Kant the possibility of synthetic *a priori* judgements spells out the possibility of a science composed of these. This would be the critique of pure reason, a transcendental philosophy which is a philosophy occupied with modes of knowledge.[13] Kant hopes to have knowledge of experience which is *a priori* and hence impervious to Humean scepticism.[14] The first *Critique* is divided into 'The Transcendental Doctrine of Elements', and 'The Transcendental Doctrine of Method'. Here it is mainly the former that is relevant. The doctrine of elements is itself divided into three parts: the *'Transcendental Aesthetic'*, *'Transcendental Analytic'*, and the *'Transcendental Dialectic'*. Of these it is the first two that primarily concern us.

The *Transcendental Aesthetic* deals with the capacity for perception. This capacity is possible, according to Kant, because of intuition, for it is in intuition that an object is given to us; the word 'intuition' is a translation of the German *'Anschauung'* which means looking at. The receptive mode in which objects are given to us is called sensibility. It is sensibility, as a receptive mode, that enables affectation, which is referred to as sensation. Intuition is immediately in relation to an object by way of sensation which affords us the capacity to be affected, while concepts are mediately, though ultimately, related to objects.[15] The undetermined object of an empirical intuition is an appearance which consists in matter and form. The matter of appearance is that which is related to sensation, and consequently it is *a posteriori*. Conversely, the form of appearance is the relational ordering of the same and it is *a priori*. Intuitions are singular representations, unlike concepts which are general. If we break down any singular representation we will be left with what is referred to as the 'pure forms of intuition' or 'pure forms of sensibility'. They are 'pure' because they are free of sensation, that is, they are *a priori*. They are of sensibility in that these forms are the very 'shape' of receptivity, the place within which reception can achieve the requisite permanence with which to construct its own identity. The *Transcendental Aesthetic* concerns these pure forms of sensibility, for it is about the possibility of sensibility.[16]

Space, it is argued by Kant, is a pure form of sensibility. This view distinguishes him from both Newton and Leibniz who held that space was absolutely real and self-subsistent, or merely relational, respectively. Kant instead argues that space is not derived empirically but is instead *a priori*: 'Space does not represent any determination that attaches to the objects themselves.'[17] Space as a form of appearance lies between sensation and thought, for it is neither of the understanding, as it is intuitional, nor is it from sensation as it is *a posteriori*.

The first argument Kant proffers for the appellation of space as a pure form of sensibility is that space is not derived from outer experience, since we require space to locate the outer. Hence the 'representation of space must be presupposed'.[18] This is not to argue that space is required for the spatiality of objects (this will be the job of the understanding), but only that it articulates the location of inner and outer: this distances Kant from Newton.[19] The second argument states that 'space is a necessary *a priori* representation, which underlies all our intuitions'. The point of this argument is that space is a condition of appearance and is not determined by appearance: this goes against Leibniz, for whom space is found in non-spatial relations between objects; hence the need for objects. For Kant, we do not need a world of outer objects, for we can never represent to ourselves the absence of space, and yet the absence of objects offers no difficulty.[20]

The third argument claims that we have only one space, so that space is unitary, single. This means that all parts are but parts of one space, and this one space precedes every part. This is important for the Kantian project because he must ensure that the *a priori* nature of space is not a result of the understanding but is, instead, a form of intuition. We must remember that intuition is always singular. Concepts are general and offer many instances of themselves. An instance of the concept dog does not provide us with 'parts of dog' so to speak, whereas a part of space does offer us a part of space, in terms of a limitation of the *one* all-embracing space. A part is only a part within its relation to this whole (the importance of this will only transpire towards the end of the chapter).[21] The fourth argument tells us that space is an 'infinite given magnitude'. Kant suggests that parts of space are contained within the one space, whereas instances of a concept fall under it in a fashion other than containment: the reason for this is that a concept is not something with an infinity of parts but only with an infinity of instances. Hence a concept does not have to be of infinite magnitude, but only of infinite possibility in terms of its representation; if a concept contained an infinitude of parts within itself it would take an infinite mind to comprehend it.[22]

There is a fifth argument to be found not in the first *Critique* but in the *Prolegomena*, referred to as the argument 'from incongruent parts'. This states that spatial difference cannot be conceptually represented but must be intuited. Kant argues that if two things are fully the same in both quality and magnitude, then each should be able to take the place of the other. Kant gives the example of a hand and its image: although they are the same they are incongruous. In other words, they are identical yet one cannot replace the other. Think of your left hand, and its reflection in the mirror. You cannot put the replica in the place of the original for one would be a left hand and the other a right hand. As Kant says: 'Now there are no inner differences here that any understanding could merely think; and yet the differences are inner as far as the senses teach, for the left hand cannot, after all, be enclosed within the same boundaries as the right (they cannot be made congruent), despite reciprocal equality.'[23]

Space is, then, *a priori* and not empirical, yet it is but the subjective condition of sensibility. Space does not refer to things-in-themselves, for it does not speak about 'objects' as such. (If it did, the reformulation of experience as experience for me would no longer count and Kant would be guilty of contradiction.) This leaves space as both empirically real and yet transcendentally ideal. It is the former because it is the possibility of the 'outer'; there is no 'outer' or empirical realm without it. But its transcendental ideality means it is also 'nothing'.[24]

Just as space is a pure form of sensibility so too is time. Kant argues that while space is the form of outer sense, time is the form of the inner sense. For this reason it must, like space, be *a priori*, it too arising from an intuition and not by discursive understanding.[25] We cannot have time as experientially derivative, because the derivation of time would itself require time; both succession and coexistence presuppose time. Consequently, time underlies all intuitions, for we can do without appearance but are unable to be without time; we could only articulate this *lack* of time using time.[26] Just as with space, there is *one* time and all particular times are but limitations of this one time.[27] For this reason the infinitude of time is but the infinite division of the same underlying time. Time is also not something real, that is, something subject-independent. For time as inner sense is the passage of the subject. Space is required to enable a subject to persist, but this persistence is, in a sense, measured by time. Thus the place of the subject is the time of that subject. Kant therefore refers to time as the mediate condition of outer appearance.[28] These twin subjective conditions of space and time are what allow Kant to bring the *a priori* into the empirical. Meanwhile the division of sensibility into objective matter and subjective form enables Kant to import the 'empirical' (synthesis) into the *a priori* in the mode of synthetic *a priori* judgements.

When we reach the second part of the doctrine of elements, the *Analytic*, the understanding is introduced.[29] There are two types of logic for Kant: general and transcendental. The former concerns only the logical form of knowledge in relation to itself; for this reason it does not relate to objects of any kind. The latter does concern itself with objects, by way of the manifold afforded it by the *Transcendental Aesthetic*, namely the pure forms of sensibility. The 'contamination' of intuition with pure *a priori* forms allows a certain interaction between the understanding and sensibility, thus enabling the transcendental logic to deal with empirical as well as pure knowledge of reason; what 'empirical' means has, of course, been fundamentally altered. Knowledge consists in sensibility as the capacity for receptivity, and understanding which spontaneously generates concepts. Sensible intuition provides an object, while the understanding will think this object. It is for this reason that Kant makes his famous remark that 'thoughts without content are empty, intuitions without concepts are blind'.[30] Only through the union of the two can knowledge arise. Intuitions are based on affections, while concepts are in a sense functional. By this Kant means that they spontaneously produce concepts which synthesise various representations under one common representation.[31] Synthesis is the act of gathering manifold elements by giving them a certain content.

First we have the manifold of pure intuition, and second the synthesis enabled by the productive imagination, which is for Kant a 'blind but indispensable function of the soul'.[32] The imagination produces concepts but these do not yet yield knowledge. This requires the pure understanding which will take the 'concepts' of the imagination and subject them to judgements. Understanding is in fact a faculty of judgement.[33] Judgement can be either a judgement of perception or one of experience.[34] The former merely combines perceptions in relation to the subject, while the latter applies pure concepts of the understanding and moves beyond sensory intuition towards objective validity. We always begin with the judgement of perception, which is then subjected to pure understanding as it seeks to be universally valid. Every judgement is stripped of content until we are left with only the form of understanding. A judgement is a function of unity, and for Kant there are four divisions of judgement, each with three moments:[35] these are the twelve forms of unity or judgement. But these forms are purely formal and lack content. Hence the title of this section is *The Clue to the Discovery of All Pure Concepts of the Understanding*. If we are to move beyond the clue, then we must link these forms of judgement with content. The only way to do this is to relate them to intuition. This would, of course, provide insoluble difficulties for Kant if it were not for the pure forms of sensibility, since otherwise there could not be any *a priori* knowledge, and the understanding as formal and sensibility as empirical would be immiscible. The pure manifold of intuition is that which is *a priori* yet sensible; by redefining experience in terms of the subject, sensibility permits this mixing of the sensible with understanding. As a consequence the pure concepts, which understanding requires, become categories since they are now related to intuition.[36]

The *Transcendental Deduction* is the philosophical endeavour to have subjective conditions of thought gain objective validity.[37] How does what the subject requires extend to include objective validity?[38] Kant offers us a choice: 'either the object alone must make the representations possible, or the representation alone must make the object possible'.[39] Yet Kant is prepared to redefine what an object is, in order to broker a third option. The *Transcendental Deduction* of the first edition of the *Critique* is articulated in terms of cognitive powers. We have the *synthesis of apprehension*, the *synthesis of reproduction*, which is that of the imagination, and the *synthesis of recognition*, which is the synthesis provided by the understanding. These relate to 'the object in general = x',[40] the transcendental object which concerns the requisite unity needed to produce an object as such. This unity is therefore transcendental: for any object to be given to us it must arise within the workings of this unity. The unity turns out to be that of apperception: apperception 'underlies the possibility of all knowledge'.[41] This apperception is transcendental, as it is self- consciousness, and self-consciousness is obviously a prerequisite for experience. Without the transcendental unity of apperception there cannot be any unity of the manifold of sensibility, so there cannot be any knowledge. The 'abiding and unchanging "I" forms the correlate of all our representations, in so far as it is to be at all possible that we should become conscious of them'.[42]

The concentration of the *Transcendental Deduction* (A) on the subject's cognitive powers leads Kant to refer to it as the 'subjective deduction', while the second edition, by contrast, offers an 'objective deduction'.[43] In this deduction the necessity of the transcendental unity of apperception is nonetheless also expounded, for the 'I' must be able to accompany all one's representations.[44] But in addition to arguing that certain conditions must be so, for objects to be represented, Kant now also argues that objects *per se* require these conditions. Objects of intuition require the categories in order to be objects. It is not, then, a matter of representation but of constitution (which is a strange understanding of what the term objective means). The unity of the synthesis of the categories as functions of unity is the prerequisite of any object 'without or within us'. Categories prescribe laws *a priori* to appearances; hence objects cannot be objects without their functional unity. These laws are related objectively by recourse to the pure intuitions of Space and Time which present a manifold; this requires the operation of the understanding orientated towards the transcendental object in order that this manifold achieve a unity. It is this which accords Kant's deduction its objective validity.[45]

This link between understanding and sensibility, categories and intuitions, is readdressed in Kant's discussion of *Schemata*. According to Kant, the subsumption of an object under a concept is only feasible if the object is 'homogeneous' with the concept. What Kant means by this is that there must be something in a concept which an intuition could represent; something which enables intuitions, in a sense, to blindly concur with concepts. But since concepts and intuitions are heterogeneous, 'never' the twain shall meet. Kant proposes the existence of a 'third thing', namely schemata. These are mediating representations of the imagination which are the product of the occult workings of the soul, 'a secret art'.[46] However, schemata are not to be thought of as simple images, because an image can never be adequate to a concept.[47] The schema of a triangle, for example, is of an *a posteriori* concept and cannot relate to the concepts of pure understanding. How could it, since these relate to every object *qua* object? Therefore any schematic image would be inadequate.

These transcendental schemata are but determinations of time; time is the form that all intuitions of sense must take. Time to be time must involve succession, even if that is the succession of coexistence, duration as such. This involves a movement between part and whole, in an almost Hegelian sense. It is the transcendental schemata which enables this determination, as it includes both conditions (permanence; one time) and example (succession; different times), *viz.*, application. The imagination as related to sensibility spontaneously produces from one time. Hence it intimates the division of the same. This may well allow understanding to apply itself in terms of temporal determination. Time is always succession of the same, but this requires variation within time, *viz.*, time is unitary. Without the schemata the categories are but functions of the understanding for concepts, and these do not relate to objects.

This leads us to the analogies of experience.[48] These arise from the difficulty we face in representing objects as beings in time, while transcending the temporality of our own representations. Kant endeavours to overcome this by establishing particular analogies which merely regulate our experience. Each of the three analogies acts as a rule from which a unity of experience may arise, relating our perceptions to each other within the *a priori* condition that all perceptions stand under the rules of universal time-determination. Any particular perception can only be known because it is related to time in general, which has three modes: duration, succession, and coexistence. These modes enable appearance to be articulated in terms of time in general, and they alone permit the operation of consciousness, as the site of finite unity. Time, as the form of inner sensibility, requires the synthesis of apperception, for this is the form of inner sense. Equally, the form of inner sense is the unity of apperception. The manifold of empirical consciousness is but a result of the synthesis of apperception that is itself related *a priori* to time as the pure form of intuition. For Kant the principle of the analogies is that 'experience is only possible through the representation of a necessary connection of perceptions'.[49] This connection is located between time in general and the transcendental unity of apperception, as time is the form of the manifold of empirical consciousness. What is required for the experience of a necessary connection between perceptions is the form which the manifold must take. This relates the manifold to the unity of apperception, which is in this way itself in relation to inner sense as the 'sum of all representations'. The unity of apperception, which is the form of time in general, is the basis for the analogies. All changes in time are changes of *one* time, just as every appearance *for me* is of the *one* subject, that is, as a determination of inner sense. To have experience we need unity of apperception so that there is an experiencing subject. This subject, then, unites the manifold in line with the form of its inner sense. Hence all experiences are in relation to time in general, and are merely determinations of this inner sense.

The first analogy is that of substance: 'the principle of permanence of substance'.[50] This analogy relates to the first mode of time, namely duration. As Kant says, 'in all changes of appearance substance is permanent; its quantum in nature is neither increased nor diminished'. The substance about which he speaks is the form of time. Time is one, and all alterations are of this one time which does not itself change. Such permanency provides us with a frame of reference within which we can notice alteration and experience as such: 'Without the permanent there is therefore no time-relation.'[51] All determinations of this substance are but accidents betraying the essential sameness of time in the mode of duration.[52] For this reason Kant says that 'all that alters persists'.[53] This is easy enough to understand, for there must be something there which alters.

The second analogy is that of causality: 'All alterations take place in conformity with the law of the connection of cause and effect.'[54] The apprehension of the manifold always involves succession. This requires a permanent substance and the internal relation between the determinations of the one time. Causality is a necessary rule of apprehension, without which the mode of succession would be impossible. Certain appearances in order to be *those* appearances require a rule of necessity. Kant provides an example of a ship travelling down a river. To perceive the ship downriver from where it was necessitates an order which must be itself immovable. To perceive the ship as lower down the river excludes the possibility that the ship could have been anywhere but upstream before. We could not place the ship lower than it is before it was here and still successfully have the same perception; succession requires irreversibility.[55]

The third analogy is that of coexistence, or reciprocity.[56] This involves the interaction between different substances. This interaction is possible because all things coexist in one time. If there was no causal interaction, no 'community', then there would be different times. This would mean that every single experience would be its own world, a monad as such. But since we can experience many things and different things at once, they must stand in a community of apperception, which is a result of a unitary time.[57] (These analogies of experience, as regulative rules, would not cause Hume any dismay. They hold only for the subject in its experience. Humean habit, imagination and so on would suffice. The experience seems the same because all that is sought is a localised result, namely the experience of experience.)

When we come to the end of the *Transcendental Analytic* we find the infamous dichotomy, phenomena/noumena.[58] A discussion of this will be left until later. It is sufficient to say for now that this division does seem to correspond to that of appearance and things-in-themselves, and that the duality does seem to leave us seeing nothing in seeing some thing. Every visible determination will be merely phenomenal, so we are left bereft of true adequation with the advent of every perception. In consequence each phenomenon lies always elsewhere, for in being merely an appearance its ontological ground 're-locates' it. The noumena are somewhat akin, however anachronistic this may sound, to the nothing outside the Derridian text. (See Part I, Chapter 7.) For it is this nothing which, in some sense, allows the advent of signification, while it is this nothing which also renders any particular signification a participant in an endless deferral. (See Part II, Chapter 10.)

To Do: Nothing

The second *Critique* re-deploys the dichotomy phenomena/noumena.[59] With the first *Critique* Kant had to employ the term *noumenon* to avoid Berkeley's idealism. The employment of this term meant that, in effect, a *nothing* was required to speak of objects. Objects were required to be *mere* appearances and there was to be, practically speaking, nothing outside them: a nothing because every experiential category is rendered inapplicable. Hence the object is literally no-thing. This nothing can be taken, on one reading, as merely a limiting concept – that is, as something nominal: noumena would have then only a negative existence.[60] In the second *Critique*, however, Kant utilises noumena to escape the mechanistic determinism of the phenomenal world. Nature is to be rendered merely phenomenal in order to allow for another realm which underlies it. This indeterminate realm allows the Kantian subject the latitude necessary to carry out an action, for to do something is to do something free. Indeed, without this requisite freedom there could not be a subject as such, or rather the subject would merely be an 'object', if we think of this as something lacking volition or self-determination.

In his second *Critique* Kant wishes to establish a pure faculty of practical reason. The first *Critique* limited our theoretical reason to appearance alone; we were to deal solely with the phenomenal. Yet this inhibition now becomes opportunity, since in dealing *only* with appearances we are left with another realm. In other words, theory concerns only phenomena, which means that theory no longer gives access to the whole realm of being. Here we find all our actions begin on the brink of this demise. Practice discloses the deeper realities beneath appearances.

Likewise the theoretical self, in being merely phenomenal, disappears. Yet for there to be a subject who acts there must be a noumenal self who has experience, if only at a phenomenal level. Kant asks us to regard this self in-itself in terms of freedom. Freedom arises, for Kant, already in this subject who has experience where it gives objective reality to the ideas of reason such as God and immortality. Inversely, freedom is itself an idea of reason; the only one which can be established *a priori* by pure practical reason and revealed by the moral law. Yet the use of such ideas does not extend theoretical knowledge but merely enables our actions to be 'ours', and only in the negation of the causal order and the phenomenal self can we regard ourselves in such a manner and affirm a *causa noumenon*,[61] which (somehow) interrupts the apparent causal order.

All moral action, which is action for which we are responsible, is issued by this noumenal self which escapes the restraints of phenomenality and is autonomous. In this way the determining ground of our will is transferred to an intelligible order of things, instead of an empirical order. In free will, the numinous surfaces, since will is self-given and produces even the reality to which its decrees or autonomous laws are to correspond.[62] For this reason the moral law is a formal law.[63] This circumstance frees the law from any empirical conditions which would have to be heteronomously presupposed, thus compromising its self-determination. In this fashion empirical conditions are formally ignored. The will can be self-determined by a number of practical rules: these comprise subjective rules which Kant refers to as maxims, and objective rules, or imperatives. Imperatives are hypothetical if they causally determine the will in relation to an effect, while they are categorical if they determine the will without recourse to the question of adequate causality, and are consequent on freedom as such. They alone enact the moral law. At this point Kant introduces the famous definition of a categorical imperative: 'Act such that the maxim of your will could always hold at the same time as the principle giving universal law.'[64]

In the second *Critique* we see that Kant posits the existence of certain practical postulates, which are prerequisites of moral law. The first of these is freedom, which we have already mentioned. The second is that of immortality, for only this postulate provides the 'requisite duration' for the fulfilment of the moral law. The last postulate is that of God, as the highest independent good. These are pure concepts of reason; consequently they cannot be accompanied by an intuition, for this would be a matter of cognitive significance which would relate to the extension of theoretical knowledge.[65] A noumenal self 'causes' moral actions by acting according to the categorical imperative, along with the practical postulates of freedom, immortality and the existence of God. The world to which we give such moral law is that of appearance. This world is not created by God, who is a practical postulate. God can only be said to create the noumenal, and indeed only noumenal beings can be said to be created.[66] (This is somewhat similar to the Neoplatonism of Avicenna for whom only the first intelligence is created by God.) Yet this uncreated phenomenal realm of the senses requires 'man' to give it meaning and in this sense to give creation meaning. Indeed, according to Kant, of the third *Critique*, without man nature would be in vain.[67]

To See: Nothing

In the third *Critique* Kant is concerned with the disparity between natural concepts of theoretical knowledge and that of the concept of freedom, which is of practical knowledge.[68] Kant attempts to unify the two realms by way of the beautiful and the sublime. The first *Critique* presents us with phenomena and the second with an intelligible realm from which no cognition is forthcoming. Yet the first also relies on this noumenal realm for it must, as Kant says, employ the idea of things-in-themselves 'as the basis of the possibility of all those objects of experience'.[69] For this reason 'our entire cognitive faculty is, therefore, presented with an unbounded, but also inaccessible field, the field of the supersensible'.[70] Such a field, although inaccessible, provides the intimation of a possible union of the two cognitive realms. The *Critique of Judgement* is the means by which Kant seeks to cross the 'broad gulf' which separates the practical and the theoretical.[71]

Judgement is the thinking of a particular under a universal. For Kant there are determinate and reflective judgements. The former present us with a universal under which the particular falls. The latter does not provide this universal, and yet it sets us in the direction of it, so to speak. The reflective judgement 'stands in need of a principle'. The purpose of reflective judgement is to seek the unity of empirical principles, a unity which would allow for a harmony between the two realms: the practical and the theoretical. Reflective judgement acts 'as if understanding contained the ground of unity of the manifold of its empirical laws'. This adopted stance is the 'as if' of finality, the finality of nature. Finality is itself directly related to pleasure; to attain an end provides pleasure in order to achieve a judgement. Consequently, the finality of nature is marked by pleasure. For this reason the principle of the finality of nature given by reflective judgement is strictly given *via* the subject. Hence it is an heautonomous 'law'. Heautonomy is the giving of the principle of nature to oneself. It is in some sense heteronomous to nature but is presumed to be 'natural', in that it is about nature. Aesthetic quality is that which is purely subjective in a representation of the object. The prescription of a law of finality to nature by a reflective judgement is, then, an aesthetic matter; the prescription is subjective, it concerns the object and it provides pleasure. When such pleasure arises we have, it seems, participated in a harmony between the practical and the theoretical. Representations of that which is final are accommodated by pleasure. And since the reflective judgement in representing the object to itself presents pleasure, this suggests that there is also a cognitive harmony between understanding and imagination.

When we cognise and achieve pleasure of this sort we must, therefore, be experiencing a harmony between the noumenal and the phenomenal (although Kant does not express it in this way). The understanding, in enabling phenomenality, directs us to the noumenal, in that understanding insists that we *only* cognise the phenomenal. What we experience is but *mere* appearance. A reflective judgement by contrast leaves us before the phenomenal in a noumenal manner, so to speak. It does so because we are left before a something which is no-thing. The object, which we now call beautiful, is no longer perfectly subsumable by the phenomenal. It is before us but not as appearance. It is for this reason that this cognition is subjective 'taste' and that it tells us nothing about the object; the cognitive faculties are in this way thought to experience something in experiencing without experiencing objectively. This means that the subject who experiences the beautiful object *experiences an appearance noumenally*, because the pleasure indicates that what is experienced is not merely appearance, a phenomenon. Furthermore, the subject in being the recipient of such pleasure escapes its own phenomenality. The pleasure 'I' have retains the subject in its experience of the beautiful: my pleasure directs me towards my own noumenality. Yet while this pleasure is subjective it remains universal; Kant refers here to the notion of a *sensus communis*, that allows for a subjective universal.[72] This sounds paradoxical, but the pleasure does not provide information with which one could disagree, *viz.*, taste does not refer to *something*. If taste does not refer to something then we cannot disagree over this or that object. Instead, the subjective pleasure indicates a universal subjective capacity which may lead us to a universal subjectivity, what Kant calls the 'supersensible substrate of humanity'.[73]

Here we have the isolation and bounding of the phenomenal. The subject takes pleasure in no-thing. In so doing, this subject becomes aware of the noumenality underlying the phenomenal and in turn of its own noumenality, which it has as a free moral agent. Only in withholding a concept does the subject solicit pleasure from appearance, that is, from no-thing. If a concept could be found, then the pleasure would be empirical, local, and related to the understanding. We would merely take pleasure in an appearance *qua* phenomenon. This would be a cognitive experience which would keep us apart from the noumenal realm of pure practical reason.

For Kant, therefore, any cognitive undertaking points to nothingness, and on two accounts. First, it informs us that what we know is *merely* appearance. Second, in presenting us with a phenomenal realm it points us towards the noumenal realm as the supersensible substrate. The noumenal is no-thing, in the sense that it lies outside every cognitive or epistemic category. When it comes to judgements of taste, the subject is able to experience this nothingness and so comprehend the nothingness which *is*. The beautiful object is an object precisely of nothingness: its phenomenal appearance betrays a dis-appearance, for it is beyond every concept yet remains before us, quickening our cognitive faculties.[74] We are, in a sense, able to see the noumenality of appearance: to see no-thing. In so doing, we participate in our own noumenality while dealing with the phenomenal. This allows us to combine the practical and the theoretical.

The beautiful object involves the form of the object, and for this reason it requires limitation. In contrast to beauty, the sublime is a representation of limitlessness with a 'super-added thought of totality'.[75] Both the sublime and the beautiful please, but do so in a different manner.[76] The latter is accompanied by a sense of the furtherance of life, while the former interrupts life, checking (*Anstoss*) its passage before 'recommencing' its arrival.[77] The sublime stops life by way of its enormity, its limitlessness, for it threatens appearance with incapacity;[78] appearance fails adequately to represent the sublime, being unable to grasp what is arriving within it. This is why the sublime is a 'check' on 'vital forces'.[79] This check, when removed, causes these forces to 'discharge' all the more powerfully. Such an increase arises, it seems, from the fact that being made aware of our inadequate capacity to represent makes us all the more aware that there is 'something' to represent. The sublime is that which is 'absolutely great (*absolute non comparative magnum*)'.[80] Its greatness causes our imagination to strain itself, becoming aware of its own incapacity. This points to a 'faculty of mind which transcends every standard of sense'.[81]

The subject who discovers that he is inadequate, unable to represent the absolutely great, is, at the same time, made aware of an unlimited faculty. The cognitive violence suffered by the subject provides its own cure, for it discloses a supersensible substrate within which the subject has a supersensible capacity.[82] Here we discover an idea of infinity which renders nature small, since it underlies both nature and the faculty of thought, *viz.*, the phenomenal and the subjective. The sublime destroys the phenomenal subject, but this destruction is a self-destruction, because the idea of the infinite in nature, of the sublime, which caused us to realise our incapacity, was our *own* idea; this violent idea issued forth from the noumenal of which the subject is itself a resident. Such destruction is the 'foundation of a self-preservation of quite another kind'.[83] The subject's phenomenal incapacity draws our attention to our experiential world as mere appearance, pointing not only the objects of sense, but us as subjects, towards the noumenal. As Kant says, 'in this way [the subject] gains an extension and a might greater [than] that which it sacrifices'.[84]

Whereas the beautiful teaches us to see no-thing, the sublime teaches us to *be* no-thing. It seems that it is the subject's vocation to hand over nature to the supersensible, by means of what Kant calls subreption. This is, nonetheless, the act of attributing to nature what actually belongs to the subject.[85] As Kant says, 'sublimity does not reside in any of the things of nature',[86] although the 'natural sublime' betrays, by subreption, its trace in nature. This is not an illegitimate imputation because we discover that nature derives from, in a sense, a unitary source, *viz.*, the noumenal. Therefore the subreption is appropriate; what is inappropriate is to think that it is the job of nature to realise this supersensible substrate, for this is rather the duty of the subject. This side of duty, of vocation, stems from respect, a respect generated from the realisation of our cognitive inadequacy.[87]

The sublime is restless, it leads us away to the supersensible, while the beautiful is still, contemplative, for its disclosure does not cause us to look elsewhere.[88] The beautiful prepares us to love something in the absence of an interest, maybe because an interest requires a *something* in which to be interested, whereas the beautiful in withholding every concept fails to provide such an end. Instead, nature appears as final and yet we do not know what this nature that is final is. All we do know is that it is not something in the object, nor is it something in the understanding; hence it cannot be thought of as some thing. Instead, the beautiful affords us a love without interest.

The sublime, by contrast, pleases not only without an interest but actually in 'opposition to our (sensible) interest'.[89] Strictly speaking the sublime negatively locates the noumenal elsewhere, in the negation of appearance, while beauty finds it positively here as appearance, or more accurately as the *appearance of appearance*.[90] (Kant persistently resorts to this phrase in the *Opus Postumum*.) If this is the case, then it may be possible to argue that the sublime discovers a no-thing above and below the world of experience, while the beautiful locates it before and beyond. All appearance comes from the noumenal and will return to it as appearance, in this sense never having left. If, then, this is the duty, or vocation, of man, it seems that it is the duty to be a *site* of dis-appearance. Beauty may well cause the world to be reduced to a particular within the world: 'I see a beautiful rose'. This holds all appearance in contemplative suspension, enabling the conjoining of the theoretical (sensible; nature) and the practical (supersensible; freedom) reduction enabled by an indeterminate univocal source, *viz.*, noumenality. The sublime may enact a reduction from a different direction. It approaches nature according to its 'fundamental measure', which is its totality, and it is nature in its totality which is subordinated to a greater measurement underlying both thought and nature. I will endeavour to increase the cogency of such an interpretation below.

To Be: Nothing

Echoing Plotinus and Avicenna, Kant insists that God does not cause the world, the phenomenal sphere. Instead, man is the 'creator' of appearance, while God is cause of noumena and the noumena is cause of man.[91] It is not, nevertheless, quite as simple as this, as we shall see. For one thing Kant is not wholly consistent with these divisions – an inconsistency which may accommodate the interpretation I am endeavouring to unfold. Man constructs appearance and this appearance is necessary, for without this input all would be in 'vain'.[92] If God, in a sense, requires man to provide such 'causation', then God seems subject to dependency. This is resolved through the ontological retraction of anything 'objective' being found in appearance. Appearance is *merely* appearance, it being nothing outside the subject. As Kant says, 'the objects of experience are never given in themselves, but only in experience, and have no existence outside it'.[93] The *necessary* appearance is bereft of independent existence; it is nothing outside the subject. So even though it is required, what is required is ontologically nothing.

Appearance is reduced to the subject. But this leaves Kant in difficulty because, as he admits himself, 'the proposition, "I think", or "I exist thinking" is an empirical proposition'.[94] The objects of experience may have been reduced, in some sense, to the subject, but this renders the subject something which is phenomenal yet apparently irreducible. As Jacobi says, 'without that presupposition *I* could not enter into the system, but without it *I* could not stay within it'.[95] Although Jacobi is here referring to the things-in-themselves, it is employed here to illustrate the quandary which the subject, 'I', faces. The subject must be there to reduce objects to experience and yet because of this it cannot be allowed to remain. Kant will have the subject posit itself as an object, and in so doing the 'world' remains merely phenomenal.[96] 'The thinkable I posits itself as the sensible.'[97] This positing takes the form of time, as Kant says in the first *Critique*: 'Time is therefore to be regarded as real, not as an object but as the mode of representation of myself as object.'[98] The subject then becomes an appearance. There seem to be two approaches to appearance: first, the subject who renders appearance as appearance, and, second, the object which is the *appearance of appearance*, to employ Kant's phrase.[99] For Kant, the subject who first 'causes' appearances to be merely appearance, then affects itself, must in consequence be the *appearance of appearance*.[100] The subject is reduced to appearance in being posited as an object. Kant has 'got rid of' appearance and then the subject, so the dependence 'God' has on these is relieved of infringing divine omnipotence.

Yet this, it seems, leaves Kant with an object ('subject-object'), and as we do not appear to have a subject, this would mean that there were indeed objects without subjects. Kant overcomes this by taking his analysis to another level, namely, to the transcendental subject and transcendental object. The object which is the object of 'subject-object', *viz.*, the phenomenal as a whole, can be thought of as the transcendental object. This transcendental is that which is thought by the transcendental subject as such. Kant is not quite sure how to term the transcendental object and subject. The former is called a cause of representation, or that which underlies outer appearance and is a ground of appearance.[101] The transcendental object is also sometimes referred to as being noumenal, as if it were a thing in itself (though Kant is not consistent here), and lastly as '= x'.[102] The transcendental subject is empirically unknown to us, yet it is the proper self, how the self is in itself.[103] The transcendental subject is also referred to as '= x'.[104] If both the transcendental object and the transcendental subject '= x', there may be only a formal distinction between the two.[105] Kant also, of course, speaks of a thing-in-itself and this is also called the subject and is equated with '= x'.[106]

It was argued above that appearances are reduced to the subject and that this subject is itself reduced to an object. This leaves us with an object without any subject, which sounds strangely pre-critical. We then became acquainted with the transcendental object and subject in all their guises. It seems that we are left with a sort of a dialectical negation between the two, as each enables the other, and each negates the other. The transcendental object allows for the subject to be affected (the appearance of appearance) while, at the same time, including the subject within its 'objective' domain. The transcendental subject enables its opposite because it allows for appearances as appearances, and so enables there to be something which will offend neither Kant's critical mind nor the God who depends on appearances to bring meaning to his creation. It seems that the transcendental subject and the transcendental object are inextricably linked. We see their 'union' to the degree that each is '= x' – a unitary source. This 'x' is also the thing-in-itself, the noumenon, 'the unknown' or 'an unknown something',[107] which is 'indeed real *per se*'.[108] The notion of things uniting around the same source becomes more interesting when we realise that there are to begin with many things which are but one. According to Kant there is but one Space and Time, both of which never change.[109] There is one 'experience' which is always the same.[110] There is one 'knowledge' of the one 'Transcendental object'. This is also called the 'whole of knowledge'.[111] There is one 'Transcendental subject' in that it = x, and in the sense of the *'sensus communis'* (although this *sensus communis* is not a postulate). There is one ideal 'Man'. There is but one 'World', and lastly there is but one 'God', if there is a God.[112]

If we look at Space and Time we see that each is one but also that each of these appears to coalesce around a common source. For example, all knowledge is but the determination of time, including knowledge of space.[113] This becomes more explicit in the *Opus Postumum* when Kant asserts that 'Space and Time, as intuitions of a whole, must always be thought of only as part of a *greater whole*.'[114] Indeed, Kant goes so far as to argue that they are one.[115] This should not sound too uncomfortable to our ears, for already in the first *Critique* Kant had suggested that both sensibility and understanding might spring from a common root.[116] The possibility of a unitary source becomes more evident if we realise that each side of the divide is always structurally 'contaminated' by the other. Sensibility has matter which, in a sense, relates to the transcendental object, but it also has a form which, in a similar manner, relates to the transcendental subject. While the understanding has concepts which obviously relate to the transcendental subject, it also has a subject which is 'empirical', and this relates to the transcendental object. Each side of the cognitive divide intimates a unicity of sorts. This unicity is arguably a univocity.

To repeat: the object is reduced to the subject, the subject to the object; each 'dis-appearing' within the perpetual dialectic between the transcendental subject and object. But these coalesce around the '= x', which can be thought of as the noumenal. If we concede to Kant that the noumenal is negative, what he calls a 'negative existence', some interesting possibilities arise.

Like Avicenna's Neoplatonist first intelligence, the noumenal, for Kant, causes appearance, but so also does man. Now if the noumenal does cause the appearance of appearance, which God cannot cause, then this noumenal (if something positive) may well threaten to infringe divine omnipotence. Appearance is required to enable creation to be creation, *viz.*, not to be in vain, a mere formal wilderness.[117] Yet God's dependence on Man appears also to lead to the negation of what is needed. Objects are merely appearance, becoming reduced to a subject who is also reduced. Even at a transcendental level a structural reduction and subsequent monistic unicity seem to arise. What we arrive at is a *noumenal nominality*, the 'x' – what Hamann called a 'Talisman',[118] and Schelling called 'nothing'.[119]

The noumenal is a negative existence, a mere limiting concept, so it may be better to think of it as a *nominal noumenality*. If appearance is reduced to a subject and then to the noumenal, this is the something reduced to nothing. Furthermore, the noumenal which is but a negative existence, a nominal '= x', is also reduced. This reduction appears to go both ways. That is, the noumenal is nothing but appearance, it exists only in this 'manifestation' (we saw this when dealing with the Kantian notion of beauty). Or the noumenal is reduced to God. We know at least that God causes the noumenal. If the noumenal is no-thing and is indeed only a negative nominal existence, a limiting concept, then it seems that God in causing the noumenal has caused nothing – certainly there is nothing efficiently caused.[120] It is indeed possible to argue that the noumenal is only formally distinct from appearance, and that the noumenal is only formally distinct from God – like the transcendental attributes in relation to the prior divine essence in Scotus. The latter is implied by Kant when he actually calls God noumenon, and when we realise that what God has caused in causing the noumena is nothing, ontologically speaking – hence its inability to remain apart from God. But if the noumenal is God, then God is either the nominal 'x' or is only formally distinct from appearance.

This becomes a more tenable interpretation when we realise that Kant invokes something called 'the totality of things'.[121] This is said to include both God and the World. Hence the unicity of the 'x' becomes a univocity. Furthermore, God becomes not a being outside man but within man. Gilson makes the point that 'having proved in his youth that we know nothing of God, old Kant was beginning to suspect that he himself might be God'.[122] (Gilson's use of the word 'youth' is strange, because Kant was certainly not young when he wrote the first *Critique*.) Indeed, the role of Man seems to be the very manifestation of both God and World. This may be the case because the formal difference between the noumenal and the phenomenal and the perpetual dialectic between the subject and the object, especially at a transcendental level, betray a unitary source which is univocal, affording only formal differences, ontologically speaking. The aspectual moment of the subject is that of the phenomenal, while the moment of the object is that of the noumenal. Kant intimates such an aspectual dialectic when he speaks of Beauty, for there we appear to 'see the noumenal' (*appearance itself becomes noumenal*!).

Kant includes both World and God within the 'totality of things'.[123] It is a *totality* revealed by 'Man'. He says that there is one God and one World and one ideal Man whose 'duty' it is to reveal the first two.[124] Man is both phenomenon and noumenon, and in so being he displays the dialectical disclosure of the totality of things ('= x') in both the World and God, which are correlates of each other. Man, in this sense, is both God and World. The sense of vocation developed in the third *Critique* out of respect for the sublime, engendered by our incapacity to represent the infinite, becomes the duty spoken about in the *Opus Postumum*. In the third *Critique* man was unable to represent the infinite and this awakened an awareness of a supersensible faculty and realm. In this realm, or by this faculty, man was able to think the infinite. But the initial idea which had given rise to the feeling of limitation was already the subject's, hence it was always self-limitation. In the *Opus Postumum* Kant states that Man's duty is to combine, connect and unite God and the World.[125] Man as phenomenon is World, as noumenon is God (in the *Opus Postumum* Kant calls God noumenon).[126] It seems that we have Man as the site of what I call 'disappearance'. He causes the object to be merely phenomenal and causes the noumenal to reside only as the phenomenal. The unitary 'x' betrays the univocity between the 'being' of noumenality and phenomenality. Each, like subject and object, *is* in the absence of the other. This also holds for God and the World. (This is Kant's Spinozistic lesson.) Hence we have an aspectual differentiation which, due to the univocity of the 'totality of things' ('= x'), affords but formal distinctions. It seems that Jacobi was correct to see critical idealism as itself the most extreme form of idealism, one which led to nihilism and has Fichte as a corollary,[127] for Fichte only spells out more clearly what was already in the Kantian corpus. We started with a subject and ended up with a monistic 'x' which mystically generates what has here been seen as the entire set of formal distinctions.[128]

It seems, then, that Kant was also guilty of having the something reduced to nothing, and then having this nothing 'be' *as* something. The phenomenal is supplemented by the noumenal and also vice versa. But this dualism gives way to a monism, one which Kant eventually calls the 'Totality'. This had already been present as the 'x', which was the sign of the nominalism of the noumenal. Like Spinoza, Kant *provides nothing*. As Žižek says: '[T]he subject "is" a non-substantial void – when Kant asserts that the transcendental subject is an unknowable, empty x, all one has to do is confer an ontological status on this epistemological determination: the subject is the empty Nothingness of pure self-relating . . . '.[129]

The next chapter offers a reading of Hegel that suggests that he deepens the *provenance* of nihilism, in so far as he seeks to develop a positive nihilism. It is argued that this nihilism causes everything to *vanish* within the act of *provision*: nothing *as* something.

Notes

1 For Aquinas see Part II, Chapter 8.
2 Kant (1964), B1. For a commentary on the first critique see N. K. Smith (1930). See also Paton (1936).

3   Our experience is always 'in the order of time': *ibid.*, A1, B1. We will see later that time is of great significance in the Kantian project.
4   *Ibid.*, Bxvii.
5   *Ibid.*, Bxvi.
6   *Ibid.*
7   *Ibid.*, A2, B4.
8   *Ibid.*, A2, B5.
9   *Ibid.*, A2, B6.
10   Kant (1997), p. 16 (4: 266).
11   See Kant (1964), A10, B14.
12   See Kant (1997), p. 16 (4: 267).
13   Kant (1964), A11–A12, B25.
14   For a positive assessment of synthetic *a priori* judgements see Allison (1983), especially pp. 73–80. For a more critical approach see Bennett (1966), especially chapters 2–4.
15   Kant (1964), A19, B33.
16   *Ibid.*, A22, B36.
17   *Ibid.*, A26, B42.
18   *Ibid.*, A23, B38.
19   *Ibid.*
20   *Ibid.*, A24, B39.
21   *Ibid.*, A25, B39.
22   *Ibid.*, A25, B40.
23   Kant (1997), p. 38 (4: 286).
24   Kant (1964), A28, B44.
25   *Ibid.*, A30, B46.
26   *Ibid.*, A31, B46.
27   *Ibid.*, A31, B47.
28   *Ibid.*, A34, B50–51.
29   For a general discussion of the Analytic see Bennett (1974), and Melnick (1973), especially pp. 30–57.
30   Kant (1964), A51, B75.
31   *Ibid.*, A68, B93.
32   *Ibid.*, A78, B103.
33   *Ibid.*, A69, B94.
34   Kant (1997), p. 51 (4: 298–4300).
35   Kant (1964), A70, B95.
36   *Ibid.*, A80, B106.
37   For criticism of the *Deduction* see Strawson (1966), esp. pp. 74–117. See also Bennett (1966), esp. chapters 6, 8, and 9. For a different approach to the *Deduction* see Henrich (1994).
38   Kant (1964), A89, B122.
39   *Ibid.*, A92, B125.
40   *Ibid.*, A104.
41   *Ibid.*, A118.
42   *Ibid.*, A123.
43   *Ibid.*, Axvi–xvii.

44 On the Kantian subject see Henrich (1989); see also 'The Proof Structure of Kant's Transcendental Deduction', in Henrich (1982).
45 Kant (1964), B159–165.
46 This is similar to the way in which Ockham envisages the production of universals, see *Ordinatio*, d. 2, q. 7.
47 Kant (1964) A141, B181. This is similar to Berkeley's criticism of Locke's theory of abstract ideas.
48 See Melnick (1973).
49 Kant (1964), A176.
50 *Ibid.*, A182, B224.
51 *Ibid.*, A183, B226.
52 *Ibid.*, A186, B239.
53 *Ibid.*, A187, B230.
54 *Ibid.*, A189, B232.
55 *Ibid.*, A194, B239.
56 *Ibid.*, A211, B256.
57 *Ibid.*, A214, B261.
58 *Ibid.*, A235–260, B294–315.
59 Kant (1993a). For a discussion of the second *Critique*, and of Kant's moral theory in general see Beck (1960); Sullivan (1989); Velkley (1989).
60 Kant (1964), B312.
61 Kant (1993a), p. 57.
62 *Ibid.*, pp. 62, 69.
63 *Ibid.*, p. 67.
64 *Ibid.*, p. 30. A discussion of this need not hold us up. It is sufficient to suggest that this seems to be contradictory, for if we must only act in a manner which would accommodate universality, then the categorical imperative if carried out would not allow its own universality for it would then be impossible to follow it. To will the categorical imperative is to render its universal application impossible. The particular will absorbs all other possibilities. For example, if I were to steal from a deposit box, and this act were universalised, then no one would put money in deposit boxes. When we return to our original action we are no longer able to will it. If we were to will a universal act, or to will the categorical imperative, and this were universalised, then when we returned to our original action we would be unable to will the categorical imperative. The condition to will something that could be universalised is impossible. To will the categorical imperative once is to disable its further application; to will the *categorical imperative* as the willed imperative. Kant wills the categorical imperative to be the base of our moral law. In so doing we emulate, but when he comes to will this act again we see that it is no longer intelligible, because the extension to the universal disables its repetition. There does seem to be something paradoxical in the structure of the categorical imperative. This is not of particular concern to my interpretation of Kant's project.
65 *Ibid.*, p. 141.
66 *Ibid.*, p. 107.
67 Kant (1952), pt. 2, p. 108.

68 On the third *Critique* see Guyer (1979); Eliot (1968); Crawford (1974); Cohen and Guyer, eds (1982); Coleman (1974); Dusing (1990), pp. 79–92; Bernstein (1992), pp. 17–65; Derrida (1987).
69 Kant (1952), p. 13.
70 *Ibid.*
71 *Ibid.*, p. 14.
72 *Ibid.*, p. 82. Kant also calls this *sensus communis* a 'universal voice', see *ibid.*, p. 56. This universal voice is only an idea, not a postulate.
73 *Ibid.*, p. 208.
74 *Ibid.*, p. 64.
75 *Ibid.*, p. 92.
76 For the sublime see Crowther (1989).
77 *Anstoss* is later employed by Fichte.
78 According to Kant the sublime comes in two forms, namely, mathematical (which deals with measure), and dynamic (which deals with might). This distinction need not concern us here.
79 Kant (1952), p. 93.
80 *Ibid.*, p. 94.
81 *Ibid.*, p. 98.
82 *Ibid.*, p. 108.
83 *Ibid.*, p. 111.
84 *Ibid.*, p. 120.
85 *Ibid.*, p. 112. This term is used pejoratively in the first and second *Critique* and in the *Opus Postumum*, but in the third *Critique* it receives a more positive reading. See Kant (1993a), p. 123; (1964), A643, B671; (1993b), p. 107.
86 *Ibid.*, p. 114.
87 *Ibid.*, p. 105.
88 *Ibid.*, p. 107.
89 *Ibid.*, p. 119. See also p. 118.
90 *Ibid.*, p. 120.
91 'It would be contradictory to say God is the creator of appearances'; 'the concept of creation does not belong to the sensible mode'; '[God] is the cause of the existence of the acting beings (as noumena)', Kant (1993a), p. 107. 'God is not the originator of the world', Kant (1993b), p. 212.
92 Kant (1952), pt. 2, p. 108.
93 Kant (1964), A 492, B521.
94 *Ibid.*, B428.
95 Jacobi (1994), p. 33; italics mine.
96 'The subject makes itself into an object'; 'The subject posits itself as object', Kant (1993b), pp. 109, 171.
97 *Ibid.*, p. 202.
98 Kant (1964), A35, B52.
99 'The *appearance of appearance* . . . is the concept of the object itself', Kant (1993b), p. 109; italics mine.
100 '*Appearance of appearance*, in so far as the subject is affected by the object and affects itself', *ibid.*, p. 107; italics mine.

101 As Cause see Kant (1964), A288, B344; A372; A391; A494, B522. As that which underlies appearance see A358; A379; A540, B568. As a ground of outer appearance see A277, B333.

102 As noumenal see *ibid.*, A288, B345; A358; A545, B573. As '= x' see A346, B404.

103 As empirically unknown to us see *ibid.*, A544, B573. As the proper self, as it is in itself, see A492, B520.

104 As '= x' see *ibid.*, A346, B404.

105 I use this term to imply the presence of a univocity akin to that held by Duns Scotus.

106 See Kant (1993b), pp. 179, 181. Kant also equates or links the thing in itself with the noumenal; see Kant (1964), A256, B312; and Kant (1997), pp. 66, 68, 86–87, 114.

107 Kant (1964), B13; B312.

108 *Ibid.*, Bxx.

109 *Ibid.*, A189, B232; A32, B47; A32, B48; A25, B39; Kant (1997), p. 95; Kant (1993b), pp. 95, 210. For the fact that there is no real change see Kant (1964), A186, B229, and A187, B230. In this instance this is only in relation to the analogies of experience.

110 Kant (1993b), pp. 80, 88, 95, 98, 123, 210.

111 Kant (1964), A109; A645, B673.

112 Kant (1993b), p. xliv.

113 Kant (1964), A 210, B255.

114 Kant (1993b), p. 172; italics mine.

115 *Ibid.*, p. 236.

116 Kant (1964), A46, B29.

117 Kant (1952), pt. 2, p. 108.

118 See Dickson (1995), p. 521.

119 Schelling (1994), p. 101.

120 I mean this to refer to efficient causality.

121 Kant (1993b), p. 228.

122 Gilson (1937), p. 239.

123 'The totality of things contains God and the world', Kant (1993b), p. 228. See also *ibid.*, p. 217.

124 *Ibid.*, p. xliv.

125 *Ibid.*, pp. 228, 229, for 'combines'; see p. 237 for 'connects'; see p. 233 for 'unites' .

126 *Ibid.*, p. 229. Gilson (1937) makes the point that 'having proved in his youth that we know nothing of God, old Kant was beginning to suspect that he himself might be God', p. 239.

127 See Jacobi (1994), pp. 331–338. For Jacobi on Fichte see pp. 497–536. The most contemporaneous and infamous charge of idealism against Kant was known as the *Feder-Garve*, or *Göttingen*, review; see Walker (1989), pp. xv–xxiv, for a translation of this review. See also Kant's response to this review in Kant (1997), pp. 126–137.

128 Hamann also accused Kant of being a mystic. Hamann levelled three main charges against Kant. The first was that his critical project endeavoured to purify philosophy of custom. Hamann pointed out rather ingeniously that

without Berkeley there would be no Hume, and without Hume there would be no Kant. This genealogy embodied the Kantian project, inextricably linking it to custom, or history. The second criticism is that Kant seeks an escape from experience, to be free of its messy contingency. The third was that Kant sought to circumvent language. These criticisms levelled by Hamann are the purisms of custom, experience, and language. See Dickson (1995), pp. 519–534.
129 Žižek (1996), p. 124.

5

HEGEL'S CONSUMMATE PHILOSOPHY

The univocity of *Geist*

To vanish

The concept of pure absolute exodus and return (from nothing, to nothing, for nothing, into nothing).[1]

(F. H. Jacobi)

We are Nothingness . . . [S]hadows are nothingness, space and time do not exist . . . everything is Nothingness.[2]

(G. W. F. Hegel)

Hegel endeavoured to enable nothing to *be*, since he understood nihilism as not merely negative.[3] We know from earlier chapters that if nothing is to be, it must *provide* all that 'something' could be said to provide, preventing itself from being lack. If nothing is but lack, then nothing cannot be said to *be*; for its non-provision will present a space for the otherness of transcendence, one which would provide. If Hegel is to be read as attempting such a nihilism then we must examine his moves in rigorous terms of ontology, not merely attending to various ontic peculiarities or methodologies. For any examination that concentrates on the merely ontic will be too caught up in the movement of his 'system', and only look to see *where* things are going, not *that* they are going, and in what way.

On the whole, direct discussion of Hegel's views on religion is avoided. That being said, I will briefly spell out a general concern about Hegel's approach to religious language, before going on to develop the main purpose of this chapter. This slight elaboration on Hegel's treatment of religion is relevant to the overall aim of the chapter because it is what I call Hegel's 'nominalism' that forces us, not to look at *where* we are going, but instead to notice *that* we are going, and in what way!

Hegel's univocity of *Geist*

The thing to avoid, I don't know why, is the spirit of
the system.[4]

(Samuel Beckett, *The Unnamable*)

There are various approaches to Hegel's reading of religion. Kojève
considers Hegel's philosophy to be atheistic, while Rowan Williams finds
the theology in Hegel's work to be central, denying a merely secularist
understanding.[5] What tends to govern such interpretations is the
distinction between *Vorstellung* and *Denken*. *Vorstellung* is generally related
to religion, while *Denken* is attributed to philosophy. According to Hegel,
picture-thinking is the representational mode of thinking to be found in
religion. This picture-thinking does not think the truth, which is
implicitly present, explicitly: in 'this picture-thinking, reality does not
receive its perfect due . . . it does not attain to what it ought to show forth,
viz. Spirit'.[6] That is, representational thinking does not afford insight the
rights it deserves: 'Insight has its rights that can no longer be denied.'[7]
Hegel's philosophy intends to offer such insight a more explicit
manifestation. Such a thinking of truth is successful only to the degree
that it is *nothing but Spirit*.[8] What I intend to bring out is that Hegel
threatens to leave us with a problem: what is Spirit? As Walter Jaeschke
says, 'Spirit is an empty word unless one says what it means.'[9] It will be
suggested below that because everything becomes Spirit in Hegel's
philosophy, what Spirit means becomes hard to articulate without the
threat of a certain nominalism. As Lobkowicz says, 'It is not easy to save
Hegel from nominalism.'[10] First I present the positive aspect in Hegel's
distinction of *Vorstellung* and *Denken*, before offering some critical
comments.

The problem with a representational thinking is that it encourages a
conception of God as something *over and against* creation. Hegel wishes to
escape this. In so doing he has invited accusations of pantheism and is
thought by some to be the grandfather of death of God theology.[11] There
is little doubt that this is true in an historical sense, for Altizer *et al.* do
trace a lineage to Hegel. Yet such an understanding is deeply mistaken,
for what Hegel accomplishes is nothing less than to break free of
ontotheology. He achieves this by arguing that God is dead. Such a
pronouncement is, as James Collins insists, the 'death of
representation',[12] which is the sublation of religion by Hegelian
philosophy. As a result God is no longer conceived as something over and
against creation and this is the death of God. For God's death eradicates
a creator/creation distinction read in dualistic, ontotheological terms.
This allows God to be beyond ontic categories, so bringing out the radical
nature of creation.

Rowan Williams is correct to see in Hegel something akin to traditional theology, in so far as Hegel conceives of God in a manner similar to Nicholas de Cusa, namely as *non aliud*.[13] To interpret this conception of God as a licence to death of God theology is mistaken, because to do so is *to remain* within an ontotheological understanding of difference: something over and against something else. In this way 'radical' death of God theologians are reactively constituted by ontotheology, which is to say they propagate a 'conservative' theology.

For Hegel, philosophy gives *form* to the *content* of religion.[14] How Hegel's relationship with religion is interpreted will depend on how this philosophical contribution is conceived. Two questions come to the fore. The first of these is whether religion is surpassed by Hegel's philosophy. The second question is, does Hegel's philosophy bring religion to an end? The answer to both of these will again depend on how *Vorstellung* and *Denken* are understood. Some commentators take the contribution made by religion to philosophy to indicate that once such a contribution is made, religion is abandoned.[15] This causes others to suggest that Hegel's conception of God is not the Judaeo-Christian one.[16] What is of central concern is the notion of what is essential and what is dispensable. As Hegel says: 'The aspect of the momentary, local, external non-essential element (*Beiwesens*) must be clearly distinguished from the eternal appearance which is inherent in the essence (*Wesen*) of truth so as not to confuse the finite from the infinite, the indifferent from the substantial.'[17] Is religion no longer essential once its content has been appropriated and sublated by philosophy? To suggest that Hegel conceived of religious doctrine as nonessential may be unfair. For Hegel defended the Christian doctrine of the Trinity against Friedrich Tholuck who considered this doctrine to be decorative timber (*Fachwerk*).[18] So Hegel's approach to religion cannot be treated in any simplistic fashion.[19] Indeed, his preference for philosophy may be but a reflection of the inferior theology which Hegel encountered in his day. So it is not a surprise to find commentators such as Paul Ricœur and Louis Dupré arguing that religion is never actually surpassed by *Denken*, in so far as the content given to philosophy by religion's picture-thinking is perpetually provided.[20] In this way religion cannot simply be surpassed, there being a continual dialectic between philosophy's form and religion's content. (Although one could wonder if Hegel does not entirely surpass religion in the same Pickwickian manner as Derrida declares that deconstruction does not simply eschew metaphysics; for Derrida thinks that he can only surpass metaphysics by remaining *with* metaphysics.) There is little doubt that for Hegel Christianity was the *consummate* religion because of its Trinitarian understanding of God; this understanding allowed God to enter creation, so collapsing the representational dualism of creator/creation. The Trinitarian understanding of God also put to rest the notion of God as something static and allowed God to be thought of as self-conscious Spirit. This allowed Hegel to differentiate his own conception of God from that of Spinoza's, and in this way to defend himself from pantheism (although it must be said that Hegel did not consider Spinoza a pantheist).[21]

According to Hegel, Spinoza's notion of God as absolute substance failed to understand God as absolute person.[22] However, we should not necessarily run to embrace this absolute person, for we do not quite know if the manner in which Hegel employs words leaves them with the same meaning, or indeed with any meaning. When Hegel equates two terms we are left somewhat bereft of the meanings of either. For example, he declares that religion is the state. It is tempting to recoil from such a statement. But any such reaction is governed by something other than speculative thinking, since one presumes that one knows what a state and a religion respectively are. The refrain of the speculative question suspends the meaning of two apparently disparate terms by equating them. Similarly, when Hegel speaks of God being the absolute person, we must not presume that in this speculative economy we know what a person is. Indeed, Hegel's main contention with Spinoza is not that his substance is too impersonal, but that it is insufficiently speculative and so is ill-defined. Hegel does not deny that Spinoza is fundamentally correct. What he does deny is any limitation that substance receives, for limitations will restrict what such a philosophy can *provide*. Hegel calls substance a subject, but here again through this equation we do not know what either term means. Such ambiguity allows Hegel to keep his philosophy perpetually open. Consequently, he can construct a more positive nihilism which is able to *provide more*. Or, more accurately, he is able to not provide less.

Hegel defined pantheism as the doctrine which asserted 'that everything, the whole, the universe, this complex of everything existing, this infinity of many things, individual things, that all this is God'.[23] There is little doubt that Hegel took his resistance to pantheism in a serious manner,[24] and that he was not pantheistic to the degree that the 'world' is in a sense unavailable to us in his philosophy. However, if it is inaccurate to assert that Hegel propagates an embryonic death of God theology and that he is not a pantheist, can it be argued that Hegel is a panentheist?

Panentheism was a term coined by Karl Krause[25] to designate a position for which God is not separate from the world but nonetheless is not *exhausted* by the world.[26] A chorus of commentators take Hegel to be a panentheist;[27] indeed, one calls panentheism the new orthodoxy concerning Hegel.[28] There is a large amount of textual evidence to support this interpretation. For example, Hegel asserts that God *cannot be God without the world*.[29] The German word for without (*ohne*) does not necessarily exclude a notion of transcendence,[30] but it must be said that it does not tend to invite one. Likewise the Universal for Hegel is referred to as the 'absolute womb'.[31] This finite exists *within* the infinite, for it is *contained* in the infinite,[32] and, furthermore, the infinite *absorbs* the finite.[33] This causes Reardon to suggest that the universe 'must be conceived as existing in God'.[34] Does this mean that Hegel does nothing but reformulate Spinoza's panentheism, as Butler argues?[35]

Hegel's position may be the result of a reading of the creator/created difference in terms of the ontological difference, the 'proximity' between God and World being a corollary of this understanding. Nevertheless, it must be asked whether Hegel's philosophy reduces the Father and Son of the Trinity to the Spirit, a reduction that may leave us unable to discern what Spirit is – a predicament that suggests a certain nominalism. (To cite Baudrillard again: 'there have always been churches to hide the death of God and to hide the fact God is everything which is the same thing'.)[36] This nominalism is not only caused by the reduction of the Trinity to one, but also results from the distinction between *Vorstellung* and *Denken*. It is possible to suggest that this distinction is *itself* guilty of merely representational thinking. For Hegel only *represents* religious thinking and its relation to the speculative. In so doing he ossifies language in terms of a univocal thought of *Geist*, a thought differentiated (remotely following Scotus) only in terms of two modes: finite and infinite. This univocity comes to the fore if we reconsider the Hegelian aphorism 'God is dead'.

It was suggested above that the idea of God's death helped Hegel to escape an ontotheological understanding of difference. God, in being dead, is not over and against the world. This is to be beyond representational thinking, a surpassing enabled by the consummate religion. But this aphorism can also be interpreted in another way which threatens the cogency of Hegel's project. God, in being dead, is indeed not over and against creation, but this can also mean that creation is *set free* of God. The aphorism read in this way allows the gift of creation its difference, and independent reality. This world is in fact so real, so different because of its given-ness, its intimacy with God, that God can be crucified in it. Thus for orthodox Christianity the Crucifixion was actual, real, bloody, and it happened to a human who was God's Son. Thus God's death identifies God with the world but equally distances the world from God, since the world is *so* distant that God dies there. This 'being in itself' of the world once again introduces ontotheology, since now in the infinite God lives and in the finite dies, and therefore they are two ontic planes. This would not be the case if he had remained with Chalcedonion orthodoxy for which God only dies *as man*; the death of a man being the life of God respects the ontological difference. Hegel therefore harbours a residual onticity in so far as he seems to conceive the world as ontologically (not just contingently, because of sin) as the place where God dies; this suggests that finite and infinite are two 'rival' spaces wherein the absolute is differently disposed. Equally, however, if God only achieves his true infinitude for himself through this finite death, then there is after all pantheistic identity. Hegel, therefore, offers either or both ontotheological distance between finite and infinite placed in relation within univocal being, or else semi-monistic identity. He lacks the distance of participation.

For Hegel there is a production of infinite and finite only in the place of the other, and within the monistic univocity of *Geist,* just as for Spinoza we saw that God was made manifest in Nature, while Nature manifested in God, both within the univocity of Substance. (Part II, Chapter 10 re-examines this nihilism, offering a more positive reading. It argues that nihilism is instructive for theology, since theology, in terms of creation, will endeavour to have the nothing *as* something. As a result it may be apt to consider nihilism as the *consummate philosophy* for theology, and Hegel certainly embodies this positive element that may emanate from the logic of nihilism.)

The remainder of this chapter will refer mainly to two texts of Hegel's. The first is the *Phenomenology of Spirit*; the second is *The Lesser Logic*, which is the first part of the *Encyclopedia of the Philosophical Sciences*.

Collapsing dualisms: Nothing is Something

Hegel adopts a number of general strategies in the establishment of his 'positive nihilism'. The first and most important strategic principle is *a war against all dualism*. The second is the *immanentisation of all that is*. The latter can only be accomplished if what *is* is nothing, but this nothing is *as* something. The reason why such a strange-sounding proposal is of the utmost philosophical importance is that if it is something to be, or if it is significant to be something, then a dualism will arise: nothing/something. The significance attributed to the idea of something will engender its opposite, in a static and rigid manner: the something will imply a nothing and these will remain perpetually immiscible yet dualistically linked. If this is so, the nihilistic philosopher will remain at the mercy of this dualism, unable fully to immanentise what *is*, because the dualism will disable the attempt completely to exclude transcendence. 'Something rather than nothing' – this metaphysical *mantra* will aporetically escape Hegel's avowedly immanent system because its articulation presumes a meta-level which, of course, it is unable to locate. (Not that I am here advocating dualism *per se* as desirable.)[37] Instead, the something must be nothing and this nothing must be *as* something. This renders both terms unstable, and disables primary location (meaning the understood definition of a term: blue is a colour of a certain wavelength. Secondary location is the combination of terms in a manner that allows for the significance of primary terms to be considered: is colour a primary or secondary quality, and if so what are the philosophical implications of that?). With regard to the terms something and nothing a one could ask the metaphysical question: Why something rather than nothing? To ask such a question one must presume the legitimacy of the primary location – the definition of the terms, whereas the inability to locate at a primary level will prevent any articulation of this metaphysical question. For what reason would one appeal to transcendence? If something is nothing, there is nothing here about which to speak, or appeal. Furthermore, if nothing is *as* something, there will be no privation, or non-provision. Consequently, there would not be any shadow cast by a loss. This idea of loss could nostalgically collude with the idea of transcendence, which would remove the loss. In this way to have the nothing *as* something eradicates the need for transcendence. That is to say, the metaphysical question no longer makes sense.

As said, the task of having the nothing *as* something will require that Hegel collapse every dualism. For each and every dualism threatens to generate the notion of an elsewhere, which also speaks of a stable 'here' as opposed to a 'there' of the elsewhere. Consequently, nothing will be unable to be *as* something, because nothing will again be set in absolute opposition to something. But to get rid of such dualism involves the disabling of stable terms, for if one secure term remains then the attempt to have the nothing *as* something will be scuppered. Any 'this' as opposed to a 'that', or a 'here' to a 'there' will foil this nihilistic nothing by being something. These are what could be called Hegel's *unhappy* dualisms, unhappy because they leave every nature in opposition to itself. The most obvious Hegelian example is that of the unhappy consciousness. This is the religious mind which has a natural vocation over and against a supernatural one, so dividing himself in half. To prevent this Hegel seeks to collapse every dualism by setting each term adrift within the dialectical procession of the Absolute Idea, or *Geist*, which sunders itself into the particularities we experience every day. This procession will remain fully immanent and will allow for the nothing to be *as* something (presuming I can express the nothing as *Geist* or the Absolute Idea). I will endeavour, however briefly, to trace this procession of the nothing *as* something.

For Hegel, the world, nature and life are the manifestation or externalisation of *Geist*, or of the Absolute Idea. The particular (which we will see is never available to us) is the result of *Geist*'s self-alienation. The Absolute, as *Geist*, sunders itself, and it does so because the Absolute must 'result'.[38] Hegel gives the example of a flower bud which gives forth a flower. The flower as bud is *An-sich* (in itself), it is not yet for itself (*Für-sich*), and it will be the job of the Absolute to be in-itself-and-for-itself (*Für-*

sich-ein), in an externalised yet fully immanentised state.[39] For this reason the Absolute cannot merely be at some abstract beginning.

Hegel mediates the beginning by forcing us to think of the Absolute as that which *results*. But he threatens his system with a problem: if that which *is* must result, how is it the same thing as it was at the beginning? How can something result and be that same thing? It seems that it must have been already what it is to become, and so there is no real becoming. That which results must already have resulted if it is to be that which results. If it is not the same then there are two different things: that which is before the result and that which is the result.

In overcoming this dilemma, Hegel first of all prohibits a merely abstract, or absolute, beginning. Instead Hegel advocates a mediated Absolute, for it is the power of *Geist* to other itself, to expand beyond itself into an alterity in which it will retain its integrity. In a sense, this integrity will not be the same, in that it will be transformed by this procession, as it will become mediated. As Hegel says, 'the power of the Spirit is only as great as its expression, its depth only as deep as it dares to spread out and lose itself in its exposition'.[40] *Geist* must 'win its truth', and it does so in a state of 'utter dismemberment'. For there in complete difference it finds itself, and consequently it is Absolute.[41]

So Spirit becomes Absolute by remaining the selfsame Spirit in its externalisation.[42] This self-alienation collapses a dualism, the first of many; each dualism collapsed will reflect the overall project of collapsing the opposition between nothing and something. In so doing, Hegel commences his attempt to have nothing other itself *as* something. The dualism involved here is that of subject and object. By othering itself, Spirit becomes its 'own immanent content'.[43] This means that the terms subject and object as typically conceived are put under threat; if Spirit is both subject and object we will find it hard to articulate, philosophically, a stable dualism. Hegel defines Spirit in terms of this perpetual task of self-alienation and return: 'Spirit becomes object because it is just this movement of becoming other to itself, i.e., becoming an object to itself, and of suspending this otherness.'[44]

Otherness is generated by the negative power of the understanding and reflection. For Hegel understanding is the absolute power of dissolution.[45] It separates and so allows for a negative form of differentiation or dissolution, which is a mode of death because *Geist* is the power to look 'the negative in the face . . . this tarrying with the negative is the magical power that converts it into being'.[46] In this way there is a movement beyond an abstract formalism which ties us to immediacy and is both epistemological error and ontological insufficiency. Thus Hegel argues that *Geist* must be understood as (a) subject which continually externalises itself as object: hence it is restless.[47]

Geist does not inhabit some static, eternal, repose, which is immediately self-identical and absolute, without remaining in a kind of 'real error'. Instead, substance must be re-cognised as subject. But if this is to happen our understanding of what this means must not itself rest in immediacy: rather, finite thought must echo the dynamism of the real which is also infinite logos.

The movement from the Absolute as substance to the Absolute as a subject therefore cannot be circumvented by thought: we must progress with it. The mediation of the Absolute, as a result, is the true actual arrival of the Absolute, for it is the provision of what *is*. To ignore the reality of such a journey is to inhabit the night in which all cows are black, by forfeiting all differentiation, all mediation. This forfeiting hands all finite configurations over to the darkness of immediacy.[48] It is for this reason that we require form and essence; each form as an expression of the divine essence is necessary and, in some sense, irreplaceable. (This will be shown below to be more of a ruse than a reality.) This is what Hegel refers to as the 'whole wealth of developed form',[49] and it is this wealth which represents the patient suffering of the Absolute.[50]

I am: Nothing

Each articulated cognition – each alienation – is absolutely necessary. The sameness which results from the fact that all is *Geist* is itself mediated. It cannot, however, be simply asserted, but must be discovered: the absolute is not absolute until it becomes mediated, even though it is the site of necessity. Hence God, as the Absolute, requires the 'world' (*Ohne Welt ist Gott nicht Gott*).[51] Finite embodiment is necessary, God requires it. But if God requires it, then, is not God, as Absolute, compromised? The requisite mediation appears to threaten the status of divinity.

It seems, then, that there is still a double move *à la* Spinoza. The finite is necessarily posited, so, in a sense, reducing God. Yet, simultaneously, the finite is reduced to God, since here alone God 'becomes' and thereby 'is'. The finite qualifies the infinite and the infinite qualifies the finite.[52] The dialectical necessity at work renders the finite nothing because it is nothing but God – of course in a mediated sense. The world must be nothing but it must be so *as* something. As Hegel says: 'True knowledge of God begins when we know that things, as they immediately are, have no truth.'[53] Indeed, the finite is evil to the degree that it presumes, in its immediacy, that it is something other than God (this is an immanent version of God as *ipsum esse*).[54] All finite things involve an untruth, for their concept and their existence do not tally.[55] Consequently, they must perish (this is in effect a 'pagan' version of the real distinction between essence and existence that pertains to creation). Death, in this sense, is an ontological and an epistemological liberation, and has, in this sense, veracity for finitude: 'The single individual is incomplete Spirit.'[56] For this reason it must suffer dissolution as it is forced beyond itself towards the infinite. Hegel instigates such a dissolution by giving up the 'fixity' of the subject, and of all finite things. They are, as said, set adrift. We struggle to locate the bare particular, but for us it is unavailable – we will see later why this is so.[57] Knowledge of God, then, begins with the loss of the particular, but the particular is preserved in this dissolution, although in the opposite direction (*Aufhebung*). For just as it must be dissolved so it must be posited, since it is a requisite embodiment of the Absolute. The particular 'discloses' knowledge of God to us by remaining in its dissolution *as* God, as mediated infinitude, just as God remains in the necessity of 'his' embodiment because what is embodied *is* nothing.

Let me repeat some of the salient points from above. Finite things are necessarily posited. Because of this they are nothing, nothing but God. Yet God is only God through that which is necessary; the finite. We know that what is posited is nothing, but God needs this nothing; indeed this nothing is God. Just as with Spinoza, God and Nature are aspectually 'provided' by the absence of the other. For Hegel, it seems we are to know God by knowing finitude. But in knowing finitude we know the nothingness of finitude, a nothingness preserved aspectually in the necessity of the divine self-alienation. The Absolute, as he declares, is the identity of identity and non-identity.

The double movement of positing the finite and the simultaneous dissolution of the same (for the truth of what is posited is this dissolution), helps us to understand the different approaches of infinitude and finitude. Finitude can be characterised as a *positing dissolution*, because in asserting itself, in being what it is (which is the that-it-is), a dissolution is enacted. Finitude is, in this sense, a site of dissolution; this site allows the Absolute to arrive. For the Absolute employs these necessary embodiments, which are but emanations of the infinite Spirit, to facilitate its own mediation. Hence finitude is what Hegel calls in the *Lesser Logic* a vanishing factor.[58] The existence of a finite being is merely the mark of infinite mediation, which finitude complies with and, in a sense, enables. The finite will say *I am*. The positivity of such an assertion allows the Absolute to *be there*, colonising this place. But this occupation reveals the ontological status of such a place, and we find that finitude in truth says *I am-nothing*. This positive dissolution is exactly what a dependent divinity requires of its finite emanations. Conversely, infinitude may be characterised as a *dissolving postulation*. Infinitude as *predicative being* (employing Hogrebe's term), which is to say expansive, always says more.[59]

The move from infinity outwards is the movement from nothing to something, while the movement from the finite to the infinite is the move from something to the nothing (this is *pronominal being* which is contractive).[60] As such, every finite location is problematised. As Hegel says: 'the infinite only expresses the ought-to-be elimination of the finite'.[61] What this means is that the 'fixity' of, for example, the self, is given up. The untruth of the finite is its nothingness, and its pretend yet provisional somethingness is dis-located by the fact that this finitude is infinitude, ontologically speaking. This means that finitude is always elsewhere, and so its dis-location results in a dissolution that ushers in the arrival of the Absolute. Because we cannot find the finite it can, or could, be the infinite. As a result Hegel can argue for the necessary embodiment of divinity without fear of lessening this divinity. Hegel need not fear the finite, since he need not fear mediation.

Yet the mediation of the infinite by finitude in Hegel's work threatens to set up a dualism, because the untruth of the finitude points to an elsewhere, at least by legitimate implication. This means that it becomes 'unhappy', *viz.*, dualistic. Or it threatens an 'immediate monism' which would fail to 'provide', and so would itself allow for a dualism. The 'here' speaks of a 'there', an elsewhere. If this is the case then there will not be a nothing *as* something and reality will not achieve the appellation *fully immanent*. To resolve this quandary, Hegel must ensure that Divinity is nothing but this finitude; there can be no residual identity which could permit an appeal to transcendence, positing an elsewhere. There can be no residual divinity outside finitude, just as there cannot be a residual finitude beyond its reduction to the infinite. This double move, *à la* Spinoza, allows for the provision of the infinite (God) and the finite (Nature) in the distinct absence of both. It seems that the Hegelian dialectic, of which more will be spoken below, moves between the permanent need of having otherness in sameness and sameness in otherness. This is more profoundly articulated as the requirement that the One be many, yet the many be One. There must be finitude, yet finitude is nothing, in that it is nothing but the infinite. Conversely, the infinite cannot be anything other than the finite (this constitutive relationship renders infinitude after all ontic, in the same fashion as the 'death of God'). For Hegel, infinite substance has become finite subject while equally, subject has become substance.[62] Finitude has become the infinite at the same time as the infinite becomes the finite. As he says, this movement is a 'twofold process and the genesis of the whole, in such wise that each side simultaneously posits the other, and each therefore has both perspectives within itself; together they constitute the whole by dissolving themselves, and by making themselves into its moments'.[63] Terms such as substance, subject, infinitude, and finitude are merely sites of disclosive disappearance; they are 'vanishing' points. Just as with Spinoza, the articulation of each term is the dissolution of the same, since difference is generated 'aspectually'.

The process of dissolution, which is meant to allow the nothing to be *as* something, is epitomised by the movement of the Absolute Idea which is itself a process. It is a process which endeavours to offer itself to itself as an immanent atlas.[64] For Hegel the world is an idea which sunders itself, becoming an object for itself. The *univocity of non-being* which underlies the process, ensures a *reditus*, which can in some sense be said to precede the *exitus*, which is but its other aspect.[65] Indeed, it is arguable that the univocity of non-being affords us only these sort of formal distinctions. These distinctions are not unreal, but they remain less than real. Such a Scotist characterisation will appear more appropriate as this chapter unfolds. The sundering of the idea into particularity causes life to be an aspectual contradiction of formalities (for example, finite as infinite; infinite as finite; subject as substance). All which *is* resides in contradiction; arguably this is a result of the nothing being *as* something.

I am Thinking: Nothing

> The Man of Hegel . . . is the Nothingness that annihilates given-being existing as world and that annihilates itself (as real historical time or History) in and through that annihilation of the given.[66]
>
> (Alexandre Kojève)

Hegel continually collapses dualisms so as to immanentise reality; we have already paid witness to this. What is important for Hegel is to employ terms and then let this employment effect a dissolution, enacting sites of disappearance. In the *Phenomenology of Spirit* we see Hegel render substance a subject, and subject, in a sense, substance. This causes each term to be set adrift, dis-located, consequently dissolved. In the *Lesser Logic*, the effort to collapse terms by way of examined use is taken to new heights. As we said earlier, it is imperative for Hegel to be rid of every 'this' or 'that', and every 'here' or 'there'. This, however, merely reflects the programmatic endeavour to be rid of something and nothing so as to have the nothing *as* something. For Hegel, in the *Lesser Logic*, the problem is the divorce between reality and the idea and the notion that they are not the same.[67] This means that there is an impervious dualism that will resist the immanence of the Hegelian system.

Hegel's first move is to argue that mind makes thought its object.[68] Here we have a typical conception of what *thought* is and what an *object* is being suspended. Hegel argues that thought as object is intrinsically concrete.[69] Again this causes our conceptions to suffer. If thought is the object of mind and thought is concrete, then the division between idea and reality, along with subject and object, becomes problematic. We cannot, it seems, locate either side of the dualism without a certain amount of violence. What is to count as spiritual or material is set adrift. For Hegel indeed, the spiritual is what is actual, while matter is but an abstraction. So any endeavour to locate 'solid' matter as opposed to ephemeral spirit or thought, suffers defeat, since it will be forced to pick out an abstraction as its materiality.

Thought, which is a concrete object, is at times expressed as subjective, that is, as Man. But Man is itself an object. As the quotation from Kojève above suggests, Man for Hegel is a site of dissolution. (Part I, Chapter 6 argues that Heidegger's Dasein enacts a similar effect.) Hegel argues that when we speak of Man as a thinker all we mean is that he 'feels' his universality. This universality is not some ephemeral cognition, but a concrete re-cognition of Man as the expression of a universal idea which is itself reality. When Man feels his universality he feels the universe as object. Furthermore, Man enables 'an expansion' of the object: in feeling his universality he expands the one finite point out to include all points. The one limited point finds within its own finitude the presence of infinity.[70] In other words, Man in thinking the universal, which is for Man to think, expands the 'I' so as to include the universe as the object. (This is an Hegelian version of *capax omnia*.)[71] Again we must remember that thought is an object. So Man as thinker thinks 'materially' so to speak. The finite subject 'includes both the universality of their sense of life, and the individual mode which is in negation with it'.[72] Hence when Man speaks, he speaks his own demise; the particular configuration which Man is, is the initiation of its own dissolution. In addition, Man, as thinker, thinks the universal object as the *thought of thought*; to think is to think this object. But Hegel risks a dualism because of the alteration effected by this thinking: not to think/to think. This is avoided because the alteration is merely the aforementioned expansion of the 'point'. The thought of Man is but the universality of the object, which is alienated Spirit. There is, in this thinking, no subject, because what thinks is but what is thought, or is only formally, aspectually, distinct from what is thought. Equally, there is no object because the object is the thinking, or the thought.

In thinking, which is but to think the universal, Man thinks his own demise, because he is nothing but what is thought. In other words, the enacted expansion of the finite point, Man, is but the point of its collapse: 'Living beings possess within them a universal vitality which overpasses and includes the single mode; and thus, as they maintain themselves in the negative of themselves, they feel the contradiction to exist within them.'[73] Man is to unthink thought as something, by thinking it as material; our implicit metaphysical presuppositions about thinking are brought to ground. What is it to think? We must presume it to ask it. The form which this requisite presupposition displays is more akin to the shape of an 'object'. We literally think nothing in thinking, but this nothing is *as* something, something universal, namely the 'object'.[74] Yet this object suffers a similar reduction and so a dissolution.

As mentioned earlier, Hegel strategically thinks a non-identity into propositions (speculative thinking).[75] What this means is that in any equation of two terms both are suspended, if not dissolved. For example, thought equals the concrete. Or, to give more famous examples from the *Philosophy of Right*, religion equals the state, or the real equals the rational, while the rational equals what is real. Hegel thereby presents us with propositions which say an 'unsaying', to employ an awkward phrase. For example, the proposition that thought equals the concrete does not tell us anything. Instead it prevents us from saying anything. In a sense, the body of the proposition occupies the place of its asking, preventing any actual communication of 'information', knowledge and so on. Speculative propositions, which is what these are, employ each term in such a manner that they suffer an implosion. They literally collapse as they dance between the dynamic or aspectual poles of the proposition.

We no longer know what thought is nor what the concrete is. Furthermore, we cannot escape the proposition and so make it to *the other side* until we answer, or re-locate, the terms. But the aporetic form of the speculation will keep us suspended within the veridical assertion, holding our terms hostage, until, as in the Kafka parable *Before the Law*, our discourse dies of old age and the door is shut. The doorway to the *Law* had been designed with us and only us in mind, since we are of course those that can have discourse. Hegelian speculation stops our speech speaking, our discourse discoursing. Consequently, it is possible to argue that nothing but silence resides in the rise and fall of our syllables.

I am: Speculation

Hegel's logical doctrine has three sides and three parts. The first part is understanding, the abstract.[76] This is rigid and fixed, articulating its sense by supposing terms to be static. The second part is that of negative reason, which comes in the form of dialectic.[77] This mode disturbs and disrupts the stable. By doing so it produces movement, which is similar to the sundering of the idea, differentiating the whole by way of negation. However, dialectic will fall into scepticism if we remain in the negative.[78] More importantly, if negation is thought of merely negatively then a dualism will be possible, for the negative will be set over and against the positve (nothing and something). Instead, in the realm of dialectic 'finite characterisations . . . supersede themselves, and pass into their opposites'.[79] For Hegel, dialectic is the 'soul of all knowledge'.[80] Thus the initial negative is in turn negated. Dialectic will find *all* in contradiction, and so every one-sided finite expression of the Absolute according to the

113

mere understanding will be forced beyond itself. But this could generate a dualism because this negation may well develop the 'unhappy' notion of a 'there' engendered by the negated 'here'.

It seems that Hegel must avoid linear progression, as it appears to allow for the notion of a 'here' and a 'there' to develop. Because the progression leaves *here* to get *there*, the very reason for negation seems to be this elusive 'there', an 'elsewhere'. This means that the contradiction cannot be merely negative. Here we come to the third part of Hegel's logical doctrine: the speculative.[81] We have already touched upon the form of speculative thought above. Speculative thought is the positive reason to be found in dialectic, in the sense that the contradiction is not a cause of disunity, since speculative thought discovers identity in identity *and* nonidentity. The mystery found in such a manoeuvre is indigenous to the understanding,[82] in the sense that only understanding employs terms in such a manner that mystery could be possible; for example the opposition between nothing and something.

This leads us to the three subdivisions. The first of these is the doctrine of Being.[83] Being is what is immediate, and as a result it is empty. For Hegel, pure Being marks the beginning of the movement of the idea. Generally Being is approached as what is fundamental, or as that which is most important. But, for Hegel, it is addressed as *mere* Being because Being is an abstraction which instead of providing 'absolute plenitude' is but 'absolute emptiness'.[84] The problem with Being is that it cannot articulate itself, in the sense that it cannot be located. Any attempt at location requires a term of specification, a 'concrete characterization'. In other words, Being to be located must become *this* or *that* being, but this means that Being to be Being has to become other than what it is. We must remember that Being is the most general of all, pure immediate self-identity. As Hegel says, 'every additional and more concrete characterisation causes Being to lose that integrity and simplicity it has in the beginning'.[85] Being, to be, must other itself. But the other of Being is Nothing. This means, it seems, that Being must become Nothing in order to be in a sense beyond *its own* emptiness (nothingness). Hegel asserts quite forcefully that Being is Nothing. Yet he also follows Spinoza in the belief that *omnis determinatio est negatio*. Being must unite with Nothing to be and this unity is called Becoming. So there are two nothings: the 'native' nothing of Being itself, and the nothing which negates Being. At the same time, of course, two nothings are but one nothing: *because* Being is nothing it finds itself in the 'other' nothing and only itself. Here again is the 'double shuttle' of nihilism, whereby the nothing that provides always 'is' only through the provided, which as derived is also in itself nothing.

Every beginning for Hegel involves becoming. This negative determination of Being is pervasive. Every finite being is what it is only in contrast, by way of its limit.[86] Being becomes determinate, moving away from abstraction by assuming 'quality', which is the first of the three primary characteristics of Being. Quality is being-for-another.[87] Quality is for-another because it is, in a sense, the beginning of communication. Being for another is 'an expansion of the mere point of being determinate, or of somewhat'.[88] Abstract Being unites with the finite Nothing: it thus becomes for another, but it moves to the stage where this other is itself. What is altered is the other; 'it becomes the other of the other'.[89] The other as different from Being is itself othered and so this difference is only aspectual. As Hegel says: 'Dualism in putting an insuperable opposition between finite and infinite fails to note the simple circumstance that the infinite is thereby only one of two, and is reduced to a particular to which the finite forms the other particular . . . the being of the finite is made absolute being, and by this dualism gets independence and stability.'[90] Instead, we must realise that Being, which is only by way of its other, *viz.*, Nothing, is not really other than its other. The other is the other of itself, hence every other is an aspectual ideality. Consequently, Hegel argues that the truth of the finite is its ideality and that true philosophy is then idealism.[91] The finite is ideal because it is, ontologically speaking, the infinite, and so to generate its own determinateness it must become ideal, separating itself and establishing another.

Consequently, for Hegel, everything which *is* must become its other. In so doing its actuality will be possible. Hence, every concrete thing is beyond itself. The understanding, the stable self-identical thing of reason, moves to the dialectic in which *it must not be itself in order to be.* This leads us to the speculative mode in which the finite thing finds sameness in otherness. The other being othered, hence aspectually determined, is a functional ideality.

For Hegel the unity of Being and Nothing speculatively effects a dissolution. Both terms are suspended, set adrift. Furthermore, becoming, which is the unity of Being and Nothing, threatens to provide a linearity which could well accommodate a dualism by generating an elsewhere, because of the very negation of the two terms. The *here* of Being, its self-identical understanding, gives way because of *somewhere* else. This, in a sense, reinforces both terms. Hegel must avoid this linear progression by preserving the two terms, just as the dissolution of every finite thing must also contain a positing and a repositioning. The finite is repositioned within the onward movement but also, so as to avoid linearity, it must itself be *a stage reached by another*. The finite, which is overcome, must atemporally be repositioned within the overcoming of another. If this is not the case, the dialectic will become merely linear and spatial – spatial because it would treat the overcome thing as given, stable, fully locatable. This would render the next stage the same as the preceding one. Here Hegel must reverse the direction to avoid *contamination*. This means that each thing, and every direction, must be conceived aspectually. Each thing is an infinite aggregate of possibilities. Consequently, any realisation of one possibility will only be articulable within a particular, aspectual, suspension of the others; this is a sort of epistemological *epoché*. If Hegel is to have true mediation in the absence of dualisms, both *things* and *direction* must lack substantial form (this echoes Scotus). That is to say, they must be unavailable in any bare sense, whether that be a particular thing or progression.

The second characteristic is quantity. Quantity is pure Being, and magnitude is this Being expressed determinately.[92] Quantity expresses Being as if it were external to Being itself, while Being as quality is internal. The third characteristic is that of measure, which is a 'qualitative quantum'.[93] Measure combines the internal and the external. For this reason measure is implicitly essence, for essence combines sameness and otherness. Essence is the second subdivision of the logic. While Being is immediate, essence is mediate. Indeed, essence 'is the being coming into mediation'.[94] For this reason essence is the *form of identity*. Consequently, it is a *show* of identity, a shining forth of what is – hence it is determinate, less abstract.[95] Indeed, essence is best characterised as difference. Essence is an immanent self-mediation because essence negates the negativity which Being has necessarily suffered in its move away from abstraction. In other words, the nothingness which Being found itself to be is itself negated.

We now no longer think that Being has lost something in losing itself to nothingness. For the determination which arises from negation is transformed by essence into the basis of identity. The negation of the negation is the shining forth of self-identity, its display. Essence as the *show* of itself dispels the pejorative connotation of negation by the fact of its mediated identity. This self-reflection, which defines essence, contains a relativity as it involves a continual self-repulsion, since it must repel that which is other to it. For that which is repelled is itself, since in terms of infinitude there is no possibility of any real difference: 'The essence is not abstract reflection into self, but into an other.' The essence, in the manner of its repose, is a ground: 'The immanence of essence thus defined is Ground.'[96] The essence affords a configuration that enables a showing forth, a *show* of identity: 'Ground is the essence in it own inwardness; the essence is intrinsically a ground; and it is a ground only when it is a ground of somewhat, of an other.'[97] What Hegel appears to mean by this is that essence, in being what it is, aspectually, surveys its own reposed configuration and considers it as existent. The categories of such a constitutive reflection are identity, difference and ground.[98]

This is a particularly abstruse part of Hegel's *Doctrine of Essence* in the *Logic*. I shall endeavour to keep what is intractably difficult as simple as possible. An extract may help with navigation.

> The ground works its own *suspension*: and when *suspended*, the result of its negation is existence. Having issued from the ground, existence contains the ground in it; the ground does not remain, as it were, behind existence, but by its very nature supersedes itself and translates into existence.[99]

The essence, in its own self-reflection, forms an identity by way of a marked difference. The *marking* of this difference acts as an immanent ground. But this ground in performing its task does so within its own suspension. Let me try to elucidate. An essence only proceeds from a ground, and a ground is the combination of unity and difference.[100] By combining these, the simple immediacy of Being is overcome. A ground that mediates the requisite other manages to maintain the identity of that which depends on what is other. This is achieved aspectually, because the truth of all finitude is the infinite. That is to say, *the other is never really other, because every finite being is the infinite*. For the ground implicitly includes the understanding that the infinite needs the finite. Yet the ground also includes the truth that every finite being is nothing, nothing but the infinite. This is the difference which the ground unites in itself, thereby allowing an essence to proceed from it. But this would not work if the ground did not *suspend* itself, or did not work in its own suspension. Why? Because if the ground did not work in its own suspension that which was afforded by grounds would be merely an immediate nothing. Consequently, the Absolute would not really be mediated. Such a failure would be witnessed in the lack of provision, in that the Absolute would not have provided existence in any rich sense. The Absolute would be but a dark night of nothingness, pure lack. Hegel appears to avoid this by suspending the ground. This means that the provision is both rich and real. *Rich* because difference is provided. *Real* because the ground does not remain; if it did then the existent would not escape the ground. That is to say, what proceeds from the ground would not be different from the ground, and that would mean there was no real difference, but only pure immediacy.

Yet at the same time *it is the ground which works in its own suspension; the ground is not suspended by the existent*. This is important because it may well carry the reminder that ontologically only the infinite is, the finite is not. When the ground presents an essence it nonetheless supersedes itself and in this way the ground translates itself into existence.[101] In translating itself into existence there is some-thing: 'The thing is the totality, the development in explicit unity of the categories of the ground and of existence.'[102] What exists is the totality of what is afforded in this configuration which is aspectually maintained.[103] Consequently, this existent is relative: 'The existent . . . includes relativity.'[104] The thing is this 'solidified' configuration, and the essence, which this thing has or displays, is the show of an existent, which is the event of appearance: 'To show or shine is the characteristic by which essence is distinguished from being – by which it is essence; and it is this show which, when it is developed, shows itself, and is appearance.'[105]

Below, the term counterfactual is used. This term is, of course, not Hegelian, but is employed to help illustrate what I take to be central to Hegelian logic; namely, that each existent both is and is not. The term counterfactual is meant to draw out the situation in which every finite configuration of infinitude finds itself: a finite being is counterfactual because it does not exist, yet it does not *not* exist. Consequently, finitude is simultaneously suffering dissolution and re-positing.

I am: Counterfactual

Each existent, or thing, not only *shows* itself, but *shows* another: Essence 'has Being-reflected being, a being in which another shows, and which shows in another'.[106] As Charles Taylor remarks, 'each object is an aggregate of objects without intrinsic connection'.[107] In this sense, every existent is only aspectually determined, as it is always an aggregate of possibilities, all of which are not realised in this configuration but must, it seems, be realised aspectually. This establishes an *immanent counterfactual*. Consequently, every thing lacks substantial form. In this way every expression of infinitude, which becomes re-cognised as a thing, contains within itself an infinity of simultaneous things and aggregates of things. *These are not merely waiting to be realised but are continually being realised, and yet are not.* Maybe it is for this reason that Hegel says that the 'existent includes relativity'.[108]

This relativity is so profound that, for essence, 'there is no real other, but only diversity, reference of the one to its other. *The transition of Essence is therefore at the same time no transition.*'[109] The notion of counterfactual is itself in dispute as it suffers, as a concept, a counterfactual realisation, and dissolution: thus the idea of the counterfactual is in certain respects itself counterfactual. We understand this more when we grasp that, for Hegel, a possibility is but the 'mere *inside* of actuality, it is for that reason a mere *outside* actuality, in other words, contingency. The contingent is . . . what has the ground of its being not in itself but in somewhat else.'[110] It is possible to suggest that this is the *contingency of contingency*. This sounds a little like Scotus when he says: 'I do not call something contingent because it is not always or necessarily the case, but because its opposite could be actual at the very moment it occurs.'[111] Furthermore, Scotus says: 'I do not say something is contingent but that something is caused contingently.'[112] We can only locate contingency by de-limiting what we survey; we locate it by creating a location, so to speak. This configuration is contingent, a contingent expression of infinitude which is nothing in itself. As Hegel says, finitude's possibility is the *inside* of actuality. It must be inside actuality, it must be in actuality, but in so being it is nothing (for it is necessary, and necessarily nothing). Hence, according to Hegel, it is also *outside* actuality. The realisation of possibilities is always complete for they have always happened, since the *univocity of non-being* only affords us formal distinctions. Possibility resides in every actuality because of the lack of substantial being, but the legion of possibilities are realised aspectually, and not just by *this* configuration (which is itself nothing). For this configuration is but one of those possibilities inside another actuality. For as Hegel says, being inside an actuality is to be outside actuality, for it is not realised. This actuality, which has this possibility, has not realised it. But every possibility which is unrealised, which is inside actuality and so outside, is realised by infinitude. So possibility *qua* possibility is not possible. This is the aspectual constitution of contingency, the contingency of contingency.

It follows that my contingency is your necessity, which includes the necessity of my contingency, so each has the identity of the configuration which they are. It is for this reason that Hegel complains of the unwarranted elevation of contingency:[113] 'Contingency is actuality in its self-immediacy.'[114] What this seems to mean is that the immediacy required for an identity is contingent, if not arbitrary. Identity as *existent actuality* is contingent because it is not, in the sense that it does not exist. Furthermore, because it is a finite expression of the Absolute there is no real difference, and any actuality is contingent, because it is contingent where the constitutive limitation is constructed. Furthermore, this delimitation is dependent on the contingent cognition of a particular perspective if it is to be seen at all; in other words, the existent actuality in being known is a result of a re-cognition of the infinite in finite terms. But this mis-cognises the finite, ontologically speaking.

We mis-cognise the finite in re-cognising the infinite in finite terms because the finite, which is aspectually afforded, is nothing – nothing but the in-finite. A correct cognition will disclose this nothingness, and so will reveal the contingency of the so-called finitude as the necessity of infinitude. This is made manifest in the nothingness of the finite, a nothingness re-cognised as contingency. The finite will remain a 'real aspect' of the infinite, being preserved in this dissolution, so as to prevent a linearity that could generate a dualism.[115] For Hegel, as for Spinoza, freedom is necessity and we free ourselves by learning of that necessity.

In doing this we discover our own nothingness, as we are but a finite expression of infinite Spirit. As Hegel says, 'man is most independent when he knows himself to be determined by the absolute idea throughout. It was the phase of mind and conduct which Spinoza called *Amor intellectualis Dei*.'[116] Necessity is freedom, because in knowing we are determined we know that *we are the Absolute*, or nothing but the Absolute. So we are independent of the need for a self, of the need to be free from determination. If we are nothing, yet a nothing *as* something, then we have no need of any autonomy; our nothingness liberates us from such requirements.[117]

If the actual contingency of contingency is, in some sense, contingent, and freedom is necessity, the idea of the counterfactual is counterfactual. For if everything which *is* is nothing, a nothing *as* something, and if all that *is* is necessary, then the thought of counterfactuality is necessary. Furthermore, the space which something 'occupies' presents an infinity of unrealised possibilities. Consequently, this space is itself counterfactual, since it only exists in a counterfactual manner. For every existent lacks substantial form and so accommodates other arrangements. Because every thing is ontologically no-thing, it is the same in any realisation (a univocity of non-being). Furthermore, infinity must realise itself infinitely in an infinity of ways. Such a realisation must problematise every 'this' or 'that', and every 'here' or 'there'. This means that the requisite spatial stability and linearity, in terms of the progression, alternating a 'here' with a 'there', is unavailable.

Counterfactual realisation is, then, itself only counterfactually realised. The *space* in which something which has not been realised is to be realised, is itself only realised in a space which contains the *unrealised, non realised, counterfactual realisation* of this possibility.[118] If a thing has an infinity of unrealised possibilities which can be counterfactually realised, it would have to be a certain something which is 'here' rather than 'there', being 'this' rather than 'that'. But any finite expression of the infinite, which is a particular configuration, is never in isolation. As it realises its own configuration it is itself suffering dissolution in an infinity of ways and directions. (For this reason it is erroneous to interpret Hegel as an advocate of a simple linear progression in history.) The configuration will participate in an endless figuration and re-figuration. The notion of concrete sides of an identity which would allow us, it seems, to speak of counterfactuals is mistaken, because every alternative state of affairs is both actual *and* not actual. An alternative state of affairs is both alternative *and* not alternative, since cognitive lack generates the appearance of unrealised compossible states. For Hegel, everything happens, has happened, and is happening. Conversely, nothing happens, nothing has happened, and nothing is to happen. Hegel must assert both aspectually distinguished propositions simultaneously so as to avoid dualism, and to have the nothing *as* something.

I am: Vanishing

Essence as the *show* of appearance, which I argue is the appearance of nothing *as* something, presents us with this show. But all that is presented *vanishes*. We already know that according to Hegel, Being, Nothing, and becoming are vanishing factors, self-erasing, but so also is the content of every show, *viz.*, appearance. The appearance of appearance[119] vanishes because content is a 'vanishing element'.[120] Every object is involved in an expansion, a move towards infinity, which is both the reason for its arrival and its disappearance. It is a *vanishing show*. What the finite shows is its nothingness. We reach the third subdivision when essence moves into the notion (the speculative order of thought). The notion is essence reverted to the simple immediacy of Being. This is similar to the move in the *Phenomenology of Spirit* from the *an sich* (Being; understanding; rigid immediacy), to the *für sich* (essence; dialectic; mediation) to *An-und-für-sich* (the notion; speculation.) The third subdivision finds identity in identity and non-identity. The notion, as reverted Essence, is a *show* of itself in itself and for itself: the sameness in otherness, and the otherness in sameness. The notion is the mediated return of nothing to itself *as* something, indeed everything. As Charles Taylor comments, 'everything is an emanation of the concept';[121] Taylor is here translating the noun *Begriff* as concept instead of as notion, which is how Wallace translates it. This emanation is, according to Michel Henry, the disappearance of everything: 'The Concept is itself disappearance. It is the Night of disappearance . . . [M]anifestation is the movement of perishing.'[122]

The 'notion' has three moments. The first of these is the universal, the second is particularity, while the third is individuality. Judgement is the notion in its particularity. It is an expression of finitude. Taylor states that 'the concept can have no use except in the making of a judgement'.[123] Judgement is 'born out of diremption' because the infinity of finite emanations from the notion embody degrees of perfection, or imperfection, by how much or how little they correspond to the concept. Again this sounds like Scotus: 'From the plenitude of its "virtual quality" the infinite is measuring everything else as greater or lesser to the degree that it approaches *the whole* or recedes from it.'[124]

A finitude which fails to realise that it is nothing but an expression of the universal will be a poor 'fit'. That which approaches the concept approaches the universal, and so its own self-dissolution. Difference, by definition, re-cognises itself as different *from*. In this sense, diversity is born, one which will be reunited with its source by the act of judgement which will declare sameness in otherness. But this declaration is itself the arrival of the difference. Judgement separates. In so doing, unity is envisioned. If, for Hegel, reality is at bottom the sundering of an idea, then judgement in separating re-enacts this reality, which simultaneously reinforces the unity. This unity, or sameness in the otherness, is mediated infinity. For every judgement, in asserting that what is separated is united, is faced with fundamental incommensurability. Any judgement finds that the two terms it endeavours to unite are different and so incommensurable. The particular (e.g. 'this rose') is not the universal ('red'). The problem lies with the copula 'is'. This copula remains too narrow, final, or rigid: it reduces the reality which it endeavours to describe. To overcome this we move from judgement to inference; that is, to the realm of syllogism and we pass into syllogism through apodeictic judgement. Hegel's example of this is 'this house . . . being so and so constituted . . . is good or bad'. This allows for a 'mediating specification'.[125]

For Hegel, everything is syllogism.[126] The reason for this is, I suggest, that everything is nothing *as* something. This means that there can be no absolute particulars, or dualistic divisions, which allow a 'this' or a 'that'. Everything, in being a syllogism, is never a 'this' or 'that', and it is never 'here' nor 'there'. We have instead a mediated specification. Syllogism 'brings the notion and the judgement into one'.[127] 'The real is Syllogism because it is of itself diversified, and yet the elements of this diversity are internally related so that they unite themselves', argues Taylor.[128] The particular finite expression can only be located by inference. This means that Hegel adopts a strongly descriptive approach, because the centrality of syllogistic logic involves us in the show of a perpetual description, which we can call appearance.[129] If we think of the universal, the particular, and the individual, we can see that the task that syllogism performs is the provision of each of these specifications through the mediation of the other two. We can think of the universal as the provision of all, the particular as provision of difference, or differentiation, while the individual provides unity. The universal requires particularity, so that its universality is not merely an immediate indeterminacy; it further requires individuality to enable its self-unity as the universal. The universal, as individual, is the universal in terms of self-identity. Furthermore, this individuality unites the particular differences in the sameness of that universality. Each term can act as the whole, as each leads to the others because its own articulation requires their mediating presence. Any notion of particularity will require the operation of individuality and universality. There is only a formal, aspectual, difference, since Hegel holds each term within its own mediated absence. This is the nothing *as* something.

Syllogism helps to realise the notion because it leads each aspect as nothing onto the Absolute. This realisation of the notion is referred to, by

Hegel, as 'Object': 'The Object in general is the one total, in itself still unspecified, the objective world as a whole, God, the Absolute Object.'[130] Objectivity contains three forms: namely Mechanism, which is the immediate undifferentiated object; Chemism, which is the propensity for differentiation, mediation; and Teleology which unites the first two. Teleology is syllogistic, for it unites the objectivity of the whole with the act of differentiation, which allows us to think of the whole *qua* whole. 'The subjective end coalesces with the objectivity external to it.'[131] The propensity to difference we find in the form of the object, called chemism, leads us to the notion of design.[132] What we see here is the combination of the subjective and objective, thought and reality, Hegelian idealism, *viz.*, the idea. The idea is truth in itself and for itself, the absolute unity of the notion and objectivity. What *is* is the concept, the idea as object and subject, aspectually differentiated. The idea's 'ideal content is nothing but the notion in its detailed terms: its "real" content is only the exhibition which the notion gives itself in the form of external existence, while yet by enclosing this shape in its ideality, it keeps it in its power, and so keeps itself in it.'[133] This is a case of mediated immediacy and an immediate mediation – the going out of the same, which is the *reditus* that precedes every *exitus*, the univocity of non-being, with formal distinctions generated by the nothing *as* something. The nothing *as* something which is Hegel's Absolute is but the infinite self-return and self-identity of the abyss. Rowan Williams suggests that Hegel differs from Fichte because there is not a return of the same, or the Absolute.[134] This is correct, but only because the Absolute cannot be located in a manner that would allow for such a return. But this means that both the infinite and the finite are unavailable. Consequently, it is a return only of the abyss (which is also the case for Fichte).

For Hegel, all the stages through which we have progressed are not permanent but are merely dynamic elements of the idea. As such they vanish, and with them all real difference. This is the ideality of reality. All that *is* is but the sundering of the Absolute Idea which means that everything is nothing but the idea. Yet the idea is nothing *but* these finite dissolutions. The idea is the concrete because it is the ideal. We saw earlier that thought was merely the expansion of the object called Man, by way of a particular or aspectual feeling of universality. This expansion ends in the dissolution of Man, for he must realise his nothingness in realising that he is but a necessary expression of the Absolute. This finite expression expands itself to universality, occupying itself with its own dissolution. Thought is rendered concrete, the event of this 'objective' dissolution. But this finite expression will be preserved because the Absolute is nothing but its infinity of finitude. Any failure to preserve the finite would 'unhappily' speak of the Absolute as an elsewhere, because it would have presumed a 'here' in the act of dissolution. The finite must instead be preserved in its finitude as the place of infinitude. If this is not achieved then we would likewise presume a given finitude as locatable, a 'this' which is 'here' alongside an infinity thought to reside elsewhere. This will, of course, give rise to an unhappy dualism, so Hegel must continually generate finitude as infinitude and the infinite as the finite.

To accomplish this feat, thought must be brought to ground. This is why there is a unity of the subject and object in the idea, for thought is reality, while reality is thought. If this is the case, then thought has nowhere else to go. It remains immanent to its own act, while the concrete finds its own location lost in its speculative equation with thought. The Absolute Idea, as the concurrence of concept and reality, leaves no space for transcendence. Every place of real difference is carried away by vanishing points. Like Spinoza, Hegel disposes of terms by using them: each perpetually perishes in its speculative use. This demise is perpetual because it is never fully realised and never was. Any location is provisional and so is the dissolution. We have in this vanishing the show which is an appearance. Being, nothing, becoming, content as essence, Man, finitude, infinitude, the practical and the theoretical, substance, subject, object, reality and thought, all vanish. This is fundamentally because the idea as 'process' provides us with only formal differences. As Hegel says, 'the different modes of apprehending the Idea as unity of ideal and real, of finite and infinite, of identity and difference, etc., are more or less *formal*'.[135]

Kojève appears to be correct in so far as Man causes thought to 'concretise' in Man's demise. When we think that something finite *is*, we fail to comprehend aspectually the finite as nothing but a corrupt, because limited, expression of the Absolute Idea. When we think that the Absolute is, we fail to realise that it is nothing but the finite. Each resides within the constitutive absence of the other. If we think something is we fail to realise the nothingness of all. If we think nothing is we fail to realise that nothing is only *as* something (infinity requiring the finite). The actuality of the nothing *as* something is enabled by the Hegelian system because everything is nothing, but the nothing *qua* nothing is *provisional* (in both senses of the word). We are unable to locate a particular or a universal, as each is an underdetermined aggregate. Any aspectual distinction plays host to an infinity of equally legitimate possibilities, which are *qua* possible, impossible. For they are only inside an actuality, and all actuality is unified by a *univocity of non-being*: this is Hegel's *meontotheology*, his univocity of *Geist*. Furthermore, this univocity affords only formal distinctions, which are nonetheless not unreal, because we cannot locate the real as opposed to the unreal. We are caught in the perpetual asking of the speculative 'question'. Here, in this asking, the opposition between Being and Nothing is suspended. It is a suspension which allows the emergence of a plenitudinal nihilism: nothing is *as* something. (Part II, Chapters 9 and 10 consider the possibility that there nevertheless might be a somewhat positive element in this logic of nihilism.)

There is little doubt that Hegel is similar to both Plotinus and Spinoza. For example, Charles Taylor says there are certainly 'affinities' between Hegel and Plotinus, while also asserting that Spinoza is an 'important philosopher for Hegel'.[136] Étienne Gilson characterises Hegel's 'idea' in terms of Plotinus: 'As with the One of Plotinus, the Idea which thus alienates itself in nature is finding its way back through the successive moments of its dialectical realization.'[137] And Hannah Arendt calls Plotinus Hegel's 'strange precursor'.[138] Taylor nonetheless qualifies the similarity between Hegel and Plotinus and Spinoza, by saying there are 'important differences'.[139] The difference between Hegel and Plotinus is that for Hegel 'finitude is a condition of the existence of the infinite life',[140] while Hegel differs from Spinoza because of Spinoza's alleged *acosmism*. My interpretations of all three thinkers would lessen these differences. With regard to Plotinus it was argued that the One was the idea of the finite as such. In terms of Spinoza it was argued that he is not guilty of a simple *acosmism*, but rather of *pan(a)theistic acosmism*. We know this because we saw that both God and Nature existed in the absence of the other, and this negation was more equal than Hegel allows. What, it seems, we have seen in Hegel, is rather an exacerbation of the nihilistic logic of the *reditus* which paradoxically precedes the *exitus*, the something made nothing and then the nothing approached *as* something.

The next chapter discusses the work of Martin Heidegger, offering a reading of his philosophy as a *meontotheology*. This being the case, Heidegger develops and furthers the impulse witnessed above, namely, to provide *everything* without giving *anything*.

Notes

1   *Jacobi to Fichte*, in Jacobi (1994), p. 508.
2   Quoted by Michel Henry; see Henry (1973), p. 698.
3   This positive embrace of nihilism can be witnessed in Hegel (1977b), p. 168.
4   Beckett (1955), p. 292.
5   See Kojève (1969), p. 71; Williams (1998), p. 119.
6   Hegel (1977a), p. 412.
7   Hegel (1962), vol. 1, p. 131.
8   Hegel (1977a), p. 412.
9   Jaeschke (1992), p. 8.
10 Quoted in Butler (1992), p. 133.
11 See Fabro (1968), p. 534; Taylor (1975), p. 495.
12 Collins (1967), p. 341.
13 Williams (1998), p. 120.
14 Hegel (1962), vol. 1, p. 154.

15 'The realization rather than the vehicle remains the important thing for Hegel', Findlay (1958), p. 139. Williamson commenting on this passage says, 'It was Hegel's belief that this realization originated from this particular vehicle, that was his Christian faith; but his philosophical position did not depend on this vehicle, for, philosophically, it was the realization that was essential, and the vehicle by which it was achieved was irrelevant', Williamson (1984), p. 171; 'The Christian religion, is therefore incapable of satisfying the highest concern of spirit, and has thereby reached its end', Jaeschke (1992), p. 15. Also see Fackenheim (1967), p. 162.

16 See Pomerleau (1977), p. 219.

17 Quoted in Rocker (1992), p. 34.

18 See Hegel (1962), vol. 1, p. 157; Tholuck (1826).

19 For Hegel on the Trinity see Schlitt (1984), (1990).

20 'Philosophy does not abolish but legitimates all the shapes that lead to the ultimate stage; furthermore, *Denken* is but the ability to recapitulate the inner dynamism of representation', Ricœur (1982), pp. 86–87. 'The development of the mind never leads beyond Christian faith: . . . faith continues to provide the content of philosophical thought', Dupré (1984), p. 128.

21 See Hegel (1988), p. 263.

22 Hegel (1975), p. 214.

23 Hegel (1988), p. 123. Hegel also argues that Spinoza is not a pantheist, see p. 263.

24 See Williams (1998), p. 121.

25 See Edwards (1967), 4.363, 364.

26 See Cross and Livingstone (1974).

27 See Merklinger (1993), p. 160; Harvey (1964), p. 172; Whittemore (1960), pp. 134–164; Williamson (1984), ch. 12.

28 Harris (1983), p. 86.

29 'Without the world God is not God', Hegel (1962), vol. 1, p. 200.

30 See Williamson (1984), p. 258.

31 Hegel (1962), vol. 1, p. 95.

32 *Ibid.*, p. 200.

33 Hegel (1975), p. 73.

34 Reardon (1977), p. 102. Colletti argues that the finite is within the infinite; see Colletti (1973), p. 16.

35 Butler (1992), p. 138.

36 Baudrillard (1976), p. 35.

37 See Part II below for an articulation of what is understood here to be a theological approach to such questions, one which endeavours to overcome nihilism.

38 'The absolute is essentially a result'; 'The result is the same at the beginning'; 'Having its end also as its beginning', Hegel (1977a), pp. 11, 12, 10.

39 'The bud disappears in the bursting forth of the blossom . . . yet at the same time their fluid nature makes them moments of an organic unity in which they do not conflict', *ibid.*, p. 2.

40 *Ibid.*, p. 6.

41 See *ibid.*, p. 19.

42   *Ibid.*, p. 490.
43   *Ibid.*, p. 32.
44   *Ibid.*, p. 21.
45   *Ibid.*, p. 18.
46   *Ibid.*, p. 19.
47   'Spirit is indeed never at rest but always engaged in moving forward', *ibid.*, p. 6.
48   See *ibid.*, p. 9.
49   *Ibid.*, p. 11.
50   *Ibid.*, p. 10.
51   Hegel (1962), vol. 1, p. 200; 'Without the world God is not God'.
52   This is similar to Spinoza because as I argued above Spinoza is better understood as an advocate of what I referred to as *pan(a)theistic acosmism*. In the sense that both God and Nature appear within the absence of the other. Fabro (1968) refers to Hegel's philosophy as 'transcendental Spinozism', p. 108. Hegel (1959) himself argues that 'being a Spinozist is the crucial point in all philosophical thinking', p. 337.
53   Hegel (1975), p. 164.
54   See Hegel (1977a), p. 588.
55   Part II, Chapter 10 argues that nihilism is characterised by a Fichtean war of all against all.
56   Hegel (1977a), p. 16.
57   As Taylor (1975) says, 'the unavailability of the bare particular is not just an epistemological truth, it reflects the ontological one that the particular is doomed by its very nature to disappear', p. 144.
58   See, for example, Hegel (1975), pp. 133, 134, and 213. The only vanishing factors, or vanishing elements, which Hegel explicitly names are that of Being, Nothing, becoming, and content. But the function which they perform is shared by earlier terms used in the *Phenomenology of Spirit*. Consequently, I have employed the terms in discussing the *Phenomenology of Spirit*.
59   The term *predicative* being comes from Hogrebe (1989), pp. 83–84. Hogrebe employs the term *predicative* being in opposition to *pronominal* being which he suggests is contractive.
60   The idea that being is pronominal reappears in Deleuze: see Part II, Chapter 10.
61   Hegel (1975), p. 137.
62   Hegel, like Spinoza, employs the term 'in so far as' to mark the transition from substance to subject and so on. He does this so that every positive assertion is underwritten by a rather apophatic reversal which disallows any metaphysical veridicality, as this may permit the construction of a dualism. See, for example, Hegel (1977a), p. 10.
63   Hegel (1977a), pp. 24–25.
64   See Findlay's introduction to Hegel (1975), xxiv.
65   This univocity of non-being is akin to what Fabro refers to as Hegel's 'radical ontological monism'; (1968), xxxi
66   Kojève (1969), p. 574.
67   See Hegel (1975), p. 9.

68 *Ibid.*, p. 15.
69 *Ibid.*, p. 19.
70 This is similar to the Spinozistic and Kantian subject.
71 See Part II, Chapter 9, where the notion of intelligence in relation to becoming all things is discussed.
72 Hegel (1975), p. 92.
73 *Ibid.*
74 See Part II, Chapter 10, where the idea of thinking nothing, and doing nothing with words is examined.
75 For a more positive reading of this speculative methodology see Rose (1981).
76 See Hegel (1975), p. 113.
77 *Ibid.*
78 *Ibid.*, p. 116.
79 *Ibid.*, p. 115.
80 *Ibid.*, p. 116.
81 See *ibid.*, p. 119.
82 See *ibid.*, p. 121.
83 See *ibid.*
84 *Ibid.*, p. 128.
85 *Ibid.*, p. 127.
86 *Ibid.*, p. 136.
87 *Ibid.*, p. 135.
88 *Ibid.*
89 *Ibid.*, p. 139.
90 *Ibid.*
91 *Ibid.*, p. 140.
92 *Ibid.*, p. 145.
93 *Ibid.*, p. 157.
94 *Ibid.*, p. 162.
95 This is, in a sense, the same *show* we find in both Heidegger and Wittgenstein. See Conor Cunningham (1999). This *show* reappears in Alain Badiou; see Badiou (2001), xi.
96 Hegel (1975), p. 175.
97 *Ibid.*
98 *Ibid.*, p. 180.
99 *Ibid.*, p. 180; italics mine.
100 *Ibid.*, p. 179.
101 *Ibid.*, p. 180.
102 *Ibid.*, p. 181.
103 *Ibid.*, p. 176.
104 *Ibid.*
105 *Ibid.*, p. 186.
106 *Ibid.*, p. 165.
107 Taylor (1975), p. 321.
108 Hegel (1975), p. 180.
109 *Ibid.*, p. 161.
110 *Ibid.*, p. 205; italics mine.
111 Ord. I, d. 2, p. 1, q. 1–2, n. 86; cited by Knuuttila and Alanen (1988), p. 35.

112 Ord. I, d. 2, q. 1, a. 2, ad. 2. This encourages Burrell to call this view of contingency 'voluntarist': (1990), p. 252. For a different view of Scotus' understanding of contingent causality see Sylwanowicz (1996).

113 Hegel (1975), p. 205.

114 *Ibid.*, p. 207.

115 See Taylor (1975), p. 325.

116 Hegel (1975), p. 220.

117 This freedom is a sort of philosophical Buddhism.

118 Unrealised because it is the more of the something, the counterfactual of the factual; non realised because nothing is realised; counterfactual realisation because everything is realised counterfactually: this is the infinite, the Absolute, as *Abgrund* or as *das Nicht* of Heidegger. Indeed, the Absolute appears to be similar to Derrida's nothing, which resides outside every text. For the infinite is that which resides outside every finite configuration, doing so as the truth of that configuration. In a similar manner the nothing outside the text is the truth of the text. See Part I, Chapters 6 and 7.

119 The phrase 'appearance of appearance' is used by Kant in the *Opus Postumum*; see Kant (1993b), p. 109. For a discussion of Kant see Part I, Chapter 4.

120 Hegel (1975), p. 213.

121 Taylor (1975), p. 301.

122 Henry (1973), p. 698.

123 Taylor (1975), p. 308.

124 *Quodlibetal Questions*, q. 5.57; italics mine.

125 Taylor (1975), p. 312.

126 Hegel (1975), p. 244.

127 *Ibid.*

128 Taylor (1975), p. 313.

129 This is similar to Wittgenstein's descriptive shows; see Conor Cunningham (1999).

130 Hegel (1975), pp. 256–257.

131 *Ibid.*, p. 270.

132 These somewhat odd terms, mechanism, chemism, and teleology, are just as appropriate as any theological terms which Hegel may use elsewhere. This is important because it may then be possible to conceive such terms as merely nominal, registering their 'truth' within a univocal mantra of intensity, qualitatively bereft. What I mean by this is that when Hegel speaks of chemism or the incarnation both are reducible to a quantitative realisation. Consequently, we must not think of them in particular qualitative terms. The bare particular is unavailable to us for just this reason. Those who analyse Hegel's use of theological terms looking for something theological, as such, run the risk of ignoring the de-differentiating effect of the nominalism of Hegel's univocity.

133 Hegel (1975), p. 274.

134 See Williams (1992), p. 75.

135 Hegel (1975), p. 278; italics mine.

136 Taylor (1975), pp. 102, 280.

137 Gilson (1937), p. 244.

138 Quoted in Alliez (1996), p. 82.
139 Taylor (1975), pp. 281, 102.
140 *Ibid.*, p. 102.

6

ON THE LINE

Martin Heidegger and Paul Celan

The line is also called the zero *meridian*[1].
(Heidegger, 1955)

I find something as immaterial as language, yet earthy,
terrestrial, in the shape of a circle, which via both poles,
regains itself and on the way serenely crosses even the
tropics: I find a *meridian*.
(Celan, 22 October 1960)

Introduction

This chapter does not attempt to offer a comprehensive reading of either
Martin Heidegger or Paul Celan. What will be offered is a short analysis
of Heidegger's philosophy and a slight and tangential comparison
between Heidegger and Celan. My reading of Heidegger will argue that
the logic of nihilism, at least as it has been defined here, is fundamental
to his philosophy. The purpose of the comparison between Celan and
Heidegger is to draw out the precise nihilistic nature of Heidegger's
work.[2] Most commentators of Paul Celan suggest a strong link between
Heidegger and Celan (for example, Baer, Felstiner, Gadamer, and
Lacoue-Labarthe).[3] The interpretation offered here considers Heidegger
and Celan as each being a *pole* through which the circular line passes on
its way to the *meridian*. Celan and Heidegger are no doubt poles apart:
one was a Jew, and a survivor of German atrocity, while the other was an
erstwhile member of the Nazi party. How could these two conspire to
similarity? The work of Heidegger will be examined before concentrating
on his use of Angelus Silesius' flower which blooms without reason,
arguing that a similar theme is deployed by Celan.[4] The first two sections
of this chapter offer a brief reading of Heidegger's text *Being and Time*.
Expressions used and terminology employed will generally be
Heidegger's.

Ladies andgentlemen,[5]
Martin Heidegger: taking care of Being

The disaster *takes care* of everything.[6]
(Maurice Blanchot)

Heidegger . . . follows Duns Scotus and gives renewed
splendour to the univocity of being.[7]

(Gilles Deleuze)

Throughout Martin Heidegger's career, the question 'why something
rather than nothing' was continually articulated and explored. It was
Heidegger's contention that throughout Western history the question of
being had been forgotten. Philosophy had suffered from a form of
amnesia. Any understanding of Being which we do have remains in the
dark with regard to the meaning of Being (or later the 'truth' of Being).
Indeed, Heidegger refers to Being as the darkest of concepts and it is this
darkness which forces us to raise again the question of being.[8] We must
reawaken an understanding of this question, this time in a way that will
recall its meaning.[9] Tradition, which hands down to us our categories
and concepts, blocks our access to the 'primordial source' of these.[10]
Consequently, we are to destroy this tradition until access to primordial
experience is forthcoming.[11] For it is there at the mouth of the
primordial, where we originally formed our determinations of Being,
that a better understanding of the meaning of Being may be offered.
Tradition has hardened over time, as it begins to *presume* Being, failing to
take proper care with our determination of its nature. The destruction of
this tradition allows for a more fluid, ancient yet nascent, approach to our
understanding of Being.[12]

According to Heidegger, we are always within an understanding. Yet
there are some understandings which pertain to an ossifying amnesia
and there are those which do not. Heidegger employs a number of clues
to help engender a better understanding of Being: basic concepts such as
existence, anxiety, throwness, care and Time.[13] Indeed, it is Time which
will point us towards Being in a primordial sense, as it is Time which
points us towards the lived reception of Being in terms of what is called
the existential analytic of Dasein.[14] It is this which acts as our
fundamental ontology from which all ontologies stem.

Da-sein (being there) is the mode of being which is to permit us an
approach to Being, in a primordial sense. Dasein is the being in the world
which is ontically distinguished from all other entities, as Being is an *issue*
for it. Even at this pre-ontological stage Being is approached in a
distinctive manner, because for Dasein the ontic is already suggestive of
the ontological; Dasein comports (*verhalten*) itself towards an

understanding of Being which is ontological. But this pre-ontological comportment can fail to reside in a proper understanding of Being, as it may reside only with the realm of the *existentiell*. The *existentiell* is the life which Dasein must live, a living which need not consider the very 'structures' of this existence. If Dasein does enter into an investigation of its very Being then it becomes existential (*existenzial*). Heidegger lists three distinctive features of Dasein with regard to this unique comportment. The first is the ontical: Dasein's Being has the determinate character of existence. This is why Being is already an issue for it. The second is ontological: because Dasein is pre-ontologically 'ontological', existence is determinative for it.[15] The third feature is an ontico-ontological priority towards Being, as it is Dasein's fundamental ontology that allows for other ontologies. It is the ontical source of this prioritisation which is the most basic and distinctive.[16]

If we are to restate 'the question of Being' in a way that differs from the tradition, then it is Dasein which may help us. Dasein is ontico-ontologically comported towards the question of Being most essentially, because of Time, its time of being-there. It is this ontologico-temporal approach which allows us to go beyond mere 'presence' (*Anwesenheit*), and to inhabit what can be called phenomenological 'arrival'. The 'da' of *Da-sein* implicates Time for Dasein, as being-there occurs only within the arrival of Time. It seems that Being and Time are inextricably linked, and this may well be disclosive. For according to Heidegger we know it is a 'clue'. The Being of Dasein is 'historical', in that Dasein is its past, but this past historicises out of a future at all times.[17] This means that Dasein in being its past must live somewhat beyond itself, at least ontically speaking and this beyond is that of the historical future. The arrival of being-there involves an ontologico-temporal reception, one which is continuous.[18] This reception must include a past as that which is there to receive, but a past that is futurial, in that what is there to be received is its already being-there. This is why Heidegger speaks of Dasein's past as something which 'already goes ahead of it'.[19] What is received is the same lived life as that which is 'there' to receive it, as that which has received before. What comes from the future is, therefore, an echo, or trace, of the past. This past can be thought of as primordial, for it is the advent of being-there, the being of the 'there'. But this advent is also essentially futurial, as this advent never occurs, but is always ecstatically occurring.

Being: ready and present

We know that philosophy is accused of forgetting Being. It does so as a result of an ontology of *Vorhandenheit*. In other words, Being becomes understood as the merely present-at-hand of beings. This is viciously ontic, but worse than this, it is ontotheological or metaphysical. What this means is that the understanding of Being employed fails to raise the ontological question as to the nature of Being as such, and any appearances to the contrary are methodologically flawed. Philosophy approaches Being in a presumptuous manner, in that it presumes it is *present*. To presume that Being is present is to disable the asking of the ontological question. For the starting point of the metaphysical (ontotheological) question is 'what'? This reduces Being to a matter of thinghood and so excludes any possibility of articulating a 'why' is there Being. This inauthentic mode of questioning (inauthentic for philosophy) only pretends to ask a question, in that its question is the answer.[20] The framework required to render such a question intelligible is the answer which is already offered in the form of the metaphysical question. The question presumes the space it occupies, treating that about which it speaks in a similar vein: only answers ask the questions.[21] Every pretence of questioning contains this notion of the present-at-hand, precisely to the degree that it knows there is something about which we can speak. All ontotheological, or metaphysical, questioning will presume the question; it will think to itself 'why something rather than nothing' in a way that fails to understand the idea of the question itself. The metaphysician will say 'there just are metaphysical questions which can be asked', and in this way they will fail to understand the radicality of the ontological question. The starting point is forgotten, for it has become self-evident. The metaphysician proceeds to enter his constructed discourse confident in the validity of his 'questioning', a confidence which betrays its inadequacy. Only when we remain at the point of questioning, mindful of the source as such, will this arrogance be curbed. (Heidegger would not put it exactly like this, probably because he falls foul of the same ontotheological, or rather *meontotheological*, arrogance, as will be argued below.)

To overcome this ontology of *Vorhandenheit* Heidegger, as we already know, seeks to escape the tradition of metaphysics which hardens that about which it attempts to speak. This tradition becomes so familiar with what *is*, that a proper understanding of Being is lost.[22] To emancipate philosophy from this ontic incarceration, Heidegger utilises the ontic-ontological priority of Dasein. This ontic priority will allow him to approach the world in a manner which is 'within' the world. For Dasein *qua* Dasein is in the world and with the world (*mit-Dasein*).[23] According to Heidegger there can be no notion of Dasein over and against the world. Dasein is not a 'what', but is a mode of being in the world.[24] The Being of Dasein is 'mine' (*Jemeinigkeit*), because what *is* is lived as the historicised future. There cannot be any dualism, because Dasein only has the Being of a there.[25] Furthermore, Dasein has the nature of a de-severing (*entfernen*), to be understood as a bringing close, and directionality (*Ausrichtung*). For the being of the 'there' is *towards*, as it is futural.[26] The comporting towards can be thought to stem from Dasein's throwness (*Geworfenheit*). This throwness brings, and situates, every understanding of Dasein with-in the world, indeed the world becomes apparent to Dasein in a *circumspective de-severing* which disallows every notion of separateness or distance.[27] Dasein *qua* Dasein is with, only as it is with-in. Consequently, Dasein does not remain external to the world about which it speaks. But this closeness does not relate to distance, in terms of the correct understanding of a relationship. For it will, in its intimacy, include appropriate if not determinative distance.[28] The closeness which Dasein brings to mind calls a wholeness to our attention, for Dasein has a *potentiality to wholeness*.[29] Such wholeness is primordial: 'Being in the world is a structure which is primordially and constantly whole.'[30] Dasein in being understood as being-with is realised as being-with-world; the de-severing, along with the directionality, calls forth the world within Dasein's self-understanding. The throwness of Dasein prohibits the 'distance' required by any notion of a subject over and against the world: 'Throwness is needed to suggest the facticity of [Dasein] being delivered over.'[31] Instead, a correct understanding of Dasein as a mode of Being, is that of a particular dissolution. The nature of this dissolution will be explained below.

As we know, Heidegger intends to restate the question of Being in a manner which attends to the asking, unlike metaphysical versions of this question: 'The question awakens in a more originary manner.'[32] This more originary asking seeks, in a manner reminiscent of Husserl's *epoché*, to detach all beings from what they are, yet simultaneously re-presenting them in what I here call an 'arrival', one which is perpetual: 'There is constantly something to settle.'[33] The 'instrument' to perform this task is, of course, Dasein.[34] There are a number of approaches that bring Being before us by way of Dasein. The ontology of *Vorhandenheit* has already been mentioned. Here Heidegger intends to detach our perceptual understanding of Being from the mere present-at-hand to the ready-at-hand (*Zuhandenheit*). The ready-to-hand is not grasped theoretically, and the alternative 'practical' approach permits a new sort of questioning of Being. Dasein encounters the ready-to-hand in terms of *a work* which 'bears' with it a *referential totality* that allows the understanding of that which is ready-to-hand to come forth. Heidegger argues that the ready-to-hand, in not being theoretically grasped, is, nevertheless, not atheoretical. However, the promise of the ready-to-hand, as a phenomenon, to offer itself as ready-to-hand, entails a withdrawal. In this sense one cannot settle the matter, there can be no presumption, as that which *is*, is only as it withdraws.

Phenomenologically speaking

For Heidegger, the idea of phenomenology encapsulated in the motto 'to the things themselves', is the simultaneous presentation-within-withdrawal which enacts this idea.[35] As Heidegger says: 'phenomenology means . . . to let that which *shows* itself be seen from itself in the very way it *shows* itself from itself'.[36] It is for this reason that only phenomenology renders ontology possible.[37] Indeed, phenomenology as the science of the Being of entities is ontology.[38] The showing, which every phenomenon is, is a showing that withdraws as it shows, because Being is the arrival of a show, one which involves withdrawal. This means that every phenomenon presents itself in a manner which exceeds understanding, and this is the excess of phenomena as such: this excess manifests itself as withdrawal. And it is withdrawal which prevents a lapse into *Vorhandenheit*. It is for this reason that phenomenology is hermeneutical, for the event of Being must be related to the being-there of an ecstatic past, which historicises the future.[39] We remain within the showing as the show.[40]

The shift from *Vorhandenheit* to *Zuhandenheit* involves a letting go, which occurs in Dasein's concernful dealings with the world. What is let go is a particular ontic stability. The entity wrestles out from beneath its present-at-hand ontic isolation, and re-presents itself within the world – a world that is suggested by its referential totality: both Sartre and Lacan develop this notion.[41] This referential totality suggests an excess, in that presence has a certain 'thickness' to it.[42] That which is ready-to-hand can lose this appellation, becoming unready-to-hand.[43] Heidegger's example is a broken or missing tool. In negativity a mere present-at-hand is revealed, which evokes a deficient mode of concern. The awareness of this unready-to-handness becomes obvious under the cognitional modes of *conspicuousness*, *obtrusiveness*, and *obstinacy*. These reveal the presence-to-hand of what is ready-to-hand. But the ready-to-hand still shows itself as ready-to-hand within its presence-at-hand.[44] *Zuhandenheit* announces a world, but it does so more effectively when it remains ready-to-hand within an apparent presence-at-hand, so disclosing something irreducibly resistant to a merely theoretical gaze. There is a certain *weight* that escapes definition, a kind of pregnant nakedness: for Lacan and Žižek, this nakedness is an excremental remainder, the Real.[45]

Heidegger states that 'readiness-to-hand is the way in which entities as they are "in themselves" are defined ontologico-categorically'.[46] Immediately after this, he asks whether the 'readiness-to-hand is founded upon the presence-at-hand'.[47] Heidegger does not answer this question, but he does speak of the ontological pertinence of the 'freeing of everything ready-to-hand as ready-to-hand'.[48] It is, in a sense, the readiness of what is present, present as ready; this suggests a third state beyond either *Vorhandenheit* or *Zuhandenheit*. What matters ontologically is that what *is*, is ready; this is somewhat akin to the 'there' of *Da-sein*: Being is not mere presence, but involves a presensing there. It is the *strangeness* of phenomena that is the ontological clue which intimates the possibility of restating the desired question. Phenomena arrive within a world which perpetually re-enacts that arrival. Thus every entity is disclosed within Dasein's concernful dealings as that which *shows* itself in *withdrawing*; this is the excess of presence, its ontological *gravitas*. It withdraws, because every phenomenon lacks ontological stability, in terms of ontic definition. The task is thus to *unknow* what *is*, by knowing Being as an *arrival*. In this way Dasein begins to approach the ontological question in a more promising fashion. For Dasein does not now ask *what* it knows. Consequently, every some-thing begins to suffer dissolution, ontically speaking. Instead, Dasein lets its question reside within the horizon of an ecstatic arrival. This approach will become clearer when Dasein's approach to death is understood.

Being and Nothing: Time and Death

For Dasein what is definitive is 'care' (*Sorge*), but what this exactly means takes time to become apparent. Dasein through 'careful' dealings begins to approach Being with a certain concern. This care arises from the arrival of a particular *mood*. Dasein always resides within a mood, and it is mood that brings Dasein to its 'there'.[49] Mood discloses the 'there' of Da-sein, because it renders Being apparent. In this way, Dasein, in a sense, begins to *notice* its being. That is to say, a mood marks Being's whereabouts. Subsequently, Dasein realises that Being resides *here*, which is of course a Being-there. But every mood does not evoke the same awareness of the 'there'. For example, a mood in showing the 'that it is' does not reveal the 'whence' or the 'whither'. Fear itself, as a state of mind, brings us closer to anxiety (*Angst*) which is the manifestation of the nothing (*das Nicht*), which in turn is the presentation of the source of the 'there'. Dasein, through fear, becomes anxious. What Dasein fears is *the nothing*. Dasein exhibits anxiety, senses the uncanny, because it realises that Being is, in a sense, nothing.[50] Consequently, Dasein begins to care for Being. It is no longer able to presume the facticity of Being, for the nothingness which is becoming manifest prohibits such *carelessness*. Indeed, it is this care which manifests Dasein's Being. As Heidegger says: 'the Being of Dasein is to be made visible as care'.[51] Throwness (*Geworfenheit*) calls care forth, giving Dasein over to this arrival of Being which must be understood as nothing: Care 'in its very essence, is permeated with nullity, through and through'.[52] Anxiety evokes the nothing of Being, and it is only a matter of 'time' before the nothingness (as which Being is made manifest) becomes that from which Being as nothing stems. *Ex nihilo nihil fit*. This arises as the first motto for Dasein, an ancient phrase read differently in the light of Dasein's anxiety. For Dasein this is the nothingness of the bare 'that it is'.[53] Nothing *does* come from nothing, this nothing intimating a certain ontological weight: 'With regard to Dasein, "that nothing ensues", signifies something positive.'[54] For Heidegger, I argue, *ex nihilo nihilo fit* must be understood in a new yet more ancient manner. It must be understood as: *ex nihilo omne ens qua ens fit* (from nothing all beings, as beings, come to be).

Dasein arouses, or is aroused, by anxiety, which induces due care by Being-towards-death (*Sein zum Tode*).[55] 'Dasein calls back to its throwness so as to understand this death as the null basis which it has to take up into existence.'[56] Dasein recalls its nothingness in understanding itself as Being-towards-death: 'The nullity by which Dasein's Being is dominated primordially through and through, is revealed to Dasein itself in authentic Being-towards-death.'[57] So the nothingness of Being is revealed by the Being-towards-death of Dasein. Dasein understands that its death defines it. Death is, in this, an echo of what is already, because Dasein has death as a result of its nothingness. Death allows Dasein to understand itself as nothing: Lacan echoes this with his understanding that the subject is a lack of being (*manque-à-être*). In so doing, death (as nothing) is not only definitive of Being-there but is constitutive. In this sense, death can be understood as Being, as the advent of Being. We know that Being is only correctly, concernfully approached when its nothingness becomes manifest. Consequently, death reveals this nothingness, but it does so as the advent of Being. Death speaks the nothingness which Being is, and does so as the beginning rather than the end of Being. The nothingness of death makes manifest Being *qua* Being; only with death do we know that Being is *there*. Heidegger asserts that 'Death is a potentiality for Being.' Indeed, 'with death Dasein stands before itself in its ownmost potentiality for Being'.[58] Dasein, in understanding death, can comprehend its own nothingness, and so begin to approach Being in an ontological manner, which means precisely, for Heidegger, to approach Being as nothing. We can think of Being as Death, as long as we do not misplace the event of Death.[59] Death does not occur *after* life as such. Instead Death arrives *before* 'life'. (Part II, Chapter 10 discusses a similar understanding in the work of Sartre, Lacan, Deleuze and Badiou.) Heidegger suggests as much when he speaks of Dasein calling back by calling forth.[60] Death is, Heidegger argues, 'something which stands *before* us'.[61] It could be argued that the notion of 'before us' implies an 'in front of' in terms of future, but this would leave Dasein as something over and against the Nothing which will arise. Yet death, as potentiality for Being, must rather approach as the beginning of Being. Heidegger suggests that 'ending as dying is constitutive for Dasein'.[62] If Death is essential or constitutive, it must be there from the beginning, as that beginning.

If we begin to understand Death as Being, as the manifestation of the nothingness of Being which allows Being to be-there, we can also understand Time. Heidegger asserts that 'Being is not something other than time',[63] and he would insist that the nothing is to be 'understood as Being itself'.[64] If Death, as the manifestation of the Nothing, equals Being, and Being and Time are equivalent in some sense, then Time itself must be thought of as Nothing. Heidegger at least suggests that Time itself is not, or is Nothing, because he speaks of 'temporalising temporality', in a manner to be echoed later by Derrida.[65] We must remember that Being is not different from Time, and we now understand Being as Nothing. If, then, we do consider Death as the beginning for us of Being, and we understand the nothingness of Death as the Being-there of Being, then Time itself is death-drenched. If we are to differentiate Death and Time then Death can, to invoke Derrida, be thought of as the nothing outside the 'text' as such, while Time is the nothing within the 'text'.[66] It is this 'internal' nothingness which may well be that which marks the passage of Being as nothing, preventing what could be termed 'entropy'. (This will be explained in a later section.)

Language: to say nothing

For Heidegger, Dasein is the 'space' within which Being becomes unconcealed truth, as *aletheia*: 'the unconcealedness of what is present, its Being revealed, its showing itself'.[67] The *showing* of what is present takes place in or as language. Heidegger does not, in a sense, think that something other than the *showing* is shown, because *showing* is but a saying, *viz.*, the activity of language: 'Dasein is essentially determined by the potentiality for discourse.'[68] Indeed, the 'asking' of the ontological question, which Dasein enacts, is 'a mode of Being'.[69] But the *showing* is the movement of language itself. The *showing*, as saying, is the utterance of language, and language utters itself as it utters Dasein. As Heidegger says, 'it is not we who play with words; rather, the essence of language plays with us'.[70] In what Dasein says, we must look to understand what is shown in, or as, that saying. Indeed, that which we are to listen for is the *showing* of language, 'to hear what language really says when it speaks'.[71] The *showing*, which is a saying, lets us see the arrival of what comes to language as language. Heidegger says that 'showing [is a] . . . letting appear'.[72]

For Heidegger 'something comes to language'.[73] What can come to language, what would this *something* be? It seems that what is to come to language is language itself: We are 'to bring language to language as language'.[74] It is for this reason that what must be heard in language is language speaking itself, and in so doing 'language shows itself'.[75] What arrives to language is language. Just as Time is not, yet temporality is temporalised, language is languaged. Every saying as a *showing* begins to suggest a certain 'substantiation', *viz.*, language as the arrival of language becomes almost 'bodily'. We know that Dasein is essentially languaged, and that the show of Dasein is the utterance of language. Consequently, with the arrival of Dasein language is brought to language. In saying language Dasein says itself, but Dasein is not in control of this saying. When Dasein says language, Dasein is shown itself. Language, in being languaged, will simultaneously say Dasein while Dasein is saying language; each is brought to itself in the same *showing*. Consequently, it begins to be possible to think that each is nothing appearing *as* something by way of a peculiar 'movement' towards the other. (Maybe this is similar to Spinoza's *Deus sive natura*?)[76]

If the first motto was *ex nihilo nihilo fit*, then the second is *nihil sine ratione*. If nothing is without reason, and if we read this with a particular strength, then we can understand this as the site of the saying/showing arrival. From nothing comes nothing, and this nothing, as the principle of Being, is *without* reason; hence the ontological question can be restated. There will be no closure effected upon the question. Indeed, it will become appropriate to consider this restated question as the un-questioning question of the nothing *as* something, if I may put it so. The epitome of this asking is that of Angelus Silesius' rose:

> The rose is without why; it blooms because it blooms,
> it pays attention to itself, asks not whether it is seen.[77]

This rose will signal a mode of discourse which is 'non-saying', or a 'not-speaking'. For Heidegger, we 'must first learn to exist in the nameless'.[78] He does not appear to mean that we initially exist in the nameless and then do not, but rather that the most basic starting point is to exist and remain in the nameless. Here we can clearly see Heidegger rendering something nothing and then composing a 'discourse' which will enact the nothing *as* something. The rose is shown to be in a manner which is a saying without 'words'. In a sense, it is language without language, as it is the very arrival of language. In other words, it is the languaging of language. This is the bringing of language to language, *the something* which comes to language. The rose *shows* itself as the saying of the nameless, that which is without words, the non-saying which says. We know that Being is understood only when it is considered as nothing, yet a nothing which is for Dasein 'positive'. Time is similar in that temporality must be temporalised, and that Time is not different from

Being. Likewise the rose presents a language without words, in so far as it does not say *something*. Consequently, this discourse is always just *before* language, as the not-speaking, the non-saying, *viz.*, the nameless. To say without saying, to be without Being, and so to temporalise and language the Nothing – this is the show of a pure arrival, the arrival of arriving.[79] Part II, Chapter 10 will argue that this arrival is the elimination of every particular as it is the 'war of all against all'. For every existent is simultaneously prohibited and permitted – *à la* Hegel.

For Heidegger, the rose has a relation and a *dis-relation* with grounds. When it is said that the rose 'blooms without why', we understand that there is a giving up of grounding – the 'why' shows this lack. But it is not privative, to the degree that the 'because' in 'it blooms *because* it blooms' and so lets appear a 'relationship to grounds'.[80] The rose lacks grounds, yet this lack still bespeaks a relationship to grounds, because the saying of grounds is the actual *showing*, or arrival, of the rose *qua* rose.[81] What is happening here? For Heidegger, what happens is happening itself: 'happening itself . . . is the only event. Being alone is. What happens? Nothing happens, if we are pursuing that which happens in happening. Nothing happens, event e-vents.'[82] This is the arrival of arriving. *Nothing does come from nothing, and that which comes is without reason.* This is the discourse which is a show-ing. The ontological question of Being, which I have characterised as an un-questioning question, makes us inhabit a perpetual arrival: Nothing *does* arrive.[83] What is this that arrives as *the* arrival? It seems that maybe 'the nihiliative nothing, the essence of the nothing in its former kinship with "being", can *arrive* and be accommodated'.[84] We are *shown* the arrival of arriving, which is the perpetual saying of the nothing *as* something: 'Being no more is than nothing. Yet there is a giving of both.'[85] We can see this 'rosy' discourse in the crossing of ~~Being~~: 'Like Being the nothing would also have to be written – and that means thought in the same way.'[86] This is the nothing *as* something; the *Abgrund* as ground.

Heidegger is confronting a general *aporia* that is pervasive in all thought, an *aporia* which has already been mentioned. Nonetheless it may be benefical to reiterate its logic. Thought requires a supplement, for if we do not supplement thought then we remain merely ontic – that is, our *answers ask the questions*. At the same time if we do supplement thought we can do so only with another thought which will induce an infinite regress, or we can supplement it with something other than thought. Yet this would mean that thought is grounded in an absence of thought, for it would be grounded by what is thoughtless, or what is nonthought. Deleuze later occupies such a position, arguing that sense is produced by non-sense.[87] Here, employing a similar logic, Heidegger is grounding Being in the Nothing.[88] Furthermore, Heidegger develops this logic in relation to the rose that blooms without a why. This is important because Heidegger is endeavouring to take thinking or language beyond ontic presumptions and the rubric of the metaphysical question. Celan, it will be suggested, does something similar. I will now offer a brief interpretation of a particular impulse which I take to be present in the writings of Paul Celan, one which arguably brings Celan close to Heidegger before *necessarily* moving them apart. At the end Heidegger will be re-examined in light of this reading of Celan.

Language: of the Stone

Celan completes Heidegger.[89]
(Alain Badiou)

Ignoring Adorno's precept, that there could not be any poetry after Auschwitz, Celan moves to write in the shadow of the Holocaust.[90] Indeed, Celan appears to write *because* of the Holocaust; his language takes its shape in the light of this horror. Celan seeks refuge in language itself, and it is his particular understanding and use of language that affords some comparison with Heidegger.

Paul Celan spoke of language in a particular manner, one which gave language a certain autonomy: a life in terms of potentiality, a life of its own. Language bears the scars of what has been uttered, yet this *collaboration* leaves some space that intimates the possibility that this collaboration is without *total* complicity. For Celan this possibility offers the poet or the person *something*, something besides the Holocaust, because there is language other than that of the Holocaust. Language, in a sense, resists reduction to what has been perpetrated upon the Jews of Europe. As Celan says:

> Only one thing remained reachable, close and secure amid all losses: language. Yes, language. In spite of everything, it remained secure against loss. But it had to go through its own lack of answers, through terrifying silence, through the thousand darknesses of murderous speech . . . It gave me no words for what was disappearing, but went through it. Went through and could resurface, enriched by it all.[91]

What this quotation communicates to us is the need, in Celan, for something to have remained 'real', to still be there in spite of the murder. Celan endeavours to acknowledge the incomprehensible evil of the Holocaust while not wanting it to dispose of all *reality*. This reveals the central ambiguity of Adorno's prohibition: there cannot be any poetry after Auschwitz. Does this mean that there is still poetry but that it cannot take place outside the shadow of Auschwitz? In this sense there cannot be any poetry that does not speak from within the sides of the Holocaust. Language must reside there, speaking from within the trauma, the wound – every articulation being shaped by the scars, the holes in the ground, the graves which are also in the sky as ash darkens all perception. Alternatively, this prohibition may insist that there just cannot be any more poetry (a declaration later retracted by Adorno on reading Celan). The worry we may have with this is that Auschwitz becomes *reality*, in that it defines what *is*. If this is the case then the Holocaust does not, in one sense, take place, and this is exactly the *shape* of Nazi propaganda. Celan appears to be aware of this problematic as he stubbornly refuses not to write poetry – even though he is more aware than most of the dangers and contradictions involved in speaking after the Holocaust. In one poem he asks: 'How / did we touch / each other – each other with / these / hands.'[92] We can imagine Celan looking at his raised hands as if they had committed the murder. How are we to speak with language, language which spoke death for millions? How to use words to speak of death, rather than words to speak death? Celan's ploy, it seems, is to keep pursuing something else, something real; indeed, Celan is looking for *reality*.

If it can be said that Celan does seek a *reality*, there is no doubt that this *reality* is not uncomplicated, for Celan speaks of the *strange*. If language is to remain in spite of what occurred, it must have some notion of *autonomy*, as it must reside outside man's total control. As Walter Benjamin expresses it: 'Language has its own word.'[93] In that case there may be a reservoir of the aforementioned potentiality, which can speak beyond, or after, the Holocaust. The form which this discourse takes is tactical, extremely deliberate.

Celan develops what can be termed the language of stones, which Adorno calls hermetic or anorganic.[94] This is the language of dead matter. The reason for this is that it is before theses, before discursive or veridical assertion, and it is before the embellishment of what could be termed 'iambic convolutions'. The language of stones offers us a certain solidity, one which may withstand the catastrophe of murder. Celan considers poetry as if it is like the language of a stone.[95] Language is to occur before the 'split of yes and no', words are to remain unsplit.[96] In this sense, the *reality* which Celan may well be pursuing will provide a place other than Auschwitz, surviving the flames of fascist discourse, with its requisite reductiveness. Celan speaks of being 'racked by reality and in search of it'.[97] For him poetry is an encounter with an other. Maybe, he says, a *wholly other*.

Poetry is a conversation because it moves *towards*. Poetry speaks in hope, a hope of an other, a hope for a reality and conversation within that *reality*. A poem sent out is sent *towards*, in hope. Towards what, asks Celan? He answers 'toward something open, inhabitable, an approachable you, perhaps an approachable reality'.[98] The reality of a 'you', a person as such. One should speak using personal pronouns because this is the language of survival, as one commentator puts it.[99] One should speak of a person because the Holocaust is an impossibility of persons. For the Holocaust cannot afford the Jews to be people; consequently, people are reduced to the homogeneity of ash. This is one reason why Celan, it seems, will not assent to the prohibition of poetry. He uses Georg Büchner's Lucille from *Danton's Death* as an example of *Dichtung*.[100] When Camille is to be executed, dying an iambic death, Lucille protests at his arrest. This protest takes the form of words: 'long live the King'. These words do not speak politically, they do not convey an opinion with regard to republics and monarchies. Instead these words embody the notion of *singularity*. Before Lucille utters these words she says, 'when I think that they – that this head! . . . The world is wide, there are so many things in it, why just that one? What would they want with it?' The reality of suffering and the particularity of life reduce the theatricality of discourse, if not art, to absurdity. For Celan, Lucille's words of protestation are poetry. They speak of *reality*, doing so as an act of freedom.

Lucille's words are mindful of dates, that is, they refer to a *here* and *now* which cannot be dispensed with or substituted. Celan endeavours to return words to the *now* of poetry, to particularity: 'With words I fetched you back, there you are / all is true and waiting / for truth.'[101] Truth as reality is essential for Celan's anorganic poetry: 'A rumbling: Truth / itself has appeared / among humankind / in the very thick of their flurrying metaphors.'[102] Truth must be before the *yes* and *no* split, it must reside before discourse, but not before language. Celan constantly probes at the possibility of such a reality, one which Lucille would recognise, maybe one which those who entered Auschwitz believed in. The language of the *stone* is there to speak those who speak. This is to be spoken by an other, a reality: 'A tree must again be a tree, and its branch, on which the rebels of a hundred wars have been hanged, must again flower in spring.'[103] Man, as he who speaks, cannot be allowed to define *reality*. Language, as an anorganic *reality*, must unsay what has been said: 'The gallows has, for this one minute considered itself a tree, as nobody had looked up we cannot be sure that it was not.'[104] The inhumanity of humanity's discourse cannot be allowed to become definitive, otherwise the very flaws and danger we witness in discourse become *reality* : 'There are / still songs to be sung on the other side / of mankind.'[105] Celan makes poetry pull 'itself back from an already "no-more" into a "still-here"'.[106] It is an effort to re-turn words to mouths, to return *reality*. Like the suitcases removed at train stations with polite promises that they will be sent ahead, Celan appears to give these 'suitcases' back. The person who was put on a train to Auschwitz had a reality, and it is the *unreality* of the Holocaust which stole this. (Indeed, it can be suggested that Celan wants there to have been murder, to have been theft, so that lives and suitcases can be returned, if not physically, at least potentially.) By contrast, discourse which has split the *no* and the *yes* seems to take words from mouths, transporting them endlessly elsewhere.[107] Like suitcases which are promised to be returned, only the infinite anonymity of death is offered. Celan speaks of the *Atemwende,* the breath-turn.[108] Words are said, uttered, leaving the mouth, but their sense, their life, requires the turn of breath between words. Such is the replenishment of air to be donated to words, so as to enable and animate the passage of words ('from me to you'). It is the place of conversation, which is the aforementioned encounter. Discourse is unable to detach itself from life, as it must, like Lucille's words, arise and return to an enracinated life. This refusal to give words up, even on the promise of a later return, disables the disengagement required by the giving up of 'suitcases', lives, and so on, within the discourse of National Socialism. Words only reside, as poetry, within the crevice of the turn. It seems that we can characterise this notion of breath-turn as a movement between in-spiration, ex-piration, re-spiration. The sense of words remains within the rise and fall of the chest. This is the strange possibility of poetry, this conversation in spite of the Holocaust.

Flowers: for no one[109]

> I owe my existence to *no one*.[110]
> (Samuel Beckett, *The Unnamable*)

The remit of poetry is specifically to 'speak on behalf of the strange'. What is strange is the unsplit words of the stone, the reality of Lucille, the suitcases returned. The hermetic character of Celan's poetry betrays the danger of discourse. Celan is fully conscious of the Holocaust, yet he refuses it the last word.[111] However, he abandons the phrase *the strange*, asserting that 'I can no longer use this word here – on behalf of the other, who knows, perhaps of an altogether other.'[112] This wholly other is the possibility of the anorganic language, the unsplit reality. It is here we meet again Silesius' flower: 'the stone / the stone in the air / . . . we bailed the darkness empty, we found / the word that ascended summer: / flower'.[113] The first word one of Celan's sons uttered was flower. And this appears to have been the occasion for writing this poem. The word flower, uttered so, appears to resemble the poetry of Lucille's 'long live the King'.

The unsplit stone of the flower resists reduction.[114] Instead it proclaims its bodily reality. This flower seems to reappear throughout

Celan's poetry, sometimes negatively: 'I see the poison flower / Is all manner of words and shapes.'[115] We cannot be sure if poison is flowering or if what is spoken of is a poisonous flower. More importantly, with regard to Heidegger, the flower appears in the poem 'Psalm', written in 1963, after Heidegger's *Principle of Reason*, and after Celan had read 'What is Metaphysics' which pays homage to *no one*, no one's rose.[116] This is the rose which flowers for *no one*. Celan, like Heidegger, gives this a strong reading.[117] The flower does actually flower and this for no other reason than for itself, or for *no one*. This *no one*, like Heidegger's nothing, takes on a particular positivity: 'Praised be your name, no one. / For your sake / we shall flower. / Towards / you.'[118] *No one* (*Niemand*) is personified, and becomes the desire that advents a direction, a shape, a towards, *viz.*, poetry.

It is *no-one* who moulds us again out of earth and clay. *No one*, like Heidegger's nothing, 'creates' us: 'A nothing / we were, are, shall / remain, flowering –, the / no one's rose.' For Celan, it seems, this *no one* signals the possibility for which he appears to have been searching, namely, the unsplit reality of poetry, the hermetic language of stones or a writing of stones, to use Roger Caillois' phrase.[119] Recalling Heidegger's assertion that 'only a god can save us', and his veneration of the nothing, we can understand Celan's *no one* as the hope of this god. Celan takes us beyond, or before, the distance of discursive reason with its questions and answers. Such reasoning presumes its sense, which allows it to 'travel', leaving behind all origins, taking its reasons to other lands and places; this mobilisation is the prerequisite for every *invasion*. Celan's language of stones instead reminds us of the 'thought of thought' which is unthought, or which is the unthinking of thought. For Celan this other of thought invokes a proximity that limits thought yet enables its very movement. For such movement does not lead thought away, even though it is a movement. It does not display the transcendental mobility of a fully deracinated thinking. There is little doubt that the language of 'no one's rose' was developed under the influence of Heidegger, especially his understanding of Being as nothing. But such influence did not remain constant, nor did it bring each to the same place.

Waiting: In Line

> What the life of a Jew was during the war years I need not mention.[120]
>
> (Paul Celan)

Heidegger invited Celan to visit him, and the invitation was accepted. Celan visited Heidegger on 25 July 1967. A poem called 'Todtnauberg', the name of the place where Heidegger lived, resulted. It is possible to argue that we see a departure in this poem from Celan's previously sympathetic reading of Heidegger's work (especially if we consider that for Celan he and Heidegger were the two poles which the *meridian* crossed promising a new language). Hölderlin may have indirectly encouraged Celan's somewhat positive reading of Heidegger, for there was a line of Hölderlin's, used by Heidegger, which suggested that where the poison lay was also the cure.[121] Maybe Celan read Heidegger, the former Nazi, because he waited for the cure to arise, hoping that Heidegger's characterisation of language, especially in his later works, intimated such a possibility. The essay which had employed the phrase the 'zero meridian' was an essay written in honour of Ernst Jünger who wrote about the line. He may well have been the author whom Celan disliked so much that he changed publishers, Fischer, in 1965, when they anthologised his work with the latter's. It was two years later when the visit took place. Heidegger kept a visitors' book and Celan's poem appears to revolve heavily around the signing of it. We can, I suggest, think of the line in the book on which he is to write his entrance as the *meridian* about which he had already spoken. But there was consternation at the idea of involving himself with this line. He worried about taking this line: 'the line / – whose name did the book / register before mine?' (Felstiner translates it as 'whose name did it take in before mine?')[122] The line remains blind to what has gone before, the line stands indifferent. Who (maybe Nazis) had signed the book before? Whom had the line welcomed? A certain complicit promiscuity surrounds its blank willingness, so detached from dates. This zero point appears atemporal, while Celan is always 'mindful of dates', speaking of 'a now of the poem and the poem only has this one'.[123] The zero point seemed to erase dates, in a sense taking words away from open mouths (this zero point could be analogous to Heidegger's *das Nicht*, or *Abgrund*, and maybe Derrida's *différance*.) Celan had written an inscription about the hope in a coming word. This word could be Heidegger's asking to be forgiven for what is unforgivable, or the hope that Heidegger's silence on the Holocaust will be broken.

Celan appears to smuggle a reference to fascism into his poem. He does this with reference to woodlands and meadows. The German used by Celan for 'woodlands, meadows, unlevelled' is '*Waldwasen, uneingeebnet*'. As Ulrich Baer points out, the word '*Wasen*' is an eccentric choice and is really only used in northern Germany.[124] And '*Wasen*' is interchangeable with *Faschine*, designating 'fascine', which means a bundle of sticks. Such bundles of sticks are often used as ceremonial props.[125] The point that Celan may be making is that Heidegger's understanding of the land in relation to Germany must pass over the *reality* of the land, its contours, dialects and so on. That is to say, the land abstracts from this and every real land. This is the requisite abstraction for the construction of Fascist discourse. In so doing, its land is like the bundles of wood used in ceremonies in so far as the 'ritual' of fascist discourse can only locate its land by burning that land. Such land is left scorched, flat, silent, just as a war-torn land will be blackened by the abstract indiscriminate logic of bombs. Heidegger, the lover of Germany, can only love such a place by passing over its regions, dialectics, its beings, that is, its inherently disparate nature. Consequently, Celan walks with Heidegger, but he is only able to go half way. Celan's words must re-turn, while Heidegger's endlessly disseminate, waiting within the arrival of the Being of nothing. Let me explain the movement of this Heideggerian arrival before returning to Celan.

What prevents an 'entropic' homogeneity in this perpetual arrival is what is here called the 'alterity of nothing': nothing *as* something. Whatever *is*, for example Dasein, moves towards Death (towards the nothing) which is a move towards Being. That which *is*, moves always on, hence everything it is somewhat escapes it; this is an almost Derridean delay of infinite indecision. Dasein, in being, must move towards the Nothing which is the truth of Being. We know that Dasein is Nothing, but we know also that Being is Nothing. So as Dasein moves on towards the Nothing, realising its own nothingness, Being is advented. The nothingness of Dasein, towards which Dasein moves, is, therefore, Dasein. Everything which *is* must understand itself as nothing, and it is this endless comprehension which provides differentiation as movement, in an otherwise entropic 'system'.

What *is* moves within the *alterity of nothing*, an alterity which cuts both ways. First of all, Dasein moves towards its own dissolution: realising its own nothingness. Second, the Nothing (or nothingness) of Dasein others itself *as* something, doing so to present its immanent plenitude, disallowing any notion of privation. This aspectual reduction performs the task of differentiation. In this way Dasein is only ever in the arriving-arrival of its own aspectual dissolution-constitution.[126] (This is 'structurally' similar to a Spinozistic attribute.) Dasein has Death as the external infinitude (the infinity of nothing), and Time as the internal infinite nullity. It has collapsed all language and meaning, along with Being itself, into the Nothing, each existing only *as* the 'bodily' expressions of this immanent plenitude. This is Being beyond Being, a nothing without privation. The perpetual un-questioning question[127] of the something rendered nothing, and the nothing *as* something. Heidegger's words disseminate in this endless manner.

Maybe Celan is unwilling to toe this line. He can only go half way along the log paths; the word used for logs (*Knüppel*) also means 'bludgeon'. The two men, Jew and former Nazi, remain separate: 'orchid and orchid, single'. The line, *meridian*, does not produce a new calculation, as Jünger had thought, because the line is the void of detached words, removed by way of a certain 'iambic' civility: 'ladies and gentlemen, would you please sign the book'. The *das Nicht*, the *Abgrund*, erases particularity, tradition and history. The arriving-arrival is blank, a perpetual movement of the same. Celan continues: 'now the hassocks are burning'. Hassocks are tufts of grass, yet they are also the name for kneeling mats used in churches. It seems that there is no need to kneel, forgiveness will not be asked for. Heidegger will not bow. Hubristically he perpetuates his silence. Celan announces, 'I eat the book / with all its / insignia'.[128] Celan may be returning the words to mouths, removing the pretence of discursive distance. Maybe the mouths to which he returns are Nazi. As a result, the proper historical 'reality' of those uttered words, by those persons, those who signed up, toeing the line, is remembered. Hence they are eaten. But also Celan eats the book so as to be rid of this detached discourse, the philosopher's book. Rather than signing the line it is eaten, and this is the reality of poetry. (In this way we can think of the words of the Eucharistic liturgy as this reality, for they *are* because they eat the Word – their words are but the time of this feast.)[129]

In the end the hopeful word, and the hope in Heidegger's words, seems impossible. Celan parts company with the philosopher of Being, rather than beings. Celan's *no one* cannot act as Heidegger's god, it cannot save the nihilism of his Nothing, nor the nihilism of his arriving god or the god of pure arrival. The supplement that Heidegger thinks into the question of Being, going beyond the ontic philosopher, fails to resist reduction, since this supplement is that of the Nothing. Each being is reduced to this Nothing which both precedes and succeeds. This reduction manifests itself in Heidegger's 'suturing' of philosophy to poetry – the consequence of which is to render thinking susceptible to a 'poem' such as National Socialism.[130] Celan's poetry does not do this because, it seems, the idea of reality (one which is there but is unavailable as such) prevents a slide into *a* poem, without undoing the possibility of poetry itself. Things are messier in the world of Celan, things do not just arrive, they depart, are deported and so on.[131] In this way Celan writes within the shadow of what Adorno calls the 'non-identical', which is to say the incongruity of thought and being; this is Celan's no-one.[132] This is not the case for Heidegger, who requires, after all, an ontotheological god for the salvation of Being and of his own words about Being. But this deity is always, it seems, the god of the blank line, the zero point, the *Abgrund* of *das Nicht*. The perpetual arrival is like the suitcases that never come, this is the Being of Nothing. Theology cannot believe in either this god or this understanding of Being. Yet Heidegger is correct in so far as only God can save us.

> With words I fetched you back, there you are,
> all is true and a waiting
> for truth.[133]

The next chapter discusses the work of Derrida. It is argued that Derrida carries the logic of nihilism to new extremes. Derrida appears to take Heidegger's *das Nicht* and place it outside every text. In so doing he combines Plotinus' *meontological* impulse with a Spinozistic dualism. For Derrida has a dualism of Text and Nothing, which I construe as equivalent to Spinoza's Nature and God. Consequently it is suggested that Derrida's philosophy is the combination of Plotinus and Spinoza, while carrying further the *provenance* of nihilism witnessed in Kant, Hegel and Heidegger. That is to say, Derrida rests his philosophy on the logic of the nothing being *as* something.

Notes

1 Heidegger is here addressing the work of Ernst Jünger. Heidegger contributed to a publication in Jünger's honour. This contribution was originally called 'Über die Linie'. This text was later altered and renamed, 'On the Question of Being'. This text can be found in Heidegger (1998), pp. 291–322.

2 For Celan's poetry see Celan (1995). For Celan's prose see Celan (1986). The above quotation is from Celan's 'Meridian' speech and can be found in Celan (1986); the 'Meridian' speech can also be found in Celan (1978).

3 See Felstiner (1995), pp. 72–75, 140. 'It would be an understatement to say Celan had read Heidegger', Lacoue-Labarthe (1999), p. 33; 'Heidegger's presence in Celan is far more prevalent than the word "backdrop" conveys', Fioretos (1994), p. 111; see also Gadamer (1997), Baer (2000).

4 Silesius' flower, which blooms without why, can be found in Silesius (1986), p. 54.

5 The phrase 'ladies and gentlemen' is that used by Paul Celan in his infamous *Meridian* speech. Celan used this phrase fifteen times in 'The Meridian'; this is understandable as he was addressing an audience on the occasion of his receiving the Georg Büchner Prize on 22 October 1960. Celan appears to employ this phrase with the particular purpose of invoking the pretence of civility, even of culture itself, used by the Nazis to 'shepherd' people into cattle carts, leaving their suitcases behind: 'Ladies and Gentlemen, please leave your suitcases, and board the train, your belongings will be sent ahead of you.'

6 Blanchot (1986), p. 3; italics mine.

7 Deleuze (1997), p. 66. It must be remembered that Heidegger did his *Habilitationsschrift* on a work that he thought to be by Scotus, but this is in fact a work of the Scotistic school by Thomas of Erfurt; see Heidegger (1970).

8 Heidegger (1962), p. 23.

9 *Ibid.*, p. 21.

10 *Ibid.*, p. 43.

11 *Ibid.*, p. 44.

12 In the hands of Derrida this destruction (*Destruktion*) became deconstruction.

13 Heidegger (1962), p. 25. I write Time with a capital to suggest its equivalence with Being.
14 *Ibid.*, pp. 38, 39.
15 *Ibid.*, p. 32.
16 *Ibid.*, p. 34.
17 *Ibid.*, p. 41.
18 The word reception is not Heidegger's.
19 Heidegger (1962), p. 41.
20 I would agree with Heidegger on this point. Theology can certainly learn from this, nihilism certainly does; see Part II, Chapter 10.
21 This is my own phrase.
22 Heidegger (1962) p. 107.
23 *Ibid.*, p. 155.
24 *Ibid.*, p. 67.
25 *Ibid.*
26 *Ibid.*, pp. 139, 143.
27 *Ibid.*, p. 139.
28 *Ibid.*, p. 141.
29 *Ibid.*, p. 277.
30 *Ibid.*, p. 225.
31 *Ibid.*, p. 174.
32 *Ibid.*, p. 232.
33 *Ibid.*, p. 279.
34 However, we will see that this move to restate the question will be but another identical repetition of the ontotheological (*meontotheological*) asking, which embodies the nihilistic logic as articulated above. Heidegger will continue this Plotinian-Spinozism, for the something is rendered nothing, then this nothing is made to perform *as* something.
35 Heidegger (1962), p. 50.
36 *Ibid.*, p. 58; italics mine. This sounds like the show about which we heard in the previous chapter.
37 Heidegger (1962), p. 60.
38 *Ibid.*, p. 61.
39 *Ibid.*, p. 62.
40 The employment of the notion of a *show* can be used to relate Heidegger to Wittgenstein and Hegel who both utilise the idea of a *show* to speak of appearance. For Wittgenstein see Conor Cunningham (1999); for Hegel see Part I, Chapter 5.
41 See Part II, Chapter 10.
42 This might be similar to Clifford Geertz's notion of 'thick description'.
43 Heidegger (1962), p. 103.
44 *Ibid.*, p. 104.
45 See Part II, Chapter 10.
46 Heidegger (1962), p. 101.
47 *Ibid.*
48 *Ibid.*, p. 117.
49 *Ibid.*, p. 173.

50 'That nothing which is equiprimordially the same as Being', *ibid.*, p. 318. The most interesting texts involving *das Nicht*, are 'What is Metaphysics' (1929), 'Postscript to What is Metaphysics' (1943), and 'Introduction to What is Metaphysics' (1949), and 'On the Question of Being' (1955); all of these can be found in Heidegger (1998), pp. 82–96; 231–238; 277–290; 291–322.
51 Heidegger (1962), pp. 83–84.
52 *Ibid.*, p. 331.
53 *Ibid.*, p. 321.
54 *Ibid.*, p. 324.
55 'Care is Being towards death', *ibid.*, p. 378.
56 *Ibid.*, p. 333.
57 *Ibid.*, p. 354.
58 *Ibid.*, p. 294.
59 Death is capitalised because it is argued to be equivalent to Being.
60 See *ibid.*, p. 333.
61 *Ibid.*, p. 294; italics mine.
62 *Ibid.*, p. 284.
63 *Ibid.*, p. 285.
64 *Ibid.*, p. 290.
65 *Ibid.*, p. 278.
66 This is similar to the internal–external infinitude of a Spinozistic attribute; see Part I, Chapter 3.
67 Heidegger (1972), p. 79.
68 Heidegger (1962), p. 47.
69 *Ibid.*, p. 27.
70 *'What Calls for Thinking'*, in Heidegger (1978), p. 388.
71 *Ibid.*, p. 389.
72 *Ibid.*, p. 401.
73 *Ibid.*, p. 408.
74 *Ibid.*, p. 398.
75 *Ibid.*, p. 399.
76 See p. 69 above.
77 Quoted in Heidegger (1996), p. 35. See Silesius (1986), p. 54.
78 Heidegger (1998), p. 243.
79 It is possible to suggest that this is somewhat similar to what Kant calls the 'appearance of appearance'. See Kant (1998b), p. 117; also see Part I, Chapter 4. Furthermore, such a show is related to Hegel who also employs the term in relation to his notion of essence; for example, see Hegel (1975), pp. 186–187.
80 Heidegger (1996), p. 42.
81 This is somewhat similar to an Ockhamian singularity, and the occult generation of meaning, and universals within the sides of 'supposition'.
82 Heidegger (1984), p. 485.
83 Derrida says something similar: 'this occultation . . . this disappearing of the ground necessary for the appearing', (1978), p. 138. I would argue that this appearance of appearance, within a constitutive disappearance, is Kantian.
84 'On the Question of Being', in Heidegger (1998), p. 310; italics mine.
85 *Ibid.*, p. 317.

86 *Ibid.*, p. 311.
87 See Deleuze (1990), p. 71.
88 Heidegger refers to this ground as the *Abgrund*, which can be translated as 'abyss'. He also refers to nothing as *das Nicht*, translated as 'the nothing'.
89 Badiou (1999), p. 77.
90 Adorno had issued the precept that poetry after the Holocaust was barbaric in the 1950s and had restated it in 1962 and 1965. But he withdrew the prohibition in 1966: 'Zur Dialektik des Engagements', *Neue Rundschau* 73/1 (1962) p. 103; repr. in *Noten zur Literatur* III (Frankfurt, 1965); see Adorno (1966), p. 353; (1973), p. 362.
91 This is an excerpt from Celan's 'Bremen' speech, see Celan (1986).
92 'The Straitening', in Celan (1995), pp. 141–153, especially p. 145.
93 Benjamin (1979), p. 117.
94 Celan does in one conversation refuse the label hermetic; see Felstiner (1995), p. 253. See also Adorno (1997), pp. 443–444.
95 See 'Radix Matrix', and 'Confidence', in Celan (1995), pp. 191, 107.
96 See 'Speak, You Also', Celan (1995), p. 101.
97 Celan (1986), p. 35.
98 *Ibid.*
99 Felstiner (1995), p. 152.
100 See Büchner (1979).
101 Celan (1995), p. 165.
102 *Ibid.*, p. 271.
103 Celan (1986), p. 5.
104 *Ibid.*, p. 13.
105 Celan (1995), p. 235.
106 Celan (1986), p. 49.
107 It could be argued that Derrida's *différance* initiates a similar dissemination.
108 This is the name given to a collection of poems.
109 Part II, Chapter 10 argues that for Sartre, Lacan, Badiou *et al.*, this No-One is a negation of the One; no One.
110 Beckett (1955), p. 294; italics mine.
111 Similarly, and under the influence of Celan, Alain Badiou argues that to speak of the 'end of philosophy' because of the Holocaust is 'tantamount to making the Jews die a second time'; Badiou (1999), p. 31.
112 Celan (1986), p. 48. Glenn translates this as 'wholly other'. This seems more sensible as Celan had just bought a book by Rudolph Otto, which he had read before giving this speech, and Otto employs the phrase wholly other; see Celan (1978), pp. 29–40; Otto (1925).
113 'Flower', in Celan (1995), p. 117.
114 Under the guidance of Badiou the language of stones, that which is unsplit, appears, I suggest, as the 'objectless subject'. For Badiou poetry is 'disobjectifying'; Badiou (1999), p. 72; see also Badiou (1991), pp. 24–32.
115 Celan (1995), p. 169.
116 Lacoue-Labarthe insists that '"Psalm" is indecipherable without Heidegger's meditations on nothingness . . . it is indecipherable without the pages of *Principle of Reason*'; Lacoue-Labarthe (1999), p. 33.

117 Hamacher suggests that there is a tendency in Celan in his early work to hypostatise nothingness. Hamacher goes on to argue that this is overcome in Celan's later work; see Hamacher (1997), pp. 344, 348.

118 Celan (1995), p. 179.

119 See Caillois (1985).

120 Quoted in Felstiner (1995), p. 59. Heidegger is generally accused of not mentioning the Holocaust.

121 Such a sentiment is to be found in Hölderlin (1998), p. 243, in a poem called 'Patmos'.

122 See Felstiner (1995), p. 246.

123 Celan (1986), p. 50.

124 See Baer (2000), p. 229.

125 *Ibid*.

126 On aspectual perception in Heidegger and Wittgenstein, see Mulhall (1990).

127 What Heidegger calls 'persistent questioning', see 'On the Question of Being', in Heidegger (1998), p. 294.

128 Celan (1995), p. 302. This calls to mind the words of Revelation 10, vs. 9–10. See also Lacan (1992), p. 322.

129 See Part II, Chapter 1.

130 See Badiou (1999), pp. 61–77.

131 Heidegger's notion of 'withdrawal' (*das Sichentziehende* or *Sichentziehen*) is merely the withdrawal involved in the perpetual arrival, because what arrives is nothing.

132 I would not articulate the non-identical in these terms, because to argue that the non-identical arises from an incongruity between Being and thought contains a hyper-resolution. Instead the non-identical arises because thought and Being are not incongruous; this is our Hegelian lesson, in terms of speculative thinking.

133 Celan (1995), p. 165; 'Your / being Beyond'.

7

DERRIDA

Spinozistic Plotinianism

Nothing is outside: the text

For both Plotinus and Heidegger, the Nothing is the
impetus of our approach to what is most real in the world,
although beyond essence and existence: the One, or Being.
This is also an important point in Derrida's analysis.[1]
(Eli Diamond)

In a certain way thought means *nothing*.[2]
(Jacques Derrida)

This chapter does not offer a reading of any particular text of Derrida's.
Instead it analyses the implications that can be discerned from what is
deemed to be a central claim of Derrida's philosophy, namely that there
is nothing outside the text.[3] From this almost axiomatic claim this chapter
extracts a logic that brings Derrida close to both Spinoza and Plotinus.
The idiom which Derrida's philosophy assumes invites complication and
often obfuscation. Instead I shall endeavour to keep the terms used and
the logic employed as simple as possible. But the endeavour to critique
this most slippery of thinkers will require some difficult moves, which
unfortunately are unavoidable.

Derrida argues that language cannot have an *outside*; he also asserts
that nothing is *outside* language, that is, the text. As a result, language is
left in some sense bereft. Language, because it is linguistic, cannot have
an outside yet, in a sense, language is but the movement towards an
outside. Language is the 'embodiment' of the desire for an *outside*. This is
true because language desires to say *something*, for language hopes that its
significations actually bear significance. The *outside* is maybe the secret
name for this desire. Language, in that it endeavours to communicate or
to say something, wishes there to be something in what is said. In desiring
thus, language desires that which is not reducible to itself. Language is in
this way the desire for something *other* than language. But this other is

forbidden by Derrida. Furthermore, it is declared to be impossible. It is impossible because language *is* language. Language as language is, then, its own limitation. Language would need to be other than language if it were to have an outside. But language is always itself, language is always language. Consequently, all signification is *inside*. Only *nothing* is *outside* language. As there is no *outside* available, language must generate one. Indeed, for Derrida language is the movement of this generation.

Outside: in

Thought-that-means-nothing . . . the thought for which there is no sure opposition between outside and inside.[4]

(Jacques Derrida)

Language is defined by nothing in two ways. First of all, language is the pursuit of an *outside* which is nothing. Second, language *in not being able to have* an outside, is nothing. This means that language is, then, the same as the *outside*, for both are nothing. In this way the *outside* which is forbidden, yet in some sense attained, is language itself. In this sense, for Derrida, language is the sundering of the something that renders it nothing; it does this because an *outside* is prohibited. Consequently, when language says something, this something is nothing, in that it is nothing but language. But, paradoxically, in being nothing, it is indeed the same as the *outside*. Hence this nothing, which language says in every signification, is nothing *as* something. The *outside* pursued and forbidden is language itself. This means that language does not say something, but instead says nothing *as* something. (It is up to Derrida to present such a conundrum *otherwise* than negatively.)

As a result, to say, signify, or do, does not require that one say, signify, or do something. Indeed, significance starts only in the absence of something, as a some-thing would be death, at least according to Derrida. Language is, in this sense, *post-linguistic*. But so also is Derrida. For Derrida comprehends language.[5] In so doing, Derrida is beyond language. We witness such post-linguistic ruminations in the very articulation of the prohibition: there is nothing outside language. Derrida is post-linguistic in that Derrida is using the opposition inside/outside in terms of the demarcated sides, or extent, of language. This means that Derrida uses language alinguistically – not in a pre-linguistic manner but in a post-linguistic one. Yet the metaphysics of either position are similar. For *this* language, *a* language, indeed a voice – that of Derrida's – defines all language, in that it pretends to comprehend *all* of language, for it both locates and demarcates in terms of a foundational circumscription. There is, then, a univocal text, for there is but one text, because Derrida's Plotininan heritage permits only one effect to emanate from the nothing. I return to this in the section 'Inside: Out'.

I will now examine this nothing which Derrida knows is outside the text in an effort to show that it comes inside every text. One consequence of this arrival will be the reduction of all significance to the level of the diacritical.

There is: nothing inside the text[6]

Violently inscribing within the text that which attempted to govern it from without.[7]

(Jacques Derrida)

Here we return to the non-being of Plotinus, which may be the nothing of nihilism. This nothing can be compared to the nothing outside the Derridian text. It is Derrida's hope that *'différance* produces what it forbids, makes possible the very thing that it makes impossible'.[8] We could not wish for a more 'modern' statement which encapsulates the dissolution of the something making the nothing generate as something. There are at least four ways of approaching this Derridian-Neoplatonic nothing (a nothing deeply indebted to Lacan, Sartre, and Heidegger, if not to Husserl, Hegel, Schelling, Kant, Spinoza and Descartes).[9]

First of all, for Derrida, we know there is 'nothing outside the text', just as for Plotinus there is 'a' non-being outside being,[10] the 'One' beyond being. Second, this means there is 'a text outside the nothing', just as for Plotinus the 'text' of *nous* comes from the non-being of the One. So, in an analogous sense, Derrida's text comes from the nothing, for without this nothing language could not say anything. Third, there is a 'nothing within the text'. This nothingness is the result of the text actually *being*; for being is a mode *less* than non-being, since the text, or Intelligence, which has come from 'the One', exists in an inferior manner to the non-actual referent. There is a nothingness in the text because the text itself does not exist in a true manner, *viz.*, beyond-being; the text is 'not' to the degree that it has (signifying) being. We can see this in Derrida's economy of *différance,* for there any existent must reside within the shadow of infinite difference and deferral. This means that *an existent is in opposition to the truth of this infinity when it says 'I am'.*[11] Fourth, there is a 'text inside the nothing'. If there is nothing outside the text then we can conceive this as an exteriority surrounding the text. In this way to say that there is 'nothing outside the text' is to say that the text is within this nothing which surrounds it. The text outside the nothing is the text within the nothing. This being the case every text is permeated with nothingness, for this nothing is outside the text and this text is inside the nothing. In this way we can see both that language says nothing and that thought thinks nothing. The Derridian text *is* without being. Consequently, it remains as nothing (which is the nothingness within every text).[12] In *Of Grammatology*, Derrida says that 'the outside *is* the inside'.[13] I take this to mean that the nothing, which resides outside, comes within every text because every text actually says nothing. I shall return to Derrida's relation to language below. First I wish to argue that Derrida's 'text' displays similarities with Spinoza as well as Plotinus.

Derrida's Spinozistic Plotinianism

Derrida's position illuminates Spinoza's position.[14]
(R. Harland)

It is possible to argue that Derrida is a Plotinian disciple of Spinoza (a discipleship which is here referred to as *meontotheology*). We can begin to see this Plotinian Spinozism when we read Derrida insisting that 'in order to exceed metaphysics it is necessary that a *trace* be *inscribed* within the text of metaphysics, a *trace* that continues to signal . . . in the direction of an entirely other text'.[15] It is this inscription that may allow 'an entirely other question'.[16] But this question remains where it was by the very fact of it being an *inscription*. This question is, I suggest, *why something rather than nothing*? Why do we need something when the nothing will *be* more than sufficient? So this question takes place in the 'displacement of a question, a certain system somewhere open to an undecidable resource that sets the system in motion'.[17] This question will be the un-questioning question of *différance*; *un-questioning* because it does not ask *something*, yet an unquestioning *question* because it *does* ask *nothing*.[18] Derrida argues that this question is older than the ontological difference.[19] *Différance* will 'provide' or generate the nothing *as* something. The question of *différance* risks 'meaning nothing'[20] – an un-meaning which allows meaning to come after it, but such an un-meaning, this *différance*, is not before as it is before every before. (This is similar to Deleuze who grounds sense in nonsense.)[21] Hence, 'the name origin no longer suits it'.[22] It will be this un-questioning question that will make presence and absence possible.[23] Furthermore, it will allow language to say nothing and thought to think nothing; we will be without being. Oppositions *qua* oppositions arrive within the active movement of *différance*.[24] If *différance* renders the nothing as something, then the question of being cannot come first and the idea of origin is indeed problematised. The nothing *as* something is 'first', but this nothing *as* something detaches itself from these oppositional logics. Derrida is here endeavouring to escape ontic categories, yet still provide what those appeared to provide: language, thought and being. (Being is an ontic category in so far as it is trapped by the notion of the something.)[25]

Derrida appears to *provide*[26] continually semantic performances of the nothing *as* something: *pharmakon* is both cure and poison, the *hymen* is marriage and virginity. (Each side supplements the other, thus allowing Derrida's text to *provide* all that it does under erasure: to be without being.) The most important example is that of the Plotinian *ikhnos* (trace). The unquestioning-question of *différance* 'goes without saying . . . remaining silent'.[27] That is, language does proceed, but does not say *something*. It does not seek *something*; instead it treats the nothing *as* something. This lets it escape ontotheology, yet without lack. The silent 'a' of *différance* passes by unheard, like the intonation of this modern question: why something rather than nothing? This inscribed trace, which 'continues to signal', is the non-productive production we found in Plotinus and in Spinoza. (In Plotinus the One was the all, while the all was the One; in Spinoza God is Nature, Nature is God.) The trace is, according to Derrida, 'nothing'.[28] It is for this reason that 'in a certain sense thought means nothing'.[29] Just as 'deconstruction is nothing'.[30]

In a sense the trace, like *différance*, is before presence and absence, as it is a non-origin that is originary.[31] This is the nothing *as* something, which for Derrida is an occultation, a 'disappearing of the ground necessary for appearing itself':[32] this sounds like Hegel and, as we shall see later, also resembles moves made by both Sartre and Lacan. From where does this *trace* issue without origins? It proceeds from the work of Plotinus, who tells us that the '*trace* of the One makes essence, being is only the *trace* of the One'.[33] We know that, for Derrida, the trace is nothing and that this trace, according to Plotinus, is the trace of the One which is itself otherwise than Being and therefore nothing. This double bind resides within *différance* as 'primordial non-self-presence'.[34] (Maybe this is a hyper non-being, an immanentised negation that becomes 'plenitudinal'.) Derrida speaks of this Plotinian transgression:

> In a perhaps unheard of fashion, *morphe*, *arche*, and *telos* still signal. In a sense, or a non-sense, that metaphysics would have excluded from its field, while nevertheless remaining in secret and incessant relation with this sense, form would in itself already be the trace (*ikhnos*) of a certain nonpresence, the vestige of the un-formed, which announces-recalls its other, as did Plotinus . . . The closure of metaphysics, the closure that the audaciousness of the *Enneads* seems to indicate by transgressing.[35]

For Derrida we must think of '*différance* as temporalization, *différance* as spacing'.[36] It seems that this is another Plotinian trace.[37] It was Plotinus who may have initiated a 'new subjectivity', a new temporality.

This temporality is the audacity of 'subjectivity'. Audacity, as the unquiet faculty of the soul stirs a desire, initiating a progression. The soul *refusing* to see all at once, all as the One, generates an endless alterity, an otherness which is the act of procession away from others (*aie heterotes*).[38] (We find this Plotinianism in Alain Badiou's notion of the 'Two'.)[39] As Plotinus says, 'time begins with the soul-movement'.[40] It is with Plotinus' use of the word *parakolouthesis* that 'a term translatable by "consciousness" appears in philosophy'.[41] Furthermore, the term *synaisthesis hautou*, meaning self-perception in the sense of self-consciousness, also appears for the first time in the Plotinian text. Time is no longer the image of eternity, there is no Cosmic time, or recollection of eternal truths.[42]

Plotinus tells us of this new time: 'So it stirred from its rest and that state too stirred with it; they stirred themselves toward a future that was ceaselessly new, a state not identical with the preceding one but different and ever changing. And after having traversed a portion of the outgoing path they produced time.'[43] Soul moves itself audaciously away into difference; alterity being the principle of procession.[44] Motion measures this 'subjectivity'. What we find is that time is an intensive expression of heteronomy as endless consciousness. This expression pays witness to the silent *provision* of that which is. By this is meant the *provision* of being in the absence of being. Contemplation causes this passage of time as it produces the production of bodies: 'I contemplate and the lines of bodies realise themselves as if they fell from me.'[45] But that which is produced is produced within a 'silent vision'.[46] It is here that we notice the heritage bequeathed to *différance*. *Différance* silently produces language (doing so by silencing language), for it 'goes without saying', like the 'a' of the written *différance*, to 'speak of a letter' which cannot be heard nor apprehended in speech.[47]

Différance is the trace of the Plotinian One, which is non-being. Furthermore, *différance* temporalises and spatialises. It is for this reason that Derrida will announce that 'at this very moment in this work here I am'.[48] In this moment Spinoza and Plotinus are conjoined. *Différance* is 'transcendentally' generating the space for time and the time for space, in terms of a certain 'subjectivisation' of reception. The temporality of time and the spacing of space are found in the 'I am', 'which goes without saying'. 'I am time', a *possession* which is a *procession*, allowing space to measure itself within this endless arrival: to occupy its own space. The space which space occupies is that of an audacious 'work', an *ergetic* generative becoming. (By this term I intend to imply work: Descartes' 'I think therefore I am', is an example of this in so far as the *cogito* must *do* something to be. In this case, the *cogito* must think.) This 'I am' is comparable to the *Deus* of Spinoza's *Ethics*. God is immanentised within the arrival of a 'work', which can be thought of as 'nature'. Nature and God arrive together, each as the other. This divinity is the effect of the trace, just as we saw that the Plotinian (and Avicennian) One requires the finite, arriving only within the finite (as the arrival of the finite). The arrival of the effects, which are always already within the movement of *différance*, belies the differing and the delay of all that does 'come'. God is different and deferred, in that God is an endless act of Nature, while Nature is an eternal God. Consequently, it too remains different and delayed. As with Spinoza, both terms cancel each other out yet, in so doing, an appearance is 'allowed'. This is the nothing *as* something.

Inside: out

To repeat: we know that language desires what it cannot have. Furthermore, the inability to have this external reference causes language to say nothing and this nothing is the Nothing outside Derrida's Text. This being the case, language in saying nothing says its outside; consequently language has an external 'reference'. But such strange possibilities were only achieved by a foundational circumscription, for Derrida had been *beyond* language so as to tell us what was outside it. He returns with bad tidings, for Derrida tells us that there is nothing outside.

Instead of this transgressive demarcation, this sceptical comprehension of language, we must realise that we can never comprehend language (at least we must remain agnostic on the point). For language in being language cannot comprehend itself in terms of its possibilities, plenitude, or lack. Any single linguistic articulation takes language out of its own control. In other words, in speaking I cannot say language, nor can language say itself. Indeed, language could be characterised as the very inability to demarcate an inside or an outside, as it would require a prior language which would not be linguistic (one such as *différance*). In this way language is always, as language, beyond itself; language *qua* language is itself excessive. But this excess does not open language out into more. Instead this is the excess of what is already. (To open it into more, a pure other, would be to isolate language and the other, which would be to lose both.)[49] In this way we understand that difference arises from sameness. (Part II argues that for theology creation arises from the sameness of divine interiority, to the degree that, for Aquinas, creation is not a change. For theology the Word has become flesh; this, it will be argued, lets language escape this philosophical *aporia*.)

Returning to Derrida we can suggest that Derrida does, in an inverted sense, realise that difference comes from sameness. For Derrida allows that language as nothing is *as* something. But this simply means that language is the outside it desires; language is the nothing outside the text. This is the most sophisticated element in the logic of nihilism.

(Part II, Chapter 10 explores this.) For it points to the possibility of language saying without the need for something. If this is the case, nihilism will escape the incarceration that results from the ontotheologians' something, a something which precedes every question. By preceding every question, the something suffocates every existent that falls within its criteria of identification. If nihilism manages to avoid this while still providing meaning, significance and so on, then, theology's doctrine of creation *ex nihilo* is presented with a somewhat legitimate rival. Indeed, creation *ex nihilo* may appear to be be less creative than nihilism because creation *ex nihilo* may still seem to arrive, or fall into, *a space* that remains unquestioned.[50]

For Derrida the nothingness outside the text is the requisite space for the movement of signification. There is a degree of truth in this, but Derrida still operates within a metaphysical system, hence the dualism: Text/Nothing. This metaphysics is what has been referred to as *meontotheology*. It is named thus because Derrida *et al.* recognise the aforementioned *aporia*. As a result they do endeavour to elude, and so escape, ontotheological categories and logics which suppress the need for thought to be supplemented. Otherwise every question asked is only asked by answers. Yet the manner of this escape is *meontotheological*; consequently the problem is merely transposed to another level. Part II examines and explains this *meontotheology*. It is sufficient to say here that such a logic replaces the reductive ossification of the ontotheological something, which has but an infinity of answers or answering, with the *meontotheological* nothing which has but the infinite sameness of an infinite questioning: a perpetual asking that coagulates into silence.

In this way Derrida's questions, like the ontotheologian's, fail to ask anything, for they are predicated on a foundational nothing. We see this when we realise that for Derrida all difference is the *same* difference and for this reason it is indifferent. Derrida's *meontotheology* takes him beyond language, beyond being, beyond the attempt to say something. Instead he resides in the post-linguistic heavens of the One beyond Being. This One provides Derrida's monism that covertly supersedes his dualism of Text and Nothing. The One beyond Being is but one difference, one question asked an infinity of times: Derrida names it *différance*; 'Primordial non-self-presence'.[51] Such monism results in the elimination of every particular, as there is a war of 'all against all'. Because difference is the same difference, the other the same other, every existent is eliminated for the sake of this blank anonymity and in the name of a greater alterity. (See Part II, Chapter 10.) For this reason we can agree with Peter Dews when he makes the point that Derrida 'is offering us a philosophy of *différance* as the absolute'.[52]

Part II of this book presents what is taken to be a theological alternative to nihilism. Chapter 8 offers a preliminary critique of nihilism, one that is heuristically benefical, but less than sufficient. This chapter also begins to construct a theo-logic by employing notions such as analogical language, transcendentals, divine ideas and a doctrine of participation. This theo-logic is developed in Chapter 9 by examining knowledge, arguing that it involves an eschatological realisation of the *beatific vision*. This chapter outlines how theology allows for difference, a possibility that is unavailable to philosophy. Chapter 10 nevertheless re-examines nihilism in an effort to present a positive element implicit in its logic of nothing *as* something. Finally, a Trinitarian theology is presented as the possibility to overcome nihilism, for it manages to elude the dualisms which appear to plague philosophy. In so doing, monism is also avoided, for, as we have already seen, each of these philosophical dualisms collapses into a monism.

Notes

1 Diamond (2000), p. 201.
2 Derrida (1987b), p. 14.
3 Derrida protests at being accused of being a linguistic idealist: 'It is totally false to suggest that deconstruction is a suspension of reference. Deconstruction is always deeply concerned with the "other" of language. I never cease to be surprised by critics who see my work as a declaration that there is nothing beyond language, that we are imprisoned in language; it is, in fact, saying the exact opposite. The critique of logocentrism is above all the search for the "other" and the other of language'; see Kearney (1984), p. 123. The problem with such protestations is that Derrida, under the charge of consistency, cannot recognise such oppositions. Of course, deconstruction does not say we are imprisoned in language for that would be to accept a metaphysical opposition between outside and inside. For Derrida language is not simply linguistic. That is to say, language must be otherwise than linguistic if it is to be beyond metaphysical dualisms. There is certainly something positive in this. I shall develop my disagreement with Derrida below. For an excellent critique of Derrida see Pickstock (1998).
4 Derrida (1987b), p. 12.
5 In Part II, Chapter 9 I make a distinction between knowing and comprehending. What I suggest is that when we come to know something we comprehend it less. Let me give an example: the more one comes to know a lover the less one comprehends the person. In this way do we know God, who is love, in the *beatific* vision. We *know* all of God's essence for God is simple, but we do not *comprehend* that essence.
6 See Derrida (1974), p. 158.
7 Derrida (1987b), p. 6.
8 Derrida (1974), p. 143.
9 Each of these philosophers is discussed here at length, except for Descartes, Schelling and Husserl, each of whom is only mentioned in passing. So let me state briefly that the Nothing to which Derrida is indebted is found in

Descartes' work in the guise of his omnipotent God who allows for hyperbolic doubt; a God inherited, to some degree, from both Scotus and Ockham. Descartes is able to construct the 'text' of the *cogito* because all else is nothing, or can be thought of as nothing. In this way the nothing outside the *cogito* allows for the 'text' of the Cartesian subject. Likewise, Schelling, of *The World of Ages* (especially the second draft), for whom God's word follows after God. In this way God, as absolute freedom, acts as the *Ungrund*, one that is certainly nothing, but a nothing *as* something. Heidegger's *Abgrund* seems almost mild compared to this; for Schelling's use of the phrase 'nothing as something', see Schelling (1994), pp. 114–118. For God as *Ungrund* see Schelling (1997). Husserl's *epoché* suspends the question of being, negating the existential realm. In so doing, the 'Text' of the phenomenal is forthcoming.

10 For Bataille this is the nothing outside the game. It is this nothing which desire pursues. And we know that Derrida is keen to play. See Bataille (1993), pp. 377, 379.

11 See Part II, Chapter 10.

12 This is like an Ockhamian *res absoluta*; see Part I, Chapter 2.

13 Derrida (1974), p. 44.

14 Harland (1991), p. 154.

15 Derrida (1982), p. 65; italics mine.

16 *Ibid.*, p. 173.

17 Derrida (1987b), p. 3.

18 This will become clearer in Part II, Chapter 10.

19 Derrida (1982), p. 22.

20 Derrida (1987b), p. 14.

21 See Part II, Chapter 10.

22 Derrida (1982), p. 11.

23 Derrida (1974), p. 143.

24 *Ibid.*

25 Part II, Chapters 9 and 10, argue that theology can treat being in a manner which is neither ontotheological nor *meontotheological*.

26 As explained in the Preface, the term provision becomes increasingly important in this dissertation. I use it to describe nihilism's *meontotheology* which is without being. The word provides stems from the word *pro*, meaning before, and *videre*, meaning to see. I use the word in relation to nihilism to suggest that nihilism provides before, or without, what is provided. For example, nihilism provides existence before, or without, being. This is the *provenance* of nihilism: to be without being.

27 Derrida (1982), pp. 5, 4.

28 Derrida (1991), p. 47.

29 *Ibid.*, p. 53.

30 Derrida (1988), p. 5.

31 See Derrida (1978), p. 203; (1974), p. 143; (1982), pp. 66–67.

32 Derrida (1962), p. 138.

33 *Enneads*, V, 5, 5.

34 Derrida (1973), p. 81.

35 Derrida (1982), p. 172, fn. 16.

36 *Ibid.*, p. 9.
37 Derrida employs the term trace, in response to Levinas, who, like Plotinus, remained *otherwise than being*; because he could not think being *otherwise* than philosophically, see Levinas (1991); 'The One which every philosophy would like to express is beyond being', (Levinas, 1996), p. 77.
38 This 'endless alterity' reappears in Badiou: see Badiou (2001), p. 25.
39 See Part II, Chapter 10.
40 *Enneads*, III, 7, 13.
41 Alliez (1996), p. 32.
42 *Ibid.*, p. 42.
43 *Enneads*, III, 7, 11. Plotinus finishes this passage with the claim that this making of time still includes *anaionos eikona*, but this, as Alliez (1996) suggests, is to 'mask his iconoclastic audacity', p. 48.
44 Alliez (1996), p. 35.
45 *Enneads*, III, 8, 4.
46 *Ibid.*
47 See Derrida (1982), pp. 3, 5.
48 See Derrida (1991), pp. 403–439.
49 See Part II, Chapter 10.
50 This is an almost Kantian *a priori*. If creation (the something) is pictured, it is imaged within an emptiness which is itself a space that conceptually precedes the creation. Nihilism may well have creation *ex nihilo* in a more radical sense, in so far as creation not only comes from nothing but remains nothing: nothing *as* something. See Part II, Chapter 10.
51 Derrida (1973), p. 81.
52 Dews (1990), p. 24. Dews compares *différance* with Schelling's notion of the absolute.

Part II

THE DIFFERENCE *OF* THEOLOGY

Even I, God, am surprised by hope.
(Charles Péguy)

Only because of the hopeless is hope given to us.
(Walter Benjamin)

8

TO SPEAK, TO DO, TO SEE[1]

Analogy, participation, divine ideas and the idea of beauty

This chapter argues that nihilism is not lack, but, indeed, the extreme *provision* of intelligibility, values, gods, and so on. Yet what it provides is only nothing after all. It may be wise to recall the particular meaning given here to the word provide. Earlier in the book it was mentioned that the word provide stems etymologically from two words: *videre*, meaning to see, and *pro*, meaning before. One can infer from this that the provenance of nihilism is a provision which occurs in the absence of that which is supposed to be given. For example, *to be without being*. (Chapter 10 develops this notion of provision.) This provenance gives its provisions before they are *seen*, that is, in their absence. We see this nothingness in the predicament in which modern discourse finds itself, namely that it cannot speak without causing that about which it is speaking to disappear.[2] By contrast, it will be argued that theological discourse will enable us to say, to do, and to see.

Initially it is argued that nihilism is not possible, but it is conceded that it can be 'a' possibility for someone. Following on from that the form of a theological discourse is outlined. Chapter 9 develops this theological understanding. The last chapter returns to an examination of nihilism in an effort to re-examine its legitimacy, after which I present my final understanding of theology (an understanding that is now, I hope, cognisant of nihilism's sophisticated logic).

The choice: of nihilism

> Nothingness or God . . . The Philosophical Knowledge of the nothing.[3]
>
> (F. H. Jacobi)

John Milbank explicitly argues that nihilism is an intellectual possibility, having successfully exposed the nihilism of a great deal of modern thought. In Milbank's book, *Theology and Social Theory: Beyond Secular Reason*, nihilism is called an 'intellectual stance'.[4] Because Milbank thinks of nihilism as an intellectual stance he refers to the 'possibility of nihilism'.[5] It is the idea that nihilism is possible, that there is a possibility involved in nihilism, or, indeed, that nihilism is a 'possible alternative' (Milbank) which is questionable.[6] This is not to disagree with Milbank's overall thesis, but merely to introduce a certain nuance.

Nihilism is the most 'uncanny of guests' (Nietzsche), so how do we approach it? How does one choose nihilism? These types of question are 'wrongheaded', because if nihilism were the case then it could not be chosen. Indeed, nihilism is the absence of all choice. But this absence comes in the form of a particular 'plenitude'. For nihilism to be 'possible' it must not be a choice, but must be, in a sense, every choice, in that every choice must be available to it. The reason for this is quite simple. Nihilism is typically characterised in terms of 'lack'. Nihilism, it is argued, is a lack of values, a lack of God, substance, horizons, and so on. If this were the case then nihilism would not amount to much. If nihilism were to be found *wanting*, then we could easily surmount an attack, utilising this perceived lack as the basis for such an offensive. This is wholly to miss the point. If nihilism is the case then it does not lack anything, or more accurately, it does not 'lack in lacking'. This conundrum merely points to the obvious fact that nihilism may lack God, but it also lacks this lack of God. Accompanying any radical absence is an absence of absence, and so to attribute a negativity to nihilism is one-sided. This type of accusation articulates its protestation only 'within the sides' of a metaphysical imputation, since it must presume the absence of nihilism so as to be able to accuse it. Such accusation takes the form of deeming nihilism nihilistic, and this, it is argued, need not be the case. Indeed, Chapter 10 suggests that nihilism can be read as promising us something positive.

If we are to speak seriously of nihilism we must, it seems, understand nihilism precisely to be an absence of nihilism: nihilism is not nihilistic. Indeed, it may well be best to characterise nihilism in plenitudinal, rather than negative, terms. If we realise that nihilism can be understood as a negative plenitude – what has been referred to throughout as the nothing *as* something – then we can realise that nihilism will not fail to provide what it is usually supposed to preclude. Nihilism will provide values, gods, and most of all, it seems, intelligibility. Indeed, as we shall see, nihilism generates an excessive intelligibility. If nihilism cannot provide something then it can be found lacking and so a space for a critique arises, precisely because it then appears as a choice, a possibility, an intellectual stance. What we can witness in the *form* of nihilistic discourse (which is in 'reality' the nihilism of discourse, in the sense that it is nothing to discourse), is the constant provision of 'all choices'. Nihilism is not a choice but all choices. It endeavours to be so in an attempt to avoid lack. This is 'possible' because what is provided is nothing *as* something. It must be understood that for nihilism it is nothing to provide *something*, just as being is nothing, or it is nothing to be. This is a sophistication of nihilism which surpasses the usual caricatures. What does it mean to be intelligible, to believe, to speak, to see? Nihilism can provide language, intelligibility and so on in a most refined manner. To observe this we only have to listen to any particular atheistic cosmologist. For such people provide something which would typically be considered to be beyond the preserve of nihilism, but here there is no incongruity. The cosmologist will provide a universe in the absence of creation. How, then, are we to critique nihilism? The answer may lie in rendering nihilism possible, *viz.*, after all a choice, rather than all choices. In being a choice (the etymology of heresy stems from the word for choice, *hairesis*),[7] then it will be *a* reality. In being 'a' reality it will be but a reactive discourse which is better referred to as 'sin'. After the initial critique offered here, Chapter 10 will re-examine nihilism, arguing that it can mount a challenge to the negative reading of its logic offered in this chapter. I proceed in this manner so as to develop an initial understanding of nihilism and theology, both of which will be forced by the sophistication of the other to develop further. Before a critique of nihilism is attempted, let us examine the *form* of nihilism, if it is possible to speak of such a thing.

The form of nihilism

In the wake of the axis fashioned, however unconsciously, by Henry of Ghent, Scotus and Ockham, that which exists was taken outside the divine essence. Consequently, that which was expelled became nothing, a nothing that allowed the invention of *a priori* realms, and tales of things called logical possibilities (a Scotist fantasy). It also generated a virulent synchronic contingency that led to a de-existentialised existence, as it became first essentialised, and then factualised. This in turn facilitated a methodological *lateralisation*, as non-existence settled alongside existence. What we find is that this expulsion of that which exists outside the divine essence permitted the emptying of existence of any inherent or, in a sense, 'natural' theology.

The *lateralisation* referred to renders being existentially neutral. This is indeed the advent of a given. It is a given that will soon fully immanentise itself, ignoring any pietist-voluntarist veto. In a sense it was the voluntarism of the late middle ages that conceived God's power in such a manner that creation became so little. But it is the reduction of creation, under the subjection of divine *fiat*, that in an inverted sense allows creation a residual independence. Creation is *so little* that it escapes all relations with divinity.[8] Such a strange consequence is reflected in the development of logical possibilities independent of God's essence. A veneration of the *a priori* follows. The nothingness of creation, which is a reflection of divine omnipotence, eludes a need for causality because *it is nothing*. Logical possibilities are in a sense this emptiness turned back onto, and into, itself until an immanent plenitude is composed. Aprioricity is an expression of this immanent realisation. There is now no place left for transcendence to occur (except as a private belief which is completely immanentisable). We 'moderns' continually betray the operation of a given within our discourse. It is this given which re-enacts the logic of the fall: to have a-part of the world apart from God. This given expands to include all creation and here lies the foundation for the development of a negative plenitude which issues from the sides of this virulent immanence. What this immanence effects, in its very self articulation, is an absence of immanence, in the sense that all particularity will suffer erasure, as it is made to *disappear*, or *vanish* (as we saw with both Kant and Hegel). *Any* description that modern discourse proffers will enact such a disappearance. Let us see why.

An example may help. If we describe a leaf, looking to modern discourse to provide such a description, we will see nothing. We will see nothing but the disappearance of the leaf as, and at, the utterance of every 'word'. The leaf will always be subordinated to structures and sub-structures.[9] The leaf will never be seen or said. Any apparent sightings will be but nominal–noumenal formalities, that is, epiphenomenal results of concepts or ideas. (Here we witness a line running from Scotus to Descartes and from Descartes to Kant, no doubt with significant differences remaining.) The leaf is carried away through its discursive subordination to the structures and sub-structures of systems of explanatory description. By explanatory description is meant that a particular entity will be explained away by the descriptions its being suffers, for it will be reduced to a list of predicates, properties and so on. The inherently excessive nature of a being will be ignored. Chapter 10 discusses this excess.)[10]

Any difference we find in a being, or in the leaf, will fail to register, except at the virtual level of data. To seek to describe this leaf, of course, involves a somewhat arbitrary selection and separation. Why this leaf, why a leaf, and why stop or begin at a leaf? We must decide, somewhat arbitrarily, to separate a leaf from a branch, a branch from a tree, and a tree from all existent materiality. We will see that the nihilistic form of modern discourse will be unable to provide criteria for this selection and will be unable to provide real difference, individuation, specificity and so on. There can, it seems, only be a *Heraclitean stasis* which merely registers arbitrary expressions of its unitary–plurality (whole–parts). The leaf, which is there, is not a real leaf, but simply a formal distinction, arbitrarily but successfully constructed, or, more accurately, generated by systems of explanatory description. (These can be formal, conceptual, idealistic, empirical, yet they all tend to be diacritical. By this is meant that all difference is nominal, ontologically speaking.) René Guénon argues that finitude is indefinite, a consequence of which is that it remains susceptible to perpetual multiplicity. For the indefinite is analytically inexhaustible, and according to Guénon Hell is the passage of this division.[11] Indeed Hell can be thought of as a bad infinite, one which is 'otherworldly', offering a false asceticism, because the object of every desire disappears into the infinite night of this multiplicity. In this way desire is forbidden 'intercourse'. And Hell is the black night of this dissolution; the very loss of the immanent under the reign of quantity.[12]

What would the opposite look like? It would look like the immanent – a leaf; an appearance that could not be subordinated to knowledge systems, for its visibility would be anchored in the Divine essence as an imitable example of that transcendent plenitude. It would be an imitability located in the Son, as *Logos*. We could then speak of cells, molecules, and so on. In nihilistic discourse even the cells of a leaf are further reduced, methodologically, *ad infinitum (ad nauseum)*. This is the place of Heaven – a place which is one of this world, of the immanent. For only through the mediation of immanence by transcendence can the immanent *be*.

The form of this discourse of epistemic disappearance is analogous to the internal–external infinitude of a Spinozistic attribute. Every description literally takes the place of that which it describes; reducing it to nothing, except the formal difference of an epistemic signification. This is also analogous to the nothing which resides outside Derrida's text – a nothingness which comes within the text in the form of the effected disappearance.[13] The intelligibility, the signification, rests on this internal–external nothingness.[14]

The aforementioned leaf is carried away by the wind of systemic description. As a result we will have nothing *as* something. It is possible to argue that systemic erasure is the basis of modern knowledge – in all its postmodern guises. The truth of this argument will not really become apparent until Chapter 10. For the moment let us tentatively, yet somewhat insufficiently, endeavour to develop an understanding of this disappearance; a disappearance referred to as a 'holocaust', because every being which falls under such description is lost, and every trace erased.[15] Such a term is not completely satisfactory but it does help to some degree in expressing the idea being developed in this chapter. (Chapter 10 argues that the argument presented here is not wholly fair, and that the situation may actually be somewhat more complicated.)

Those who are made to disappear

What we may begin to realise is that the *form* of nihilism's discourse is complicit with a certain 'holocaust'. It will speak a 'holocaust'. But how can one speak a holocaust?[16] We do so if when we speak, something (or someone) disappears, or if our speech is predicated only on the back of such an erasure. We have to think of those who are 'too many to have disappeared'. They must have been made to disappear; we may be able to discern three noticeable *moments* in modern discourse which encourage the speaking of a 'holocaust'.[17]

The first moment is when the systemic description effects a disappearance. This is accomplished by placing what is described outside the divine mind, rendering it ontologically neutral – a given rather than a gift. The notion of a given allows for the invention of such neutrality. That which 'is' becomes structurally amenable to experimentation, dissection, indefinite epistemic investigation.[18] For the first time there is something which can render the idea of detached, de-eroticised, study intelligible. There is now an *object* which is itself neutral, the structural prerequisite for 'objectivity'. This 'holocaust' is the *a priori* of modern knowledge. The second moment comes when modern discourse describes the initial disappearance, the first moment. Consequently, the first moment, the event of disappearance, disappears. Modernity will ask us 'what can it mean to disappear'? Any 'hole' is filled up, every trace erased.[19]

More obviously, but with greater caution and difficulty, we see modern discourse describe the disappearance of a 'number-too-great' to disappear, in terms that are completely neutral. It is unable to describe this *dia-bolic* (meaning to take apart) event in a way that is different from its description of the aforementioned leaf.[20] The loss of countless lives can only be described in neutral terms, however emotionally.[21] But discourse is predicated on a nothing to which every entity is reduced.[22] (For example, a human is reduced to its genes, while consciousness is reduced to chemicals, atoms and so on.)

Our knowledge of a 'holocaust' causes that 'holocaust' to disappear (like leaves from a tree in a garden fire: *kaustos*). We see the disappearance of a 'holocaust' as it is erased by its passage through the corridors of modern description: sociology, psychology, biology, chemistry, physics, and so on. All these discourses speak its disappearance.[23] 'Holocaust', ice-cream, there can be no difference except that of epistemic difference, which is but formal. Both must be reducible to nothing; the very possibility of modern discourse hangs on it. In this sense all 'holocausts' are modern. The structures, sub-structures, molecules and the molecular all carry away the 'substance' of every being and of the whole (*holos*) of being.

The third moment comes upon the first two. We see modernity cause all that is described to disappear, then we see this disappearance disappear.[24] In this way a loss of life, and a loss of death is witnessed. It is here that we see the last moment. If we think of a specific holocaust, the historical loss of six million Jews during the Second World War, we see that the National Socialist description of the Jews took away their lives and took away their deaths. For those who were killed were exterminated, liquidated, in the name of *solutions*. The Jews lose their lives because they have already lost their deaths.[25] For it is this loss of death that allows the Nazis to 'remove' the Jews. That is to say, if the Jews lose their deaths then the Nazis, by taking their lives, do not murder. This knowledge, that is National Socialism, will, in taking away life, take away the possibility of losing that life (death becomes wholly naturalised). This must be the case so that there is no loss in terms of negation. In this way National Socialism emulates the 'form' of nihilistic discourse. There is nothing and not even that. There is an absence and an absence from absence. (This *is* the form Nietzsche's joyous nihilism took.) So we will not have a lack which could allow the imputation of metaphysical significance:

> The mass and majesty of this world, all
> That carries weight and always weighs the same
> Lay in the hands of others; they were small
> And could not hope for help and no help came:
> What their foes liked to do was done, their shame
> Was all the worst could wish; they lost their pride
> *And died as men before their bodies died.*[26]
> W. H. Auden, 'The Shield of Achilles'

The life that is lost is always lost before its death. They who lose their life are already lost in terms of epistemic description. When their life is 'physically' lost it is unable to stop the disappearance of that life, and the death of that life. So the living-dead are always unable to die; death is taken away from them before their life, in order that their life can be made to disappear without trace and without 'loss'. Thus, the living are described in the same manner as the dead. Modern discourse cannot, it seems, discriminate between them. In some sense, it takes a loss of life and a loss of death to engender 'holocaust'. For it is this which forbids the registration of any significance – any significant difference between life and death. 'Modern' description has no ability to speak differently about lost lives, because before any physical event 'dissolution' has already begun to occur (all that remains is for the bodies to be swept away). The preparation is carefully carried out so that a 'nonoccurrence' can occur.

The fundamental, and foundational neutrality in modern discourse is here extremely noticeable. Its inability to speak significantly, to speak 'real' difference, carries all peoples and persons away. In 'modern' death there are no people, no one dies. Here we see the de-differentiating effect of nihilism. Bodies come apart as different discourses carry limbs away. This cool epistemic intelligibility of a Dionysian frenzy fashions whole systems of explanatory description.

In order to give an example of nihilism's ontological myopia, let us think of nihilistic eyes gazing across a piece of land; this land upon which nihilism gazes is full of shapes, pointed configurations, odours, ratios, proportions, smells, noises and so on. Modern discourse, I suggest, cannot see or say death.[27] For it cannot see pits full of bodies and twisted limbs, as there can be no loss, there being only an immanent 'plenitude'. As Adolf Portmann says, 'For pre-modern thought, death was the great puzzle of human existence; for us, today, life is the great puzzle.'[28] Witness the descriptions offered by biology, chemistry, sociology, physics and so on. They provide only formal distinctions, or differences, *à la* Scotus. These all must have *a loss of loss* just to function. The immanent reductionism of their nihilistic 'form', the 'hole' with which they fill the world, cannot but cause difference to disappear. For example, when biology comes to describe what lies before it, there will not be any *visibility*. As one commentator puts it, we are but 'meat puppets run by molecular machines [which is] the transformation of the organism into an effect of *a univocal language of life*, an *Esperanto* of the molecule'.[29] This is what Colin McGinn calls 'meatism'.[30] Indeed, as one Nobel prize winning biologist argues: 'Biologists no longer study life today [because] biology has demonstrated that there is no metaphysical entity behind the word life.'[31] Everything remains unseen and, in this sense, unsaid; for what difference is there, biologically speaking, between an organism that is biologically now in one way and now in another? The system of explanatory description will offer only nominal or diacritical difference because its immanent identity relies on this inability. As Doyle argues, such discourse is predicated on the ability to say 'that is all there is'.[32] For as Guénon declares: 'The modern mentality is made up in such a way that it cannot bear any secret nor even any reserve . . . [This is] the suppression of all mystery.'[33] (This mystery is analogous to Péguy's *mystique*.)[34] Likewise, as Foucault says: 'Western man could constitute himself within his language, and gave himself, in himself and by himself, a discursive existence, only in the opening created by his own elimination.'[35] Indeed, *life*, according to Foucault, 'is a sovereign vanishing point within the organism'.[36] For this reason Smith argues that physicalism should adopt the ontology of nihilism: 'True, a physicalist ontology is ontologically simple; but it is another question as to whether it is ontologically adequate. The ontology of the ontological nihilist is even more economical: nothing exists at all. If considerations of solely ontological economy dictate our world making, then the physicalists are recommended to become ontological nihilists.'[37] (Chapter 10 returns to a discussion of biology.)

These discourses depend upon a descriptive reduction that perpetuates a structural plane of immanence, which is but an identical repetition of *the same*. Biology *must* reduce that which it describes to nothing, that is, nothing outside its descriptive abilities (DNA, etc.). This is the 'text' which biology is, and this text has nothing outside it (recalling Derrida's aphorism).[38] Indeed, George Gamow, who heavily influenced Francis Crick, describes DNA protein as a 'translation'.[39] The Word has not become flesh, rather flesh has become 'words' (in an almost Hegelian manner). When biology studies life (*bios*), it does so on the axiomatic assumption that life does not exist. Affirming life would require a meta-level as it displays an excessive moment that breaks free of immanent description, *yet validates the immanent*. Biology can neither afford nor provide such a meta-level. All modern discourse, it seems, reduces that which is described to the description and its particular 'mode' (these modes are somewhat akin to Scotistic intrinsic modes which differentiate univocal being, without themselves having to be). This is the extreme erasure that has already been mentioned.

Each discourse appears to conjure up intelligibility within the nothing upon which they are predicated – returning only ever to themselves. That which is described therefore becomes only the internal logic or intelligibility of that discourse (an intrinsic mode, so to speak). The difference between that which describes and that which is described collapses, for only in this way can nihilism occupy every place and everything. As it speaks, as intelligibility is gained, the nothingness that surrounds and perpetuates this signification draws it always back to a double disappearance; a nothingness which is always *within* every description. Biology cannot *see* the loss of life. Death is never seen, again no one dies. This is to re-enact a 'holocaust'. Here in this modern world nothing happens, nothing is or is not. The 'cancer' of my body is a world unto itself. My leg becomes apart from me, it grows as it re-narrates my body, in a manner of which Kafka would be proud. Our bodies come apart as knowledge rips them asunder, even though it may keep them intact. Our very being is carted away, to live and breathe as 'humus' would. (Chapter 10 argues that the living are treated as cadavers.)

The instructive reductionism articulated above displays the 'form' of nihilistic discourse. This form is to some degree the inheritor of a legacy which has been outlined in earlier chapters: Plotinus' *meontotheological* constitution of finitude; Avicenna's necessitarianism; Ghent's Avicennian essences, and analogy of the concept, which, following Avicenna, places '*res*' as the highest transcendental name; Scotist plurality of forms, and

177

intrinsic modes with their univocity of being; Ockhamian cognitions that appear only within the sides of supposition, and the logical function, or performance, of propositional terms; the intensional modality of the Ockhamian-Scotist-Ghentian-Avicennian axis, with its 'extended' world of logical possibilities; the external–internal infinitude of Spinozistic attributes; the Kantian subject-object, and noumenal–nominality, which causes all phenomenality to disappear in its very appearance;[40] the Hegelian absolute that is a site of a perpetual vanishing, and an ending of discourse; the Heideggerian *show* of Being and Time as an external–internal nothingness, that is but Death; Derrida's economy of *différance*.

The rest of this chapter offers a preliminary critique of nihilism before going on to articulate a theological approach that appears to speak otherwise than nihilistically.

Approaching nihilism[41]

How are we then to approach nihilism? We can approach it on two counts; the latter resting within the internal consistency of the former. First of all, we know nihilism must be able to *provide* what non-nihilistic discourse can.[42] To accomplish this all that *is* must be nothing, but nothing *as* something. This is the diabolic infinite plenitude of nihilism. As we saw above, some accuse nihilism of being a lack of values and so on, but this does not succeed in saying anything significant; since nihilism removes the negative aspect of a perceived lack. In this way, nihilism does not exclude the generation of values; moralities pay witness to this. Indeed, Nietzsche's nihilism called for values so as to overcome nihilism. Nietzsche's nihilism was an endeavour not to be nihilistic, so we cannot accuse nihilism from the outset of failing to provide x or y, but what we can do is render it 'a' choice, a possibility. If this can be achieved, then, nihilism may be merely an intellectual stance, one which may be reactive.

If nihilism is to allow everything, and forbid nothing, then it must not have a particular 'form' that excludes this or that (we saw this in Hegel's positive nihilism). If nihilism is found to have a certain form it becomes identifiable, for it will display certain characteristics. These will force it to become more solid and particular. In this way it will become a choice, but if nihilism is a choice, or a stance, then to make this choice, or to take this stance, is to be somewhat reactive. It is reactive because the reasons for such *a* choice will be shaped by other choices and so on. One can endeavour to render nihilism a choice by comparing it with the circularity of certain forms of discourse, for example faith, in that faith is a mode of speaking with certain grammatical rules, displaying a particular form of discourse. What the structure of such discourse provides is an *irreducible assertion*.[43] For example, if we say 'something', nihilism will cause this to disappear. But if we say something *is*, then a transcendental circularity will resist, if not disable, reduction.[44] For an excess will be brought to the fore. This excess will both enable and elude descriptions, forcing every description to remain agnostic about its own success. This circularity will take all creation within its positive plenitude, and so re-present everything which *is*, as something irreducible.[45]

Of course the immediate appeal by nihilism will be that this is another example of metaphysical imputation, merely circular. This does not matter though, if the imputation is consistent. The problem is that nihilistic discourse cannot effect a disappearance upon the transcendental circularity of being and faith; this does not mean that faith is correct, so to speak, but simply that it manages to attain a moment of difference, by circular means.[46] But the consequences of such an 'event' is to leave nihilism as *a* possibility and a choice, and so it is no longer nihilism. This being the case nihilism would now *be* nihilistic, which would mean that nihilism is for this perspective (and even in a sense objectively) but a heresy, that may only be reactively constituted; this would cause it to remain a parasitic discourse, full of metaphysical complicity. The nihilist, in this sense, will need to borrow 'faith' in order *to be*. Nihilism could argue that faith is imputing its significance and constructing its circularity, but this will be a position of faith on its own part. It will then be a 'this' not a 'that', a 'here' not a 'there' (this echoes the problems that faced Hegel). So John Milbank is correct to say that nihilism is 'a' possibility. The depth of this 'possibility' is examined in Chapter 10.

To speak, to do, to see

> All knowers know God implicitly in all they know.[47]
> (Aquinas)

> God is at the centre of what I think and of what I do . . . to
> go from myself to myself, I pass through Him constantly.[48]
> (Maurice Blondel)

This section examines analogical language, causation, and participation, in an effort to present a theological manner of speaking that is otherwise than nihilistic; one which understands the need for mediated transcendence. More generally this section argues that it is not possible to speak, do, or see without appealing to transcendence. To some degree, we have already paid witness to the disappearance of all within the articulations of modern discourse, but discourse need not deliberately cause something to disappear to be complicit with nihilism.

For example, if we were to ask someone what they saw in seeing a tree, they would reply in a most obvious manner. Yet the same person may fail to appeal explicitly to transcendence. The problem with this is that they are not aware of the implicit appeal already employed, just to be able to see or speak of the tree. It is the obviousness of the phenomenal world that seems to encourage us to presume its actuality and consequent availability,[49] but let us ask how anyone can see a tree unless transcendence is appealed to? Any person who says 'I see a tree', or 'I said', or 'I did' such and such, presumes the actuality, and more importantly the significance of such entities or events. On each occasion we presume that we see, say and do *something*. This something is not another thing besides that which we have cognised, for that would induce an infinite regress. Instead, the something about which we speak each time is that of *significance* or meaning. (By meaning, I do not imply an epistemic concern, for this is a metaphysical matter.) To see a tree we must see something, but what does it take to see something in seeing a tree (and so see a tree)? The answer is an *eidos*, a form that is 'meaning'. This may seem abstruse, if not otiose, but it is of paramount importance. Without the recognition of this requisite significance then the tree, like the aforementioned leaf, may well disappear within the flurry of our words and perceptions. To see a tree requires a *significance,* an *eidos,* so that it can be cognised, but in so being it cannot become merely data or a given. The *significance* required to see a tree, and seen in seeing a tree, is infinite. It takes an infinitude of delicate *significance* to enable the presentation of the tree, while it takes an infinity of transcendent significance to preserve the tree in that cognition, to make it something irreducible, something which requires an eternity to be fully known. (See Chapter 9.) This tree is temporal in being corporeal, but this apparent limitation implicates eternity itself, because the tree endures, in other words, it takes time. (See Chapter 10.) In so doing, we must refrain from carrying the tree away in the guise of information, for the time of the tree demands time, if we are to 'know' it; its significance, though finite, is implicated in the tree's infinite links through time and space, with their indefinite extension and infinite divisibility. Furthermore, in each passing moment the tree demands a cognition that can know its infinite ways, in being *this* tree: its shades, contours, textures, leaves, branches, molecule and sub-molecule, roots and soil hidden; all recapitulated within the temporal form of its dynamic repose, that is, its being.

How then can we say, do, or see? Maybe in this way only God sees, knows, does, and we, by way of analogous participation, receive the gifts of knowing in part. Theological discourse will involve us in the plenitude of the object.[50] We will see how theology can be considered a pedagogy of perception, cognition, and utterance. For there are ways in which theology teaches us to speak that will allow us to better consider the *aporia* of actuality and its temporal infinitude

Analogically: speaking

Aquinas offers no theory of analogy.[51]
(D. Burrell)

It is traditional, at least in Thomist circles, to pit analogy against univocity. This is not something with which to disagree, but in Chapter 10 it is argued that univocity appears to embody the 'spirit' of analogy, while analogy runs the risk of generating a peculiar form of univocity. This section will confine itself to a discussion along traditional lines; such confinement is not meant to suggest that this approach is unwise.

Analogy has received much attention within Thomist circles.[52] Theologians have often endeavoured to make analogy a mode of speaking that is veridical, a manner of speaking that allows the creature to speak of the Creator. Analogy was supposed to enable such a feat because there were mechanisms involved in its construction, and articulations, that took into consideration the Creator's transcendence. There are many things wrong with such an understanding of analogy, which I do not have the space to explore; suffice it to say that such a doctrine of analogy is rather exsanguinate. That is, it is disengaged from its proper environment, its interpretive community. Consequently, analogy is approached with only epistemic concerns in mind, and these concerns have little, if anything, to do with the place of analogy within theological discourse. The main problem is the notion of a neutral epistemic 'situation', which is meant to provide 'knowledge' about God. In terms of theology, analogy is part of a metaphysical doctrine, and so it is cosmological, rather than epistemological, and only as such can we appreciate its position and function; a function which is also more pedagogical than epistemological.

The main target for contemporary theologians who are endeavouring to understand what Aquinas had to say about analogy is Thomas de Vio, otherwise known as Cardinal Cajetan. Cajetan's short work *De nominum analogia* was for centuries taken to be the true Thomistic understanding of analogy,[53] but this, it is argued, is far from the case.[54] Cajetan concentrates his reading of Aquinas on a passage from his commentary on Peter Lombard's *Sentences*.[55] This passage spells out three types of name: a name according to intention (or reference), which, for Cajetan, becomes an analogy of attribution; an analogical name that is according to being and not reference, which Cajetan baptises the analogy of inequality; finally the name that according to being and reference, and for Cajetan this is the analogy of proportionality. This last type is the only correct analogous name; consequently, Cajetan takes it as his bench mark. What Cajetan seems to do is to take Aquinas' words *'aliquid dicitur secundum analogiam tripliciter'* a little too literally. As McInerny says, Aquinas 'is not providing us with a threefold division of analogous names'.[56] An obvious reason why Aquinas is not doing this is that the first and the second member of the division are not analogical at all. Hence it can hardly be supposed to be a definitive list of analogous names. Accordingly Cajetan places a 'straitjacket' on the Thomist understanding of analogy, a 'straitjacket' that leads to an *analogy of the concept* instead of an *analogy of judgement*. As Bouillard suggests, if we were to present Cajetan with the proposition *'conceptus entis est univocis'*, Cajetan would reformulate it as *'conceptus entis est analogus'*.[57] Instead, analogy is to operate at the level of judgement, because being itself is analogical, as it is created by a transcendent God who is *ipsum esse* and gives to created being this ungivable gift of himself, so ensuring that every *ens* is like him as unlike, unlike as like.[58] Analogy is therefore itself analogical as it seeks by likeness and unlikeness to trace this situation.

At the heart of analogy lie causality and participation. The latter expresses the former in a particular and telling manner. Indeed, participation, causality, and analogy are, in a sense, a dynamic trialectic which keeps our understanding of each in check, helping us to understand as creatures should.[59] There are three main texts which base analogy on causality, and I will consider one here.[60] In the *Summa Theologiae*, Aquinas first of all considers univocal causality as allowing for univocal predication (*synonymy*). He argues that a univocal understanding would be impossible because such a predication would require that God causes an effect that is the same as *He* is, and this would entail creatures possessing perfections without composition. Second, Aquinas suggests that equivocal predication (*homonymy*) would not be adequate as we would know nothing of God – even that we do not know. It is then that Aquinas suggests analogy, meaning proportion. God is spoken of in neither a univocal nor a purely equivocal sense; instead analogical predication is employed. The reason for this is that God, understood as transcendent Creator, is cause and principle of creation. This is an order of cause and caused; *ordo causae et causati*, and if God is cause of the world then the cause communicates something of its likeness to the effect. It does not do this univocally because that would infringe transcendence, nor is it done in a purely equivocal manner, for that would imply that God created in a manner unsuitable for an agent. It is axiomatic for Aquinas, following Dionysus, that *omne agens agit sibi simile*.[61] God creates by his intellect as well as his nature: *ars agens per artem; agens per naturam*; for this reason the Neoplatonic principle of one effect resulting from God is mistaken, because it is based purely on the latter aspect of divine creation. As God creates using intellect it is appropriate to refer to God as *agens analogicam*.[62] If causation were purely equivocal then the notion of causation could easily become univocal, in an inverted sense. It must be understood that the notion of cause itself is analogical, because there would be no such thing as cause unless there were an ontological difference, for what would it mean for one thing to cause another? We see this *aporia* even at the ontic level of natural causation: for example, fire causing heat; it is possible to argue that transcendence is required to render such a notion intelligible.[63] Causation at all levels is dependent on analogical causality, or on causality being analogical. Only this permits actual intelligent causation, in other words, effective communication. It is this which provides natural causality with a realm within which to do, or be, what it is; this is why Aquinas calls God both cause and principle. It could be thought that we can prove God's existence by proving that God is a first cause, but this is somewhat mistaken. For what such an idea entails is a certain univocity, or at least onticity, for God would be contained by the ontic logic of such an idea. This can be understood if it is realised that being first, in terms of cause, still leaves God within a series which in a sense He shares with man (as is the case with the God we find in Plotinus, Avicenna, Scotus, Spinoza, Kant and Hegel). If man were to prove the existence of this first cause, all man would find is himself (see Chapter 10). In this regard Feuerbach is correct, for if we reeled in the line (which is the shared series), we would find the hook stuck in our own hands, so to speak: Hamann may have meant something similar when he spoke of 'the unbelief of theism';[64] which would here be called ontotheology. For this reason Aquinas appeals also to the Good as the cause of causation, which is to invoke God as both cause *and* principle of creation.

This helps to ensure that causality remains analogical, as it is essentially linked to intellect. Therefore it must be remembered that divine causality is the intelligible birth of all forms of causality; for this reason analogical causality means causality *par excellence*, as it is intentional and intelligent, which means that effects are best considered as examples of art, both deliberate and particular. If causality depends on the analogical causation of art and nature, then effects must communicate to us knowledge of God. It is said that an effect participates in its cause if it is less than the cause, that is, if it is not equal to the power, or inferior to the efficacy, of the cause.[65] As Aquinas says: 'The form of an effect exists in a certain way in the higher cause but in a different mode and with a different nature.'[66] In terms of effective communication Aquinas also considers this to be analogical. As a result, he argues that there are a number of different types of communication akin to causality: perfect communication, which communicates in the same form, by the same formality and mode (e.g., two things equally white); a less than perfect communication, which is the same as before except that it is of a different mode, that is, measure; and the communication offered by a non-univocal agent, which is the same form, but according to a different formality. Every agent acts within its form, hence it must, in causing, communicate some of this form to that which it causes; this can be within a species (man causing man), or by genus (sun causing heat). Yet God is beyond genus and species, so we, as effects of a causation that causes according to its form, participate in a certain likeness, but only analogically.[67] Analogy is here indicating the peculiar nature of creation, a peculiarity arising from the fact that the recipient receives itself in the reception – including its form, matter, and being. Analogy here requires creation, which implies intelligence, and the utter dependence of participation. The distance attested to by the phrase 'some sort of analogy' does, in this instance, bring an ultimate intimacy; in other words, we only *are* as we participate in God. Hence being is analogical, there being no analogy 'of being'. The latter will always presume at least one ontic term; for this reason Burrell and his colleagues are right to insist that analogy is itself analogical.[68]

Generally we can think of Aquinas' approach to analogy in terms of proportion, in a broad sense, as a relation of 'many to one' (*unum alterum*), and one to another, or two to one of them (*unum ipsorum*). The latter modes are applicable to theology as a discourse since it indicates derivation, while the first would fail to signify transcendence, since it does not. The *unum ipsorum* mode of proportion is the same as being by participation, and being by essence. An example of 'one to another' would be how being is said of substance and accident; accident refers to substance, consequently when being is said of both the being is referred to substance, accidents only having being by reference to substance. There is, nonetheless, a problem here, because in the realm of the creature, being can be said in terms of priority for substance, as it is known, and in nature. Theological analogy does not have this happy coincidence, for the creature can only know God by first knowing the effects of God. This means that the *ratio* of the name belongs to God, but is arrived at gnoseologically after the creature by posteriority. Perfections are first known of the creature, even though they ontologically belong properly to God. It is here that the distinction between the mode of signification and the thing signified can be employed.[69]

As has already been said, for Cajetan there is only one notion of analogical naming that deserves that appellation, and that is an analogy of proper proportionality. It is interesting to note briefly that Aquinas defines univocal predication in a manner almost identical with that of Cajetan's understanding of analogical naming: 'When something is predicated univocally of many it is found in each of them according to its proper *ratio* . . . but when something is said analogically of many it is found according to its proper notion in one of them alone, from which the others are denominated.'[70] McInerny, commentating on Cajetan's version of analogical naming, and bearing this text in mind, argues that Cajetan ends up with an analogical predication that is for Aquinas univocal.[71] A consequence of this is an analogy of a concept, rather than an analogy of judgement. The former is found, to some degree, in Henry of Ghent, Duns Scotus and Suarez. Furthermore, it is not impossible to trace Karl Barth's understanding of analogy from this version of analogical predication, especially when this is coupled with his almost explicit Kantian understanding of knowledge. As Chavannes argues, knowledge for Barth involves a grasping of the known by the knower. This Kantian idealism is not too distant from the univocal functioning of concepts which we witness in Cajetan, Ghent, Scotus and also Suarez. Such an understanding is found in Suarez because he alters the understanding of Aquinas' real distinction.[72] There is not the space to discuss this except to suggest that there does seem to be a legacy passed down which involves the hegemony of the concept. As a result Barth, like Levinas with regard to being, is unable to think knowledge *otherwise* than philosophically (ontotheologically), and consequently his thinking was forced to remain *otherwise* than knowledgeable.[73]

For us, what is important is to realise that analogy rests on causality, and causality, as a concept, already requires a notion of creation. For this reason it seems apt for Ross to refer to analogical use as 'craftbound'; in other words, something which modulates life or activity.[74] McInerny, on the other hand, goes so far as to suggest that analogy is not metaphysical but merely a logical concern.[75] This seems to be correct if what we mean by metaphysics is really epistemology, but this would require a Kantian view of metaphysics. As we shall further see below, it may be preferable to understand analogy as an expression of the metaphysical doctrine of participation – a modulated and modulating recognition of divine causality. Participation prevents the provision of a purely ontic and so univocal understanding of causality. As Fabro says, 'the Thomistic notion of participation founded in *esse* as supreme intensive act makes it possible to pass from finite to infinite being through analogical discourse, which has in participation its beginning, middle, and conclusion'.[76] Likewise Paul Ricoeur asserts that 'it is creative causality . . . that establishes between beings and God the bond of participation that makes the relation by analogy ontologically possible'.[77] In a similar fashion Pierre Rousselot spoke of analogical participation in God,[78] while W. N. Clarke speaks of an analogy of causal participation.[79] Participation suggests the efficient causality of being, along with the intimacy of intelligent, or artistic, creation. If there is no idea of causality, or of being, outside of God, then a purely ontic logic is avoided. This again opens up the analogical relationships of cause and caused with an effective communication of form, but not *in* form. Indeed, Aertsen makes the point that participation excludes the possibility of predicating 'being' univocally of God and creature.[80] As Aquinas says, 'God alone is subsistent being . . . therefore nothing is predicated univocally'.[81] What is it that participation brings out that reinforces, or enriches our understanding of God as subsistent Being? It seems that participation keeps 'being' analogical, just as it renders causality analogical.[82] Cause is imaged in terms of 'A' causing 'B', but with participation we understand the utter given-ness involved in causation, because God is as 'Goodness', the cause of cause. This draws to our attention the presumed, or unaccounted for space within which 'B' occurs; hence we can fully image only an ontic causality, for we have presumed causality. (See Chapter 10.)[83]

For Aquinas, participation implies the real distinction of *esse* from *essentia*, because this allows a participation in God's goodness, which is *His* being, a participation that allows the creature to possess this intrinsically.[84] The convertibility of being and goodness bids us to remember the analogical nature of causality; a nature that precludes causality being measured, or understood, in quantitative terms. In other words, the way something is caused coincides with its nature, its power, and this defines that which is actually produced. Aquinas argues that 'the quantity of power of a cause is measured not only according to what is made but also according to the mode of production'.[85] This qualification disables a univocal, or equivocal, understanding of being, just as it will prohibit occasionalism. Aquinas says that 'while granting being God simultaneously produces that which receives being; and so it is not necessary that he acts on the basis of something pre-existing'.[86] In so doing, God does not deny secondary causality, because although God may not depend on anything pre-existing, that which is created is created in such a manner that it has a certain causal integrity: 'The first cause grants from the eminence of its goodness not only to things that they are, but also that they be causes.'[87] The nature of causality is such that it is not flat or univocal, but varied and specific; God causes natures with their own powers and so on. Indeed, as Chavannes says, 'every perfection we attribute to the secondary causes increases the glory of the Creator, the first cause, and gives us an occasion of glorifying him'.[88] This ontological, or causal, integrity afforded creation is a communication of the divine source: a communication which manifests itself in the possible analogy between divine subsistence and creaturely subsistence, for we are determinate beings with our own act of to-be, and so resemble our Creator.

This relationship does not infringe transcendence, instead it forces us constantly to consider causality in analogical terms. Therefore the intimacy of analogical similitude, at the level of secondary causality, precludes both univocal and equivocal notions of causality. Instead we are, in effect, left thinking of causality more in terms of artistic intention. This does afford us a greater knowledge of causality, but we are left comprehending it less – since efficient causation cannot now be simply imagined in terms of power, for it is conjoined with finality, the more ultimate reason for causation. An efficient cause is only efficient in so far as it is towards an end, and for this reason the good also is a cause of causation.[89] Like Dionysus, Aquinas affords a certain primacy to the good,[90] a primacy that 'lies in the teleological order'.[91] It is this teleological order that causes cause, although in the ultimate theoretical order which complements the ultimate practical order, being has primacy. As Aquinas says, 'every excellence in anything belongs to it according to its being. For a human person would have no excellence as a result of his wisdom unless through it he were wise.'[92] Yet God causes out of goodness, because of an end, an intention. (Chapter 10 argues that this divine intention manifests an open finality.) This causation causes beings with secondary causality, yet at the same time God as the primary cause – universal cause – is *magis causa*; a cause that exerts a deeper influence than the secondary causality.[93]

Here we are invited to develop a more sophisticated understanding of causality (one which will be radicalised in Chapter 10). On the one hand, this understanding is more variegated and rich, that is, analogical, and on the other it is more ultimate, for we are led to reconsider our understanding of causality through the intimacy accrued from the artistic intention of an end. This very intimacy forces us to lose all *comprehension* of causality. This is our analogical participation in the first cause. God has given *so much* that we are left suspended in mid-air, so to speak – but not as an occasionalist would understand it. The given-ness of creation disturbs all our concepts because of its intimacy – an intimacy that can extend to incarnation. For Deleuze and Guattari the artistic intention of creation is interpreted pejoratively, in so far as order is thought to 'strangle' creation: '[A] God at work messing it all up or strangling it by organising it.'[94] But it is possible to argue that Deleuze has misunderstood the notion of intention, interpreting it in rather ontic terms. For we shall see in the following chapters how divine intelligence manifests itself in an open finality that affords creation an openness that includes a co-creative aspect.

Returning to the issue in hand, it is of benefit to recall that traditionally the *viator* is said to approach knowledge of God in terms of a *triplex via*: *via positivia*, the cause is the cause of the effect; *via remotionis*, the cause is not the effect; *via eminentia*, the negative does not cancel the positive. Consequently, we can think of the effect as contained in the cause in a superior fashion.[95] This can usefully be compared to causality, participation and analogy. The positive is that we are caused, and negatively speaking we are not the cause, we do but participate. Even so, this participation does not negate the principle of causation. Rather, it affords us our analogical participation in God, for if the negative cancelled out the positive, that is, if participation resulted in occasionalism, then an equivocal notion of causality would be assumed, and this would be ontologically univocal. Here we see there is only an aspectual difference between occasionalism and pantheism, because causation is being understood here in terms outside artistic intention, and so we have an unaccounted ontic logic at work in our notion of utterly equivocal causation. What would it mean to cause except in the manner of a loving God who creates out of his divine art? Any notion apart from this results in univocity, which collapses the ontological difference. Hence, not even a 'natural' mode of causation can be successfully intelligible. In other words, if in being caused we were not a deliberate effect – loved creatures – then there would not be any causation; this is already suggested by the primacy of the Good in the order of causality.[96] Indeed, we begin to see how all metaphysics, and its terms, are subalternate to theology. (We shall see in Chapters 9 and 10, how this subalternation works, and how it induces a particular *agnosticism* which leaves space for a form of dialogue.)

Being *qua* being can only be articulated in terms of love,[97] which is to say, that being must begin in love, before it can be afforded a metaphysical level of understanding, one that relies somewhat on the theological level to enable its very articulation; for only love knows difference, and being *qua* being is an epiphenomenal registration of this originary difference. The problem with such a secondary level is that it suffers a philosophical *amnesia*, presuming it understands difference, while in reality it must be gifted such an insight. This insight is certainly inchoate, but this is because our natures, operative at the level of secondary causality, have been created thus. We are left, then, approaching the intimacy of causality in a manner which leaves it completely unfathomable.[98] We see this when we realise that final causation sets being in 'relief', for it maintains the ontological difference, in so far as any simple understanding of causality is problematised, because causation requires causation. This prevents the generation of a purely ontic conception of causation which inevitably fails to consider the unnoticed – immanent – space within which something is efficiently caused, and the terms and categories employed, the significance of which is presumed to possess an indigenous self-given worth, which is to forget the ontological difference and to conduct an analysis only at the level of the ontic. Likewise, yet conversely, efficient causality frees final causality from the closure feared by Deleuze by opening it up with the brute 'space' of given-ness. Yet it must be remembered that the Good is convertible with Being, and this informs us that the relief provided by

Being to the Good and vice versa is not foreign to either. In this way, a dynamic and open balance is provided between purpose and freedom – openness and being. Furthermore, beauty, as formal cause, is the space – the breadth – between efficiency and finality. In this way it is the place of each. (See Chapter 9 for an elaboration of this.)

Form integrates efficiency and finality. I agree with te Velde when he makes the point that 'Form is something of God in things created by God.'[99] Why is this the case? It is possible to suggest that God as an agent causes, or makes, in some analogous sense, by way of His form, by some reference to His form. Aquinas argues as much, because for him something is only good in so far as it is actual, and form is the act of something, so consequently it is that which is like God in everything that is; form is essentially act, and God is *actus purus*.[100] As Aquinas says, 'the more form each thing has the more intensely it possesses being'.[101] Furthermore, form as act is the source of intelligibility, and only that which has form can be known, or intelligible. For this reason God gives creatures form so that they can know and be known. The form given by God to man, as rational creature, is of such a nature that man's soul, which is the form of the body, can, in a sense, both know and be all things.[102] This may be the reason why Rousselot refers to the rational intellect as the 'faculty of otherness'.[103] Likewise, Pieper, echoing this Aristotelian sentiment, suggests that 'to know is to become another'.[104] This means that the form, which is our similitude to God, and our intellect, which is particular to our form – which is how we are in the image of God – is able to lead us into a vision of God (a notion developed in the next chapter). As Mark Jordan remarks, 'the richest kind of causality is the causality by which God brings rational creatures into participation of the divine life'.[105] Furthermore, according to Aquinas, it is the procession of the Trinity which is the 'cause and reason of every procession'.[106] Consequently, we are led by way of causality up to the very vision of God,[107] but if this is causality we now no longer presume to comprehend causality as we are, it seems, analogical participants in the eternal procession of the Trinity which is love.[108] It seems, then, that cause, participation, analogy, can be thought of as a trialectic which leaves metaphysics in need of love. (See Chapters 9 and 10 for a defence of this proposition.)

Ideas: of the Divine

The Aristotelian notion of act may be combined with the Platonic notion of participation. But it is the notion of the ideas within the Christian theology of creation which alone explains the diversity of participants in the participated.[109]

(V. Boland)

189

Following a long tradition before him, Aquinas argues that there is a plurality of ideas in God's intellect, and they are of what he intends to create, or in speculative terms what God could create.[110] These ideas are God's self-knowledge, for in knowing the divine essence, God knows how it is imitable, and it is this knowledge of imitability which is the basis for the divine ideas. From this it follows that each creature in being, and so having form, is an example of God's essence, not as that essence is in itself, but rather a privative example. In other words, the creature is defined in terms of how 'less' it is than the divine essence, and it is precisely this 'distance' which is its specific form; a plant may be like God in having life, but it is not like God in that it does not 'know'. God's essence as *principium actus intelligendi* means that when God comes to create, the essence can be a *terminus actus intelligendi*, in the sense that the understanding, as understood, can proceed to combine and divide that understanding. This means that God is the principle of His own understanding, and is therefore the terminus for every creative act, which means that because God's own essence acts as the *terminus*, extrinsic plurality is avoided: 'God who makes all things by means of His intellect, produces them all in the likeness of His own essence. Hence His essence is the idea of things, not as an essence considered as an essence but considered as it is known.'[111] An idea is a form, and as a form it is the end of a generation. This form can pre-exist according to an agent's natural being, or according to intelligible being.[112] As the world was not made by chance, or by an equivocal cause, there must be form to which the world was made, which exists in the intellect of God. That by which God understands is His wisdom, and that which God understands by that wisdom is the idea. Consequently, God understands His essence perfectly and understands that He understands His essence; for this reason God understands the plurality of ideas. [113]

There is, however, a shift in Aquinas' thinking, for in *De Veritate* the presence of exemplars is extended to speculative knowledge, yet by the time we reach the *Summa Theologiae* only practical knowledge has exemplars – and, although there are *rationes* for what could be made by God,[114] it is possible to consider *rationes* as purely informed by what *is* the case. The *Summa Theologiae* emphasises the imitability of the divine essence more than earlier works do. On this point Jordan comments, 'Thomas is moving away from the term "idea" and toward a greater emphasis on the unity of the divine essence as variously imitated.'[115] It should also be noted that Aquinas did not mention the divine ideas in either the *Compendium of Theology* or the *Summa Contra Gentiles*; although an earlier redaction of the latter text had.[116] Aquinas, it seems, was moving towards a stronger understanding of God's Word as exemplar of all creation.[117] This shift in emphasis is attributed by Boland to a heightened sensitivity for the issue of God's simplicity.[118]

The Word, *Verbum*, is God's self-knowledge; hence it is the image (*eikon*) of God, through which God makes all of creation, for the Word is the knowledge of this creation. The *Verbum* is co-eternal with God, and is of the same nature as God, hence the Word is the Son of God, which is to imply that God the Father is not before the Son, rather they are co-eternal.[119] The Son is the knowledge of the Father, hence there is nothing in the Father which is not the Son and vice versa. As the Word is God's knowledge of God, it is pure cognition, and because of this it is act from act. Therefore God, who is *actus purus,* cannot be without the Word, for if that were the case God would be in potency, in that God would know in potency. Instead the Word is the intellect of God and God is His intellect. God looks to the Word, who is, as Son, the art of the Father (*ars Patri*).[120] Furthermore, the Son, as the art of the Father, is the brightness of God's glory,[121] and the Word, as pure cognition, is pure light, resplendent with the form of intellect.[122] If, as was argued earlier, only love knows difference, then the Word, as intellect of the Father, is the knowledge of difference, and the communication of that knowledge. The Son is the knowledge of the Father's love, so the Son is the knowledge by which God creates, which by implication means that the Word is the knowledge of difference, hence it is the knowledge of love. The Son informs the Father that the Father is love, and the Son, as image of the primordial difference of the Trinity, is the image of love. It is for this reason that creation is through the Word and preserves its being in the Word.[123]

Following Augustine, I argue that to be known by God is to *be*.[124] In this sense, creation only is as it is in the Word. Furthermore, creation pre-exists in the Word from eternity as its eternal utterance. Creation pre-exists in the Word in a manner which is superior to its mode of existence *in via*, and for this reason Aquinas says: 'A thing is known more perfectly in the Word than in itself, even as regards its own particular shape and form.'[125] Knowledge of a thing in the Word is superior in a number of ways; in the Word the creature has uncreated being, life itself, and also the particular nature is more clearly expressed in the Word. Yet Aquinas points out that in the order of predication the creature exists better in creation than in the Word, because it exists according to its own mode of existence. Nonetheless, the likeness of the creature in the Word is, in a sense, the 'very life of the creature itself'.[126] More importantly, as the creature is in the Word, it in some sense brings about its own existence: 'The likeness of a creature existing within the Word in some way produces the creature and moves it as it exists in its own nature, the creature, in a sense, moves itself, and *brings itself into being*.'[127] (This notion will be examined as we progress, especially in Chapters 9 and 10, where it will be argued that this idea will present us with a better understanding of creation, but it will also bring theology closer to nihilism, or nihilism closer to theology. Such gravitation of one to the other will be the site of a tense, yet less than deliberate, dialogue between the two, which is implicit throughout the book, but will come to the fore towards the end.)

Knowledge which is had of a thing as it is in the Word is called by Augustine 'morning knowledge', while knowledge had of a creature in itself is called 'evening knowledge'.[128] Aquinas adopts this terminology and to some degree extends it. Creation is created through the Word, and 'holds together' in the Word. Consequently, superior knowledge is to be gained by knowledge in the Word, because the Word is the supreme intelligibility, and, as already said, the Word is the brightness of God's glory, for the Word is a resplendent light, just as God is light. In the *Summa Contra Gentiles*, Aquinas makes the point that the origin of the word God (*theos*) stems from the word *theaste*, which means to see.[129] This makes the words of the author of the *Liber de Causis* less surprising: the 'reality of a thing, in a way, in itself is its light'.[130] Consequently, it may be beneficial to consider light as the ultimate reality of a creature, because light is the possibility of its intelligibility – of its being known and its being able to know – and this requires it to be in act, an act arising from form. The light of a creature can be interpreted as a sign that it is from love (God) and towards love;[131] it is knowable – so it is from love, and it can know – so it is towards all things. Hence the creature is essentially of the other. (Chapter 9 develops this understanding of intelligence and knowledge.)

To know is, in a sense, to be towards an other – who is also the unknown; just as ultimate intelligibility is afforded to creation at the same time as it lies beyond it.[132] In this way, the ability to know requires the aid of God, for only God can know, because only God is love.[133] Likewise, only as we know in the Word, which is to attain *morning knowledge*, do we know aright, in so far as the life and knowledge of the creature lies in the Word, and it is only in our participation in the eternity of the Word that we can hope to know. We will see below what this entails. Let us end this section by noting that knowledge involves difference – otherness – and so it is ultimately love. Only God is love, and our participation in God's being is a participation in God's love, for it is this love which knows us, and so creates us.

Beautiful ideas: the idea of beauty

Man's ability to see is in decline.[134]
(Joseph Pieper)

Late have I loved You, Beauty so ancient and so new, late
have I loved You . . . You called and cried out and broke my
deafness; You shone forth and glowed and chased away my
blindness; You blew fragrantly on me and I drew breath and
I pant for You; I tasted You, and I hunger and thirst for
you; You touched me, And I was inflamed with desire for
your peace.[135]

(Augustine)

We have learned that to know a creature, as it is in the Word, is called
'morning knowledge', and that it is of a superior nature to that of
'evening knowledge', which is knowledge of the creature as it is in itself.
What complicates such a distinction is the co-creative aspect evidenced in
De Veritate, for there the creature is said *to bring itself into being*.
Furthermore, the Word is with the creature as it is, because not only is
creation through the Word but it is held together in it. This complication
is fundamentally exacerbated when we recall creation as not only
through the Word, held together in the Word, but also as including the
Word itself became flesh. In other words, the Incarnation presents us
with a new understanding or, as Borella puts it, a new vision.[136] What is
important to us here is the effect that this can have on our notion of
cognition, knowledge, and being *qua* being.

It is said by some that for Aquinas beauty is a transcendental; in other
words, beauty is co-extensive, and so convertible, with being, in the same
way as both goodness and truth are. Other commentators argue that
beauty for Aquinas is not a transcendental, because it is reducible to an
aspect of the good, which is itself a transcendental.[137] We cannot afford
the space to offer a thorough discussion, but for the sake of balance we
will examine briefly what Aquinas does say concerning beauty – keeping
Romanus Cessario's observation in mind: 'The custom of reading
Aquinas as if he were Bonaventure is gaining increasing respectability,
and therefore must be considered one of the evolutions to which
Thomism submits.'[138]

For Aquinas the good and the beautiful are based on form. But they
differ in reason, or operate by a different *ratione*. The reason for this is
that the good refers form to appetite and ultimately to will, while the
beautiful refers form to cognition, knowledge, and so ultimately to the
intellect. (See Chapter 9.) Beauty brings the appetite to rest in the
contemplation of beauty, while the good does not. Beauty consists in
integritas sive perfectio; debitita proportio sive consonantia; and *claritas.* Yet it
must be emphasised that these three characteristic features should not be
taken as canonical.[139] This becomes obvious when we realise that along

193

with the list of the transcendentals, the typical constitutive features of beauty alter, for at times there are only two features. Notwithstanding this less than canonical treatment, beauty can still be said to be related to cognition, while the good refers to the will. As Gilson says, 'beauty is to knowledge what the good is to desire of the will'.[140] It is for this reason that Aquinas argues that beauty involves that of which the mere apprehension is pleasurable.

For Maritain beauty is the splendour of all the transcendentals, while for Eric Gill it is the splendour of Being.[141] Yet it may be best to consider beauty as the *nubility* of Being, and indeed it may well be this *nubility* which is its splendour. The word *nubility* is employed so as to invoke two notions. The first of these is eros, which is meant to recall the desire involved in cognition, while the second is that of in-visibility. Chapter 9 discusses this idea of in-visibility in greater depth. It is sufficient to say here that *nubility* is intended to bring to our attention that our knowledge of something is inversely proportional to our comprehension of it. For example, in the *beatific vision* we will know all of God's essence, but we will not comprehend all of it. This idea of incomprehension is invoked by the term *nubility* because it comes from the Latin *nubilis*, which in turn comes from *nubere,* and this means to veil oneself. This is important when it is argued that only love can know – because only love can know difference – and difference can only be known if it is known by a lover. This, in some sense, means that knowledge has its own veil, but one that arises from the plenitude of the object. Coincidentally, Walter Benjamin appears to advocate something similar: '[B]eauty can only appear as such in the veiled . . . [For] only the beautiful and nothing besides can be essentially veiling and veiled, the divine ground of the Being of beauty lies in the secret.'[142] (And we saw earlier that, according to Réne Guénon, modernity cannot stand secrecy.)[143] When we relate the *nubility* of being to God's essence, which is utter knowability – yet incomprehensible – and bear in mind that *theos* comes from *theaste*, meaning to see, the in-visibility of creature and creator comes to the fore – this is the veil of beauty, the *nubility* of being.

Beauty relates to form, so it is of little surprise that *formosa* is the Latin word for beautiful. Form is itself related to act because it is related to divine clarity.[144] Every form participates in this divine clarity, and it has form because of, and through, this participation: 'All form through which things have being is a certain participation in divine clarity.'[145] It is for this reason that Maurer argues that for Aquinas, beauty is closely related to actuality.[146] Consequently, beauty is the *formositas actualitas*[147] – the splendour of form, which is the *splendor intellectus.* It is for this reason that vision is knowledge, in the sense that to see is to know being, because being is that which is to be seen – to be known (yet it is not that which is to be comprehended).[148] Cognition and knowledge involve an *irreducible* visibility, that resists the epistemic reduction of a pure informatics which renders reality virtual. This irreducible visibility escapes every description, hence it can be expressed in terms of *nubility* with its implication of veiling. Beauty as the *nubility* of being suggests that creation is an act of communication – one of love[149] – but it is a communication that entails the breadth of an eternal repose, a contemplation which is the *place* of the Good.[150] Beauty takes time, it implicates eternity, and so can be thought of as the very substance of being. In a sense beauty is a 'holocaust' of time just as liturgy is, as Pieper suggests.[151] In this way, being is not something reducible to information, or data. A resistance is made manifest in beauty as the very time of being – involving a *nubility* that erotically demands that we remain *with* being, the loved one. For, as Augustine tells us: 'Only the beautiful can be loved . . . *we cannot stop* loving what is beautiful.'[152] The time of beauty gives 'breadth' to the communication which being is. This breadth precludes idealism or a reductive 'message'. Instead the purposive nature of being manifests itself in a temporal excess. In other words, purpose – to be purposive – resides, as itself, in an otherwise than definitive manner, which is to say that it displays an 'open finality'.

As we saw above, beauty, in relating form to cognition, involves 'light'[153] that can be thought of as the *claritas* of beauty, which is the *claritas* of form – an act of ontologico-cognitive differentiation.[154] But if being is disengaged from beauty, then being can be supposed to be merely epistemic. Any sundering of being from beauty would generate a purely ontic realm that could be conceived in predominantly epistemic terms. Here again we see that Deleuze is employing a flimsy conception of form. For it is formal causality, which beauty is, that forbids the incarceration of being. It does so because beauty introduces a temporal infinity – if not eternity – into the mundane. Furthermore, beauty – in letting us know being – renders us more 'agnostic'. In other words, the temporal infinity of the corporeal, introduced by beauty, allows us to know being but prevents us from comprehending it. To know is to know an other, and it is, in a sense, to become that other; but this does not violate alterity, because knowledge – arising from the *nubility* of being – is essentially related to love.[155] This is the case because if love is not the supreme 'metaphysical' term, then difference cannot be articulated, cognised, or perceived. As Pieper says, lovers of beauty are simply known as lovers.[156] This being the case we understand how beauty, as the ontological reference to cognition, involves desire – we cannot know unless we love. In other words, to know we must know an other, and must become that other, but unless we love that other we will destroy this other – failing to know. As we saw above beauty is the temporality of being, which is the *breadth of its breath*. As Keats says:

> A thing of beauty is a joy forever:
> Its loveliness increases; it will never
> Pass into nothingness; but still will keep
> A bower quiet for us, and a sleep
> Full of sweet dreams, and health, and quiet breathing.[157]

Any entity involves time, and in so doing it implicates eternity; as de Lubac argued, this world is the 'matter of eternity', and so it cannot be abstracted from in an otherworldly manner.[158] Therefore beauty is the *substance* of being, and any other candidate would fail to uphold the 'open finality' of being's temporal plenitude.[159] If *substance* were anything else a nihilistic act of de-differentiation would ensue. For how could difference be known, how could difference be? Even a lack of substance – the reality of a flux – would coagulate into a Heraclitean stasis.[160] For this reason only beauty can be the *substance* of Being, for only beauty is the substance of relationality. It is quite traditional in Christian theology to consider being convertible with the good, but in the absence of beauty there is the threat of a narrative foundationalism (which would confirm Deleuze's aforementioned fear). In other words, the Good involves a description of what is good and so, in a sense, it leads us somewhere for some reason. The structure of such a movement *could* carry being away[161] (Hegel's system appears to do this). But beauty as the *substance* of Being offers a breadth to the act, or form, of Being and an openness to the finality of the Good. Being, then, by definition involves, and demands of its participants, a dynamic repose.[162]

It was suggested earlier that to know properly involves love, for only love will allow for difference. To know, then, involves an incomprehension as the known is approached in terms of the eternity of its source – the Word – in which it pre-existed in an eminent fashion. But the Word is the Word of God, which is an eternal *now*, and so the being remains, in a sense, in the Word. This means that knowledge is knowledge of the Word, and to approach a being in its beauty recalls this excellent inhabitation: 'The Word is, in a fashion, the word of the creature, because creatures are manifested by means of the Word.'[163] Creation is the *verbum Verbi*.[164] If we come from the Word, are held together in the Word, and are only known by reference to the Word – beauty being the substantial breadth of this referral – we can understand why beauty is traditionally 'referred' to the Son: 'The Son has clarity which radiates over all beings, and in which all beings are resplendent.'[165] Beauty is identified with *species*, an aspect of form, and species in terms of beauty is linked to the Son.[166] The Son has integrity or perfection, because he is God; proportion as the image; and *claritas* as the light and splendour of the intellect – which is the truth and glory of the Father. The Word, as beauty, is also, then, the truth of cognition – supreme intelligibility – for it is the brightness of the Father's glory. As Jordan says, 'to give light is to give a means of understanding'.[167] The given light is the light of God: 'In thy light do we see light.'[168] God is light and we are to be children of light.[169] This means that to know is to participate in the light of God, just as to be knowable is also a participation. God as light, and the Son as the brightness of that light – the splendour of the intellect – is the source and possibility of all knowledge. The Son is the difference of the Father, the Father's love. In so being, the Son is the gift of love, which is the ability to know and be known. In relation to beauty, we can agree with Navone when he says, 'to be or not to be is the question of beauty'.[170] Gilson concurs, saying that 'to make things be and to make them beautiful are one and the same thing'.[171]

The next section discusses the notion of the Word becoming flesh, before returning to a discussion of divine ideas in the light of Charles Péguy's understanding of repetition, a combination which may begin to point towards a better conception of language and knowledge (the latter will be developed in Chapters 9 and 10).

The language of difference

In the beginning was the Word, and the Word was God
. . . and the Word became flesh . . .

The Word became flesh, and as Aquinas says, 'he was written on our flesh'.[172] All materiality is the result of the Word, and this Word assumed that materiality – yet did so remaining as the Word. If our cognition requires the Word, if we only know because of the Word, by looking to the Word, and so to beauty, then we must understand that it is this Word which has become flesh. This Word – as beauty – enables us to say, to do and to see. As Aquinas says, it is only because of the truth of the Word that we have words, that our words are words: 'by this Truth all words are words'.[173] Without God we would, as de Lubac says, 'have to abandon speech'.[174] This truth is also that of the Word becoming flesh, a truth which cannot but 'revolutionise our ways of seeing . . . inducing us to enter a new order of reality', as Borella puts it.[175] We were with the Word, in that we were in the Word, and we helped bring ourselves into being, but now this Word has become flesh – the Word is now with us. This means that we who have come from the Word have in some sense returned; or at least turned (*metanoia*) to the Word. We have done so because the Word has come to us, and in a sense become us. The Word has become flesh and has also gathered us all to the Word.[176]

Following Borella, it is possible to argue that Christ as the Word, in becoming flesh, suffered a double *kenosis*. First of all, the Word, as God, emptied itself of Divinity, and by this sacrifice creation was divinised: 'the divinisation of the world is effected as a function of the Incarnation'.[177] (Yet we must not, as Bouyer warns us, separate the Incarnation from the Passion.)[178] This sacrifice renders us His body, or of His body, in the sense that He has become like us, and so we have become like Him. But this prepares creation for the second kenotic moment, that of the sacrifice of Christ's humanity; Christ on the Cross sheds His blood, and this blood falls on the earth, an earth, in some sense, divinised. Therefore this blood falls 'into' a new body – that of creation. Furthermore, as Christ on the Cross is lifted into the air He enters Heaven drawing all men to Him.[179]

In this way creation has become the body of Christ as it 'holds' the blood of Christ. This blood now flows through the veins of creation, a living vessel prepared by the Incarnation. We know that God creates out of love, which is God's difference; the articulation of which is the co-eternal Son. And this Son, as beauty, calls, and re-calls, all creation back to life.[180] The Son is battered, bruised, and killed; yet even the deformed and the formless is known by Christ, and so is reformed. Consequently, it is possible to understand the love which Christ both is and enacts as the ultimate in terms of knowledge. For the 'supreme beauty of the crucified' (as Jordan puts it)[181] is able even to know death – finding form in its abyss. In this way there is form in the formless, for the Resurrection testifies to such knowledge. It is important to remember that the Son's body retains the testimony of scars, and that for three days the Son, in his divinely personified humanity, was dead. This is important because it is not a violation of natural form, or forms, but their 'open finality'. If the Son remained unbruised even though beaten and so on, then there would, it seems, be but an otherworldly violation. But the Son's overcoming of death mirrors creation, for there it was God's love – God's difference – that enabled the difference of creation. In this way there was an 'abyss' of sameness at the bottom of creation's difference – yet this abyss is the ultimacy of love. In a similar fashion, the Resurrection displays the hegemony of love, for Christ's love gives breath to death. In doing so the foundation of knowledge is revealed – love. This is, in a sense, a 'metaphysical' point, not simply a theological one. For in finding life in death, Christ discloses the form of creation, because in finding difference where there is none – there being only the sameness of death – difference is made possible. The Son's ability to see form-in-the-formless is the beauty which Dostoyevsky said would save the world, a beauty that 'creates, sustains, and draws to perfection the whole of creation'.[182] For not even death could not be known by love. (It may well be for this reason that in the Book of Revelation death is thrown into an eternal lake of fire, receiving eternal existence; the annihilation it practises meets its own contradiction.) The body of Christ, which retains its scars, recalls fallen creation, halting its fall to indefinite multiplicity which is, ontologically, a lack of real difference.[183] In other words, the beauty which Christ bestows upon creation resists all analytical reduction and indefinite multiplication. For Christ brings creation within the eternal procession of the Trinity. Here we can agree with F. L. B. Cunningham when he says that 'The divine mission continues in us the eternal processions'.[184]

Two negative effects are forestalled by this. First of all, there cannot be, as we shall see more clearly, an understanding of form that incarcerates being in the prison of comprehension. For every form is *qua* form open. Yet – and this is the second effect – any simple notion of absolute openness, that is, indefinite multiplication, is disabled, because creation is the result of a Word, of a divine idea. In this way it is a specific and purposive intention of divine art as we saw earlier. Instead we are left with an open finality. (What this means will become more apparent in the next chapter.)

Before the opposition of being and nothing there is the difference of the Trinity. As Evdokimov says, 'between being and nothingness, there is no other principle of existence than the Trinitarian principle'.[185] For this reason we can agree with Aquinas that 'creation is not really a change';[186] consequently, we were in the Word in a manner superior to that in which we are in ourselves and we helped bring ourselves into being. For this reason the Word is also the word of creatures. This involves us in a manner of co-creation; not only because we were in the Word, but now because we are both within the knowledge and testimony of the Word in relation to the Father, and are the body of Christ. This co-creation occurs in our language and liturgy, our culture and practices of living, and so on; it is a co-creation important enough to implicate eternity to an ultimate degree, and it explains the divine ideas in a more promising fashion. (For an elaboration of this notion of co-creation see Chapter 10.)

As Aquinas says, 'the more form each thing has the more intensely it possesses being'.[187] Yet, as Borella argues, form is not a 'spatial configuration, except under one of its modes; but is what is meaningful in a physical being, which is to say what is intelligible (*eidos*) and therefore what enables us to distinguish it from other beings'.[188] Consequently, we, as creatures, are left to develop forms of worship and liturgy which are theophanic. Evdokimov appears to concur, saying that 'a form becomes a place of theophany'.[189] Indeed, as de Lubac says, 'each creature is a theophany'.[190] We who are in the image of the Creator are able to share in the creativity of the Creator.[191] For example, Gilson argues that it is possible to 'join in the praise of God by co-operating with the Creator's power and by *increasing* the sum total of being and beauty in the world'.[192] Likewise, Milbank suggests that 'our linguistic expressions mirror the divine creative act which is immanently contained in the *ars patris* that is the Logos'.[193]

This *poesis*, which is a co-creative potentiality, in terms of an actual participation in the very form and act of the *Verbum*, may become more apparent if we consider that we have, on receiving the Eucharist, become the *true body* of Christ. Let us first consider two guiding motifs which will lead us to a consideration of the Eucharist. Water and wine can be employed as *hermeneutical devices* that may heuristically intimate to us the very *form* of co-creativity, which may in turn instruct us how to speak, do and see.

Mary, as mother of God, utters human words that enable the Incarnation.[194] In this sense, human discourse, from the beginning, is full of grace. Mary offers her will to God, insisting that God's will be done. From this there follows the virginal Conception and the Incarnation. Allegorically speaking, the breaking of her waters can be interpreted as marking the coming of Christ. What is important to note is that the water comes *before* Christ, announcing *the way* (like John the Baptist). This water can then be thought to lead us to the wedding at Cana, where Mary instructs the stewards to do the will of her son. In so doing they repeat the form of Mary's submission. Water is then 'transubstantiated', a transformation which announces the divinity of Christ. This is the first miracle of Christ's public ministry. Furthermore, this water that now becomes wine can be thought to anticipate Christ's future sacrifice, in this way calling forth what is 'known'. The water which has become wine leads us to the upper room, a room that is located in one Gospel account by following a water bearer.[195] Only by following the man carrying a jar of water can the upper room be discerned. This can be read as recalling the water which began the story, yet it leads us on to Holy Thursday. In the upper room wine becomes blood, a transubstantiation which announces the sacrifice of Christ, and brings us to Good Friday, wherein Christ sheds his blood. The completion of this sacrifice is, in a sense, attested to by the water which comes from Christ's pierced side; this water can be interpreted as Mary's breaking water, for herein the Church is born, as it announces the coming of the Church.[196] What is important for us is that this birth is anticipated in the first birth, the first waters, which arrive after the *words* of Mary. This drama of birth and rebirth, with the Church as now the true body of Christ, cannot be disassociated from human discourse and actions. We will see how important this is below. It is sufficient to say here that this may well enable us to develop a theo-logic that overcomes nihilism.

The question of the mystical body of Christ is a much discussed and vexed question. It is sufficient for us to adumbrate two differing 'schools' of emphasis. Henri de Lubac in his two books, *Corpus Mysticum* and *The Splendour of the Church*, discusses two approaches to the locating of the mystical body of Christ.[197] De Lubac argues that before the twelfth century the Church was considered the true body of Christ (*corpus verum*), while the sacramental body was thought of as the mystical body (*corpus mysticum*). After the middle of the twelfth century the *corpus verum* became associated with the sacramental body, while the Church became the mystical body.[198] With this change there was a reduction from the ternary to the binary, as de Certeau puts it.[199] What this means is that the Church and sacrament were joined together in a manner which meant that the Church was but an invisible and nominal extension of Christ's body. This body was but the hidden effect of the Eucharist. Before this, the Church, being the *corpus verum*, was able to resist reduction to the sacramental. Yet, conversely, the Church as *corpus verum* only existed because of the Eucharist. The link was, in some sense, closer, but the three bodies were distributed in three moments. Instead, a reduction to the binary gave rise to the spectacle of the sacrament, because the Church, as an indistinct extension, could only legalistically receive, and not be, the true body of Christ. The recipient remained apart from the reception; reception was now more synchronic. Consequently, it reflected a more literalist approach, a literalism reflected in another way in the protestant version of the binary structure.[200] If, by contrast, the Church is the *corpus verum*, the recipients are themselves received: in consuming one is consumed (the importance of which becomes apparent in the next two chapters).[201] This precludes such a literalism, or emphasis on the spectacle, for the sacrament becomes, ontologically speaking, more a verb than a noun. According to de Lubac, we should look not for an object but for a sacrifical act.[202] As Catherine Pickstock says, 'The notion of the Eucharistic presence was gradually substituted for that of sacred action, giving rise to a literalist concern as to what the Eucharist is, as an isolated phenomenon, rather than an ecclesial event.'[203] Consequently, the Eucharist no longer makes the Church and instead the 'Church makes the Eucharist', to quote Paul McPartlan.[204] What this new emphasis introduces is a new 'punctuation of dogma'.[205] A *caesura* was placed between the sacramental and Church ecclesial bodies, one which had previously fallen between the historical and the sacramental bodies.[206] What is important for us is the difference this understanding has for how we see and 'read'. As already suggested, the new punctuation of dogma gave rise to a literalism of the spectacle of the sacrament, or of scripture.[207] This is more in line with a secular logic, since such an understanding of the Eucharist will be unable to know as well as it could, for it will be less able to resist reductive approaches to creation, as it now involves discrete moments or entities, and these invite endless description, and dissection. In this way the pursuit of an essence, a kernel, colludes with nominalism, affording us but diacritical signification.[208]

Returning to the upper room we recall that the words of Mary allowed for the water which announced both the birth and the divinity of her son; it also became the wine that was to become His blood. This in turn gave birth to the Church, which we are to understand as the body of Christ. In the upper room on Holy Thursday Christ, it seems, offered to those gathered His body and blood. They were allowed to partake of it, consume-and-be-consumed by it, for they would become that body. Yet on Holy Thursday Christ had not yet gone to the Cross. Nevertheless, we have what appears to be the first Eucharist. What can this mean for us? How are we to see such an event? How do we speak, and how can we do that which has not 'literally' been done? Before endeavouring to answer such questions let us recall the question of divine ideas, and our participation in the Word, before we are, and as we are, in terms of Incarnation, Crucifixion, and the Eucharist. Furthermore, we must not forget the 'liturgy' of Mary – human words made divine. We now turn to Charles Péguy's understanding of repetition in the hope that it may help us to understand both divine ideas and the co-creative aspect of our words. After this discussion we return to the issue of the Eucharist.

Charles Péguy argued that we tended to misunderstand events, because we read them in too linear a manner.[209] For example, it would be supposed that the fall of the Bastille is commemorated by Federation Day in France, which could be said to repeat that fall. Instead, Péguy suggests that the fall of the Bastille repeats and celebrates all subsequent instances of Federation Day. Another example would be a waterlily painted by Claude Monet. For Péguy, the first painting executed by Monet of his famous waterlilies repeats all subsequent paintings. These later paintings in some sense intensify the originary repetition of the first:[210] 'Everything which is beginning has a virtue which can never be rediscovered, a strength, a novelty, freshness like dawn . . . [T]he first day is the most beautiful. Perhaps the first day is the only beautiful day.'[211] This is *Clio*'s law of *vieillissement*, in that things get older and decay. What Péguy wishes to oppose with this understanding is the logic of the hoarder, that is to say, cumulation, but this does not mean that a second painting is *simply* not as good as the first. For even Péguy's own work contradicts this notion, in that his second work on Joan of Arc is better than the first. The point to be made is that the second is better *because* of the first, so in this sense is less. The intensification is not a cumulative hoarding; instead it is a lived realisation of the beginning, just as Picasso realises the potency of Cézanne and so on. All artists do, then, in a sense is realise the first artist – nature – which is itself the realisation of God's artistic intention: the Word.

Jean-Luc Marion captures this idea when he speaks of the exemplar of the creature in the mind of God: '*En fait, l'étant ne devient lui-même qu'en référence, et donc en retard sur sa vérité propre qui ne cesse, en Dieu, de l'attendre. L'exemplar anticipe sur la vérité de l'étant qui s'y reconnaît étrangement précédé en Dieu par sa plus propre essence, se découvrant comme en retrait sur lui-même.*'[212] At a mundane level, with regard to the fall of the Bastille, unless there was a certain potency in that event there would be no Federation Day. The event would not be commemorated if the fall had been followed by a reversal of royal fortune. It is the *poesis*, the potency, in the first Monet that gives rise to the non-identical repetition of all those that follow. All subsequent paintings are the event of the first, in so far as the first creates the place for these others through its own being. (Deleuze criticises Péguy's, and Kierkegaard's, understanding of repetition; Chapter 10 answers this criticism.)

Such an understanding of repetition may well be instructive for our understanding of the divine ideas, and for the way in which we are to approach reality. The *Verbum* is the knowledge of all creation, for it is the intellect of God, and we saw earlier that creatures reside in the Word, come from the Word, yet remain only because of the Word; in this sense, the Word, as exemplar of creation, yet also as eternal image of God, effects an *originary repetition* of creation – or of any particular creature. An existent creature does not repeat the exemplar, but is already within an originary repetition, of which it is the intensification. As Péguy says: 'An eternal foundation does not exclude the need to begin anew. No degree of eternal foundation alters the fact that the foundation is, in some sense, in the world and eternity.'[213] Furthermore, according to Fabro, *esse* is the ultimate intensive act, and according to Aquinas, as we read above, the more form a creature has the more intensely does it possess being.[214] It seems that the creature, as it exists, is an intensification of the Word's originary repetition, but it can enact such an intensification only as it moves *towards* the Word. This movement is twofold. First of all, it looks back to the Word because it is from the Word, and was previously in the Word; second, the Word repeats the creature, and the creature intensifies the 'potency' involved in such a repetition. How can the creature intensify the Word's repetition, and how can it look back towards the Word if it is not a repetition of the Word? It can because the Word is already a repetition of the creature. Yet how can the creature intensify its being in relation to the Word, within which it resided in a superior manner? The Word, as said, is the image (*eicon*) of the Father, and is co-eternal, inhabiting the 'eternal now' of God, but the Word is also exemplar of creation. Furthermore, the Word becomes flesh, as this is its divine mission. Therefore it seems that the intensification that the creature can effect is an echo of the Word *ad intra*. The Word enacts an originary repetition because the very form of the Son includes in eternal reality the divine mission of creation and salvation, even though this proceeds from divine decree (for any decree of God is eternal, is simply his being). And the form of the Son *ad intra*, within the eternal now, displays this form – a form that is eternal, consequently, dynamic.[215]

The creature's intensification of the repetition is itself an echo of redeemed creation, eschatologically taken up into the Son, and so into the eternal procession of the Trinity. Jean-Pierre Torrell emphasises the centrality the Trinity has for Aquinas,[216] which offers it a certain priority over the Incarnation, in that it is the eternal procession of the Trinity *ad intra* which explains the efficient causality of God *ad extra*. The procession of the Word from the Father is analogous to the divine efficacy involved in creation, just as the grace required for a return of creation to God is linked to the eternal spiration of the Holy Spirit. Creation and Incarnation only make sense from the perspective of the Trinity *ad intra*. It is for this reason that love is the 'basis' or 'possibility' of metaphysics, because only by referring to the eternal charity of the Father, in relation to the Trinity, can we hope to understand what it would mean to be at all. This eternal love is the only first principle our discourse can have. For in the absence of such a principle we will not understand what it is to say, do, or see, because difference would only ever be nominal: the difference between one and the many; between the many; between this word and that word, syllable and syllable; here and there, this and that. Therefore it takes an eternal and infinite charity for there to be a grain of sand. Furthermore, this positioning of our 'knowledge' in the Trinity disables every ontic category.

Holy Thursday precedes Good Friday. The Eucharist 'literally' takes place before the Cross. How can we understand such a conundrum? Let us take the figure of Christ as instructive. Two main approaches in the manner of how to 'see' or speak of this figure are enlightening. The first we can term the literal (somewhat akin to historicism), the second 'metaphorical' (similar, methodologically, to extrinicism). If we approach Christ in the manner of a literalist, sewing together discrete historical acts, then the very form of Christ disappears. The form of Christ will enter a cycle of perpetual dissolution, as abstract, disengaged pieces of information replace the form; a crime committed in the name of an essence, but any such substance would reside in the 'dark'. If, by contrast, we approach Christ 'metaphorically', endeavouring to extract general principles, or morals, from recorded events, we would reduce the form of Christ to a type; as with the tree, it would be an example of something more general. Here again cognitive darkness would ensue, following on the back of such a reductive dissolution. Both approaches carry Christ away *in bits* or *as a bit*. What would be of interest here would be to explore how spiritual exegesis employing a fourfold manner of interpretation (literal, allegorical, tropological and anagogic) would enable us to avoid such dire consequences.[217] Space forbidding, we can but point to such an approach under the banner of the 'analogical'. To see Christ we must see him analogically, in a sense maintaining the 'literal' and 'metaphorical', but within a non-reductive understanding: an understanding informed by an appeal to the transcendentals. Christ is, and Christ is truth, goodness, and beauty. For this reason the truth our reading explicates is *a good way and a beautiful life*. Such an approach can be understood to be that which Blondel recommends by the term 'tradition'.[218] We participate in that which we are trying to know. In this sense we realise that to know involves love, and so an irreducible supplement of 'visibility' (or *nubility*). We must, then, shape our lives as suitable vessels, which will not only hold but increase what is held in the manner of an intensification; one that reflects the grace of the original gift.

We pay witness to this somewhat strange logic when we realise that Good Friday is curiously displaced.[219] For we cannot reduce it to a merely literal identification as it was called forth by Holy Thursday, a calling forth which *remembers the future*. As Catherine Pickstock says, concerning a related matter: 'The word arrives both from the past – the remembered tradition of language – and from the future – as that which can only arrive because of the futurity of each subsequent syllable, and which ultimately betokens the futurity of the resurrection.'[220] The displacement of Good Friday does not result in dissolution, for there is a real sacrifice. (This is a positioning of the *caesura* similar to that which we find between the historical body of Christ on the one hand and the sacramental and Church bodies on the other.)[221] A consequence of this futurial *anamnesis* is that the real sacrifice, and presence, of Christ on Good Friday cannot actually be absolutely differentiated from every subsequent Eucharist. This, then, is the importance of our liturgy and our 'poetic' practices, which display the open finality of form – the breadth of being. The Eucharist cannot be separated from the sacrifice on Good Friday. Indeed, we can even consider subsequent Eucharistic feasts, which are also a real sacrifice and real presence, as an intensification of Good Friday, just as Good Friday was an intensification of Holy Thursday. This is the 'power' of liturgy, of the forms we conspire to create, which, as Gilson said, *add* to the sum total of being. Likewise, as de Certeau says, 'The Jesus event is extended (verified) in the manner of a disappearance in the difference which that event makes possible. Our relation to the origin is in function of its increasing absence. The beginning is more and more hidden by the multiple creations which reveal its significance.'[222] In this way we can understand that the words of Mary anticipate our liturgy, and that all our liturgy participates in the potency of that uttered submission ('*Deipara*'). The Church, as the *corpus verum*, is not only Christ's body, but is co-creative with the Word. Indeed, the Church, as the body of Christ, is itself in the upper room of its own Holy Thursday, as it eschatologically calls forth the *parousia*, remembering the future in its words and deeds. The Church, then, is the *sacrament of the future*, anticipating the return of all creation to God.[223] This intensification of the liturgy and sacraments, which the Church enacts and inhabits, is an echo of the Word *ad intra*, for we as creatures, with our creative words, remember (*anamnesis*) our being in the Word; recollecting in the present (*epiclesis*) that we are within the Word, and preparing, that is, re-calling (*epectasis*) the future in which we are in the Word *ad intra*.[224] As Péguy says: 'I cannot do anything temporally which is not inserted, physically, as it were, into the body of God himself.'[225]

Mary, in giving birth to God, gives birth to the Church. In so doing Mary displays the 'Church before the Church',[226] to use Paul Claudel's phrase. This co-operation with grace, this remembered, and enacted, co-creation, calls forth the Church as the sacrament of the future. The Church is before Christ in one sense (since church as Mary is before Christ, and the Upper Room precedes the Crucifixion) but in so being, a place apart from grace is not engendered. Indeed, because the Church is before the Church it will call forth its own sacrifice by *anamnesis*, in terms of the salvation of the cosmos. We are able to see the 'before', 'during', and 'after', of creation, in that we see the form which creation embodies in the Trinity *ad intra*, namely the Son as gifted by the Spirit.

The virginity of Mary can be interpreted as an allegorical repetition of creation's given-ness – the efficient causation of love.[227] Christ in the womb can be thought to represent the Church's production of the Eucharist, which signifies the pre-existence of all in the Word,[228] and the production of the Church by the Eucharist.[229] Mary who comes *before* Christ does so only in the manner in which creation pre-exists in the Word. We have in the womb the Eucharist, because we have seen that the Eucharist is always futurial in the sense of a calling forth. Christ is in Mary's body, and this can be read as being analogous with the Mass, in so far as Mary is one body with Christ. In this way the Church is already eucharistically one with the Groom – as a virgin. This is the grace of the opportunity for giving and receiving.[230] The Bride truly receives only as she remains a virgin. Her giving is always the result of a prior gift, one which is simultaneous with her own donation, which is thereby virginal – productive by virtue of what she has always already received, and which therefore has never penetrated her. Consequently, the ontic categories of before and after – of donor and donee – are insuperably complicated, for grace is the *operation of operations* – just as the Good is the cause of causes. The prior being of the Church recapitulates the Church within an eschatological economy. It is before itself, before Christ, because it came from the Word. This being the case, the Church *before* the Church becomes the Church *after* itself, which is to say that the Church is the true body of Christ, and that which displaces the historical body of Christ by consuming it, is itself consumed – displaced.[231] The Church remembers the future of Christ's sacrifice. In so doing, it becomes one with Christ, receiving the gift of this sacrifice, and this entails the Church's giving of its own body. In remembering the future the Church participates in the sacrifice of Christ by receiving His body, the receipt of which enacts an eschatological sacrifice.[232]

The *Assumption* announces the form of the salvation of creation. For as Péguy says, Mary 'is already that new universe which the Church is to be'.[233] Daniélou appears to concur with Péguy when he says, 'The mystery of the assumption teaches us in Mary the transfiguration of the cosmos . . . the dawn of the new creation.'[234] This is the form of the echo between, so to speak, the Son *ad extra*, and *ad intra*. For as Paul Claudel remarks, Mary 'brings together in silence in her heart and reunites in one single heart all the lines of contradiction'.[235] The difference between creation *ad extra* and *ad intra* is the breadth of beauty's dynamic repose, which is the open finality of form with its non-identical repetition of eternity. As Claudel says, 'Mankind in labour, once more succeeds in tearing from its heart a perfect naming.'[236] For this reason, time becomes, again in Claudel's words, 'ecstatic', as it is eschatological,[237] in that it is towards another.

Our words, and our being, in its co-creative potentiality, enact an intensification of divine truth that has 'permanence danced by movement, eternity scattered by time'.[238] This intensification is the living out of being, for being must, as Borella says, 'be realised'. Hamann echoes this, asserting that we are still in the making.[239] Furthermore, Daniélou says: 'God did not give us a ready-made world; he gave us a world to make; and consequently, our creativity, our initiative, and our responsibility are immense.'[240] God does not give us a ready-made world because, as Claudel says, God is 'a God for ever inventing the heaven in which he dwells, and whose next move we can never foresee'.[241] It seems to make sense that if Heaven is ever new so too is creation. Hence the development of new forms which 'add' to being, in order to approach the eschatological realisation of all within the risen Son, who draws all men to Himself.

Chapter 9 returns to the question of intelligence, of visibility, light and causality. It will be argued that intelligence involves becoming the other it knows, but that such knowledge includes a lack of comprehension, so allowing for proper difference. This lack of comprehension is taken to be central to being. Consequently, it is argued that being displays a particular *in-visiblity;* this is its *nubility*. The next chapter also suggests that creation is not a change, as it is a result of divine unity, and consequently difference arises from sameness. Furthermore, it is argued that any particular being is to be understood as both *res* (thing) and *aliud quid* ('another what'). Both of these represent two poles in terms of causality: the first is positive – vertical; while the second is negative – horizontal. It is argued that one without the other generates a monism, while a better conception and application of both points us towards a better understanding of creation.

Notes

1   This title refers back to the three critiques of Kant.
2   We have paid witness to this disappearing act in the preceding chapters.
3   Jacobi (1994), pp. 524, 519.
4   Milbank (1990), p. 213.
5   *Ibid.*, p. 217.
6   *Ibid.*, p. 213.
7   See Borella (1998), p. 3.
8   In the *Quodlibetal Questions* Ockham denies that relation is a real thing, and that creation *qua* creation does not have a real relation with God; see VI, q. 9 and VII, q. 1.
9   Or meta-structures, for example general types.
10   I have suggested elsewhere that Wittgenstein's advocacy of a purely descriptive philosophy was underwritten by an explanatory impulse, hence explanatory descriptions; see Conor Cunningham (1999).
11   See Guénon (2002).
12   See Guénon (1953).
13   We saw this earlier in Ockham's intuitive cognition; see Part I, Chapter 2.
14   'To risk meaning nothing is to start to play and first to enter into the play of difference'; 'in a certain way thought means nothing', Derrida (1987b), pp. 9, 14.
15   On the link between modernity, rationality and the Holocaust see Bauman (1989), and see Rose (1993), pp. 22–24, for criticisms of Bauman's interpretation. Also of interest is Rose (1996), where what is called 'holocaust piety' is defined and critiqued.
16   Hitler did so. This is perhaps why the Bible speaks of those with murderous thoughts, or words, as murderers. Such sins did not depend on outward action. One did not have to kill to be a murderer.
17   We must be careful not to be too schematic for we risk emulating the logic we hope to critique. Furthermore, we must ensure that we do not cause modern discourse to disappear. We will see when discussing theological discourse that such a disappearance will be impossible for theology to carry out. Indeed, this impossibility will, in some sense, upset the critique being offered in this book. Consequently, a certain agnosticism will arise; see Part II, Chapter 10.
18   See Guénon (1953) and (2001).
19   The hole is only ever filled with another hole, this being the form of an attributional 'plenitude', and this we saw in Spinoza; see Part I, Chapter 3.

20 This present-absence is somewhat akin to what in Scotus are real-possibles, or the intuitively cognised in Ockham, the Being of Heidegger's Dasein, Hegel's universal thinker, and Kant's subject–object.

21 For a theological critique of the notion of morality see Milbank (1997), pp. 219–232.

22 Ockhamian cognitions.

23 Theological discourse must not cause modern discourse to disappear. This we will see in Part II, Chapter 10 is our own structural 'agnosticism'. For there it will be argued that theology and nihilism have a moment of solidarity.

24 This is merely an inverted form of Kant's appearance of appearance; see Part I, Chapter 4.

25 Just as nihilism must lack its lack; see Part II, Chapter 10.

26 Auden (1994), p. 597; italics mine.

27 See Part II, Chapter 10 for a discussion of this.

28 Portmann (1990), p. 258.

29 Doyle (1997), pp. 36, 42; italics mine.

30 See McGinn (1999), p. 18. McGinn is himself guilty of propagating what is referred to in Part II, Chapter 10 as a 'Devil of the Gaps'; consequently, his is merely a 'delayed reductionism', one which may not be meatism but is what one could call a 'vegetarianism'.

31 Jacob (1973), p. 306.

32 Doyle (1997), p. 19.

33 Guénon (1953), p. 107.

34 See Péguy (1958).

35 Foucault (1973), p. 197.

36 *Idem* (1971), p. 128.

37 Smith (1985), p. 73.

38 A physicist turned biologist such as Erwin Schrödinger explicitly treats life as a 'code-script'; see Schrödinger (1967), p. 22. The chromosonal code-script contains the pattern of every life in entirety. 'Genes 'R' Us'; see Doyle (1997), p. 7.

39 See Gamow (1954).

40 We could also include Wittgenstein's systems of explanatory description with their descriptive shows; see Conor Cunningham (1999).

41 I mean this in two senses. First of all, theology is approaching nihilism in terms of examination. Second, theology approaches nihilism in that they are similar in at least one respect; see Part II, Chapter 10.

42 At least to the degree to which it does not lack in lacking.

43 Scientists such as Michael Behe and Alan Linton employ the phrase 'irreducible complexity' in an effort to problematise the Darwinian idea of evolution, for the notion of irreducible complexity resists reductive descriptions; see Behe (1996).

44 The transcendentality about which I am speaking is the trans-categoricality of the medieval transcendentals, each of which is co-extensive with being. On the doctrine of transcendentals see Aertsen (1985), (1991), (1992a), (1995a) and (1996). The transcendentals are discussed later in this chapter.

45 Yet this transcendental circle, in terms of assertion, also appears in nihilism; see Part II, Chapter 10.

46 This moment is necessarily infinite. Just as the fall can, as such, be identically repeated, in terms of its 'logic', by having a single 'part' of creation apart from God, so too can salvation arise through one moment of irreducible given-ness. We were condemned by one, so are we saved by one, so to speak.

47 *De Veritate*, q. 22, a. 1 (hereafter DV); 'Beings with cognitive ability somehow resemble God Himself in whom all things pre-exist', *Super Librum Dionysii De Divinis Nominibus*, V, 1 (hereafter Comm. DN). In this chapter I will not use year of publication to indicate the text, or edition of text; instead, for Aquinas' texts, I will use their Latin titles with an appropriate abbreviation.

48 Blondel (1984), p. 346. 'Every act, whether it is an act of knowledge or an act of will, rests secretly on God'; de Lubac (1996), p. 36.

49 We even presume the actuality of actuality, in that we can easily presume the meaning, and so the significance, of actuality.

50 Blondel (1984), p. 403.

51 Burrell (1973), p. 109. See also *idem* (1979), p. 55.

52 For analogy see the following works: Phelan (1967), pp. 95–122; Clarke (1976); Burrell (1973) and (1979); McInerny (1961), (1968) and (1996); Ross (1981); Lyttkens (1952); Mondin (1963); Mascall (1949); Chavannes (1992); Rocca (1991); Klubertanz (1960); Meagher (1970); Owens (1962); Bouillard (1968); Calahan (1970); Morrell (1978); Smith (1973); Chapman (1975); Nielsen (1976); Garriou-Lagrange (1950), pp. 87–94.

53 Cajetan (1953).

54 Gilson (1955) refers to Cajetan's treatment of Aquinas as tantamount to a sterilisation of St Thomas' metaphysics, p. 134.

55 See *Scriptum super libros Sententiarum*, I, d. 19, q. 5, a. 2, ad. 1. (Hereafter Sent.)

56 McInerny (1961), p. 12. Meagher (1970) also makes the point that such a threefold division is untenable, see p. 237.

57 See Bouillard (1968), p. 106. See Cajetan's *Analogy of Names*, which has an appendix entitled 'The Concept of Being'; Cajetan (1959), pp. 79–83.

58 Gilson contrasts Duns Scotus and Aquinas on exactly this point, arguing that Scotus has an analogy of the concept which is at base univocal; see Gilson (1952b), p. 101. See also Burrell (1973), p. 109; Chavannes (1992), p. 54; Mondin (1963), pp. 43–44; Clarke (1976), p. 65.

59 This is to understand understanding. What I mean by this is that our notions of understanding are upset because we presume what it means to understand, in that we presume that understanding entails understanding *something*. This something is there from the beginning as the beginning, and because of this we never escape this beginning, that is, we never begin. We have failed to understand anything because we have failed to put in question the something. Heidegger would not disagree with this analysis so far. Instead we must, it seems, begin to realise the meta-position required to understand, and so place understanding within a more certain, yet 'agnostic' position, *viz.* faith.

60 *De Potentia*, q. 7. a. 7 (hereafter De Pot.); *Summa Contra Gentiles*, I. 34 (hereafter SCG); *Summa Theologiae*, I, q. 13 (hereafter ST).

61 See ST, I, q. 4. a. 2; SCG, 1. 29, 2; De Pot., q. 3, a. 6. ad. 4; DV, q. 21, a. 4c.

62 See II Sent., d. 8, q. 1, a. 2c. In this passage Aquinas discusses three types of agent causality: univocal, equivocal, and analogical. God is best considered as the last because God is both efficient and exemplary cause.

63 It seems that David Hume is correct.

64 Quoted in Alexander (1966), p. 66.

65 See te Velde (1995), p. 92; Chavannes (1992), p. 18.

66 SCG, I. 29.

67 See ST, 1, q. 4, a. 3.

68 See Burrell (1973), ch. 6.

69 This is a much discussed area. I do not have the space to explore it except to briefly adumbrate what it entails. Aquinas employs such a distinction when he says 'In every name predicated by us [of God] imperfection is found with respect to the name's mode of signifying which does not belong to God, though the thing signified is suitable to God in some eminent manner', SCG, I. 30, 277. In ST, 1, q. 13, a. 3, Aquinas uses this distinction to differentiate between predications that are metaphorical and those that are perfection names, predicable of God. The former primarily signify the creaturely realm, and only secondarily are attributed to God, as in 'God is a rock'. The latter express perfections without any notion of composition, and the *ratio propria* of such a term lies in God. The mode of signification belongs to the creature but the thing signified belongs properly to God. Lytkkens (1952) thinks this distinction is unimportant. Morrell (1978) calls it a 'bogus distinction', p. 114. More generally see Rocca (1991); Aertsen (1996), p. 386; Davies (1992); Chavannes (1992); all accord the distinction a certain importance.

70 ST, I, q. 16, a. 6.

71 As McInerny (1996) says, 'True analogy and univocity are equated', p. 17.

72 'Barth displays characteristics borrowed from Duns Scotus', Chavannes (1992), p. 252, fn. 11; 'That Barth is repelled by the philosophical ideas he cites [analogy] could be explained by his too univocal understanding of them, which could also be his Kantian heritage', p. 260, fn. 142; 'Wolf, who in Kant's view represents metaphysics, establishes the thought of Duns Scotus over that of St Thomas. His affinity with Duns Scotus links Wolf with Suarez. Barth naturally displays characteristics borrowed from Duns Scotus, Suarez and Wolf', p. 253, fn. 11; 'Has Barth not accepted philosophical truths which owe nothing to revelation . . . deducing divine inconceivability from general noetic principles . . . we resemble the objects we grasp, we are masters of what we grasp', p. 179. See also Gilson (1955), p. 178, and (1952a), pp. 84–120. Analogy of the concept is the 'Scotus–Ockhamian primacy of the demand for deductive reasoning and the logical functioning of concepts', Clarke (1976), p. 65.

73 Levinas is discussed briefly in Part II, Chapter 10.

74 Ross (1983), pp. 177, 167.

75 McInerny (1961), p. 35.

76 Fabro (1974), p. 481. For participation generally see Fabro (1961); Te Velde (1995); Fay (1973); Hart (1952); Wippel (1984); Annice (1952); Clarke (1952).

77 Ricoeur (1977a), p. 276.

78 Rousselot (1935), p. 58.

79 Clarke (1976), p. 87. See also Milbank (1998), 'the possibility of analogy is grounded in this reality of participation', p. 15.

80 See Aertsen (1996), p. 384.

81 De Pot., q. 7, a. 7.

82 Causality ensures that the recipient is received in the reception of being, something which participation will reinforce. Without the efficiency of causality, analogy could easily become neo-Kantian, rather more epistemological than metaphysical.

83 Efficient causality is the given-ness of being, a given-ness maintained by final causality, for it frees causation from ontic categories, doing so by demanding a cause of causation. In this way the presumptuous use of concepts such as causality is forestalled. The personalism involved in finality upsets the self-certainty of philosophical categories which think, by employing terms such as cause, logic, truth and so on, that an immediate significance is forthcoming. We see in final causality that this is not the case. Yet the possibility of a narrative foundationalism is prevented by the use of formal causality. For this mode of causality provides the good with the place for its being. In other words, beauty gives the good a breadth, a breadth intimated by efficient causality's brute given-ness. Yet this given-ness is now otherwise than ontotheological or *meontotheological*.

84 When I speak of the real distinction I am referring to the real distinction between essence and existence.

85 ST, 1, q. 65, a. 3, ad. 3.

86 De Pot., q. 7, a. 1, ad. 16.

87 DV, q. 11. a. 1. See Gilson (1940), pp. 128–147. See also Aertsen (1996), p. 171.

88 Chavannes (1992), p. 194. See also Gilson (1994), p. 184.

89 'The end is the cause of the causality of the efficient cause, because it makes the efficient cause be an efficient cause'. *De Principiis Naturae*, 1v.22; 'End is called cause of causes', ST, 1, q. 5, a. 2.

90 See O'Rourke (1992), pp. 85–116.

91 SCG, III. 20.

92 SCG, I. 28.

93 *Liber de Causis*, prop. 1.

94 Deleuze and Guattari (1987), p. 159. Here these two philosophers are writing under the influence of Antonin Artaud's notion of a 'body without organs'; a body free from the 'judgement of God' that would make it into an organism, which is to incarcerate the potentiality involved in a body. Interestingly a somewhat similar 'body without organs' also appears in Samuel Beckett's *The Unnamable*; see Beckett (1955), p. 305.

95 See Te Velde (1995), p. 121.

96 It could be argued that God need not create out of love, or that God need not love us to create us. But this is somewhat mistaken, for if creation is not out of, from and because of love, then there will only be an ontotheological notion of creation at work, because difference *qua* difference will not have been 'invented' so to speak; instead it will be firmly in place, a situation from which God will borrow His ability, but not necessarily His decision, to

'create'. Consequently, God will be God only because of power, which means that God is contingently God, for we do, then, share a univocal plane with Him. In other words, there will not be 'real' creation. The validity of this argument will become more apparent by the end of the book.

97 See Part II, Chapter 10; see also Milbank (1997), p. 49: 'We only are as we love and remain in love, whereas God who is love cannot not be.'

98 It may be suggested that love certainly knows difference, but that this does not mean that all difference is a result of love. For an answer to this the reader should refer to Part II, Chapter 10.

99 Te Velde (1995), p. 233.

100 'The form, through itself, makes a thing to be actual, since it is essentially act'. ST, 1, q. 76, a. 7; 'Every being is due to some form', ST, 1, q. 5, a. 5.

101 De Pot., q. 5, a. 4, ad. 1.

102 The 'intellect can become all things', SCG, II. 83; 'The soul is in a sense all things', DV, q. 1. a. 1. This is directly influenced by Aristotle's *De Anima*.

103 Rousselot (1935), p. 20.

104 Pieper (1989), p. 135.

105 Jordan (1993), p. 247.

106 In Sent. I, prologue.

107 See Peter (1964).

108 It was Augustine (1991) who instructed us that the divine missions reveal the eternal processions of the Trinity. These processions are not constituted by the divine mission, but are eternally so.

109 Boland (1996), p. 261.

110 Generally see Jordan (1984); Boland (1996); Ross (1991) and (1993); Maurer (1970).

111 DV, q. 3. a. 2.

112 ST, I, q. 15, a. 1.

113 See ST, I, q. 15, a. 2.

114 See ST, I, q. 15, a. 3; De Pot., q. 1, a. 5, ad. 11.

115 Jordan (1984), p. 28.

116 See Maurer (1990), on the *Compendium of Theology*, p. 217. For an extensive discussion of the composition of SCG. I, see Boland (1996), pp. 214–225.

117 The role of *Verbum* as exemplar is central to SCG, I. But it was absent in the first redaction. See Boland (1996), p. 220.

118 *Ibid.*, p. 224.

119 It was Augustine (1991) who argued that the persons of the Godhead are their mutual relationships, which is their real, and not nominal, distinction.

120 'Even as a craftsman makes all things by means of the form or word which he has preconceived in his mind, so, too, God makes all things by His word as by His art', Aquinas' *Commentary on the Apostles' Creed*, sermon II, b, 1. See also Augustine (1991), bk. VI, ch. 2.

121 Hebrews I, v. 3; SCG, IV, 12, 4.

122 SCG, IV, 12, 5.

123 John, I, v. 13; Colossians, I. v. 17.

124 See Augustine (1984), bk XI, ch. 10; and (1961), bk VII, ch. 4, and bk XIII, ch. 38.

125 DV, q. 8, a. 16, 11.

126 DV, q. 4, a. 8.
127 DV, q. 4, a. 8; italics mine.
128 Augustine (1982), vol. I, bks 1–5.
129 SCG, I, 44.
130 *Liber de Causis*, prop. 1.6.
131 For the use of the theme of light in theology see Pelikan (1962).
132 See Jordan (1984).
133 See Part II, Chapter 9.
134 Pieper (1990), p. 31.
135 Augustine (1961), bk 10, ch. 27.
136 Borella (1998), p. 75.
137 Those who offer a positive reading of *Pulchrum* as a transcendental number among them Étienne Gilson, who in at least four works states that Beauty is a transcendental: See 'The Forgotten Transcendental: Pulchrum', in Gilson (1978), pp. 159–163; see also his trilogy on the arts, Gilson (1959), (1965) and (1966). In each of these Gilson states that beauty is a transcendental, naming its study *calology*, thus making it a branch of metaphysics, in terms of ontology. Also Eco (1986), (1988) and (1989); Maritain (1930) and (1953); Balthasar (1982–1991); Jordan (1989), who changes his mind, see Jordan (1980); Kovach (1963), (1967), (1968), (1971), (1974), (1987); Maurer (1983); Navone (1996), (1999). For other more general works on beauty see de Bruyne (1969); Chiari (1960), (1970) and (1977); Spargo (1953); Duby (1999); Nichols (1980) and (1998); Viladesau (1999); Garcia-Rivera (1999); van der Leeuw (1963); Brown (1989). The most impressive opposition to beauty as a transcendental is offered by Aertsen (1996), pp. 335–359. At one point Aertsen appeals to Kristeller (1990), pp. 163–178, in the hope of establishing that the triad 'true–good–beautiful' was only developed in the Renaissance. Both Aertsen and Kristeller appear to be employing a rather Kantian understanding, at least at this point in their work. Kristeller's main point is that beauty was not related so much to the arts, but to metaphysics. Yet this is not of real importance in terms of beauty as a transcendental; it may even be an argument for its being so. There is no doubt that beauty did become more prominent in terms of aesthetics in the post-medieval period. Cajetan also thought that *Pulchrum* was reducible to the Good. See Kovach (1963) for excellent arguments against Cajetan's position.
138 Cessario (1992), p. 297.
139 See Jordan (1989), p. 398.
140 Gilson (1960), p. 162.
141 Gill (1933).
142 Quoted by Lacoue-Labarthe (1993), p. 107. See also Benjamin (1980).
143 See Guénon (1953), p. 107.
144 'Beauty properly includes the notion of form', ST, I, q. 5, a. 4, ad. 1; 'All form through which things have being, is a certain participation in the divine causality', Comm. DN, IV, 6; 'Particular things are beautiful according to their own nature, that is according to their own form', *ibid*, IV, 5; 'Form gives a thing its beauty', in Sent. II, d. 23, q. 9. a. 3, a. 1. See also Spargo (1953), p. 34.
145 Comm. DN, IV, 6.

146 'Beauty seems to be inseparably connected with actuality', Maurer (1983), p. 7.
147 See De Pot., q. 4, a. 2, ad. 31.
148 See Part II, Chapter 9.
149 See Pieper (1989), p. 120.
150 See Part II, Chapter 10.
151 See Pieper (1987), p. 6.
152 Augustine (1961), ch. 14. 3; italics mine.
153 For a further discussion of light see Part II, Chapter 9.
154 Beauty is 'the glow of the true and good irradiating from every ordered state of being', Pieper (1966), p. 203.
155 He who knows is somewhat displaced in knowing, so there can be no notion of Kantian control. Furthermore, the subject in being able to know is already intelligible, and in this sense the subject is known, as it is in act. In this way the knower knows only by being already known, that is, by another already being that knower. To know another is, then, already, from the beginning, to be another. We are from, and towards, another, this is the *ecstasis* of our being, and so of our knowing. See Pieper (1985).
156 Pieper (1995), p. 44; he is here meditating on the words of Plato's *Phaedrus*.
157 Keats, *Endymion*, (1957), p. 42; italics mine.
158 de Lubac (1996), p. 190.
159 The plenitude of the object is attested to by its temporality. So, in some sense, every object is a temporal plenitude. See Part II, Chapters 9 and 10 for a discussion of the temporality of being, for there I will speak of the time of eternity as spoken by us in the Spirit.
160 Derrida's *différance* is an example of a Hericlitean stasis.
161 See Part II, Chapter 10.
162 Beauty intimates 'true' notions of friendship and community; see Navonne (1989), pp. 136–137.
163 DV, q. 4, a. 5, 6.
164 SCG, IV, 13. 2.
165 Sent. I d. 31, q. 2, ad. 1. See Kovach (1987), p. 227.
166 ST, 1, q. 39, a. 8; '*Species autem, sive pulchritudo*'. ST, 1, q. 15, a. 3. St Thomas is here following Augustine and Hilary of Poitiers; indeed Aquinas is actually quoting Hilary of Poitiers' *De Trinitate* 6.10.
167 Jordan (1989), p. 401.
168 Psalm 36. 9.
169 'God is light', 1 John, 1. 5; 'One must welcome the Light which is God Himself', John, 1. 9; 'Children of light', Luke 16. 8; 'Whoever hates his brother is in darkness; but whoever loves his brother is in the light', I John, 2, 9–10.
170 Navone (1996), p. 25.
171 Gilson (1965), p. 27.
172 Aquinas' *Sermon on the Apostles' Creed*, III, 2.
173 Aquinas' *Commentary on the Gospel of St John*, Lect. 1, 31.
174 de Lubac (1996), p. 37.
175 Borella (1998), p. 75.

176 For this reason we can agree with Daniélou (1962) that the 'resurrection is not simply an event of the past. It constitutes our present', p. 103.
177 Borella (1998), p. 85.
178 Bouyer (1962), p. 158.
179 'When I will be lifted up from the earth, I will draw all men to me', John, 12. 32. 'Salvation is both human and cosmic *metanoia*, raising up the whole of nature to the fullness of the Kingdom', Evdokimov (1990), p. 111.
180 The Greek word for beautiful is *kalon*, which is itself derived from the verb *kaleo*, which means to call, or beckon. The Greek word for the good is also linked to beauty: *kalokagathia*. The word for the good in Latin also betrays a link to the notion of calling.
181 Jordan (1989), p. 407.
182 Navone (1996), ix.
183 As Guénon says: 'Indefinite repetition is nothing but the pure multiplicity towards which the present world is straining . . . a gradual reduction of everything to the quantitive . . . [B]odies can then no longer persist as such, but are dissolved into a sort of "atomic" dust without cohesion; it would therefore be possible to speak of a real "pulverization" of the world . . . the final return to the indistinction of "chaos" . . . the realm of death and of a dissolution without hope of return . . . this constitutes "satanism" properly so called', Guénon (1953), pp. 17, 139, 199, 201.
184 F. L. B. Cunningham (1955), p. 184. 'Disassociation of the act of creation *ad extra* from the generation *ad intra* . . . sealed the displacement of the Trinity from the centre of Christian dogmatics', Milbank (1986), p. 219.
185 Evdokimov (1990), p. 243.
186 De Pot., q. 3, a. 2.
187 De Pot., q. 5, a. 4, ad. 1.
188 Borella (1998), p. 50.
189 Evdokimov (1990), p. 12.
190 de Lubac (1996), p. 88.
191 'The theophanic capacity of the world'; 'a theomorphic possibility', Borella (1998), pp. 24, 34.
192 Gilson (1959), p. 272; italics mine.
193 Milbank (1997), p. 29.
194 On Mariology see Bouyer (1962).
195 Luke, ch. 22, v. 10.
196 For a discussion of Mary as co-redemptrix see Bouyer (1962), ch. 9.
197 de Lubac (1949), (1956). See also Borella (1998), ch. 7. More generally on the mystical body see Mersch (1938), (1939) and (1951); Rubin (1991).
198 de Lubac (1949), pp. 281–288 ; (1956), pp. 87–93.
199 de Certeau (1992), p. 83. See Pickstock (1998), for an excellent reading of this shift in approach to the Eucharist, and its wider implications, especially pp. 121–166.
200 See de Certeau (1992), p. 84.
201 *Ibid.*, p. 315, fn. 15.
202 See de Lubac (1949), p. 78.
203 Pickstock (1998), p. 163.
204 McPartlan (1995), p. 38.

205 de Certeau (1992), p. 82.

206 de Lubac (1949), p. 288; de Certeau (1992), p. 82.

207 de Certeau (1992), p. 84.

208 The centrality of the individual, or the absolute singularity of beings, in the work of Ockham is argued for by Alféri (1989), Maurer (1999). Adams (1990) accords the idea of individuality a less central but still significant position.

209 'Dialogue de l'histoire et de l'âme charnelle', and 'Dialogue de l'histoire et de l'âme païenne', in Péguy (1992), 3: 594–783; 997–1214. These two texts are referred to as 'Clio 1' and 'Clio 2'. The second text is the more relevant with regard to repetition.

210 See Péguy (1992), pp. 45, 114; see also Péguy (1958); Deleuze (1997), pp. 1, 189. On repetition see Kierkegaard (1983). See also Pickstock (1998) for an excellent use of Kierkegaard's notion of repetition in relation to the Eucharist.

211 'Clio 2', quoted in Servais (1953), p. 336.

212 Marion (1981), p. 37.

213 Péguy (1958), p. 96.

214 Fabro (1974), p. 481; De Pot., q. 5, a. 4, ad. 1.

215 The eternal procession of the Son is not constituted by the divine mission, in the sense that the eternal processions are revealed, but not constituted, by the economic missions. Yet the divine missions do reveal the divine processions ad intra, in that we see our understanding of creation alter as we realise that creation is, in some sense, taken up into the eternal processions. Creation is constituted, while the eternal processions are revealed, not the other way around.

216 Torrell (1996), pp. 43–44.

217 de Lubac (1999), (2000a), (2000b); see also Wood (1998).

218 See Blondel (1995), pp. 219–287.

219 On the displaced body of Christ see Ward, in Milbank, Pickstock, and Ward (1999), pp. 163–181.

220 Pickstock (1998), p. 221.

221 'Do this for a commemoration of me', Luke ch. 22, v. 19; see also de Lubac (1956), p. 93. On the commemorative aspect of the Eucharist see Bouyer (1968), pp. 103–105; Frankland (1902), pp. 102–105.

222 See de Certeau in Ward (1997), pp. 146–147.

223 The notion of cosmic salvation mentioned above is not Origen's apokatastasis. Instead it is Péguy's hope for the salvation of all, a hope based on the fact that God has already hoped for all. See I Corinthians 1, v. 28. See also Péguy's 'The Mystery of the Holy Innocents', in Péguy (1956), pp. 69–165. Also see 'A Vision of Prayer', in Péguy (1965), pp. 183–200. On the notion of cosmic salvation see Balthasar (1988), de Lubac (1988), and Ludlow (2000).

224 On epiclesis see Bouyer (1954), ch. 10. Epectasis is discussed at the end of Part II, Chapter 10.

225 Péguy (1958), p. 120.

226 Le Miracle de l'Eglise, ch. 1; quoted in de Lubac (1956), p. 35.

227 For a meditation on the meaning of virginity see Gregory of Nyssa (1979), vol. V.

228 See de Lubac (1956), pp. 92–93.

229 *Ibid.*
230 On how the Eucharist reconfigures the dynamics of giving and receiving, overcoming postmodern *aporias* with regard to the gift, see Pickstock (1998); Milbank (1995).
231 As de Certeau (1992) says, 'Christianity was founded upon the loss of a body', p. 81.
232 On the Eucharist and eschatology see Wainwright (1981).
233 Péguy, quoted by de Lubac (1956), p. 259.
234 Daniélou, quoted by de Lubac (1956), p. 262, fn. 3.
235 Claudel (1956), pp. 198–199.
236 *Ibid.*, p. 65.
237 Claudel (1942), p. 306; 'The Liturgy takes the form of the sacrament of eternity . . . [the Word of God] as Chronocrator, the Lord of time', Evdokimov (1990), p. 137; see also Pickstock (1998), p. 221; Bouyer (1963), chs. 10–11.
238 Claudel, *Présence et Prophétie*, p. 46; see Caranfa (1989), p. 50.
239 Borella (1998), p. 85; for Hamann see Dickson (1995), p. 350.
240 Daniélou (1970), p. 16.
241 Claudel, quoted by de Lubac (1998), p. 236. This is in stark contrast to someone like Wittgenstein who thought everything was foreseen; see Conor Cunningham (1999).

9

THE DIFFERENCE KNOWLEDGE MAKES

Creation out of love[1]

Proper knowledge

As we saw in the previous chapter, before the opposition of something and nothing there is the eternal procession of the Divine Persons – the Trinity. This affords us a Trinitarian ontology, one which may allow us to speak of difference *qua* difference. Without this ontology, it is argued, difference is impossible and nihilism ineluctable. Yet it must be stated here that the arguments of this chapter will not be satisfactorily developed until Chapter 10.

According to Aquinas, 'Everything is in virtue of its proper operation.'[2] Furthermore, to operate one must be in act, while the nature of every act is to 'communicate itself'.[3] Therefore, God, as subsistent Being (*ipsum esse*), is *actus purus*, and as a result God is perfect communication; indeed, God is, in being pure act, infinitely knowable, utter intelligibility, yet incomprehensible.[4] Lower beings are less knowable, for they contain potency; hence they are always *before* complete communication. Consequently, they are less than completely knowable, but all creation – every creature – is knowable in so far as, and to the degree that, it *is*. Corresponding to modes of operation are different modes of emanation.[5] These range from the inanimate object, which can only be acted upon, to the animate, which acts within itself – to the degree that it grows producing seeds from 'juice'; while for the human, who has an intellect, emanation is greater, because the intellect can know and understand itself by reference only to itself. The intellect's emanation is, then, internal, somewhat subsistent. But the human still begins with senses. Consequently, its emanation is disrupted, and so imperfect. Angelic knowledge is even more immanent, because the knowledge of an angel does not come from without; yet the angel is still not its own being so it remains less than self-subsistent, for only God, as *ipsum esse*, is fully knowable and knowledgeable. In other words, God's understanding is identical with God's Being. Indeed, creation means to be creatively thought by God.[6] We will see below the radical implications of this. Let us for the moment take a closer look at knowledge.

According to Aquinas, we do not comprehend the substantial form of any being.[7] Instead we learn of a thing by its proper accidents; a consequence of which is, as Aquinas says, that 'The essential grounds of things are unknown to us.'[8] For this reason, St Thomas asserts, the philosopher does not even know the essence of a fly. Therefore any particular thing, which is known by listing its predicates, does not afford us actual comprehension of that thing. In knowing some-thing, a space of otherness opens up as the basis of that knowledge; indeed, as we saw in the previous chapter, the intellect is the faculty of the other, the faculty of being[9] – in that to know something the would-be-knower must become the other: for Sartre, Lacan, Badiou and Žižek, this space of otherness is horrific.[10] Intelligence insists that we become that other, for intelligence in a sense contains all things. For this reason Rousselot says, 'Knowledge alone permits oneself while remaining oneself to become the other.'[11] According to Aquinas, this is because an intellect is 'capable of taking all being into itself',[12] which is its *capax omnia*. Of course God is the ultimate intelligence, and for this reason *God's knowledge is the cause of things*. To know, we must become an other. Yet in so doing, do we not run the risk of violating difference, a danger which postmodern priests of alterity appear to warn us against? The exact opposite is the case: I in knowing do not absorb the other, in the manner of an idealistic monism; on the contrary, in knowing an other, in an intelligent manner, I not only become less subjective, for I am now more aware in a substantive and particular sense of this other, but I am more aware of what I do not *comprehend*, namely, this other. The paradox of knowledge begins to come to the fore, especially if we remember that God, who is the most knowable, is comprehended least. In knowing something we fail to comprehend its essential grounds, its substantial form – we fail to know the essence of a fly.[13] Yet we become, in a sense, all beings. That is, we become the other in knowing this other. How can we resolve such a paradox? Instead of offering a solution it may be wiser to learn from such a predicament. What we can begin to learn is a more sophisticated understanding of creation and, as a result, of difference.

Being: incomprehensible

> Being (esse), with which [Aquinas] is concerned and to which he attributes the modalities of the One, the True, the Good and the Beautiful, is the unlimited abundance of reality which is beyond all *comprehension*, as it, in its

emergence from God, attains subsistence and self-possession within the finite entities.[14]

(Hans Urs von Balthasar)

We tend to consider that in knowing something we have increased our *comprehension* of what is known. But if we do not, in knowing something, comprehend any substantial forms and if the essential grounds always elude our comprehension then maybe we should reconsider our approach. Perhaps an increase in knowledge is inversely proportional to comprehension. The supreme example of this is the *beatific vision* in which we see *all* of God's essence, because God is simple, hence to see part must be to see all; but in *knowing* all of God's essence we do not *comprehend* that essence. It must be understood that our knowledge corresponds to our own limitations; a finite, created, being knows in a finite manner – a limitation that is appropriate to a particular nature. So although we know all of God's essence in the *beatific vision*, our finitude and, indeed, our limited charity provide the form of that knowledge. What can this mean for that which we know in this life, *in via*? It is common to consider that which we see as visible, as available to comprehension. But it may be more promising to consider visibility as *in-visible* in terms of comprehension. As Gregory of Nyssa says: 'This is what it means to see: not to see.'[15] Such *in-visibility* is perhaps better conceived as *nubility*, if it is remembered that *nubility* has an etymological connotation of veiling.[16] Some, of a rather phenomenological persuasion, tend to speak of the 'invisible in the visible', in some sense relating this dichotomy to transcendence (for example, Merleau-Ponty, Jean-Luc Marion and Michel Henry). There is certainly something correct in this, but it is somewhat misleading. It is preferable, it seems, to speak of what we consider to be visible as *in-visible*, which is not meant to suggest a noumenality lurking behind appearance, but quite the reverse. As Alexander Düttmann argues: 'The imcommunicable does not hide any content, it has no meaning: it *is* communicability.'[17] In the same way, the in-visible *is* visibility, which is being's *nubility*.

If we take the example of a visually impaired person, we can understand that this person is, in some sense, less aware of blindness than the *correctly minded* visually unimpaired; the more colour seen, the more detail that becomes apparent, the more I know that I do not comprehend that which I am beginning to know – I know I fail to comprehend the blue flower and the small black fly over there.[18] If I did not *know* such rich detail it would be easier for me to pretend comprehension. Indeed, most violence, or violation, tends to stem from, or be encouraged by, a mistaken notion of comprehension. For any such idea employs a reductive knowledge which encourages, as Pieper puts it, 'a de-actualization and devaluation of the visible reality of creation'.[19] If we believe an increase in knowledge to be accompanied by an increase in comprehension then we risk such disregard. As was said in the previous chapter, each being is a plenitude, for it is an imitable example of the divine essence. Any particular being does not provide an infinite example of the divine essence, yet its finitude does not exclude a certain infinity. Therefore the nature of *this* being – as this being – resists every reductive analysis; the very *time* of its being implicates eternity. We saw earlier that 'the measure of the reality of a thing is the measure of its light',[20] and that 'the reality of things is itself their light'.[21] God, meaning to see, is the 'abyss of light',[22] within which the form of every creature rests. As Gregory of Nyssa expresses it: 'Veritably this constitutes the view of God: never to find satiety in desire. [For] God concedes the favour [of vision] by his very refusal.'[23] For light is never seen! Furthermore, we saw earlier that it is the lover, the one who is the most intimate, who knows that the one he or she loves escapes every description. And God, who is love, is the truth of this excess. This is similar to Augustine's 'knowledge with love, or loved knowledge (*amata notitia*)';[24] a notion already expressed beautifully in Plato's *Phaedrus*: '[B]y this madness he is called a lover . . . Then they are beside themselves, and their experience is beyond their *comprehension* because they cannot fully grasp what it is that they are seeing.'[25]

All that which exists is incomprehensible, for the only 'thing' which could be totally comprehensible is *nothing*. When we think we comprehend something because of our knowledge, we treat that something as if it were nothing. I cannot know nothing, or nothingness, hence I can comprehend it; in the sense that comprehension and noncomprehension are the same in reality with regard to nothing. The opacity of creaturely *nubility* gives way to transparency, *viz.*, pure 'visibility'. But this visibility is that of the dark, not of the light. The preceding chapter showed us that we increase our understanding of a being the more we look to its divine source, and so to its *open finality*. The essence of any particular thing is itself specific – final – but this finality possesses an openness arising from the plenitude of the object, which is a reflection of its source. It is for this reason that Pieper considers man's existence in terms of knowledge as a condition of hope;[26] a hope that expresses both limitations and excess.

A caveat must be served here: the disclosure of a being's plenitude must not be conceived in linear terms, for that would suggest a quantitive logic, which in turn implies a certain dubious *gnosis*.[27] Instead of a linear progress, what must be remembered is the form of a *futurial anamnesis*, as manifested in the Eucharist; and an originary repetition that offers itself in such a manner that subsequent repetitions non-identically intensify its truth – a borrowed increase, which is the grace of given-ness displayed in a co-creative open finality.

Any change?

Earlier the matter of divine causality was discussed in terms of God causing as an artist. It is from this understanding that the principle *omne agens agit sibi simile* follows. With this principle we can understand that God, who is incomprehensible, yet infinitely knowable, causes beings who are both knowable yet less than totally comprehensible. In this way, our knowledge of any particular being foreshadows the *beatific vision*. Furthermore, we must realise that creation is caused by the procession of the Divine Persons of the Trinity: 'The issuing forth of the Person in a unity of essence is the cause of the issuing forth of the creatures in a diversity of essence.'[28] As a result, creation cannot be thought of as a change, for the 'temporal procession is not other than the eternal procession'.[29] Indeed, Aquinas specifically says, 'Creation is not a change.'[30] He further argues that 'Creation does not involve any passage into being, nor any transformation.'[31] At one point Aquinas states that 'we cannot say that Being itself is'.[32] Here Aquinas is ensuring that there is no univocity of being by according a certain pre-eminence to the Good as final cause;[33] this allows us to *know* creation as having been created in the distinct absence of *comprehension*. What this disables is any ontic logic that would presume the ultimate legitimacy of certain formal logics. For example, it is tempting to think of creation as different, a difference involving a before and after, but this is to commit a rather Kantian theoretical sin. If we were to say 'creation is a change' then we must have already presumed or have in place, the concept of *change* – whereby the change literally takes place or occurs within something outside the change which is the transcendental possibility of change. However, only creation once established is the sphere of change, which is therefore a finite actuality, not a univocal possibility indifferent to finite and infinite. Not only this, but we also have, again in a quasi-Kantian manner, presumed without declaration the concept of *time*. The change which creation is thought to be has, as such, a before and after. Yet it must be asked 'where is the time of this time, from where does it issue forth'? The time of such a change would, in a sense, have to have been before the subsequent change. Such thinking usually elevates efficient causality above final causality. In so doing an implicit univocity remains, for what can it mean to cause something efficiently without a prior efficiency having already been there *ad infinitum*, and so again in indifference to finite and infinite. The fact that, for Aquinas, creation is not a change, but a way of understanding – a certain relationship – allows him to avoid such univocity. This is in line with Augustine who argued that time only arises with creation. More importantly it begins to allow a more adequate understanding of difference to arise: difference is prior to change, and so *is* different since change occurs only within the *same* framework of change. (By way of deviation, it may be beneficial to note that this balance between efficient and final causality can be compared to a balance that Hamann strikes between philosophy and history; 'Without philosophy there is no history'; 'Philosophy without history is a matter of fancies and verbiage'.)[34]

If creation is not a change, there being no passage into being, and creation is itself caused by the eternal processions of the Divine Persons, then we can tentatively argue that difference to be different requires that this difference arise from a unity, a oneness. For only in this way can any difference be real, and so resist reduction to a general concept. Neoplatonism makes a mistake on this count, for it argues that from one comes one effect, but this generates a dualism from which the originary *One* fails to escape. Indeed, it is this dualism which allows the *One*'s self-articulation; we saw this earlier in Plotinus, where the *One* was constituted by the finite. Instead the *One* must already be different, or be difference. This we see in the Trinity: God as God is difference. The Son is the difference of the Father, while the Holy Spirit is the gift of this difference.[35] The Spirit is essential as it is the 'second difference', to use John Milbank's phrase and, as a result, a reproduction of the aforementioned Neoplatonist dualism on a different plane is avoided.[36] (See Chapter 10.) Such a dualism affords only negative differentiation. God as one substance is a relationality, an originary difference.[37] Because God is difference, yet this difference is a unity, creation can be a result of this difference without having to speak of change. It is for this reason that we understand God to know creatures by knowing His own essence, and that creation is made by and through the eternal Word of God, being held together in that Word.[38] Only in creation not being a change can it really be different from God, an absolute positing that presupposes nothing (no-thing). This seeming paradox is the crux of creation, and consequently it is the foundation of all knowledge.

The Son as the Father's difference brings forth creation. Creation is *for* the Word, and is *through* the Word. Because God is love, the loving difference of the Trinity, creation is within the difference of this love. This would seem to be an odd sort of difference; would not the alterity of creation be violated? Quite the reverse. We saw above that to know something the knower must become the known, and in so doing this other is not erased but discovered and protected, for in becoming this other, this other is known, but comprehended less. God, in an analogous sense, knows creation (though he 'becomes' it entirely within himself) and in so doing creation is not violated but actually created. In this sense God's knowledge is knowledge *per se* for knowledge is to do with creation, or creating, not epistemology. (Epistemology *can never know knowledge*. This be will elaborated on below.)

God becomes the other that God knows, but creates this other in knowing it. Since creation is through the Word and in the Word God becomes that which God knows, in that God allows that which is to be. We are, then, unable to locate a basic concept which would allow us to speak of creation as a change, and for just this reason creation can indeed be a real difference. For difference can but be a result of artistic intention, and cannot be just by nature as the Neoplatonists thought: since nature is the fatality of the univocal same. Creation rather arises from the intentional unity of the divine difference. Because God is in himself the Good that is love of difference, he can posit a genuine difference outside himself, which yet is not alongside him on the same ontic plane. Just because creation is a radical difference which God bears no relation to, and cannot absorb, it all the more declares only the glory of God.

From knowing the fly we the *viator* move towards God. In becoming this other, the fly, we proceed along the inside of a circle.[39] We in becoming the other, which our intelligence knows, begin to understand the plenitude of that other. As our knowledge grows, our comprehension decreases. In so doing, knowledge of this other imitates, in an analogous manner, the difference given to a creature by divine thought, *viz.*, being. We, in knowing, begin to inhabit a realisation of being, of difference. I know the other by becoming the other, just as God creates the other by knowing it through the divine essence. Also, in knowing this other without comprehension I anticipate the *beatific vision*; the proportion of my knowledge is correlated to the clarity, or intelligibility, of this particular other, and the limits of my own intelligibility, due to both nature and charity. Furthermore, I in knowing this other know my self. For I cannot think myself except through difference: a point already made in Plato's *Sophist*.[40] As Aquinas says, 'Nobody perceives himself thinking unless he thinks something else.'[41] Just as we equally know that other by discerning difference: 'To discern is to come to know a thing through its difference from others.'[42] This means that every being relies on others to disclose its own being, a predicament which reflects the dependence of all not just on an other, but on an other other, namely the Wholly Other who is not other (as Nicholas of Cusa would put it).

Knowing me, knowing you: An aporetic heuristics

Because it is what it is (cardinal determination), a creature is also an element of universal order (ordinal determination). Thus a musical note, because it is itself, that is, such or such a specific note, simultaneously defines its place within the octave. By its very nature a creature is a nexus of relationships implying the entire universe.[43]

(Jean Borella)

Every being has an essence which is, of course, its identity – its quiddity – yet this essence is disclosed by otherness. An entity 'X' has an essence which makes it different from 'Y', but its articulation of this essence requires this other. In one sense 'X' is *aliquid*, something, or an 'other what' (*aliud quid*).[44] This is the negative pole of a being's identity. However, every being also has a positive pole to its identity, otherwise a certain monism of mutual determination would arise. For this reason Aquinas says: 'The nature or essence of any thing is contained within that same thing. Whatever, therefore, bears a relationship to what is outside the thing, is not the thing's essence.'[45] This positive pole is the being considered not as *aliquid* but as *res*. These two poles allow us to develop a better understanding of difference, avoiding the problems which plague a purely philosophical approach, as we shall see.

'X' is divided from 'Y' in being a *res*, while 'X' is undivided from itself, but this is not the end of the story. 'X' is also divided from this 'un-division', because of the real distinction between essence and being; 'X' is really distinct from 'Y', but 'X' is also really distinct in itself, for 'X's essence is not its being. This relates 'X' to God. Yet this has a somewhat strange consequence. 'X' in being related to God is divided from itself, rendering its essential subsistence somewhat aporetic. Furthermore, transcendence, which divides the undivided 'X', also directs 'X' horizontally, *viz.*, towards 'Y', since 'X', which has but an aporetic subsistence, exists through the Word, but so also does 'Y'; again the oneness of divine difference forces us to reconsider our basic logics.

Aquinas, following Augustine, distinguished between a *veritas rei* and a *veritas praedicationis*.[46] The *truth of a thing* resides in the Word ('morning knowledge'), while the predicational truth of a being lies within the ontic logics of signification ('evening knowledge').[47] But this is not such a simple division as it may at first seem. The *truth of a thing* of course lies in the Word, for the Word is the very idea of that thing, its originary difference, so to speak. And the truth of a 'saloon car' certainly lies in its predicational order. But the Word, as said, became flesh. This means that the absolute location of the *veritas rei* is complicated, just as a complete discernment of a purely predicational order suffers insuperable difficulties. This is where we can understand the place of a proper pneumatology.

The Son as Word is final since it is God, but this finality is extremely sophisticated, just as the notion of divine difference is. The finality of the Word, while being in place, is open, and it is open because of the Holy Spirit. The Holy Spirit as 'second difference', again to employ John Milbank's phrase, opens up the Word, just as it opens up every creature's essence. For the Spirit, in teaching us that the Son is in the Father and that the Father is in the Son, teaches us that we are in the Son.[48] The Spirit in endlessly interceding for us opens up the finality of the Word, and our essences while maintaining both.[49] We saw above that 'X' was divided from 'Y', and that 'X' as 'X' was undivided from itself, yet the real distinction between essence and existence divides 'X' from this lack of division. This directs 'X' to transcendence – vertical causality but also redirects 'X' towards 'Y'. It does so twice over because the Word has become flesh, offering us His body with which we are to become one. 'X' becomes one with the Word in sharing a unity with 'Y', in a sense becoming one with 'Y'. This means that the negative differentiation, in terms of 'X' as *aliquid*, becomes more constitutive. We realise the extent of this when we understand the role of the Holy Spirit. For the Spirit brings horizontal causality and mutual constitution within vertical determination as it takes us within the Trinity by teaching us the unity of the Word.[50] Our predicational order cannot now be distinguished in an absolute manner from the *veritas rei*, just as 'X' as *res* cannot be understood in an absolute manner apart from 'Y', with whom it is one in the Word before creation. Furthermore, I am now with 'Y' through creation, which is itself within the procession of the Trinity. To repeat a quotation used earlier: 'Essentially, the temporal procession is not other than the eternal procession.'[51] The Spirit, as a 'second difference' is, in a sense, the time of eternity, as it is the *'Midrash'* of the Word so to speak. Here we see the form of divine difference, for creation in its open difference actually occurs within the movement of divine difference. This is why creation is not a change, and for this reason univocity is precluded, since change would occur within a shared being common to finite and infinite. The difference of difference is the divine unity. In this way we become more ourselves, as particular essences, the more we realise that we are within the body of the Word. For in this way we become more Christlike, in that we understand creation in a proper manner, namely as not a change, but as God's thought. Aquinas, unlike Scotus and Ockham, argues that if there were no divine mind there would not be any truth. (See Part I, Chapter 1.) Furthermore, Aquinas calls time a co-inventor and it is possible to understand the work of the Spirit as just this co-invention.[52] For every essence, which we understood to be but an aporetic subsistence in terms of vertical causality, is also within the horizontal pull of a *plenitudinal heuristics*. Each essence finds itself within the open finality of the Word as testified to by the work of the Holy Spirit.[53] As Borella puts it: 'Creation . . . proceeds like a musical score: the staff and notes have been composed by the Logos, but it is the Holy Spirit who sings it.'[54]

The dynamics of identity witnessed in the movement and complication, in terms of location, of the two poles of differentiation, offer us a theological manner of understanding difference which is maybe the only way in which difference can be different. If negative differentiation, or determination, was the only mode of identity then a *Heraclitean stasis* would arise, which is in reality a monism – a univocity of non-being. This is true because such negative determination (as can be witnessed in Spinoza, Hegel, Saussure, Sartre, and Derrida), affords us only formal differences, which upon their first articulation coagulate as the one eternal moment of the system itself. What this means is that such a differentiation cannot but provide an *immediate mediacy* whereby the creature has, in a sense, no before or after. This means that this single difference becomes *all* differences. This is what I call 'Hume's problem'. Hume introduces a plurality into what is perceived and that which perceives, and this means that a single perception is immediately, by implication, all perceptions. There cannot, as a result, be any real difference between perceptions – one perception is all perceptions. In short, a purely negative determination occurs in the absence of vertical causality.

Yet a vertical causality without horizontal reference would produce the same result, but in an obverse manner. Instead of each being but the other, a singularity resides in ontological isolation. We see this in Ockham's absolute things which are pure singularities;[55] in being isolated a singularity inhabits a dark world as a dark object, but this renders *this* singularity all there is. The Ockhamite pole gives us a *monistic monad*, while the Spinozistic pole provides a *monadic monism*. Without horizontal causation we arrive at Ockham, without vertical causation at Spinoza. Theology eludes this dilemma by not only having both a negative and a positive pole, but in avoiding a dualism. For there can be no absolute discernment of either pole, hence a true dynamic is generated. This dynamic understanding of identity – an aporetic subsistence within a plenitudinal heuristics complicated by divine procession – embodies divine difference. For exteriority of identity proceeds from the form of interiority.[56]

I know 'Y', I realise an-other is, but I become this other. Furthermore, this other allows me to think myself, yet the other and I are from the same Word, and are still within this Word; this is especially so when we realise that creation is not a change, and that we are, as the Church, the Body of Christ. Indeed, Christ on the Cross, in some sense, lifts the earth in to Heaven (the horizontal into the vertical, exacerbating its validity). I am a *res* and *aliquid*, both positive and negative. The negative horizontal aspect of my identity, or essence, signals the openness of that essence without reducing its positivity, while this negative determination is, in some sense, as open, positive. For the very negativity of horizontal causality is the result of a perpetual plenitude; the reason why I am open to constitutive determination by way of otherness, is that I and the other are from the Word; a Word which has become flesh, gifting creation with both the divinity and humanity of the Son. This precludes the immediate mediacy of purely negative determination, or *Heraclitean stasis*. The nature of the negative is, in a sense, transformed – transubstantiated – just as we saw with our understanding of difference outside the context of change. Creation is not absorbed as a result of not being a change, since difference is not something over and against an other; difference is, then, some-thing else – another thing. Difference is not ontic; rather we are distinct from God because of our ontological real distinction, in that we are as creatures distinct from ourselves.

We have seen that the negative pole drives us always on, because it stands within the openness of the Word's actual finality, as spoken by the Holy Spirit. This helps us understand the dynamism of the Trinity. For we understand that the Father and Son are not involved in the mere negativity of a dualism, as is the case with Neoplatonism. The positivity of such mutual determination is shown in the eternal gifting of the Word by the Spirit. This is the difference of divine sameness. For us creatures our essences remain open, in an analogous sense, for we inhabit the movement of a plenitudinal heuristics within an aporetic subsistence, which is our participation in divine difference, in that we are thought creatively by God. (Here Berkeley is certainly correct; indeed what I am advocating is a form of 'Berkeleyan realism'). If this negative development was not positive then the aforementioned monism would result, which would fail to provide any negative determination, being the immediate mediacy of a pure positivity. In the same way the redirection of 'X' to 'Y', because of vertical causality, prevents a similar monistic immediacy, one generated by a pure dualism of 'X' over and against God; a dualism which would risk a univocity of being, in that the difference which 'X' was would not resist absorption, for it would understand its difference as consisting in another thing – some-thing else.

So the dynamic identity of creation and every creature renders the positive pole somewhat negative and the negative pole positive. Thereby, the horizontal and the vertical causalities are inextricably intertwined. The aforementioned Humean problem of eternal moments, which results from an introduction of plurality into both subject and object, is avoided. Likewise, there is neither an Ockhamian nor a Spinozistic monism. Instead difference remains difference, every knowledge of which anticipates the beatific vision and remembers divine creativity.

Traditionally speaking

Tradition anticipates and illuminates the future and is disposed to do so by an effort which it makes to remain faithful to the past.[57]

(Maurice Blondel)

> Tradition provides us with the the model and secret of
> spiritual resistance.[58]
>
>   (Jean Borella)

Tradition can be thought to embody a balance between the vertical and the horizontal, for it inhabits an aporetic subsistence within a plenitudinal heuristics. As a result, tradition provides a form of discourse that resists introducing a plurality into the 'subject' and 'object'. What is meant by this is that, for example, the Christian faith-tradition does not suffer the *Humean problem of eternal moments* consequent upon the ultimacy of the 'passage' of succession and sensation. This is a problem repeated by postmodernists when they espouse a grand methodology, that is, a univocity of non-being; Derrida's *différance* is such an example, for *différance* is always before and after all that is, being wholly transcendental.[59] This renders all signification atextual, erasing all linguisticity, in so far as Derrida *comprehends* language.[60] So any narrative about the importance of language, which Derrida appears to advocate, is a narrative to which he remains external and of which he remains in control: he is in control of the lack of control. Instead, faith-tradition enacts a narrative that narrates and re-narrates those who narrate. Therefore Christian faith-tradition forms and is formed by its narratives. Tradition, rather than *différance*, differentiates and unites without introducing a simultaneous plurality, and so precipitating a *Heraclitean stasis*, which is but a univocity of non-being.

Christian faith-tradition achieves this by being a 'religion' of the *Book*; although we must heed de Lubac when he reminds us that 'Christianity is not, properly speaking, a "religion of the book". It is a religion of "the Word".'[61] Derrida castigates the idea of a Book, deeming a Book a self-contained, self-identical, immediacy, which violates difference. But this is to perpetrate an atemporal circumscription of difference and language. By contrast, the inhabiting and explicating of the faith-tradition of a *Book* upholds textuality because the dynamic repose required to prevent a simultaneous plurality, and so foundational sameness, is provided by the skills developed by such a tradition. We are made by *the Book*, yet we make *the Book*, and for this reason *the Book* is the lived resistance to reductive circumscription. This is an ontological plurality as opposed to an epistemic one, which Derrida appears to advocate. We say appears because we cannot be sure, a hesitation engendered by the *Book*; although if this hesitation is merely the banality of promiscuity then an atextuality is introduced, rather than the practised living of a tradition. The promiscuity of such an atextuality is what is here called a 'Protestant reserve'.[62] This 'Protestant reserve' can be witnessed in those theologies which denigrate creation under the shadow of an omnipotent God, for this renders creation so little, so undivine, unmediating, that a residual certainty is generated. Furthermore, this residual certainty is an inverted onticity. Indeed, this residue is a result of its being so little, of creation being 'nothing'; the nothing *as* something. This 'Protestant reserve' is, of course, not simply Protestant, in terms of denomination: it can also be located in Roman Catholic Counter-Reformation thinking. On occasion the form of this type of reactive, and indeed reactionary, thinking enacts a similar inversion. We witness this when it fights against such notions as 'grace beyond the Roman Catholic Church', in terms of salvation, apostolic succession and so on. The problem with this is not the advocacy of tradition, but rather the foundational circumscription which sometimes accompanies and undergirds such extolling. The Roman Catholic Church can certainly locate itself. Yet the Roman Catholic Church is but the participation in, and partaking of, the body of Christ, so it too is consumed. Consequently, foundational location, or circumscription, appears somewhat heretical. (Since we do not comprehend all the truth of Christianity, we cannot exclude for sure 'other' religions. For that is to comprehend them as purely other, which is to presume the comprehension of both self and other.) Heresy in a sense stems from the possibility to *choose*, absolutely, between 'Christian' churches,[63] as it is predicated on a foundational circumscription; circumscription which threatens to render the Body of Christ ontic, so to speak. In so doing, there is a loss of mediacy and a fall into an immediacy that threatens the ontological difference. This sort of onticity is that of a 'Book' which threatens to become atextual, for example the *text* which replaces the Book in the work of Derrida.

We suggested above that Derrida's *différance* enacted an atextuality, made manifest in the *promiscuity* of infinite difference and deferral, which is the same as the *chastity* of the self-certain, for both perpetrate an epistemic ossification as all is 'comprehended'. Those inside and outside are united by the univocity of such an epistemic self-certainty; by knowing yourself fully, absolutely, you know *all* difference as different, and so as the same difference. In other words, in knowing all as difference, in knowing all difference as different, all is the same. Instead, faith-tradition knows itself, but not all of itself. Furthermore, it knows difference, but it does not know all difference as absolutely different; faith-tradition, informed by a Trinitarian ontology, knows a different difference proceeding from the understanding that difference arises from divine interiority, and as a result is not a change.

Yet this same insight forces us to soften the critique of nihilism offered here. For we now find that this logic is not different from theology in an absolute sense; it could even be said that there is a strange analogy. Maybe such a discovery is a more interesting model for 'dialogue' than is usually proffered. This being the case Christian faith-tradition waits and welcomes, resists and desists, within the skilled practices of living which it develops, and which develop it.

> What you have as heritage, take now as task; for thus you
> will make it your own.[64]

(Goethe, *Faust*)

The next chapter re-examines the logic of nihilism, re-presenting it in a more positive manner, arguing that its endeavour to have the nothing *as* something generates a strange analogy between nihilism and theology; for the nothing *as* something *can* be read as a notion of given-ness, one which any doctrine of creation *ex nihilo* would be pleased to advocate.

Notes

1   For a different redaction of this chapter see Conor Cunningham (2001b).
2   ST, 1–2, q. 3, a. 2. c.
3   De Pot., q. 2, a. 1. c.
4   *Super evangelium S. Ioannis lectura* I. 11. 213; ST, 1, q. 12, a. 7, c.
5   See SCG, IV, 11.
6   See Pieper (1957), pp. 56–57.
7   See ST, 1, q. 77, a. 1, ad. 7.
8   *Comm. De Anima* I, 1. 15.
9   See Rousselot (1999), p. 16.
10   See Chapter 10.
11   *Ibid.*, p. 20.
12   SCG, I, 44, 5.
13   *In symbolum Apostolorum, scilicet 'Credo in Deum', expositio*, prol. 864.
14   Balthasar (1982–1991), vol. 5, p. 12; italics mine.
15   Gregory of Nyssa (1978), I, 377.
16   *Nubility* stems from the word *nubere*, which means to veil oneself. A woman would veil herself in preparation for marriage. In this sense the *nubility* of being invokes the *eros* involved in knowledge. Since desire is the ground of knowledge, that which is known will not be comprehended. That is to say, the greater knowledge that is had of the loved reveals a loss of comprehension. For it is typical of the lover to exclaim that the loved lies beyond description.
17   Düttmann (2000), p. 43; Düttmann is discussing Walter Benjamin in this quotation.
18   It must be stressed that this is not simply an occularcentric bias; by sight is meant any of the senses. For a blind person, in being deprived of sight, may be even more aware of that which is not seen. The only possible problem with this is that it implicitly presumes that if the deficiency were removed sight would be attained, and that is misleading, because in having sight restored, 'blindness' is revealed.
19   Pieper (1957), p. 37.
20   *Commentary on the Epistle of Timothy*, VI, 4.

21 *Commentary on the Liber de Causis*, I, 6.
22 Pieper (1957), p. 99.
23 Gregory of Nyssa (1978), I, 404.
24 Augustine (1991), bk. 9, ch. 15.
25 Plato (1995), 249e–250b.
26 Pieper (1957), p. 74.
27 For an exploration of the term *gnosis* see Borella (1979).
28 Sent. I, d. 2.
29 *Ibid.*, I, d. 16, q. 1, a. 1, c.
30 SCG, II, 18.
31 De Pot., q. 3, a. 3, c, p. 43.
32 See *Expositio libri Boetii De hebdomadibus*, lect. II.
33 'If the end is taken away all that remains is emptiness', Sent IV., 1, prol. For this reason the Good is the 'causa causarum', ST, l, q. 5. a. 2, ad. 1.
34 Quoted in Alexander (1966), p. 175.
35 See Augustine (1991), bk. 5, chs. 2, 3.
36 See Milbank (1997), pp. 171–193.
37 'The Persons are the subsistent relations themselves', ST, I, q. 40, a. 2, ad. 1.
38 See Colossians 1, v. 16–17.
39 See Rosemann (1996), ch. 9. This is an excellent book to which I am indebted.
40 See Plato (1993), 255–260.
41 DV, q. 10, a. 8, c.
42 Sent, I. d. 3, q. 4, a. 5, c.
43 Borella (2001), p. 37.
44 See DV, q. 1, a. 1. See also Wood (1966); Rosemann (1999), pp. 135–137; *idem* (1996).
45 ST, l, q. 59, a. 2, c.
46 See DV, q. 4, a. 6.
47 *Ibid.*, q. 8, a. 16.
48 See John 14, v. 25, and John 15.
49 See Romans 8, v. 26.
50 On vertical and horizontal causality see Fabro (1961), pp. 319–343; Rosemann (1996), pp. 279–306; Milbank and Pickstock (2002) pp. 51–58. See also Plato's *Sophist*, 255 c–d; Plato (1993).
51 Sent. I, d. 16, q. 1, a. 1, c; 'The processions of the divine Persons are the cause of creation', ST, I, q. 45, a. 6, ad. 1.
52 *Sententia libri Ethicorum*, lib. 1, lect. II.
53 See Milbank (1997), p. 188.
54 Borella (2001), p. 39.
55 See Maurer (1999), ch. 1. See also Alféri (1989), pp. 15–106.
56 See Geiger (1953), pp. 205–219. In more general terms we make a mistake when we treat interiority as a principle of a subject instead of a principle of ontology. One invokes interiority as an apophatic measure, for we can never locate that which is interior, so to speak. See Part II, Chapter 10.
57 Blondel (1995), p. 268.

58 Borella (1998), p. 45. For a valuable overview of the notion of tradition see Pelikan (1984). See also Guénon (1963) for an interesting, if not eccentric, view.

59 As Wood (1988) comments: 'Derrida either uses transcendental forms of arguments in explaining the term *différance*, in which case he undermines his whole project, or he does not, in which case the force of all he says about *différance* (and its intelligibility) evaporates', p. 65; Dillon (1997), p. x also accuses Derrida of being transcendental; see also Dillon (1995), p. 184. It does seem that Derrida is guilty of transcendentalism, but in Part II, Chapter 10 the significance of such a crime is challenged, by arguing that it may not be the sin we presume it to be. For it is argued that Derrida espouses a transcendentalism which is not transcendental. Such a conundrum is common to the logic of nihilism; for an explanation see Part II, Chapter 10.

60 As does Wittgenstein; see Conor Cunningham (1999).

61 de Lubac (2000b), p. xx.

62 An example of a 'Protestant reserve' can be witnessed in language which suggests an 'overflowing' of grace, or of the Eucharist. What I mean by this is that the idea of overflowing has already demarcated its boundaries, which are now being overflowed. This is an inverted onticity. Instead, eschatological plenitude is an inability to locate the extent of divine grace, salvation, Christ's true body. In being able to see (say, or do) we cannot foresee; *contra* Wittgenstein, see Conor Cunningham (1999).

63 The word heresy stems from the word for choice (*hairesis*); see Borella (1998), p. 3.

64 Quoted in Pelikan (1984), p. 82.

10

PHILOSOPHIES OF NOTHING AND THE DIFFERENCE OF THEOLOGY

Sartre, Lacan, Deleuze, Badiou and creation out of no-one

Introduction

So far I have endeavoured to offer both an accurate description and a critique of nihilism, but this is to ignore the possibility that nihilism may offer a *promise* of genuine creation, and this challenges the theological critique offered so far. The question is, then, not only 'can theology overcome nihilism' but also, 'does it sublate it?'

This chapter has four sections. The first discusses the *aporia* which this book takes to be central to the task of discerning a genealogy of nihilism. The second and third sections endeavour to identify what is central to nihilism. In so doing, both a positive and a negative evaluation of nihilism are presented, concentrating on the notion of creation *ex nihilo* which nihilism appears to propagate in the guise of the nothing being *as* something. The second section articulates this idea with reference to many of the philosophers discussed so far, but with particular reference in addition to Gilles Deleuze and Alain Badiou. An initial, yet replete, critique is made. However, the third section re-presents nihilism's strange doctrine of creation, with special reference to Jean-Paul Sartre, Jacques Lacan and Slavoj Žižek. The purpose of this repetition is to further confront nihilism's similarity and difference with theology. Following this, it is argued in the fourth section that a difference remains between theology and nihilism, but one which is somewhat more agnostic; an agnosticism of the faithful, for it is but the agnosticism of a tacit 'dialogue'.[1]

An *aporia*, so to speak

What am I to do, what shall I do, what should I do, in my situation, how proceed? By *aporia* pure and simple.[2]
(Samuel Beckett, *The Unnamable*)

I think *x* or *y*, but what is it to think either of these or what is it to think? When we think, do, or see *something*, we presume a certain significance for each of these events. Yet this significance cannot, it seems, be accounted for within the immanent realms of any of them. In other words, how am I to decide that the sound emitted by my mouth is different from the sound of waves, the silence of stones, or dogs barking? An answer may be that one communicates in a sophisticated and extremely complicated fashion while the others do not; but such a reply attends merely to the mechanics of the procedure. Consequently, this does not explain, or even address, the presumed *significance* of this no doubt complicated act. Therefore a further edition of the same question must be issued; what is it to communicate, why should it be considered important?

Such questions bring us face to face with the aforementioned *aporia*: if we lean back in our chairs declaring that there *just are* metaphysical questions to be asked, then we have not attended to the significance required, and so presumed, in this utterance. It seems we require a *thought of thinking*, or a *thought of thought*. In other words, a meta-level is required. But the identification of such a need does not escape the *aporia*; instead, it deepens it. If thought requires its own thought, then it can either be another thought or something other than thought; the former would initiate an infinite regress, for the supplementary thought would require its own thought and so on. Such a thought would be reducible to the previous thought, failing to escape, and so explain, the immanent act. The latter would ground thought in that which is not thought, but this means that all thinking would rest upon its own absence, as its foundation would not be the same as itself. Yet this returns us to the previous position, in which thought had not addressed its own immanent activity, simply presuming its significance. But if thought does endeavour to think itself, it then bases itself on what is *not* thought. As a result all thinking would, as before, fail to think. We have paid witness to this quandary in earlier chapters, where the dualisms employed to cope with this *aporia* (which was the fundamental problem bequeathed to German idealism by Jacobi) display the difficulties involved.

It may be instructive to recall some of these dualisms: Heidegger grounds Being in *das Nicht*; Deleuze, sense in nonsense, thought in nonthought; Hegel, the finite in the infinite; Fichte, the I in Non-I; Schopenhauer, representation in will; Kant, the phenomenal in the noumenal; Spinoza grounds Nature in God, and God in Nature. Each of these dualisms collapses into a monism as each dualism resides within a symbiotic unicity; a unity which is at times named, alluded to or ignored. For example, Derrida employs a dualism of text and nothingness, or presence and absence, but these are the by-product of a 'higher' name – *différance* – although such a name is immanent to the dualism. According to Derrida, *différance* is the 'primordial non-self-presence'.[3] Furthermore, '*différance* is . . . what makes this presentation of the being present as such'.[4] Indeed, '*différance* makes possible the opposition of presence and absence possible'.[5] Derrida indicates the fundamental nature of *this* supplement when he argues that 'it is the strange essence of the supplement not to have essentiality'.[6] Yet this simply transposes the *aporia* to another level. Similarly, Schopenhauer collapses his dualism of will and representation into what he terms 'nothing': 'After the complete abolition of the will . . . is nothing, [indeed] this very real world of ours, with all its suns and galaxies, is *nothing*';[7] the world is but objectified will, but will is itself nothing.[8] As we saw in an earlier chapter, Hegel names his single ultimate *Geist*, into which the finite and infinite slide.[9] Likewise, Heidegger's Being and Time fall into the *das Nicht*, or alternatively Being and Nothing rest upon and within the *Abgrund*, while Gilles Deleuze rests his dualism of sense and non-sense on what he calls 'the groundless ground [which] engulfs all grounds'.[10] And the name of this groundless ground is the One-All,[11] for which there is but a single voice (univocity). Consequently, there are not, argues Alain Badiou, really 'thoughts in the plural'.[12] Incidentally, Badiou names the One-All *the void*, which he deems the proper name of being.[13] The monistic nature of these names becomes more obvious if we take the example of Deleuze as instructive.

For Deleuze the absolute *outside* is 'an outside more distant than any external world because it is an inside deeper than any internal world'.[14] This outside which is not external, is the supplementation of sense by nonsense, or thought by nonthought. What Deleuze is endeavouring to do is to avoid transposing the *aporia* onto a new level, which would identically repeat the problem. Likewise, Derrida endeavours to elude the *aporia* in a similar fashion, arguing that *différance* is thought that '*means nothing* . . . the thought for which there is no sure opposition between *outside and inside*'.[15] The success or otherwise of such philosophical moves is explored below following a re-examination of nihilism. This re-examination presents the possibility that nihilism offers a positive 'element', one which theology can sublate as part of its fundamental content. In this way, the Hegelian sublation of religion is reversed and radicalised. In other words, just as Hegel took philosophy's content from religion, theology can take some of its content from nihilism, recapitulating it within the form of faith-tradition as explicated by theology.

Nihilism: the consummate philosophy?

The moving desert

The desert is squeezed into the tube-train next to you. The
desert is in the heart of your brother.

(T. S. Eliot, *The Rock*)

There is a poem by Shelley called *Ozymandias*. In this poem a traveller
comes across the remains of a statue in a desert, upon which there is an
inscription that is still readable. It reads:

My name is Ozymandias, King of Kings;
Look on my works, ye Mighty, and despair.

Such an inscription can be taken as a critique of vanity, the pretension of
importance. Someone like Derrida takes the mobility of the sign to be the
iterability of the sign; signs are repeatable by definition outside any
particular context in which they were first uttered. In other words, signs
are acontextual, hence they can be employed and re-employed at
different times or in different places. For example, the inscription in the
poem can still signify, yet its significance has altered, even though the
signifiers remain the same. This is relevant to nihilism, because if we take
this iterability of the sign seriously, then all signs always signify in a *desert*,
which is analogous to the nothing *as* something. If nihilism is correct, we
inhabit cities which resemble the sets of Western films, for there is only
façade, so to speak. Indeed, the fact that thought cannot, it seems, think
itself, indicates that thought is somewhat lacking; since it is full of
something other than thought. Every signification is, then, underwritten
by an 'in-signification', for we do not travel to the desert as it is always,
already, before us. Interestingly Deleuze refers to the One-All as a
moving desert.[16] Of course, this movement would be 'on the spot',
otherwise there would be places other than the desert, and such places
would be outside the One-All; an outside that could possibly evade
Deleuze's Scotistic–Spinozistic advocacy of a univocity of being. This will
be elaborated upon below.

Postapocalyptic

The end of the End.[17]
(Alain Badiou)

> The death of metaphysics or the overcoming of philosophy
> has never been a problem for us; it is just tiresome,
> idle chatter.[18]
>
> (Gilles Deleuze and Felix Guattari)

Nihilism is *postapocalyptic* in more than one way. First of all, nihilism declares that nothing is. Second, and more importantly, nihilism reads this assertion with a particular strength, which is to say that nihilism is arguing that nothing *is*. Throughout this book I have endeavoured to explore this strange logic, but maybe its more positive aspects have not been presented. Mark C. Taylor intimates the positive aspect of nihilism when he argues that 'ontotheology leaves nothing unthought by not thinking nothing'.[19] This sounds abstruse, but it is making an important point; ontotheology presumes the significance of its categories and concepts, and in so doing it fails to think the thought of thought. As a consequence, it employs only logics of an ontic nature. In other words, it fails to think any ontological difference: we saw this earlier when discussing causality; ontic models of causation forget to question the space into which that which is being caused is from: cause of causation. Instead they remain at the superficial level of the ontic. With regard to ontotheology, it is possible to suggest that Taylor is arguing that it – in thinking everything – thinks nothing. In this way it perpetuates what Adorno calls the 'lie of the question mark';[20] or as Samuel Beckett expresses it: 'Where now? Who now? When now? Unquestioning'.[21] Ontotheology has an exhaustive – yet unchecked – knowledge of everything. For such ontic logics, to borrow a mathematical analogy, always have a *domain*. A 'potential infinite' in mathematics always has a domain of which its variable is a value; in this sense the potential is always actual, it is already, so to speak – this is what Hallett calls the *domain principle*.[22] It seems that Taylor endeavours to both critique and escape these ontic questions. For him, ontotheology has thought everything and so it has thought nothing; it has not thought at all. This being the case, a *space* appears to open up within the corpus of ontotheology. For in leaving nothing unthought, ontotheology leaves us 'something' to think, and so leaves us the chance to think, which is to think difference. Taylor wants us to *think* nothing. The same could be said for Derrida, who argues that 'in a certain way thought means nothing'.[23]

> In reality I said *nothing* at all, but I heard a murmur,
> something gone wrong with the silence.[24]
>
> (Samuel Beckett, *Molloy*)

For Taylor, we are to know we cannot know. In other words, we are to think *nothing* in an effort to escape the ontic grip of *the something*. For this

239

something will eschew specificity, that is, difference. Consequently, every *reditus* will precede any *exitus*, so to speak. In this way, to think something is to know nothing, while to think nothing may be to know 'something'. Similarly if our thought has a ground – foundation – it will fail to 'get off the ground'. Any height that such thinking attains will still reside on the ground upon which it rests. In other words, the perceived height is illusory; an illusion that distracts thinking. The *opiate of the something* keeps the thinker on the ground. Therefore thought, it seems, must be groundless. Here we are in the midst of a strange logic – that of nihilism. This is a logic that offers a seemingly fundamental challenge to theology, because the theologian thinks of creation as *ex nihilo*, yet this may turn out to be somewhat ontic. In contrast, nihilism urges us to think of 'genuine creation' (Deleuze's phrase) *as* nothing.[25] Before considering such an idea it may be profitable further to elucidate the nature of this nihilism.

Nihilism is postapocalyptic, because it is past being apocalyptic. That is, it is otherwise than merely negative. The apocalypse, which is passed through, or passed over, is that of the *disaster*. This is Maurice Blanchot's phrase; he speaks of 'writing the disaster'.[26] This is a disaster which is itself always postapocalyptic, because 'when the disaster comes upon us it does not come'.[27] More instructive is the understanding of the disaster as that which 'ruins everything, while leaving everything intact'.[28] What is this disaster? What is it that could both ruin and keep that which it ruins intact? Predictably the answer is nothing; nothing does actually, in a sense, ruin and keep intact everything. For this is 'to be without being', a state of affairs Blanchot refers to as 'possibility itself'.[29] Why is this possibility itself, what does it make possible? It seems that this *nothing* may well make creation itself possible, and it will be at such a juncture that nihilism and theology approach each other.

To crown anarchy

The Absolute of Nothingness as the univocity of Being.[30]
(Uhlmann)

The disaster is to *be* without being, and this is to issue in a certain univocity, which was referred to earlier as a *univocity of non-being*. What this means is that everything *is* not, or rather, that all *is* nothing. For this reason the disaster is posthumous, in that our suicide precedes us.[31] Therefore, we only *are* after being nothing, but not in the manner of *ex nihilo*, for that implies that we are no longer nothing. Instead we remain nothing, but as we have seen, we are nothing *as* something. For the nihilist, language *says* nothing, and for Derrida what is *outside* the text is nothing, or the nothing (*das Nicht*). But as Deleuze and Guattari say, this outside is the 'not-external outside and the not-internal inside';[32] it is, so

240

to speak, the outside-in. Mark C. Taylor tells us that the question is 'How to do nothing with words'.[33] But language, it seems, is doing just this, for language is saying nothing. And as we saw in an earlier chapter on Derrida, if language says nothing it has *uttered* its outside, for it is nothing which is outside the text. In other words, language has, in a sense, attained a 'reference' other than itself, a 'reality' of sorts. Such a reality will lie beyond the purview of the ontotheologian, and so it will be *otherwise* than ontic (or otherwise than being). This is the language of the disaster, for it is without being; a *crowned anarchy*.[34] What could rule in such a land, who would be the monarch? Surely it must be nothing, for nothing rules in the disaster, but make no mistake, it does rule. Yet it must still be asked, what can such a kingdom provide?

To provide nothing: Nihilism as genuine creation

What is forever excluded . . . is a pure and simple repetition of the philosophers of participation.[35]

(Paul Ricœur)

Can we not conceive a reconciliation between analogy and Univocity?[36]

(Gilles Deleuze)

We can begin to see that nihilism may well provide all that theology can. It has already been pointed out that nihilism cannot afford to be lacking, as it must be plenitudinal. This is exactly what we are starting to witness here. Consequently, it is possible to argue that nihilism endeavours to donate real creation, so to speak. This creation will no doubt be in the absence of both Creator and creature. But this will now be assessed in a partially positive manner. Let us see why. Theology conceives of creation as *ex nihilo*, but nihilism can try to make the point that such an idea is ontic since the nothing will always be an empty *space*, or as Bergson might say: nothingness is but the suppression of an absent something.[37] For this reason Bergson argues that 'The representation of the void is always a representation which is full.'[38] According to Kolakowski, Bergson means that:

> It is the practical attitude of our intellect which fabricates the nonsensical idea of 'nothing'. The absence of something we expect or wish to see is the foundation on which the abstract idea of total absence, of nothingness, is built. Since we can mentally abolish any particular thing, we imagine that we can abolish the whole and think of an empty abyss. . . . [A]bsence is a category relative to our recollection . . . with no ontological meaning.[39]

Furthermore, nihilists such as Lacan, discern in the doctrine of creation *ex nihilo* a particular atheism: 'The creationist perspective is the only one that allows one to glimpse the possibility of the radical elimination of God.'[40] Nihilism does not say that creation is from nothing, but that it *is* nothing and remains so. This may seem to be contradictory, yet it is not; certainly it is counter-intuitive, but not obviously illegitimate. Creation is impossible, and is only possible if it can be without prior existence; and we saw above that Blanchot considered that to be without being was possibility itself. The fear is that if creation stems from transcendent being then it will be merely ontic, as being comprising an eminent presence of everything ontic will be presupposed.

It seems that for the nihilist it is the univocity of non-being which ensures that creation is nothing, and this in turn allows creation to be truly different. This is what Deleuze appears to call 'Genuine creation',[41] one that is a 'presence made of absence', as Lacan puts it.[42] Univocity is defined by Deleuze as the single voice of the single event, and in the same sense;[43] the very clamour of being.[44] It was mentioned above that for Badiou there are not really thoughts in the plural; a consequence of univocity. But this univocity does allow for dissimilar production,[45] as all resides unequally in the equal One.[46] Here we see a challenge to the analogical notion of participation advocated earlier, because this univocity allows, in a sense, for difference-through-sameness, just as it was argued earlier was the case for creation without change; creation originating from the interiority of the Godhead. The fact that creation, in terms of the univocity of non-being, is nothing, presents, as it were, a radical and almost inconceivable notion of participation. This is one which is somewhat similar to the narrator in Beckett's *The Unnamable*: 'I can't go on, you must go on, I'll go on.'[47] This encapsulates the sheer impossible possibility of creation *as* nothing, in a postapocalyptic sense. For nothing is no longer taken apocalyptically, that is, negatively. As Blanchot argues, the disaster 'is that which does not have the ultimate for a limit: it bears the ultimate away in the disaster'.[48] If we take the ultimate as the opposition between nothing and something, we can see that in the postapocalyptic tone of the disaster, the question is no longer 'to be or not to be', but, as said, to be without being. In other words, to *be* nothing: the nothing *as* something. Like Beckett we cannot go on, but we do, we will, we must. Such is the positive discourse of nihilism.

In this way nihilism becomes, in a plenitudinal sense, provisional. For not only will it offer us the possibility to think otherwise than ontically, but it gives us the surprising *promise* of creation, even a strange participation. What is interesting is how classical philosophical concepts are provided by sophisticated nihilists such as Deleuze, yet are presented in an atypical fashion. (Incidentally, both Badiou and Deleuze refer to themselves as classical philosophers.)[49] It was suggested earlier that we cannot participate in a sight that sees, a saying that says, and so on, without the mediation of transcendence. But what nihilism ingeniously does is to grasp the negative aspect of this type of assertion, and transform it into something positive. In other words, nihilism will endeavour, in the name of 'creation', to provide sight without seeing, thinking in the absence of thought, existence without being.

As we saw in the preface, the word *provide* stems from the Latin *pro* meaning before, and *videre* meaning to see. Provide can, then, be taken to mean *before* sight, or before that which is seen. In this sense nihilism tries to provide that which is yet to arrive; that which will not arrive. For the nihilistic provision will, in a sense, occupy its place. Therefore nihilism gifts us sight before, or without, seeing. This may help us to understand why a philosopher such as Badiou speaks of 'objectless knowledge'.[50] Indeed, Badiou argues that 'every truth is without an object',[51] just as every subject is 'objectless'.[52] What can this mean? It seems that Badiou is attempting to have the nothing *as* something; to *be* without being. He employs Cantorian mathematics to develop an ontology of the multiple, along the lines of what Cantor would call an inconsistent multiple: a multiple that cannot be counted as a unity. As Cantor puts it, 'A collection can be so constituted that the assumption of a "unification" of all its elements into a whole leads to a contradiction, so that it is impossible to conceive of the collection as a unity . . . such collections I call absolute infinite or inconsistent collections.'[53] Badiou combines this notion of an inconsistent multiplicity with the Cantorian idea 'that the parts are more numerous than the members (Cantor's Theorem)'.[54] Badiou calls this a 'wandering excess'[55] (presumably he gets this from Cantor who spoke of wandering limits).[56] Cantor showed that there were different 'sizes' to infinity or that there were different infinities with varying powers.[57] What is relevant to us here is Badiou's use of such ideas to develop what he calls a theory of 'the Two'.[58]

What this means is that the *One* contains a number beyond itself, so to speak. When Badiou speaks of the Two he means to suggest that any set has already within itself a *space of more*. We recognise such an excess in the Two, who have, through desire for example, subjectivised themselves in terms of an amorous encounter, which defies and escapes any unity. The Two escapes the One, or rather the Two is an escape from the One since multiplicity cannot unify. But more profoundly, the Two in escaping 'does'[59] not leave, for it does not establish another unity. Instead its subjectivity can be tied to what Badiou calls *an event*, to which the Two is the display of a 'post-eventful fidelity'.[60] Badiou gives St Paul as example: St Paul remained faithful to the event of the Resurrection, but this does not mean it happened; instead it is happening in St Paul, as it *is* St Paul; just as Lenin *is* the revolution, and the Two lovers are the event of their amorous encounter; they are formed from and by it, as a witness to it, yet they are not different from it. These lovers do not look externally for verification, they – as Two – are verified. The point is not to expound the thought of Badiou; rather, it is merely to give an example of nihilism's provision. Here we have realities which function in the absence of the *Real*.[61] We have reality, but it rests in a space before or without the *Real*. Indeed, if there were such a thing as the *Real* then there could not be a reality, or so the nihilist might argue. For Badiou, events diagonalise out of the unity of the One, discovering it to be inconsistent, since there is no function available to provide unity or closure. In mathematical terms there can be no bijection; in other words, there cannot be any one-to-one mapping between sets.[62] In this way, there is a wandering excess, or what Badiou calls an additional signifier.

To repeat: what is important here is the attempt to provide reality without the *Real*; just as there are subjects in the absence of objects, which allows Badiou to have both without either. For each subject is, as such, the embodiment of an event, a quasi-object. The event is not an object, for there is no subject apart from it, to which it could become an object. In this way, the subject is a trace of an event, being only formally distinct from it, and vice versa; we *are*, then, in the absence of both subjects and objects, but within the substantive shadow of each. Nihilism, in this sense, provides before that which is provided. This is the *provenance* of nihilism.

We saw this logic also epitomised in the logic of the disaster, which occurs-without-happening. As Deleuze and Guattari say, 'nothing happens yet everything changes'.[63] This is because the nothing *actually* happens; this is the disaster. Nihilism provides us with endless examples of its provisional logic. For example, Badiou's objectless truths: we have what is true before the truth, or Blanchot's suicides which precede us, allowing the living without life.[64] In a similar fashion, Deleuze and Guattari seek to have 'transcendence within the immanent', which means that we have transcendence but no transcendent.[65] Conversely, these two philosophers argue that: 'Immanence is immanent only to itself, and consequently captures everything, absorbs All-One, and leaves nothing remaining to which it could be immanent.'[66] This appears to mean that we have immanence, but nothing immanent. Such a logic can be repeated *ad nauseum*, applying itself to many concepts, a further illustrative number of which are offered below. These examples challenge parts of the critique of nihilism which I have also offered, while at the same time indicating ways in which it can be strengthened.

Part I, Chapter 7 accused Derrida of being a transcendentalist. This is not untrue, but the significance of this criticism must be reappraised, because Derrida, in a sense, can be a transcendentalist while not having anything transcendental (or having *nothing* transcendental!). Consequently, the legitimacy of the negative assessment is challenged because nothingness 'underwrites' the provision. In other words, so long as transcendentalism is provided before it is 'seen', or before something transcendental is 'seen', then Derrida may well escape the criticism. The same can be said for metaphysics, for the philosopher can have or provide a metaphysics without, or before, being metaphysical. Someone like Badiou is quite conscious – in spite of postmodern prohibitions – of providing a metaphysics.[67] In this light do we understand his opposition to all those fashionable brokers of 'the end'. Instead, as we saw above, he calls for 'an end to The End'.[68] Yet, for Badiou, being metaphysical does not stop one from being a nihilist. Maybe it is for this reason, or because of this logic, that we also hear of a *God without Being*, for all the intended difference between Marion's Catholic orthodoxy and nihilism.[69] For in this way the nihilist can have a god who is not divine. We see this not only in persons such as Jean-Luc Marion, but more significantly back in Descartes whose God cannot doubt and so deceive, because this God is not any longer exactly 'conscious'; this God is already dead.[70] The nihilist can provide a god without, or before, divinity; for example: Caputo's 'Religion without religion'; Mark C. Taylor's 'Atheology'; Žižek's 'Faith without Belief'.[71] Such a logic is epitomised by the words of Blanchot when he speaks of 'the night lacking darkness, but brightened by no light'.[72] Brightness without light – night in the absence of darkness – this is the provenance of nihilism. Just as for Deleuze and Guattari the void is not nothingness, and chaos, which is the One-All, is not to be defined by disorder,[73] because it is not chaotic. Likewise for the nihilist, the void is *plenum*, because the void is the 'proper name of being'.[74] This is the nothing *as* something. Mark C. Taylor in the end, or after the end, has his 'prayer' answered – he is allowed to '*do* nothing with words'.[75]

How can this be? How does the nihilist manage such a feat? It seems there is a secret supplement at work. For example, in the work of Deleuze and Guattari philosophy is supplemented by non-philosophy, just as art is said to be supplemented by non-art, science by non-science.[76] This supplementation is important enough for Deleuze and Guattari to argue that 'the non-philosophical is perhaps closer to the heart of philosophy than philosophy itself'.[77] Furthermore, they endeavour to keep such a supplement internal. For example, they assert that the 'pre-philosophical . . . [is] something that does not exist *outside* philosophy'.[78] Why do they require such a supplement? This supplement is required to enable them to provide that which they endeavour to provide: if art depends on non-art then we can have the aesthetic without beauty. For art does not have to account for its own excess, an excess arguably present in all immanent realms. Think of a Shakespeare sonnet; it is always more than the paper and words. Indeed, it is arguable that all behaviour – and all beings – are the embodiment of such an excess. But if art cannot account for the significance, or signification, of its own realm, then it will have to be *accounted* for elsewhere. Taking account in this manner tends to manifest itself as a *discounting*, which involves a *deflation* of the immanent existent by the employment of other terms or concepts.

To take a previous example: 'Biologists no longer study life . . . [indeed] biology has demonstrated that there is no metaphysical entity hidden behind the word "life".'[79] If such a discourse is presented with a dead body how will it speak of death? Furthermore, if science is to remain 'atheistic', that is, fully immanent to itself, in the sense of not requiring the mediation of transcendence, so that it says what it does say by itself, then it makes a trade-off with philosophy leaving such concepts as life and death to the latter's domain. This might lead us to the conclusion that science incurs a loss of independence. But this is not the case, because science *takes account* of the excess by *discounting* it, reducing it, carrying it away, transferring any residual significance into neutral terms. Then science will have, after all, borrowed *nothing*. Hence the cadaver is dead, but there is no *death* to be explained, described or negotiated. To reuse a quotation from Richard Doyle: one is 'a meat puppet run by molecules, [which is an] effect of a univocal language of life, an Esperanto of the molecule';[80] this is what McGinn refers to as 'meatism'.[81] For this reason it is possible to argue that biology cannot tell the difference between a dead body and a living body – death escaping its discourse – as all is reduced to biological terms, which fail to register, in a significant manner, any real difference. Therefore there are but formal distinctions, which are only 'parochial' articulations. Consequently, we can agree with Adorno: 'Our perspective of life has passed into an ideology which conceals the fact that there is life no longer.'[82]

> The tears stream down my cheeks from unblinking eyes.
> What makes me weep so? From time to time. There is
> nothing saddening here. Perhaps it's *liquefied brain*.[83]
>   (Samuel Beckett, *The Unnamable*)

Like nihilism, biology, to a degree, escapes the critique offered here by embracing the apparent negativity and turning it into a positive or at least indifferent matter. Biology allows a non-science, philosophy, to cart the body away in terms of death. Then philosophy in its turn deflates any excessive signification, arguing that there is no death, no soul and so on; or that death occurs before birth. In this way death occurs, but does not happen; instead nothing happens. And this allows biology philosophically to have the dead in the absence of death. (It is not surprising that thinkers as disparate as Dennett and Deleuze employ an idiom that refers to humans as machines.) Consequently, the biologist meets us only after death, for the nihilist has provided him with a discourse which includes the living and the dead without death and life.[84]

We can witness a parallel situation in the different views regarding consciousness. Antonin Artaud refers to consciousness as 'nothing',[85] while Roger Penrose speaks of consciousness as 'the phenomenon whereby the universe's very existence is made known'.[86] But as Badiou argues: 'we cannot know where the sensible finishes and the intelligible begins'.[87] Therefore any significance consciousness might be thought to possess is but the result of an imputation, one which cannot immanently account for itself; in other words, there is no *thought of thought* here to aid us past the aforementioned *aporia*. So Artaud could say to Penrose, 'You have yet to say anything intelligible. For what is existence, why is it to be deemed significant?'. Furthermore, Penrose's disclosure is empty, for consciousness is *of* the universe. Consequently, it is not the universe's existence which is disclosed, it is just the universe 'universing'; in this way, it neither exists nor does not exist. As Beckett's narrator puts it in *The Unnamable*: 'To think of myself as being here forever, but not as having been here forever . . . [T]here are sounds here, from time to time, let that suffice.'[88] Penrose smuggles in the term *existence* with an unaccounted for significance. This term should in the name of parsimony be discarded, for all is already *provided* for.

The nihilist, then, can provide a metaphysics as it is something already *discounted* elsewhere. In other words, nihilists can 'speak' safely from within their skin, for they are but genes and atoms. This is the *provenance* of a metaphysics which is not something metaphysical: nothing *as* something. Does nihilism, so conceived, actually presents us with 'genuine creation'? Is the creation proffered by nihilism so creative that it lacks both a creator and a creature, yet remains a creation *nonetheless*? For is it not Lacan's insight that creation *ex nihilo* is atheistic because a creation from nothing is so utter that every creation cannot register a need for a cause.[89] In other words, every creation from nothing remains nothing; nothing *as* something. For example, the subject, according to Lacan, is a creation from nothing, in so far as it does not have being (*manque-à-être*). Consequently, it is a nothing *as* something, which means that the idea of a creator is otiose.

Passers-by

A remarkable passer-by.
(Mallarmé on Rimbaud)

Leopards break into the temple and drink the contents of the sacrificial vessels; this happens over and over again; eventually it can be reckoned with, and it becomes part of the ceremony.[90]

(Franz Kafka)

Does the nothing *as* something offer us a promise of something positive, plenitudinal? Is the provision of signification without, or before, significance, as is the case in the work of Derrida, creative? If so are the confines of ontic logics evaded? In essence: should we read nihilism's *form* positively or negatively? Before attempting to answer, it may be wise to note that there does seem to be a crossroads at which Scotus (in the form of Deleuze) meets Aquinas; theologians such as John Milbank and Catherine Pickstock do appear to cross the path of Deleuze and Derrida respectively. For it is true that in the acknowledgements of his *magnum opus* Milbank pays tribute to Deleuze.[91] And there can be little doubt that Derrida has encouraged Pickstock to *write* more, and better, about orality. Likewise, pagans, Jews and Arabs caused Aquinas to write better Christian theology;[92] similarly, Claudel found God in Rimbaud, yet, conversely, Lacan finds an extraordinary nihilism in Claudel.[93] With regard to Scotus, can we not, then, read his univocity as another conception of participation? A conception taken up and developed by nihilism, one which is otherwise than nihilistic, according to Nietzsche's intention? It certainly seems to be true that there is a significant but mostly indiscernible intercourse between each – theologian and nihilist – as they cross by and move on. Furthermore, it is now harder to discern who is who as they travel on. This is not to mix these thinkers up; for example, mistaking Aquinas for Scotus. There are indeed real differences between such thinkers, but this difference requires perpetual discernment.

Absolute beginnings

> I conceptualise *absolute* beginnings (which requires a theory of the void).[94]
>
> (Alain Badiou)

The *provenance* of nihilism always precedes that which is provided. In so doing, it provides in a manner which leaves us *with-out*. Yet it is possible to suggest that this causes a Fichtean battle of All against All.[95] This will be elaborated upon below, but first Dostoyevsky is employed in an effort to draw out the nature of this war.

> 'God is Dead, so everything is permitted'; nothing is permitted anymore.[96]
>
> (Jacques Lacan)

Dostoyevsky writes in *The Brothers Karamazov* that if God does not exist *anything* is permitted. This certainly appears to be true. For it seems one cannot even register suffering without an appeal to transcendence; when it is said that there cannot be a God because there is suffering in the world, it might be argued that such a sentiment, although understandable, is incoherent. For without God there would not *be* any suffering. That is to say, it would be impossible to cognise such significance. A field full of dead bodies would be regarded purely in terms of size, shapes, smells and so on. This would be done without recourse to any significant discourse that could articulate something such as suffering or loss. Likewise, without transcendence the universe is but one block of 'stone', or a 'single' insignificant flux, in so far as we cannot find reason at an immanent level to separate one piece from another; identities can certainly be constructed by 'regimes of signs', but they remain merely formal or arbitrary. Consequently, there is no real difference between a holocaust and an ice-cream, just as there is no real difference registered between the vital body and the cadaver.

This being said, there is a strange ambiguity which creeps in: if it is true that there is not any suffering without God, this can certainly be read in a different direction, namely, that God is the cause of suffering. Deleuze reads Dostoyevsky's dictum in just this manner. He, no doubt with history in mind, argues that with God *everything* is permitted; the actions of fundamentalists would seem to confirm this re-reading. But that is not the end of it. For it is arguable that if God does not exist *nothing* is permitted: this is meant in the strong sense as nihilism would have it; nothing *is*. Yet this can be interpreted to mean that having permitted nothing, *all must be eliminated*; all specificity, particulars and entities must upon birth be got rid of, as each of these illegitimately inhabits a place for the *other*; we see such 'prophylactic suicide' in the work of Levinas who, quoting Pascal, questions his place under the sun.[97] Consequently, he develops an entire philosophy so as to be *otherwise than being*.

Such *meontological*, or rather *meontotheological*, impulses are witnessed in the elimination of the particular in Hegel, whose univocity of *Geist* takes all that *is* into the counterfactual pieces of the infinite. Likewise, we witness this univocity in Spinoza, and in Bergson for whom there is a univocity of creation, so to speak. John Mullarkey captures this point well when he says that for Bergson 'each and every locus is no less real than any other as a resting place, but equally no less unreal than any other as the bearer of evolutionary movement . . . [E]ach point is *similarly* new in some way.'[98] Bergson here betrays his similarity with Hegel. This radical democracy is *bellicose*, and it is this agonism that guides Nietzsche. For Nietzsche's will-to-power is but an expression of this struggle, one prefigured in Schopenhauer and Fichte; not to mention Kant, for whom, in some sense, the noumenal was the truth of the phenomenal. Similarly for Deleuze, chaos is the infinite speed of disappearance and birth, both of which are indiscriminately simultaneous (it is possible to argue that Hegel is somewhat Deleuzian; yet conversely, that Deleuze is somewhat

Hegelian). For this reason there is only the homogeneity of *the* indeterminate, and this indeterminate is underwritten by a univocity of non-being. This means that there is indeed a suicidal *reditus* preceding every *exitus*, because the neutrality of the univocity of being[99] is in reality the *neutralisation* of every being; a neutralisation echoed in Heidegger who is the philosopher of a univocal Being, not beings.[100]

Mallarmé appears to be correct when he says '*Un coup de dés jamais n'abolira le hasard.*'[101] For what has been thrown remains ontologically equivocal, and so must await infinite deferral. It is this deferral which Derrida champions, one which ensures that that which is thrown is *thrown out*, so to speak. Such utter equivocation is the true nature of the univocity of non-being. Consequently, all distinction can only be constructed formally. This brings about a situation which affords only diacritical signification, generated by the infinite being of the void; chaos; deferral; disappearance and birth; spirit; the absolute; the indeterminate; the noumenal; the totality; *das Nicht*; the plane of immanence, and so on. Nihilism might escape ontotheology, and from this we learn much, but its flight is illusory – futile. For ontotheology is merely replaced by a *meontotheology*, which is in reality an *ouk-on-totheology*, or at least can be construed that way, where nihilism fails to recognise itself as an *election*. Nihilism's *exitus* from the ontic was itself ontic, for its own abstruse logic rested within the *domain* of pre-meditated, and so preceding, premises: answers asked the questions.

Therefore nihilism, in even its most profound guise, is arguably nothing but an ontic monism: any movement being but the aspectual fluctuation of one of its foundational dualisms; here we recall Jastrow's *duck-rabbit*, which is but *one* picture. To repeat: Heidegger has the dualism of Being and Time, which names its monism *das Nicht* (or he has the dualism of Being and Nothing, which in turn baptises its monism as *Abgrund*). Spinoza has God and Nature, the monism of which he names Substance. Schopenhauer has will and representation which gives way, as we saw above, to nothingness. Fichte's I and non-I collapse into the Absolute I; Schelling's nature and mind collapse into the absolute; Hegel's finite and infinite collapse into a monism of *Geist*. Kant has a dualism of phenomenal and noumenal, and he names his monism, at least in the *Opus Postumum*, the Totality.[102] Deleuze has the dualisms of sense and non-sense, and thought and nonthought, the second of each supplementing the first; as does Lacan, for he, too, has sense emerge from non-sense.[103] Deleuze names his monism the One-All, or chaos. In the end such monisms *threaten* to become *ouk-on-totheologies*, because the hegemony of *the nothing* sucks *all* in, allowing (only) nothingness to escape.

Indeed, Badiou is but the philosopher-king, whose 'risky supplements'[104] come down, as Lecercle says, to 'subjective decisions'.[105]

Here the void, as perpetual deterritorialisation, precedes every event. (The term 'deterritorialisation' is Deleuze and Guattari's.)[106] In this way Badiou *absolutises* beginnings or more accurately, *the* beginning, which is *the* indeterminate. This suffers what was referred to earlier as the 'Humean problem of eternal moments', these being the result of an 'infinite alterity' which is indifferent to difference.[107] For there is, then, but *one* event, that of the void – the absolutised beginning. The Cantorian inconsistent multiplicity does not serve Badiou well, for he seems to have forgotten that Cantor, in naming the absolute infinite, resorted to the language of Aquinas in calling it *actus purissimus*.[108] Therefore the appearance of radical creation – true participation – gives way to radical destruction, and absorption: the nothing *as* something.

The next section repeats some of the points made above so as to underscore the differences and similarities that nihilism's notion of creation presents to theology.

A-voiding One: creation from No-One

> Nothingness is the peculiar possibility of being and its unique possibility.[109]
>
> (Jean-Paul Sartre)

> Nothing exists except on the assumed foundation of absence.[110]
>
> (Jacques Lacan)

The idea that nothingness is the foundation of being seems strange, if not wrongheaded, but this should not surprise us, for was it not the stranger in Plato's *Sophist* who argued that nothingness was the source of difference; nothingness was the 'Other'.[111] Deleuze appears to concur, for he argues that 'Non-being is difference.'[112] Likewise, Blanchot: 'Pure absence wherein there is nevertheless a fulfillment of being.'[113] This difference of fulfilment is what Lacan refers to as 'the being of non-being (*être de non-étant*)',[114] which is an 'absence made of presence'.[115] None of this, though, dissipates the strangeness which surely accompanies such an idea.

For Lacan, the creationist perspective is essential, mainly for two reasons. First, the creationist perspective is 'consubstantial with thought';[116] second, it affords the possibility for the radical elimination of God.[117] Why should creation from nothing give rise to these two possibilities? An answer to this lies close to the central role which nothingness plays. Sartre, Lacan, Blanchot, Deleuze, Derrida, and Badiou, not to mention Hegel and Plotinus *et al.*, all approach 'creation' through a negation of what can be termed 'the One'. By 'voiding' the

One, many arise, and it is this belief which seems to guide their philosophy. For example, Badiou states explicitly, that for him, 'the One is not';[118] indeed, his philosophy is based on a 'destitution of the One'.[119] We pay witness to this voiding in the work of Lacan and Sartre, for each has man – or the subject – nihilate being so as to generate the many. Being – the One – is regarded as 'solid',[120] because it is a 'full positivity';[121] this 'compressed' One precludes difference because it is inherently 'indistinct'.[122] Consequently, only by its being 'nihilated' can existence arise. Sartre calls such a move a 'flight' from Being.[123] This flight does not go elsewhere, for where would one go? Rather, any movement is but on the spot, as being is decompressed, because the One is voided by nothingness and this allows for difference.[124] As said, according to Sartre nothingness arises in the world through man, before whom there was no world: 'Thus the rise of man in the midst of the being which "invests" him causes a world to be discovered.'[125] A world is discovered because man, as the for-it-self, nihilates being: 'It is as the nihilation of the in-itself [*être-en-soi*] that the for-it-self [*être-pour-soi*] arises in the world.'[126] Man, as the for-it-self, bores a hole[127] in being, inducing a 'break in being'.[128] This decompression is firmly based on nothingness, for man, as the for-it-self, rests on a constitutive lack; just as the subject, for Lacan, is that which lacks being (*manque-à-être*): the for-it-self 'has the being of a lack and, as lack, it lacks being'.[129] Badiou's *event* which breaks with the being of the multiple (which Badiou contrasts with the 'neoplatonism' of Deleuze's pre-ontological virtuality) follows the same trajectory.

For both Lacan and Sartre, we can only attain difference in the absence of being, in terms of nihilation. Lacan expresses this by rewriting Descartes' famous dictum, *cogito ergo sum*: 'I think where I am not, therefore I am where I do not think.'[130] This echoes Sartre: the for-it-self 'is a being which is not what it is and which is what it is not'.[131] As far as these two are concerned, being – as the One – precludes difference, because its full positivity leaves no space for otherness.[132] Consequently, difference can only exist as it escapes being, and it does this by lacking being. Badiou expresses this sentiment well when he argues that 'non-being sustains man'[133] – although Badiou more contrasts the significant *universal* difference of the event, with the meaningless ontological 'many'. Sartre tells us that 'the possible is the *something* which the for-it-self lacks in order to be itself'.[134] Why must it lack possibility? Maybe because possiblity signifies the presence of a determinate essence, one that could easily confine the would-be for-it-self in the in-it-self. For this reason, the for-it-self – man or the subject – must be essenceless, and in so being they elude the grasp of compressed being – the indistinction of Lacan's *réel* (or Badiou's ontological manifold). It is here that the full force of nothingness becomes apparent, because the name which this nothingness goes by in this situation is death.

I – who is not – am – so will not be

The frontiers represented by 'starting from zero', *ex nihilo*, is . . . the place where a strictly atheist thought necessarily situates itself. A strictly atheist thought adopts no other perspective than that of 'creationism'.[135]

(Jacques Lacan)

The Antichrist can adopt the very symbols of the Messiah, using them of course in an inverted sense.[136]

(René Guénon)

We saw above that, according to Lacan, the subject can only think in the absence of being, for only in lacking being can difference arise; a noetic structure is not possible in the One. In other words, nothingness – death – is the possibility for man (Sartre) or the subject (Lacan) to exist. Lacan argues that 'Truth is akin to death.'[137] Here he seems to be following Hegel,[138] who called Death 'the absolute master',[139] which encourages Kojève to refer to Hegel's work as a 'philosophy of death'.[140] Indeed, Kojève, taking Hegel's lead, tells us that 'there is no freedom without death'.[141] Death frees us from being, *viz.*, from every incarcerating essence and the monolithic One. Lacan, and to some degree Sartre, concur. For Lacan, death is indeed freedom from being, a freedom he sees in *Oedipus at Colonus*. Oedipus asks: 'Am I a man in the hour when I cease to be?'[142] This ceasing to be brings one beyond the world of essences and of being, and it is the analyst's job, according to Lacan, to 'make death present';[143] to encourage the realisation that we are 'already dead'.[144] In this way, freedom – existence – stems from death; we are to look into the mirror until nothing looks back. In other words, by realising we are not, we can escape being *via* the hole – the break – this truth displays in being: *you are not, so be!* The One as being is voided, its grasp eluded, and for this reason *noesis* is possible.

From where does this freedom come? It seems that language is the escape route that man takes. Blanchot argues that 'Language begins only with a void.'[145] And this void is the 'voiding' of being. 'The word gives me what it signifies, but first it suppresses it . . . It is the absence of that being, its nothingness.'[146] In other words, speech 'is the life of death'.[147] Furthermore, 'It is clear that in me the power of speech is also tied to my absence of being. I name myself; it is as if I were pronouncing my funeral chant.'[148] Why is speech linked to death? It is because, according to Lacan, the word 'murders the Thing'.[149] But this is not wholly negative, for language also makes the world of things: 'It is the world of words that creates the world of things.'[150] Why? Because language accommodates the Sartrean nihilation of being, and so affords articulating difference about which the Eleatic stranger had already spoken; it is only through this nothingness that a world is discovered. As Lacan says, 'Before speech, no-thing neither is nor is not.'[151] In other words, 'Emptiness and fullness are introduced into a world that by itself knows not of them.'[152] Furthermore, as Sartre insists, 'It is only a nothingness in-itself separating all the thises.'[153] Language is, then, to be understood as the speaking of death because it is the speaking of a separation; it separates being, sundering it. This is Lacan's murder of the Thing (*das Ding*); *das Ding* is what Silverman calls 'a non-object',[154] since *das Ding* is not some object that preceded a division, rather it is the name of *loss that is lost*. Lacan calls *das Ding* a 'primordial function',[155] which he also likens to 'nothing',[156] and also to creation: 'The notion of creation *ex nihilo* is coextensive with the exact structure of the Thing.'[157] (Badiou's Cantorian ontology of incompatible infinite multiples also belongs here.)

Two aspects conjoin to produce a sophisticated atheist doctrine of creation from nothing. First of all, we have a univocity of non-being, in the sense that univocity precludes any difference in the understanding of being. This being the case, death (always of particulars) is the truth of this monistic being. Second, this death sets us free, as it frees us from being; an escape enabled by language, for it kills the Thing, allowing for the creation of a world of *things*. Being is (a)voided, nihilated, and this affords us difference. In this way, the power that being might be thought to hold over us is eluded, for being makes us dead, and language resurrects us in this very demise; we do not look to being to let us exist, but instead language murders the Thing – being – and divides it up. Indeed, Hegel does something similar. Consequently, those who think that everything is captured by Hegel's system are quite wrong; Kojève and Lacan seem to have realised this. Hegel's system rather brings being to a halt, but this stillness – this univocity – allows for utter eruption. In other words, Hegel's system kills us to set us free; hence Kojève is correct to see it as a philosophy of death. *Geist* is exhausted, wearied, brought to ground; this being the case, existences can then 'diagonalise' out from within this 'inconsistent multiplicity': being and essence are silenced, existence speaks! Thus, for Hegel the absolute is realised in the resumption of *indifferent* choices, in a consumerist residue. This type of creation, which Lacan equates with the Thing, tells us: *being is dead, long live life*. Such creation is so radical it has no need of a creator; it is radical, simply because it is a 'true' creation *ex nihilo* or, rather, creation out of No-One.

Language shatters the Thing, and in so doing desire is eternalised,[158] for being now lies in rubble and *das Ding* is also the name of this eternity; an eternity that is the *loss of loss*, because pure and utter creation can have no place for such loss; creation is given to such a degree or in such a manner that it gives beyond loss. Indeed, with the death of *das Ding* – the voiding of being – *loss is lost* because being was itself the impossibility of difference. Yet the ontological or meontological truth of existence is revealed in death. For in existing we can now die. This mortality, marked by biological death and the endlessness of desire, which scratches out an existence within the ruins of being, displays our truth; we are not, hence we exist, consequently, we will not be. Death is the truth of our lack of being (*manque-à-être*). Nonetheless, we will have existed, doing so in the absence of God; this, it seems, is genuine creation!

The stain of existence: An indivisible remainder[159]

The One, or being, is for nihilism voided; as a result, difference escapes out from under its 'skirt'. For Sartre, this voiding was a result of man's nihilation of being, while Lacan attributes it to language. Likewise, Deleuze, here following Heidegger, understands the voiding of being to arise from a 'universal ungrounding'[160] afforded by the perpetual repetiton of a question; namely, the putting into question of being: 'Everything has its beginning in a question, but one cannot say that the question itself begins.'[161] Now, what is important here is how such a questioning not only puts being into question but does so with beings, so inducing the aforementioned war of all against all; the erasure of all specificity. Indeed, in voiding the One, beings are also voided. It is said that the One is not, but this 'vertical' pronouncement falls out of a now denounced sky onto 'earth' and horizontally negates every-one, so to speak. The voiding of the One becomes the a-voiding of everyone, as a result of the Plotinian understanding of causality which governs this movement, whereby *one comes from one*. The nihilation of the One gives rise to only one effect, which is able to escape from the plenitude of its 'desert' only by repeating a 'desertion'. We see this problem running from Plotinus, through Avicenna, and on to Derrida: Derrida has but the one effect emanate from the nothing, and this is *the* Text; the univocity of one text.

Now, this one effect that squeezes out from the nihilated, reflects its source, in the sense that difference is problematic. As Schelling says: 'What is not . . . is under what is.'[162] In a sense this is the bare existence that precedes every essence. Schelling goes further: 'If we were able to penetrate the existence of things, we would see that the true self of all life and existence is horrible.'[163] This horrible truth is what Lacan calls the Real (*réel*), which is, in a sense, *être-en-soi*, to put it in Sartrean terms. And, according to i ek, 'The Real is the unfathomable remainder.'[164] We see such a remainder becoming apparent in Sartre's novel *Nausea*: 'Existence has suddenly unveiled itself. It had lost the harmless look of an abstract category . . . all these objects . . . How can I explain? They inconvenience me; I would like them to exist less strongly, more dryly.'[165] The crisp, clean, ideality of words, categories, and so on slip from every face, revealing something that escapes us; a horrible excess, one that leaves us suspended before a sublime void; words slide from their objects, on which they had settled in a contented fashion, like a hen on her eggs. Instead, these eggs hatch a fox that eats the hen. For such words are moribund in the face of this ineluctable, indivisible remainder. This is the naked strengh of compressed being, the Real. For Schelling, Sartre, Lacan and i ek, to mention but a few, this remainder is ugly. Indeed, i ek speaks of the 'shock of ugliness',[166] an ugliness arising from the 'Kernel of reality', for this kernel is horrible; it is the 'horror of the Real'.[167] Furthermore, this kernel that remains beyond and in a sense before every essence, every idealisation, is 'excremental';[168] the Real is 'shit', as i ek puts it.[169] The neat world which we have constructed through linguistic division, in our effort to decompress being, hides the reality which it seeks to cover up; but from underneath the blanket comes the indelible stench. And we can catch sight of this reality – *the what is not*, that lies beneath *the what is*. We see it in the stain which every desire seeks to ignore, to clean up. For example, the social construction of wife and husband, which is there to disguise the *univocal nature of eros*,[170] domesticating it, by hiding desire in the clothes of legitimate relationships. But the truth of desire does not know any such distinction; like being it suffers indistinction. In other words, the truth of eros is just as much a desire for the mother as it is for the spouse. Indeed, and even more disturbingly, it is as partial to children as it is to the other parent. For example, this 'truth' can be 'witnessed' – the Real of eros is seen – as it erupts, striking out from underneath the settled hen in the form of rape; but rape is no more or less dramatic than other manifestations of univocal desire. Was this not what the great masters of suspicion had begun to tell us, for each in his own way pointed us beyond the façade of the name, to the pulsating reality that lay behind the accepted account?

Devil of the Gaps

> The curious man lacks devotion. There are many such persons, devoid of praise and devotion, though they may have all the splendour of knowledge. They make wasps' nests that have no honeycombs, whereas the bees make honey.[171]
>
> (St Bonaventure)

There is certainly a degree of truth in nihilism, to the degree that reality does exceed every idealisation that would seek to domesticate it. And it is true to point out, as Samuel Beckett does, that notions such as friendship, family, employment, money and so on distract us from life, like an insidious opiate. We are indeed sedated by the mindless chatter of gossip; call it politics, sport, economics, romance or whatever. There is a shameful absurdity in this, for do we not juxtapose incongruous bedfellows; the management consultant and the emaciated child? And is this not what both the Old Testament and the New Testament condemn? 'Happy shall they be who take your little ones and dash them against the rock' (Psalm 137, v. 9). 'Whoever comes to me and does not hate father and mother, wife and children, brothers and sisters, yes, and even life itself, cannot be my disciple' (Luke, ch. 14. v. 26). Is it not true that desire is held captive by such 'worldly' categories, making it easier to colonise? And does not the above call to dash one's children against the rock and to hate one's father and mother, life itself, not check this colonisation, disrupting the domestication of desire?

To be sure, nihilism draws our attention to this facile, yet extremely dangerous, incarceration of desire, and domestication of existence within the odourless idealities that divide up the spoils of being, while hiding us from the reality of being: 'you are not!'. We live in a world without chairs, true, and from this we learn much. But a corollary of this is that we live, then, in a world without neighbours; lives without life. Furthermore, is not the notion of the indivisible remainder, of ontological shit, not the epitome of an idealism, however perverse? For is not the Lacanian Real still the really real (*ontos onta*)? And does not this reality, this kernel, one so typical of philosophy in its endless pursuit of the essential, represent a pure ideal: pure reality, absolute shit, devoid of shape and distinction? Is this brown – monochrome – world not a univocal being or non-being? Let us hear Badiou's translator explain this philosopher's achievement: 'It is Badiou's achievement to have subtracted the operation of truth from any redemption of the abject, and to have made the distinction between living and unliving, between finite and infinite, a matter of absolute indifference.'[172] And we know already that Badiou is 'indifferent to differences'. Since all the various incommensurable events of new truth and new love still rest on the same univocal 'grace' of self-referring finite origination.[173] In this way, there is but one difference that emanates from the one void – the nothing outside the text; here we are still with Plotinus and Avicenna. There is also a blatant Gnosticism in the embittered nihilist who sees horror and shit as the kernel of reality: 'If we want to get rid of the ugliness, we are forced to adopt the attitude of a Cathar, for whom terrestrial life is a hell and the God who created this world is Satan himself, master of this world' (i ek).[174] Not forgetting the excess which does escape our idealisation of existence, is there not a whiff of *resentiment* fuelled by the bitterness of the impotent? In other words, is this nihilism not the fruit of the castration complex, of a disappointed idealist who is no longer playing the game because he cannot win: 'I cannot capture life, therefore there is no life.' Indeed, does the nihilist not, then, move to re-capture being by invoking a new name; for example, the Real, indivisible remainder, *différance*, *être-en-soi*, the void, and so on?

It is well known that Parmenides equated being and thought. To be sure, there is something problematic with this, and the history of ontotheology, as creatively delineated by Heidegger, displays this with acumen. What Lacan and Žižek seem to be pointing to is the incongruity between being and thought, and with good reason. It seems to be true *prima facie* that being does exceed thought, and that if it did not there could not be creation, so to speak. For all would suffer the paralysis of a strict idealism; as we witness in ontotheology, which confines being with its unthinking categories and presumed significance. Indeed, can it not be said that life can only take place – existentially occur – in the space between thought and being? In other words, the difference between the two allows for difference. Yet the problem with such an approach is that it invites a new idealism, in the form of a new 'name', which actually realigns thought and being by bridging, and so removing, the difference; it is arguable that this is what meontology is guilty of. These new names come in many guises. For example, because thought and being are not the same, accidents happen, tragedy arises. But the danger is that if one simply renames life as tragic, tragedy disappears, for its now 'metaphysical' status – its reality – leaves it without the requisite space for tragedy to occur. To put it another way, to say that the world is full of suffering and so is meaningless, is to dilute the very suffering that initially motivated the negative judgement: there is suffering in life, therefore life is meaningless, therefore there is no suffering. Absurdity and nihilism operate in a similar fashion, for they are names that settle into the gap between being and thought, reforging a novel chain. This is the 'Devil of the Gaps', who is a bridge to the void, after which it lusts.

The stamen of existence: An irreducible reminder

What God has made clean, you must not call profane.
(Acts, ch. 10, v. 15)

There is little doubt that being's excess becomes a pornography of the void in the works of Žižek, Lacan, *et al.*, as Graham Ward has argued.[175] For Žižek does seem to display a lust for the void based on the excremental horror he claims to discern in life's excess; the excess which life is. Hamann would surely have disagreed with Žižek's pejorative interpretation of the Real, because for Hamann all that is made is clean, in so far as what God makes is clean, so we must not call it profane.

Indeed, according to Christianity, God became man and so He had genitalia, bowel movements and so on. Consequently, Hamann rejoices in the very physicality of the body: 'It is noon and I enjoy what I eat and what I drink and also just as much the moment I become free of both and give back again to earth what has been taken out of her.'[176] Hamann goes on: 'Man must not deny the pudenda of his nature. For to do so would mean estrangement from God';[177] in a letter to Herder, Hamann continues this idea: 'The pudenda seem to me to be the unique bond between creation and creator.'[178] Dickson puts it well: for Hamann, 'God has made us, passions, desires, excrement and all; what God has made, we must not call unclean.'[179] Indeed, just because that which manifests itself escapes our categories (appearing ugly)[180] to dismiss it as horrible is to remain reactively consituted by an idealism that displays a distinct lack of *caritas*. For as Jean-Luc Marion says, 'The very disfiguration remains a manifestation.'[181] This means that for the Christian, sin is a matter of *egurgitation*, as it does not stem from the world, but comes to it. Furthermore, we cannot abandon what *is* because it appears to be less than ideal. For this reason, to name the world as horrific is to entertain the Devil of the Gaps. Instead there must be, and here I somewhat follow Adorno, a *priority of the object*. For does the object – reality – not call to us in all its rich forms; forms which, as Adolf Portmann puts it, are a 'conveyance for receivers'?[182] Indeed, is Roger Caillois not correct to speak of 'An outrageous outpouring of resources beyond vital interest'.[183] For this reason, nature is not to be deemed a 'miser'.[184] As a result, we can agree with Portmann when he calls for an *expansionist* approach to existence,[185] one that responds to what Merleau-Ponty calls an 'inexhaustible richness',[186] that lies in the perceived; a richness that is an 'urge to self-display', to use Portmann's phrase.[187] Consequently, is it not correct to agree with Caillois when he speaks of an 'autonomous aesthetic force in nature',[188] a force present in the very being of manifestation? When Adorno calls for a prioritisation of the object, he does not leave it at that. As Buck-Morss puts it: 'Truth resided in the object, but it did not lie ready at hand, the material object needed the rational subject in order to release the truth which it contains.'[189] Hannah Arendt echoes a similar sentiment: 'All objects because they appear indicate a subject, and, just as every subjective intention has its intentional object, so every appearing object has its intentional subject.'[190] The accusation of anthropomorphism can easily be levelled at such an understanding of appearance. However, this accusation is contradictory, because non-anthropomorphism is itself anthropo-morphic; just as nihilism is somewhat anthropocentric: 'I can't do it, so it can't be done.' Anthropomorphism is avoided because man is not fully present to himself; man, too, exceeds his name. This is the non-identity which Adorno finds in being. And it is this non-identity which discerns

259

the present excess, an excess that does not lead to an elsewhere, but moves – resonates – on the spot. As Adorno says, 'What is, is more than it is.'[191] For this reason we must, as Adorno suggests, view everything from 'the standpoint of redemption'.[192] Such redemption stands within the disruption that the aforementioned excess is. Interestingly, Adorno finds hope in what he calls 'the name'.[193] Yet, as Düttmann reminds us: 'A name always wants to be the only one to name what it names, that is its narcissism, narcissism itself.'[194] But, of course, this is to repeat the problem, for narcissism here threatens to become the only name; the name of every name. Instead, the hopeful name displays a certain amnesia, and therein lies its redemption: 'Forgetting always involves the best; for it involves the possibility of redemption' (Benjamin).[195] And here we can agree with Žižek when he says, in a manner reminiscent of Péguy, that 'Christianity calls upon us to thoroughly reinvent ourselves . . . Christianity enjoins us to REPEAT the founding gesture . . . '.[196] We return to the object because it calls us again, and we have forgotten the hue of its beauty, for we cannot quite recall the plenitude of its form; is such a non-identical repetition not the only way to return to the face of our lover? Indeed, is this not the rich thrust of desire, one that keeps pulling us back to the very depth of the surface? Consequently, the phenomenological resistance met in the handshake or in intercourse, is not to be read as a failure of intimacy; resistance being read as an excluding distance. For such resistance does not mock our efforts to encounter; indeed, the logic that generates such an understanding is governed by a vicious idealism that hates the body, which it deems a creation of Satan, and which it seeks to destroy; to meet the demands of pure encounter, would the hand not have to be squeezed to obliteration, which would be annihilation, not intercourse? In returning to the object we answer a call – this is our calling – doing so with the offer of a hopeful name; and we are called by a name that we too exceed. In this way, being is not beyond thought; it is the beyond *of* thought.

Created creators: such is love's difference

> Therefore I pray to God that he may make me free of God.[197]
>
> (Meister Eckhart)

Does the above quotation betray a similarity with nihilism, at least as it has been defined here? For Eckhart seems to be suggesting that we have God without God. Indeed, at one point Eckhart actually instructs us to love God as 'non-God'.[198] Is such a God the God of nihilism? Furthermore, theology construes creation as gift, and does this not mimic nihilism's nothing *as* something? In other words, does the presentation of creation as pure gift resemble nihilism's endeavour to have nothing be *as* something. (Such a question could, of course, be posed in the opposite direction.) There is certainly some similarity, and it is this similarity which induces an already mentioned *agnosticism* in our 'perception'. Recall the analogy of the crossroads where we saw Scotus and Aquinas pass by, leaving us for a moment unable to discern, in an absolute fashion, who was who. It is this uncertainty that may represent the *space* of dialogue, one which is not that of the liberal, for liberal dialogue knows who is who – as it is self-certain. Consequently, the liberal self *only* looks *across* the table at the *other*.

This dialogue, between nihilism and theology, is to all intents and purposes not deliberate. This lack of intent is not a result of refusal, but of profound confusion; one arising from the theologians' inability to know *themselves* enough to take their seat at the table of arranged dialogue, confidently looking only out or across; a look which would absorb the other, because it is unidirectional. It is true that nihilism is something that would be considered as *other* than theology; nonetheless, theology does seem to engage in dialogue, in so far as theology 'loses' its-self. In other words, theologians cannot fully locate their self. This being the case, they cannot for sure exclude nihilism from their own self-understanding. Therefore, otherness is attended to by approaching alterity from sameness, which as sameness is difference; we saw this already in terms of the Godhead. In this way, theology seems able to articulate plurality in a more satisfactory manner.

So as to better understand the form of ontotheology and *meontotheology* it may be beneficial to use Plato's simile of the cave. In the *Republic*, Plato tells us of a world in which imprisoned people live mistaken lives,[199] for these persons live in a cave, and they presume that the shadows which flutter on the wall are reality. In leaving the cave the philosopher is blinded by the sun, but eventually comes to understand this sun as the source of all change, of seasons and years. The enlightened prisoner (the philosopher) then returns to the cave in an endeavour to educate and govern his fellows; an unenviable task, as pedagogic enlightenment will be met with strong resistance, even violence. This cavernous story can be interpreted in a manner which suggests that the philosopher who has returned to the cave with 'knowledge' is the prisoner we find at the beginning of the Platonic simile. In other words, the enlightened philosopher who returns is the shackled prisoner who never left. If we do perceive a movement of departure and return, it is but the movement of initial arrival, that is to say, the actual arrival of the cave. Both the ontotheologian and the *meontotheologian* are guilty of this. The first, because of their certain categories; the second, by their compulsion to go beyond these categories towards another reality. The move to leave the cave is epitomised by the *meontological* impulse witnessed in

Neoplatonism. This is the case because the move *beyond* being, so as to *be* otherwise, is guided and motivated by a presumptuous knowledge of being; those who seek to go beyond, or to speak of a beyond, do so on the basis of their certain knowledge of being. In other words, they must, in a sense, know being to the degree to which they now know they are beyond it. But this is illusory, in so far as the question of being is simply transposed to another level, a level deftly demarcated by the being they have so audaciously traversed. They know that they are beyond; in this way they know the beyond in the same manner in which they know being. Indeed, being marks the *sides* of the beyond – of the otherwise – tracing its outline. Such an identification may only be one-sided, but this simply directs the traveller aimlessly on into an anonymous, homogeneous, ateleological desert. Leaving the cave of being may not make this give the certainty of *the nothing* instead of the certainty of the *something*. It is this *meontotheological* peregrination which violates being, for it knows itself in such a self-certain manner that it no longer looks back. It heads only onwards towards a blank horizon; like a self looking *only* across a table at an *other*. Such an other, such difference, is always the same other, the same difference. In this way all difference is *indifference*; this is *the* indeterminate.

Conversely, to stay safely in the cave, as the ontotheologian appears to, is to have already left and strayed beyond. Such a transgression is obvious, for I must know the beyond (the outside) – I must have been beyond – if I can be certain of the cave. That is to say, if I can safely know the cave, demarcating its extent, then I do this from outside; like Derrida with regard to the text. This is where the onticity of both the ontotheologian and the *meontotheologian* are indiscernible. For in knowing the cave (my self, being and so on), I have looked in only *one* direction. Instead the cave, if it is to be spoken of at all, must be understood as itself excessive; which means that the cave – my self, other, and being – is always, already, ecstatic. Just as language is. For any description of an object cannot adequately speak of the described; objects exceed language – if such an excess is not recognised, then what is described is violated, since it suffers the inadequacy dealt by a reductive logic. To some degree language, which does violate in this manner, carries the evidence of the crime with it. For example, if language is employed to capture a being in a reductive description, the excess so ignored leaves its trace in language itself: the excess of the forgotten being manifests itself in the excess of language. We see this to the degree to which we cannot control language completely: the negative determination involved in language leaves every term within the constitutive shadow of its opposite. It is arguable that this excess mimics the excess of being. Therefore, mimetic properties can be interpreted as a *memory* of the lost being, in the sense that the reason for the initial description – the being – was lost in a reductive flurry, but this being is remembered in both the supplementary excess of language and its self-denying ecstasy. In other words, the reason language *moves* is because of the being about which it speaks: *ecstasis*. Consequently, language re-calls its other twice in an ecstatic excess, which is the being of language. Here we can witness the work of the transcendentals: language speaks because of being (for the speaker must be) and beings (those about whom language speaks); language implies truth, for even a lie rests on truth (one might speak here of adequation, but not simple correspondence); the reason one speaks of *this* being, is because being is good and the manner in which this being appears is in the breadth of beauty – for each object manifests a *nubility*, both revealing and hiding, because it is erotic and plenitudinal.

'Returning' to the cave we can see that it is indeterminable – like language – yet it is not *the* indeterminate. Why is it not the indeterminate? Because the manner in which excess is conceived is not of a *more* which is spatial, because such excess thinks quantitatively. As a consequence there arises the aforementioned war of all against all, for entities give way to the *one* event of *the* indeterminate other (*Geist*, Substance, the Totality, *das Nicht*, *différance* and so on). The theologian conceives of creation as gift, but this gift is not conceived purely in terms of efficient causality, because the *gift* points to the *giver*, and so to the Good. This means that the radical nature of the gift, its utter participation, articulates itself more in the qualitative terms of final causality. It is in this way that specificity remains, yet ecstatically and excessively. The intelligent, that is artistic, donation of being resists the quantitive excesses of radical efficiency. Consequently, that which *is* cannot simply give way to an *other*, for it is there in the first place as a result of eternal intention. Yet that which does remain does not do so in a self-contained manner, since the gift is a result of the difference of divine unity. In this way, a being that *is*, which resists reduction, does so as *another*'s, in that my self *qua* self is already an other, because it is donated by an other; this is its given-ness. Here we can employ Rimbaud's *'Je est un autre'* with some benefit, in so far as it echoes Kierkegaard: 'The human self is . . . a relation that relates to itself and in relating itself to itself relates itself to another.'[200] The creature does not simply wait for another 'bigger' other, that is, a greater Levinasian alterity. Instead the creature remains as donated gift, and therefore as already another, for it subsists in an ecstatic manner.

This means that specificity cannot be eliminated, yet at the same time, and for the same reason, this specificity has an indeterminable potentiality. For the given-ness of the creature, which resists destruction yet is itself an ecstatic opening, possesses a qualitative infinity as an imitable example of the divine essence. Furthermore, it proceeds within the circle of the divine procession. Such an infinity, again to borrow from

Cantor, would best be considered as *transfinite* in distinction from the absolute infinite which incomprehensibly enfolds all sub-sets of bounded infinitude. This is the *actus purissimum* which is also in a sense beyond the infinite and the mathematisable finite/infinite contrast

So the creature as transfinite gift remains within the hyper-infinite act of the Trinity. Such an infinity opens up all finitude; yet it is not opened out onto *more*, nor is it opened up after its arrival, nor at the moment of its birth. Instead its openness is its arrival – the artistic intention of its arrival. The *open finality* of the Word – as gifted by the Spirit – is the breadth of being, for it is the beauty of trust, hope and love. In becoming one through redemption with the Word the creation enters the Trinity. Yet this is not absorption. Rather, this is the space of difference. Life is lived, and this existentiality is the *monument of love*, which is meant to imply duration, the occurrence of history, biography: the lived eternal utterance of the Son as testified to by the Spirit.

In a previous section it was argued that philosophy's response to the *aporia* of thought was the generation of dualisms; dualisms which collapsed into monism. Theology does not, it seems, suffer such duality. Yet it might be complained that the dualism of creature/creator is itself a governing dualism. This may not though necessarily be true, because creation-difference is a result of love which, precisely, does not divide. In line with Aquinas, it has been suggested that creation is a result of divine unity, and for this reason it is not a change. And the creature, as Aquinas says, 'brings itself into being'.[201] To this degree, then, the creature cannot be simply set over and against God the Creator: Nicholas of Cusa referred to God as *non aliud* (not other). Furthermore, Augustine informs us that 'God has been made man so that man might become God'.[202] Likewise, Gregory of Nyssa says: 'Man leaves behind his own nature; . . . to sum up everything in a word: from being man, he becomes God.'[203] Eckhart concurs: 'God and I are one'.[204] Consequently, there is no simple dualism between creator and creature.

It must also be understood that the Creator is the unity of three. In this way also dualism is avoided. Furthermore, Christian theology avoids the *stasis* of Neoplatonism, where the One, and all that which is below the One, cannot actually be separated or discerned. In Neoplatonism the element of necessity appears in the fact that creation is a consequence of nature, not of intelligence, and the linked view that from one follows only one. As a consequence it is argued here that what falls *below* the One falls *within* it. In this sense, an ontological difference is not forthcoming. It could still be said that this is somewhat similar to the Trinitarian reading offered here. This is false for the reason that God is in no way mingled with the creature. Creation arises because love can allow for difference; love gives in such a way, and so utterly, that what is given is not a change, and therefore divine simplicity is not offended. How could this be the case?

Love is the *invention* of difference, for love did not look to an external register from which it took its idea for difference. In this way creation can be other than God yet come within the Trinitarian procession. The Trinity is not scared of difference for all difference *is* love, and love drives out fear. By heeding Eckhart's words – approaching God as 'non-God' – we manifest the ultimacy of love, and eschew every ontotheology. Being is not something, it is nothing – nothing but love. Here we see theology's dialogue with nihilism; for being *is* after all nothing *as* something although in a manner beyond nihilism's imaginings. Furthermore, there is a *reditus* which precedes every *exitus* in theology, to the extent that creation is utter given-ness, and according to the pre-eminence of final causality as the cause of causation. But this preceding *reditus* does not , like that of nihilism, eliminate specificity. This is because the return is the ultimacy of the arrival – its eternity. We creatures were in the Word from eternity; we reside in the Word now through Christ and in the Spirit. Furthermore, the open finality of the Word speaks of the lived, inhabited, breadth of being, for it speaks of the seriousness of the here-and-now as it does of our eternal *epectasis*.[205]

In this regard Deleuze's criticism, levelled at both Kierkegaard and Péguy, that there is a desertion of true repetition in theology, because there is a once-and-for-all resurrection, is misplaced.[206] For there is, in a sense, no beginning, as creation is not a change; nor is creation ever 'over', even in the *eschaton;* while in eternity itself temporality continues in the form of an eternal *epectasis*. As Evdokimov says of Gregory of Nyssa's understanding of this: 'The *epectasis* tension of which St Gregory of Nyssa speaks is an outburst of faith which goes beyond time and even traverses eternity without ever stopping or being fully satisfied.'[207] Likewise, Péguy speaks of '[T]emporal revolution for eternal salvation. Such is, eternally, temporally (eternally temporally, and temporally eternally), the mysterious subjection of the eternal itself in the temporal. Such, properly speaking, is the inscription of the eternal itself to the temporal.'[208] Temporal being, as the time of eternity, is always more desirous, because that which is desired is God who is love, and we are from love, and we remain as lovers. Creation does not in a sense have a beginning, because creation is not a change, yet if we do conceive a beginning we must conceive of it as eternal. As Gregory of Nyssa insists, we have beginnings which do not end to the extent to which they traverse eternity.[209] There is not, then, in Deleuze's sense, a once-and-for-all resurrection. Indeed, in Deleuze's account of repetition there is but the stasis of the One-All: the void. Instead the *reditus* of theology is but the trace of God's eternal *Now,* love's movement.

Eckhart is correct, *Esse est Deus*.[210] We are left, then, bereft of *comprehension*, for all our categories have folded – exhausted by plenitude. Our words, thoughts, and deeds can but *begin* in praise, for they are already doxological;[211] this is our supplement, our supplication. We, created co-creators are truly sons of God, even of God the Father. To this end we must bear the logic of the Cross. For it is in this way that the Church is the *sacrament of the future*; in being given Christ's body, the Church must give this gift away. The Church, in consuming Christ's body, is in turn consumed. But then again, as the Church gives to the other, so does the other give. So ultimately, to be sacrificial, the Church must twice receive: from God, and from the world; indeed, the sacrificial reception of the God–Man *already* involves this double passivity. This ensures that the Church, to be the Church – the place of sacrifice – is, even finitely, outside itself, not in a defined place at all. The Church in being but the reception of Christ does not have a fully locatable self that could be laid down for the *absolute other* without return and reciprocity. By contrast, the *meontological*, Levinasian impulse to sacrifice self-for-other unto utter self-destruction, identically repeats the logic of the fall: *to find a part of the world apart from God*. In this sense, my self, which I 'ethically' give you, must have first been *stolen*; for I have *presumed that I am mine*. The Church does not follow this logic, for it can, as suggested, only give within the grace of continual reception. It is, then, our responsibility to receive ourselves for the sake of the other; only in receiving my self do I not presume *this* to be *my* place under the sun. Here we approach the balance between the self and the other – sameness and difference.

The Church, then, gives itself on two fronts: in the first sense it *receives* itself; in the second sense the self it receives is one of *sacrifice*. Hence the Church receives the event of eternal reception. In so doing, the Church cannot locate itself in an absolute manner, because it cannot *foretell* how it will be received: the ancient Jews did not foresee Christ, Christianity did not foresee Judaism. The Church, then, is open to itself, and open to itself as other. Hence it is a lived reception, which is an embodiment of sacrifice – the sacrifice of reception as testified to by the Spirit. In other words, to feed others I must also feed myself; this is my only acceptable sacrifice.

> Love bade me welcome; yet my soul drew back,
> Guiltie of dust and sinne.
> But quick ey'd Love, observing me grow slack
> From my first entrance in,
> Drew nearer to me, sweetly questioning
> If I lack'd any thing.

A guest, I answer'd, worthy to be here;
Love said, You shall be He.
I, the unkinde, ungratefull? Ah, my deare,
I cannot look on thee.
Love took my hand and smiling did reply,
Who made the eyes but I?

Truth, Lord, but I have marred them; let my shame
Go where it doth deserve.
And know you not, sayes Love, who bore the blame?
My deare, then I will serve.
You must sit down and taste my meat;
So I did sit and eat.

George Herbert, 'Love Bade Me Welcome'

Notes

1 The champion of tacit 'dialogue' or knowledge is Michael Polanyi; see Polanyi (1967).
2 Beckett (1955), p. 291.
3 Derrida (1973), p. 81.
4 *Ibid.*
5 Derrida (1974), p. 143.
6 *Ibid.*, (1974), p. 314.
7 Schopenhauer (1969), vol. I: 412; italics mine.
8 Because all is will and will, in a sense, is nothing, Uhlmann is correct to discern a certain univocity in Schopenhauer's work; see Uhlmann (1999), p. 16.
9 Part I, Chapter 5.
10 Deleuze (1990), p. 263.
11 'An unlimited One-All (*omnitudo*)', Deleuze and Guattari (1994), p. 35; see also Deleuze (1997), p. 37.
12 Badiou (2000a), p. 90.
13 See Badiou (1999), pp. 124–127; *idem* (1991), p. 28.
14 Deleuze and Guattari (1994), p. 59.
15 Derrida (1987b), p. 12; italics mine.
16 *Ibid.*, p. 41.
17 Badiou (1999), p. 121.
18 Deleuze and Guattari (1994), p. 9.
19 Taylor (1990), p. 204.
20 Adorno (2000), p. 340.
21 Beckett (1955), p. 291.
22 Hallett (1984), p. 7.
23 Derrida (1987b), p. 14.
24 Beckett (1955), p. 119; italics mine.
25 See Deleuze (1997), p. 37.
26 Blanchot (1986).

THE DIFFERENCE *OF* THEOLOGY

27   *Ibid.*, p. 1.
28   *Ibid.*
29   Blanchot (1982), p. 96.
30   Uhlmann (1999), p. 17.
31   See Blanchot (1986), p. 5.
32   Deleuze and Guattari (1994), p. 60.
33   Taylor (1990), p. 203.
34   See Deleuze (1997), p. 37.
35   Ricœur (1977b).
36   *Ibid.*
37   See Bergson (1983), pp. 272–298.
38   *Ibid.*, p. 283.
39   Kolakowski (1985), p. 64.
40   Lacan (1992), p. 213.
41   Deleuze (1997), p. 212.
42   Lacan (1989), p. 65.
43   See Deleuze (1990), pp. 179–180.
44   See Deleuze (1997), p. 304.
45   Badiou (2000a), p. 45.
46   Deleuze (1997), p. 37.
47   Beckett (1955), p. 414.
48   Blanchot (1986), p. 28.
49   See Badiou (2000a), p. 44.
50   Badiou (1994), p. 67.
51   Badiou (1999), p. 91.
52   Badiou (1991), pp. 24–32.
53   In a letter from Cantor to Dedekind, 30 August 1899, quoted in Dauben (1990), p. 245. Badiou is responding to Lacan's call for 'mathematization'; see Lacan (1998), xxxii.
54   Badiou (1999), p. 80.
55   *Ibid.*
56   *Ibid.* For Cantor's use of the 'wandering limit' see 'Mitteilungen zur Lehre vom Transfiniten', *Zeitschrift für Philosophie und philosophische Kritik* 91 (1887), reprinted in *Gesammelte Abhandlungen mathematischen und philosophischen Inhalts*, ed. E. Zermelo; see Cantor (1966), p. 393.
57   For criticisms of Cantor's views on infinity see Webb (1980); Fang (1976); and Allen (1976).
58   See Badiou (1999), p. 91.
59   I am putting inverted commas in because of my breach of grammar, for the Two should still, in a sense, be treated as a unity, not a plurality, hence I use the word *does* instead of the word *do*.
60   Badiou (1991), p. 26.
61   The *Real* is a Lacanian term for that which lies outside meaning. For Lacan the *Real* is being, but the *Real* is the excremental void. For this reason, to exist we must lack being.
62   Bijection is a combination of injection, which is when one element maps to only one element in another set, and surjection, which is the one-to-one correspondence of all the elements in a set to all the elements in another set.

63 Deleuze and Guattari (1994), p. 158.

64 See Blanchot (1986), p. 37.

65 Deleuze and Guattari (1994), p. 47.

66 *Ibid.*, p. 45.

67 See Badiou (1988).

68 Badiou (1999), p. 121.

69 See for example Marion (1991).

70 Gillespie (1995) makes the point well: 'Deception . . . is the consequence of imperfection and no such imperfection is found in God. That is to say, deception requires self-consciousness, which is the basis for distinguishing oneself from others. God, however, is not self-conscious. God thus is no deceiver . . . [Descartes'] God is an impotent God, not an omnipotent God, a God who has lost his independence and become a mere representation within human thinking', pp. 61–62. See Marion (1998).

71 See Caputo (1997); Taylor (1984); Žižek (2001).

72 Blanchot (1986), p. 2.

73 Deleuze and Guattari (1994), p. 118.

74 Badiou (1991), p. 26.

75 Taylor (1990), p. 203; italics mine.

76 See Deleuze and Guattari (1994), p. 218.

77 Deleuze and Guattari (1994), p. 41.

78 *Ibid.*; italics mine.

79 Jacob (1973), p. 36.

80 Doyle (1997), pp. 36, 42.

81 McGinn (1999), p. 18. McGinn himself, in the end, advocates a deferred reductionism. This is what I call a 'Devil of the Gaps'.

82 Adorno (2000), p. 80.

83 Beckett (1955), p. 293.

84 We can see in Badiou a somewhat parallel relation between philosophy and theology. In writing a book on St Paul, he is able, in a sense, to colonise the figure of Paul and 'discount' any theological significance thought to reside there; see Badiou (1997). This process can also be witnessed in the hegemony of cultural studies, which discounts literary works, for example, Milton's *Paradise Lost*, in the sense that theological questions are prohibited; or in a more philosophical sense, Saussure who when he argues that there are no positive elements in language discounts any meta-significance: 'In language there are only differences without positive terms', Saussure (1960), p. 120.

85 Artaud (1982), p. 72.

86 Penrose (1989), ch. 10.

87 Badiou (2000a), p. 88.

88 Beckett (1955), p. 296.

89 See Lacan (1992), p. 261.

90 Kafka (1996), p. 7.

91 Milbank (1991).

92 For example, Plato, Aristotle, Proclus, Maimonides, Avicenna, and Averroes.

93 On Claudel and Rimbaud see Paliyenko (1997); for Lacan and Claudel see Bugliani (1999).

94 Badiou (2000a), p. 90; italics mine. Badiou appropriates this notion of 'absolute beginnings' from Lacan; see Lacan (1992), p. 214.
95 See Willms (1967), p. 110; see also Gillespie (1995), p. 94.
96 Lacan (1966), p. 130.
97 See Levinas (1991).
98 Mullarkey (1999), p. 72.
99 See Deleuze (1990), p. 180.
100 Heidegger was to some degree influenced by Scotism; see Heidegger (1970): *Traité des catégories et de la signification chez Duns Scot.*
101 Mallarmé (1914).
102 'The totality of things *contains* God and the World. World means the whole of sensible things', Kant (1993b), p. 228; italics mine.
103 'Sense emerges from nonsense', in Lacan (1989), p. 158.
104 See Badiou (1999), p. 107.
105 Lecercle (1999), p. 12.
106 See Deleuze and Guattari (1987).
107 See Badiou (2001), pp. 25–27.
108 See Dauben (1990), p. 290; Aczel (2000), pp. 188–189. More generally see Cantor (1952); Small (1992).
109 Sartre (2000), p. 79.
110 Lacan (1966), p. 392.
111 Plato (1993), 255–259.
112 Deleuze (1997), p. 64.
113 Blanchot (1969), p. 307.
114 Lacan (1966), p. 300.
115 Lacan (1989), p. 65.
116 Lacan (1992), p. 126.
117 See *ibid.*, p. 213.
118 Badiou (1988), p. 104; (2001), p. 25.
119 Badiou (2000b), p. 102.
120 Sartre (2000), xlii.
121 *Ibid.*, pp. 22–23.
122 *Ibid.*, p. 17.
123 *Ibid.*, p. 123.
124 *Ibid.*, p. 74.
125 *Ibid.*, p. 24.
126 *Ibid.*, p. 138.
127 *Ibid.*, p. 79.
128 *Ibid.*, p. 78.
129 *Ibid.*, p. 102.
130 Lacan (1989), p. 166.
131 Sartre (2000), p. 79.
132 See *ibid.*, p. 23.
133 Badiou (2001), p. 14.
134 Sartre (2000), p. 102.
135 Lacan (1992), pp. 260–261.
136 Guénon (1953), p. 326.
137 Lacan (1989), p. 145.

138 Malcolm Bowie argues that there is a strong Hegelian undercurrent in the work of Lacan: see Bowie (1991), p. 95.
139 Hegel (1967), p. 237.
140 Kojève (1947), p. 539.
141 *Ibid.*, p. 556.
142 Sophocles (1947), p. 83.
143 Lacan (1989), p. 140.
144 *Ibid.*, p. 100.
145 Blanchot (1981), p. 38.
146 *Ibid.*, p. 36.
147 *Ibid.*, p. 41.
148 *Ibid.*, p. 37.
149 Lacan (1989), p. 104.
150 *Ibid.*, p. 65.
151 Lacan (1988), p. 228.
152 Lacan (1992), p. 120.
153 Sartre (2000), p. 191.
154 Silverman (2000), p. 40.
155 Lacan (1992), p. 62.
156 *Ibid.*, p. 63.
157 *Ibid.*, p. 122.
158 Lacan (1989), p. 104.
159 The term 'Indivisible Remainder' is Schelling's. Žižek makes a great deal of this notion; see Žižek (1996).
160 Deleuze (1997), p. 67.
161 *Ibid.*, p. 200.
162 Schelling (1997), p. 141.
163 Quoted by Žižek in the introduction to Schelling (1997), p. 17.
164 *Ibid.*, p. 27.
165 Sartre (1962), pp. 126–128.
166 Žižek (1997), p. 22.
167 *Ibid.*
168 Zizek (1999), p. 161.
169 *Ibid.*, p. 157.
170 The claimed univocal nature of eros is its lack of being. As Sartre puts it: 'Desire is a lack of being', (2000), p. 88.
171 Quoted in Bonaventure (1993), p. 44.
172 Peter Hallward in Badiou (2001), xix.
173 *Ibid.*, p. 27.
174 Žižek (1997), p. 25.
175 Ward (2000), p. 274, fn. 32.
176 Quoted in Alexander (1966), p. 59.
177 Quoted in O'Flaherty (1979), p. 41.
178 Quoted in Alexander (1966), p. 137.
179 Dickson (1995), p. 140.
180 It may well be the case that beauty allows for the ugly, while the ugly will only permit the aesthetic; is this not what was witnessed in National Socialism's aestheticisation of politics?

181 Marion (2000), p. 208.
182 See Arendt (1978), p. 46.
183 Caillois (1964), p. 40.
184 See Caillois (1985).
185 See Portmann (1967) and (1990). Portmann calls this expansionist project 'Morphology'.
186 Merleau-Ponty (1963), p. 186.
187 See Arendt (1978), p. 29.
188 Caillois (1964), p. 41.
189 Buck-Morss (1978), p. 81.
190 Arendt (1978), p. 46.
191 Adorno (1973), p. 161.
192 Adorno (1974), p. 247.
193 Adorno (1973), p. 53.
194 Düttmann (2000), p. 100.
195 Benjamin (1970), p. 136.
196 Žižek (2001), p. 148.
197 Eckhart (1981), p. 202.
198 *Ibid.*, p. 208.
199 Plato (1974), bk. vii.
200 Kierkegaard (1980), pp. 13–14.
201 DV, q. 4, a. 8.
202 Quoted in Borella (1998), p. 127.
203 Quoted in Balthasar (1995), p. 117. For Gregory of Nyssa, human nature is itself other than itself. For the 'water' that God gives us in terms of divinisation 'does not come from strange, far-off streams but springs from our own depths'; see Balthasar (1995), p. 127.
204 Eckhart (1941), p. 232.
205 The notion of *epectasis* stems from Philippians, ch. 3, v. 13.
206 See Deleuze (1997), p. 95.
207 Evdokimov (1959), p. 175; cited in de Lubac (1986), p. 315, fn. 79.
208 Péguy (1958), p. 67.
209 This is the proper place for a use of the notion of infinity.
210 On Eckhart's notion of *Esse est Deus* see Turner (1995), p. 163.
211 On the pre-eminence of the doxological I am but following Catherine Pickstock's lead; see Pickstock (1998).

CONCLUSION

Strange forms

Faith is the truth of knowledge.[1]
(Jean Borella)

Beatitude is service, vision is adoration, freedom is dependence, possession is ecstasy.[2]

(Henri de Lubac)

This book has endeavoured to examine, explicate and critique the logic of nihilism. The process took the form of an analysis of a number of thinkers who, it was argued, embodied this logic: articulated as the sundering of the something, rendering it nothing, and then the production of nothing *as* something. There is, however, little doubt that each of these thinkers *exceeds* the critique offered, for their work contains a potentiality beyond any reading which offers itself as definitive. Such an excess is witnessed in the progress of the text, for it began with a number of 'certainties', later somewhat qualified. For example, it was argued that nihilistic philosophy had at its centre a *reditus* which preceded every *exitus*, but a similar movement was also discerned in theology. Likewise, towards the end of the book it was argued that nihilism's logic of the something as nothing was analogous to that of theology. Furthermore, nihilism's dealings with the *aporia* of the *thought of thought* were instructive, because they pointed theology beyond the self-satisfied philosophies of the ontic thinker; the one who asserts that there 'just are' metaphysical questions to be asked (although it should be said that this *aporia* was first pointed out by Jacobi, who first defined it as a crux of nihilism, in the course of his critique of nihilism). In this way the direction of the analysis learned from that which was *prima facie* different – other – namely, nihilism.

It may be wise to suggest that this is a better form of *dialogue* than is usually espoused, because my other is not simply not me, nor am I simply not my other. In this way theologians can manifest an open finality that allows for the excess of an already ecstatic gift, which may well allow us

273

both to avoid the violence of an unquestioning ontotheology, and *meontotheology*'s infinitude of indeterminate univocity, that coagulates into the one question of the void. By contrast theology neither exhibits the imbalance of pure vertical causality, which we saw was analogous to pure fideism (in the form of Ockham); nor does it exhibit the imbalance of pure horizontal causality, which is analogous to pure reason (in the form of Spinoza). Theology cannot have a pure reason or a pure faith, because, following de Lubac, it can be understood that there is no pure nature;[3] conversely there is no pure unmediated supernatural. This means that there can be neither a natural theology nor a fideism. It is easier to see why when we realise that each contains an element of the other. Natural theology must have faith in its *reason*. That is, it must supplement rationality with a mode of faith (as an analogy, Gödel's 'Incompleteness' theorem comes to mind here). Furthermore, faith in retreating into its own ghetto does so for its own *reasons*. In other words, faith that appeals only to its own fully identifiable logics does so as natural reason writ small. In this way it is guilty of what is referred to in the philosophy of mind as the 'homunculus fallacy': those who reject consciousness succeed only to the degree to which they reproduce the functions of consciousness at a smaller level. Likewise, fideists, in rejecting reason, the clues of finite reality, and so on, do so only to the degree to which they replicate the functions these concepts provide at a smaller level. Faith alone is, then, a homunculus reason.[4] The same can be said when faith and works are separated in an absolute fashion, for this renders faith a work. Furthermore, good works will themselves only be discernible by a form of faith, as they run the risk of being done in bad faith, and so they are bad works.

Theology must endeavour to avoid these imbalances, employing the Christian tradition in a manner which allows the radical nature of creation – its difference – to present itself. Therefore, the faithful theologian, in articulating the creeds – in explicating the particularity of the faith – finds himself within *different memories*, for those in the Upper Room called forth Good Friday, in that they remembered the *future*;[5] just as the Church is the *sacrament of the future*. In being the Bride of Christ we are to find form in the formless, love in hate, blood in wine, life in death. This is 'dialogue', and it is 'agnostic', but it is the dialogue between a lover and a loved within the mystique of desire. Love always has faith in difference, that there is difference in the same, and that we are able to trust that which is otherwise.[6]

Notes

1 Borella (1998), p. 38.
2 de Lubac (1946), p. 492.

3 See de Lubac (1969); (1998).
4 de Certeau calls this retreat of faith to a pure object 'the myth of the Reformation'; de Certeau (2000), p. 168.
5 This is eschatological pragmatism; see Ross (1988).
6 Although I am here cognisant of a warning issued by Badiou: 'This celebrated "other" is acceptable only if he is a good other – which is to say what, exactly, if not the *same* as us?'; Badiou (2001), p. 24.

BIBLIOGRAPHY

Aczel, A. (2000) *The Mystery of the Aleph: Mathematics, the Kabbalah and the Search for Infinity*, New York: Four Walls Eight Windows.

Adams, M. (1970) 'Intuitive Cognition, Certainty, and Scepticism in William of Ockham', in *Traditio*, 26: pp. 389–398.

— (1977) 'Ockham's Nominalism and Unreal Entities', in *Philosophical Review*, 86: pp. 144–176.

— (1987) *William of Ockham*, Notre Dame, IN: University of Notre Dame Press.

— (1990) 'Ockham's Individualisms', in *Die Gegenwart Ockhams*, eds. Wilhelm Vossenkuhl and Rolf Schönberger, Weinheim: VCH Acta Humaniora.

Adorno, T. W. (1966) *Negative Dialektik*, Frankfurt: Suhrkamp.

— (1973) *Negative Dialectics*, trans. E. B. Ashton, New York: Seabury Press.

— (1974) *Minima Moralia: Reflections from a Damaged Life*, trans. E. F. N. Jephcott, London: NLB.

— (1997) *Aesthetic Theory*, trans. R. Hullot-Kentor, London: Athlone.

— (2000) *Adorno Reader*, ed. Brian O'Connor, Oxford: Blackwell.

Aertsen, J. A. (1985) 'The Convertibility of Being and Good in St Thomas Aquinas', in *New Scholasticism*, 59: pp. 449–470.

— (1991) 'Good as Transcendental and the Transcendence of the Good', in *Being and Goodness: The Concept of the Good in Metaphysics and Philosophical Theology*, ed. S. MacDonald, Ithaca and London: Cornell University Press, pp. 56–73.

— (1992a) 'Truth as a Transcendental in Thomas Aquinas', in *Topoi*, 11: pp. 159–171.

— (1992b) 'Ontology and Henology in Medieval Philosophy', in *On Proclus and his Influence in Medieval Philosophy*, Leiden: E. J. Brill, pp. 120–140.

— (1995a) 'Transcendental Thought in Henry of Ghent', in *Henry of Ghent: Studies in Commemoration of the 700th Anniversary of His Death (1293)*, Louvain: Publications Universitaires de Louvain.

— (1995b) 'The Beginning of the Transcendentals in Phillip the Chancellor', in *Quodlibetaria Mediaevalia*, Festschrift J. M. da Cruz Pontes. *Textos Estudos*, 7–8: pp. 269–286.

— (1996) *Medieval Philosophy and the Transcendentals*, Leiden: E. J. Brill.

Afnan, S. (1958) *Avicenna*, London: George Allen and Unwin.

Alanen, L. (1985) 'Descartes, Scotus, Ockham: Omnipotence and Possibility', in *Franciscan Studies*, 23: pp. 157–187.

Alexander, W. M. (1966) *Johann Georg Hamann, Philosophy and Faith*, The Hague: Martinus Nijhoff.

Alféri, P. (1989) *Guillaume d'Ockham: Le Singulier*, Paris: Minuit.

Allen, A. D. (1976) 'Notes on a New Definition of Infinite Cardinality', in *International Logic Review*, vol. 7: pp. 57–60.

Alliez, E. (1996) *Capital Times*, trans. G. Abbeele, Minneapolis: University of Minnesota Press.

Allison, H. (1983) *Kant's Transcendental Idealism: An Interpretation and Defence*, New Haven: Yale University Press.

Anawati, G. C. (1978) *La Métaphysique du Shifa*, Paris: Vrin.

Anderson, J. (1949) *The Bond of Being*, New York: Greenwood Press.

Annice, M. (1952) 'Historical Sketch of the Theory of Participation', in *New Scholasticism*, 26: pp. 167–194.

Aquinas, St Thomas (1932–1934) *De Potentia*, 3 vols, trans. L. Shapcote, London: Blackfriars.

— (1952) *Compendium Theologiae*, trans. C. Vollert, St Louis, MO: Herder.

— (1960) *The Pocket Aquinas*, ed. V. J. Bourke. (This contains a translation of *De Principiis Naturae*, and excerpts from *Super Librum Dionysii De Divinis Nominibus*.) New York: Washington Square Press.

— (1964–1973) *Summa Theologiae*, eds T. Gilby and T. C. O'Brien, 60 vols, London and New York: Blackfriars.

— (1975) *Summa Contra Gentiles*, eds and trans. A. C. Pegis, J. F. Anderson, V. J. Bourke and C. J. O'Neill, Notre Dame, IN: University of Notre Dame Press.

— (1980) *Super Ioannem*, trans. J. A. Weisheipl and F. R. Larcher, Albany, NY: Magi Books.

— (1983a) *Quodlibetal Questions*, 2 vols, trans. S. Edwards, Toronto: Pontifical Institute of Mediaeval Studies.

— (1983b) *De Ente et Essentiae*, trans. A. Maurer, Toronto: Pontifical Institute of Mediaeval Studies.

— (1990) 'Sermon on the Apostles' Creed', trans. L. Shapcote, in *On Faith and Reason*, ed. S. Brown, Indianapolis: Hackett Publishing Company.

— (1994) *De Veritate*, 3 vols. trans. R. W. Mulligan, Indianapolis: Hackett Publishing Company.

— (1996) *Super Librum De Causis*, trans V. A. Guagliaro, C. R. Hess and R. C. Taylor, Washington, DC: Catholic University of America Press.

— (1997) *Aquinas on Creation*, translation of Aquinas' writings on Peter Lombard's *Sentences*, 2. 1. 1, trans. S. E. Baldner and W. E. Carroll, Toronto: Pontifical Institute of Mediaeval Studies.

— (1998) *De Principiis Naturae*, trans. J. Bobik, Notre Dame, IN: University of Notre Dame Press.

Arendt, H. (1978) *The Life of the Mind*, New York: Harcourt Brace and Co.

Aristotle (1984) *Complete Works*, ed. J. Barnes, the revised Oxford translation, 2 vols, Princeton: Princeton University Press.

Artaud, A. (1982) *Antonin Artaud: Four Texts*, trans. C. Eshleman and N. Glass, Los Angeles: Panjandrum Books.

Auden, W. H. (1994) *Collected Poems*, ed. E. Mendelson, London: Faber and Faber.

Augustine, St (1961) *Confessions*, eds Betty Radice and Robert Baldick, London: Penguin Books.
— (1982) *On the Literal Meaning of Genesis*, trans. John Hammond Taylor, S.J., New York: Newman Press.
— (1984) *The City of God*, trans. H. Bettenson, London: Penguin Books.
— (1991) *On the Trinity*, trans. Edmund Hill, O.P., ed. John E. Rotelle, O.S.A., Brooklyn, NY: New City Press.
— (1999) *On Christian Teaching*, trans. R. P. H. Green, Oxford: Oxford University Press.
Averroes (1954) *Tahafut al-Tahafut*, trans. S. van den Bergh, Cambridge: Cambridge University Press.
Avicenna (1951) *Avicenna on Theology*, trans. A. J. Arberry, London: John Murray.
— (1952) *Avicenna's Psychology*, an English translation of *Kitab al Najat*, book II, Ch. vi, trans. F. Rahman, Oxford: Oxford University Press.
— (1973a) *Propositional Logic of Avicenna*, trans. N. Shehaby, Dordrecht and Boston: Reidel.
— (1973b) *Metaphysics*, trans. P. Morewedge, Chicago: Chicago University Press.
— (1974) *Treatise on Logic*, trans. F. Zabeeh, The Hague: Martinus Nijhoff.
— (1977–1980) *Liber de Philosophia Prima sive Scientia Divina*, ed. S. Van Riet, 2 vols, Louvain: Peeters; and Leiden: E. J. Brill.
— (1984) *Remarks and Admonition, Part One: Logic*, trans. S. C. Inati, Toronto: Pontifical Institute of Mediaeval Studies.
Azkoul, M. (1995) *St Gregory of Nyssa and the Tradition of the Fathers*, Lampeter: The Edwin Mellen Press.
Back, A. (1992) 'Avicenna's Conception of Modality', in *Vivarium*, 30: pp. 217–255.
Badiou, A. (1988) *L'Être et l'évènement*, Paris: Éditions du Seuil.
— (1991) 'On Finally an Objectless Subject', in *Who Comes After the Subject*, eds E. Cadava, P. Connor and J.-L. Nancy, London: Routledge.
— (1994) 'Gilles Deleuze, The Fold: Leibniz and the Baroque', in *Gilles Deleuze and the Theater of Philosophy*, eds C. Boundas and D. Olokowski, London: Routledge, pp. 51–69.
— (1997) *Saint Paul: le fondation de l'universalisme*, Paris: Presses Universitaires de France.
— (1999) *Manifesto for Philosophy*, trans. N. Madarasz, Albany: SUNY Press.
— (2000a) *Deleuze: The Clamor of Being*, trans. L. Burchill, Minneapolis: University of Minnesota Press.
— (2000b) 'Frege/On a Contemporary Usage of Frege', trans. S. Gillespie and J. Clemens, in *Umbr(a): 2000, Science and Truth*, pp. 99–115.
— (2001) *Ethics: An Essay on the Understanding of Evil*, trans. P. Hallward, London: Verso.
Baer, U. (2000) *Remnants of Song*, Stanford, CA: Stanford University Press.
von Balthasar, Hans Urs (1982–1991) *The Glory of the Lord: A Theological Aesthetics*, vols 1–7, trans. Erasmo Leiva-Merikakis, eds J. Fressio, J. Riches, B. McNeil, O. Davies and A. Louth, Edinburgh: T. and T. Clark.
— (1987) *Truth is Symphonic: Aspects of Christian Pluralism*, San Francisco: Ignatius.
— (1988) *Dare We Hope 'That all Men Shall be Saved' with a Short Discourse on Hell*, San Francisco: Ignatius.

— (1992) *The Theology of Karl Barth*, trans. Edward T. Oakes, San Francisco: Ignatius.

— (1995) *Presence and Thought: an Essay on the Religious Philosophy of Gregory of Nyssa*, trans. M. Sebanc, San Francisco: Ignatius.

Barth, T. A. (1965) 'Being, Univocity, and Analogy According to Duns Scotus', in *Studies in Philosophy and the History of Philosophy, John Duns Scotus*, eds J. K. Ryan and B. Bonansea, Washington, DC: Catholic University of America Press, pp. 210–262.

Bataille, G. (1993) *The Accursed Share*, vols II and III, trans. R. Hurley, New York: Zone Books.

Baudrillard, J. (1976) *L'Echange symbolique et la mort*, Paris: Gallimard.

Bauman, Z. (1989) *Modernity and the Holocaust*, Cambridge: Polity Press.

Beck, A. J. (1998) 'Divine Psychology and Modalities: Scotus's Theory of the Neutral Proposition', in *John Duns Scotus. 1265/6–1308. Renewal in Philosophy*, ed. E. P. Bos, Amsterdam: Rodopi, pp. 123–138.

Beck, L. W. (1960) *A Commentary on Kant's Critique of Practical Reason*, Chicago: Chicago University Press.

Beckett, S. (1955) *Three Novels: Molloy, Malone Dies, The Unnamable*, New York: Grove Press.

Behe, M. (1996) *Darwin's Black Box: The Biochemical Challenge to Evolution*, New York: Free Press.

Benjamin, W. (1970) *Illuminations*, trans. H. Zohn, London: Jonathan Cape.

— (1979) *One Way Street and Other Writings*, trans. E. Jephcott and K. Shorter, London: NLB and Verso.

— (1980) *Gesammelte Schriften*, vol. I: 1, Frankfurt am Main: Suhrkamp.

Bennett, J. (1966) *Kant's Analytic*, Cambridge: Cambridge University Press.

— (1974) *Kant's Dialectic*, Cambridge: Cambridge University Press.

Bergson, H. (1983) *Creative Evolution*, trans. A. Mitchell, Lanham, MD: University Press of America.

Bernstein, J. (1992) *The Fate of Art*, Cambridge: Polity Press.

Bettoni, E. (1976) *Duns Scotus: The Basic Principles of His Philosophy*, Westport, CT: Greenwood.

Blanchette, O. (1992) *The Perfection of the Universe According to Aquinas*, Philadelphia: Penn State University Press.

Blanchot, M. (1969) *L'Entretien infini*, Paris: Gallimard.

— (1981) 'La Littérature et le droit à la mort', in *De Kafka à Kafka*, Paris: Gallimard.

— (1982) *The Space of Literature*, trans. A. Smock, Lincoln: University of Nebraska Press.

— (1986) *Writing the Disaster*, trans. A. Smock, Lincoln: University of Nebraska Press.

— (1995) *The Work of Fire*, trans. C. Mandell, Stanford, CA: Stanford University Press.

Blondel, M. (1984) *Action*, trans. O. Blanchette, Notre Dame, IN: University of Notre Dame Press.

— (1995) *The Letter on Apologetics and the History and Dogma*, trans. A. Dru and I. Trethowan, Edinburgh: T. and T. Clark.

Blumenberg, H. (1983) *The Legitimacy of the Modern Age*, trans. R. W. Wallace, Cambridge, MA: MIT Press.

Boehner, E. (1943) 'The *Notitia Intuitiva* of non-existents according to William of Ockham', in *Traditio*, 1: pp. 223–275.

— (1945) '*In Propria Causa*: a Reply to Professor Pegis', in *Franciscan Studies*, 5: pp. 37–54.

— (1958) 'The Relative Date of Ockham's Commentary on the *Sentences*', in *Collected Articles*, ed. E. Buytaert, New York: Franciscan Institute, pp. 96–110.

Boland, V. (1996) *Ideas in God According to Thomas Aquinas*, Leiden: E. J. Brill.

Boler, J. (1973) 'Ockham on Intuition', in *Journal of the History of Philosophy*, 11: pp. 95–106.

— (1976) 'Ockham on Evident Cognition', in *Franciscan Studies*, 36: pp. 73–89.

— (1982) 'Intuitive and Abstractive Cognition', in *Cambridge History of Later Medieval Philosophy*, eds N. Kretzmann, A. Kenny, and J. Pinborg, Cambridge: Cambridge University Press, pp. 460–478.

Bonansea, B. M. (1983) *Man and His Approach to God in John Duns Scotus*, Lanham, MD: University Press of America.

Bonaventure, St (1993) *The Journey of the Mind to God*, trans. P. Boehner, Indianapolis: Hackett Publishing Company.

Borella, J. (1979) *La Charité profanée*, Bouère: Éditions Dominique Morin.

— (1998) *The Sense of the Supernatural*, trans. G. Champoux, Edinburgh: T. and T. Clark.

— (2001) *The Secret of the Christian Way*, trans. G. Champoux, Albany: SUNY Press.

Bouillard, Henri (1967) *The Logic of Faith*, trans. M. Gill, New York: Sheed and Ward.

— (1968) *The Knowledge of God*, trans. S. Feminano, New York: Herder and Herder.

— (1969) *Blondel and Christianity*, trans. J. Somerville, Washington, DC: Corpus Books.

Bouyer, L. (1954) *Liturgical Piety*, Notre Dame, IN: University of Notre Dame Press.

— (1962) *The Seat of Wisdom: An Essay on the Place of the Virgin Mary in Christian Theology*, trans. Fr A. V. Littledale, New York: Pantheon Books.

— (1963) *Rite and Man*, trans. M. J. Costello, S.J., Notre Dame, IN: University of Notre Dame Press.

— (1968) *Eucharist: Theology and Spirituality of the Eucharitic Prayer*, trans. C. Underhill Quinn, Notre Dame, IN: University of Notre Dame Press.

— (1990) *The Christian Mystery*, trans. I. Trethowan, Edinburgh: T. and T. Clark.

— (1999) *The Invisible Father*, trans. H. Gilbert, Edinburgh: T. and T. Clark.

Bowie, A. (1993) *Schelling and Modern European Philosophy*, London: Routledge.

Bowie, M. (1991) *Lacan*, London: Fontana.

Brampton, C. K. (1965) 'Scotus, Ockham and the Theory of Intuitive Cognition', in *Antonianum*, 40: pp. 449–466.

Bréhier, E. (1953) *The Philosophy of Plotinus*, trans. J. Thomas, Chicago: University of Chicago Press.

Brink, G. van der (1993) *Almighty God: A Study of the Doctrine of Divine Omnipotence*, Utrecht: Kok Pharos Publishing House.

Brown, F. (1989) *Religious Aesthetics*, Princeton: Princeton University Press.

Brown, S. (1965) 'Avicenna and the Unity of the Concept of Being', in *Franciscan Studies*, 25: pp. 117–150.

— (1968) 'Scotus's Univocity in the Early Fourteenth Century', in *De Doctrina Ioannis Duns Scoti: Acta Congressus Scotistici Internationalis*, vol. IV (Studia Scholastico-Scotistica 4), Roma, pp. 35–41.

de Bruyne, E. (1969) *The Aesthetics of the Middle Ages*, trans. E. B. Hennesey. New York: Frederick Ungar Publishing Company.

Büchner, G. (1979) *Danton's Death*, trans. J. Maxwell, London: Eyre Methuen.

— (1986) *The Complete Works and Letters*, trans. H. Schmidt, New York: Continuum.

Buck-Morss, S. (1978) *The Origin of Negative Dialectics: Theodor W. Adorno, Walter Benjamin, and the Frankfurt Institute*, Hassocks, Sussex: Harvester Press.

Bugliani, A. (1999) *The Introduction of Philosophy and Psychoanalysis by Tragedy: Jacques Lacan and Gabriel Marcel read Paul Claudel*, London: International Scholars' Publications.

Burbidge, J. (1992) *Hegel on Logic and Religion: The Reasonableness of Christianity*, Albany: SUNY Press.

Burrell, D. (1973) *Analogy and Philosophical Language*, New Haven and London: Yale University Press.

— (1979) *God and Action*, Notre Dame, IN: University of Notre Dame Press.

— (1985) 'Creation, Will and Knowledge in Aquinas and Scotus', in *Pragmatik*, I, ed. H. Stachowiak, Hamburg: Felix Meiner.

— (1986) *Knowing the Unknowable God*, Notre Dame, IN: University of Notre Dame Press.

— (1990) 'Aquinas and Scotus: Contrary Patterns for Philosophical Theology', in *Theology and Dialogue*, Notre Dame, IN: University of Notre Dame Press.

Butler, C. (1992) 'Hegelian Panentheism as Joachimite Christianity', in *New Perspectives on Hegel's Philosophy of Religion*, ed. D. Kolb, Albany: SUNY Press.

Caffarena, J. G. (1958) *Ser participado y ser subsistente en la metafísica de Enrique de Gante*, Rome.

Caillois, R. (1964) *The Mask of Medusa*, trans. G. Ordish, New York: Clarkson N. Potter.

— (1985) *The Writing of Stones*, trans. B. Bray, Charlottesville: University Press of Virginia.

Cajetan (1953) *Analogy of Names and the Concept of Being*, trans. E. R. Bushinski and H. Koren, Pittsburgh: Duquesne University Press.

Calahan, J. C. (1970) 'Analogy and the Disrepute of Metaphysics', in *Thomist*, 23, no. 3: pp. 387–442.

Callahan, L. A. (1947) *Theory of Aesthetics According to the Principles of St Thomas Aquinas*, Washington, DC: Catholic University of America Press.

Cantor, G. (1952) *Contributions to the Founding of the Theory of Transfinite Numbers*, trans. P. Jourdain, Illinois: Open Court.

— (1966) *Gesammelte Abhandlungen mathematischen und philosophischen Inhalts*, ed. E. Zermelo, Berlin: Springer; reprinted Hildesheim: Olms.

Caputo, J. D. (1997) *The Prayers and Tears of Jacques Derrida: Religion without Religion*, Bloomington: Indiana University Press.

Caranfa, A. (1989) *Claudel*, London and Toronto: Associated University Press.

281

Catania, F. (1993) 'John Duns Scotus on Ens Infinitum', in *American Catholic Philosophical Quarterly*, 63 : pp. 37–51.

Celan, P. (1978) 'The Meridian', trans. J. Glenn, in *Chicago Review*, 29: pp. 29–40.

— (1986) *Collected Prose*, trans. Rosmarie Waldrop, Manchester: Carcanet.

— (1995) *Selected Poems*, trans. M. Hamburger, London: Penguin.

de Certeau, M. (1992) *The Mystic Fable*, vol. 1, trans. M. B. Smith, Chicago: University of Chicago Press.

— (2000) *The Certeau Reader*, ed. G. Ward, Oxford: Blackwell.

Cessario, R. (1992) 'Virtue Theory and Thomism', in *The Future of Thomism*, eds D. W. Hudson and D. W. Moran, Notre Dame, IN: Notre Dame University Press.

Chapman, E. (1942) 'The Perennial Theme of Beauty and Art', in *Essays in Thomism*, ed. R. E. Brennan, New York: Sheed and Ward, pp. 333–346.

Chapman, T. (1975) 'Analogy', in *Thomist*, 34: pp. 127–141.

Chavannes, H. (1992) *The Analogy Between God and the World in St Thomas Aquinas and Karl Barth*, trans. W. Lumley, New York: Vantage Press.

Chiari, J. (1960) *Realism and Imagination*, London: Barrie and Rockliff.

— (1970) *Aesthetics of Modernism*, London: Vision Press.

— (1973) *The Necessity of Being*, New York: Gordian Press.

— (1977) *Art and Knowledge*, New York: Gordian Press.

Clarke, W. N. (1952) 'The Meaning of Participation in St Thomas', in *Proceedings of the American Catholic Philosophical Association*, 26: pp. 147–157.

— (1976) 'Analogy and the Meaningfulness of Language about God: A Reply to Kai Nielson', in *Thomist*, 40: pp. 61–95.

— (1982) 'The Problem of the Reality and Multiplicity of Divine Ideas in Christian Neoplatonism', in *Neoplatonism and Christian Thought*, ed. D. J. O'Meara, Albany: SUNY Press.

Claudel, P. (1942) *Présence et Prophétie*, Fribourg: Librairie de l'Université.

— (1950) *The Eye Listens*, trans. E. Pell, New York: Philosophical Library.

— (1956) *The Sword and the Mirror*, trans. E. Pell, New York: Philosophical Library.

— (1960) *Break of Noon*, trans. W. Fowlie, Chicago: Henry Regnery Company.

— (1968) *Five Great Odes*, trans. E. Lucie-Smith, London: Rapp and Whiting.

— (1969) *Poetic Art*, trans. E. Pell, New York: Philosophical Library.

Cohen, T. and Guyer, P., eds (1982) *Essays in Kant's Aesthetics*, Chicago: University of Chicago Press.

Coleman, F. (1974) *The Harmony of Reason: A Study in Kant's Aesthetics*, Pittsburgh: University of Pittsburgh Press.

Colie, R. (1966) *Paradoxia Epidemica*, Princeton: Princeton University Press.

Colletti, L. (1973) *Marxism and Hegel*, trans. L. Garner, London: NLB.

Collins, J. (1967) *The Emergence of Philosophy of Religion*, New Haven: Yale University Press.

Coomaraswamy, A. K. (1938) 'St Thomas on Dionysius and a Note on the Relation of Beauty to Truth', in *Art Bulletin*, 20: pp. 66–77.

Courtenay, W. J. (1984a) *Covenant and Causality in Medieval Thought: Studies in Philosophy, Theology, and Economic Practice*, London: Variorum.

— (1984b) 'The Dialectic of Omnipotence in the High and Late Middle Ages', in *Divine Omniscience and Omnipotence in Medieval Philosophy*, Dordrecht: Reidel, pp. 243–269.

— (1990) *Capacity and Volition: A History of the Distinction of Absolute and Ordained Power*, Bergamo: Pierluigi Lubrina Editore.

Crawford, D. (1974) *Kant's Aesthetic Theory*, Madison: University of Wisconsin Press.

Cronin, T. J. (1966) *Objective Being in Descartes and Suarez*, Rome: Gregorian University Press.

Cross, F. and Livingstone, E. A. (1974) *The Oxford Dictionary of the Christian Church*, 2nd edn, London: Oxford University Press.

Cross, R. (1999) *Duns Scotus*, Oxford: Oxford University Press.

Crowther, P. (1989) *The Kantian Sublime*, Oxford: Oxford University Press.

Cunningham, C. (1999) 'Wittgenstein after Theology', in *Radical Orthodoxy: A New Theology*, eds J. Milbank, C. Pickstock and G. Ward, London: Routledge, pp. 64–90.

— (2001a) 'The Difference of Theology and Some Philosophies of Nothing', in *Modern Theology*, 17:3, pp. 289–312.

Cunningham, D. (1998) *These Three are One: The Practice of Trinitarian Theology*, Oxford: Blackwell.

Cunningham, F. A. (1974) 'Averrroes vs. Avicenna on Being', in *New Scholasticism*, 48: pp. 185–218.

Cunningham, F. L. B. (1955) *The Indwelling of the Trinity*, Dubuque, IA: Priory Press.

Daniélou, J. (1956) *The Bible and the Liturgy*, Notre Dame, IN: University of Notre Dame Press.

— (1962) *The Scandal of Truth*, trans. W. J. Kerrigan, Dublin: Helicon Press.

— (1970) *The Faith Eternal and the Man of Today*, trans. J. Oligny, Chicago: Franciscan Herald Press.

Dauben, J. (1990) *Georg Cantor: His Mathematics and Philosophy of the Infinite*, Princeton: Princeton University Press.

Davenport, A. (1999) *Measure of a Different Greatness: The Intensive Infinite*, Leiden: E. J. Brill.

Davies, B. (1992) *The Thought of Thomas Aquinas*, Oxford: Clarendon Press.

Davis, L. (1974) 'The Intuitive Knowledge of Non-existents and the Problem of Late Medieval Scepticism', in *New Scholasticism*, 49: pp. 410–430.

Day, S. (1947) *Intuitive Cognition: A Key to the Significance of the Later Scholastics*, New York: Franciscan Institute.

Dejond, T. (1989) *Charles Péguy. L'Espérance d'un salut éternel*, Namur.

Deleuze, G. (1988) *Spinoza: Practical Philosophy*, trans. R. Hurley, San Francisco: City Lights Books.

— (1990) *The Logic of Sense*, trans. M. Lester and C. Stivale, London: Athlone Press.

— (1992) *Expressionism in Philosophy: Spinoza*, trans. M. Joughin, London: Zone Books.

— (1997) *Difference and Repetition*, trans. P. Patton, London: Athlone Press.

Deleuze, G. and Guattari, F. (1987) *A Thousand Plateaus*, trans. B. Massumi, Minneapolis: University of Minnesota Press.

— (1994) *What is Philosophy*, trans. G. Burchell and H. Tomlinson, London: Verso.

Deleuze, G. and Parnet, C. (1987) *Dialogues*, London: Athlone Press.

Derrida, J. (1962) *Introduction à 'L'Origine de la géométrie' de Husserl*, Paris: Presses Universitaires de France.

— (1973) *Speech and Phenomenon*, trans. D. B. Allison, Evanston, IL: Northwestern University Press.

— (1974) *Of Grammatology*, trans. G. Spivak, Baltimore: Johns Hopkins University Press.

— (1978) *Writing and Difference*, trans. A. Bass, London: Routledge.

— (1982) *Margins of Philosophy*, trans. A. Bass, Chicago: University of Chicago Press.

— (1987a) *Truth in Painting*, trans. G. Bennington and I. McLeod, Chicago: University of Chicago Press.

— (1987b) *Positions*, trans. A. Bass, London: Athlone Press.

— (1988) 'Letter to a Japanese Friend,' in *Derrida and Différance*, eds D. Wood and R. Bernasconi, Evanston, IL: Northwestern University Press.

— (1989) *Edmund Husserl's Origin of Geometry: An Introduction*, trans. J. P. Leavey, Lincoln: University of Nebraska Press.

— (1991) *A Derrida Reader*, trans. P. Kamuf, Hemel Hempstead: Harvester-Wheatsheaf.

— (1992) *Acts of Literature*, ed. D. Attridge, London: Routledge.

Dews, P. *Logics of Disintegration: Post-Structuralist Thought and the Claims of Critical Theory*, London: Verso.

Diamond, E. (2000) 'Hegel on Being and Nothing: Some Contemporary Neoplatonic and Sceptical Responses', in *Dionysius*, 18: pp. 183–216.

Dickson, G. (1995) *Johann Georg Hamann's Relational Metacriticism*, Berlin: De Gruyter.

Dillon, M. (1995) *Semiological Reductionism*, Albany: SUNY Press.

— (1997) *Merleau-Ponty's Ontology*, 2nd edn, Evanston, IL: Northwestern University Press.

Dionysius [Pseudo] (1980) *The Divine Names*, trans. Editors of the Shrine of Wisdom, Garden City, NJ: Garden City Press.

— (1987) *The Complete Works*, trans. C. Luibheid, London: SPCK.

Doyle, R. (1997) *On Beyond Living*, Stanford, CA: Stanford University Press.

Dubay, T. (1999) *The Evidential Power of Beauty*, San Francisco: Ignatius.

Duhem, P. (1985) *Medieval Cosmology*, ed. and trans. R. Ariew, Chicago: University of Chicago Press.

Dumont, S. (1995) 'The Origin of Scotus's Theory of Synchronic Contingency', in *Modern Schoolman*, 72: pp. 149–167.

— (1998) 'Henry of Ghent and Duns Scotus', in *Medieval Philosophy*, ed. J. Marrenbon, London: Routledge.

Dupré, L. (1984) 'Hegel's Absolute Spirit: A Religious Justification of Secular Culture', in *Hegel: The Absolute Spirit*, Ottawa: University of Ottawa Press.

— (1993) *Passage to Modernity: An Essay in the Hermenutics of Nature and Grace*, New Haven and London: Yale University Press.

Dusing, K. (1990) 'Beauty as the Transition from Nature to Freedom in Kant's Critique of Judgement', in *Noûs*, 24: pp. 79–92.

Düttmann, A. (2000) *The Gift of Language*, trans. A. Lyons, London: Athlone.

Eckhart, M. (1941) *Meister Eckhart: A Modern Translation*, trans. R. Blakney, New York: Harper and Row.

— (1981) *The Essential Sermons, Commentaries, Treatises and Defence*, trans. E. Colledge and B. McGinn, London: SPCK.

Eco, U. (1986) *Art and the Beauty of the Middle Ages*, trans. H. Bredin, New Haven and London: Yale University Press.

— (1988) *The Aesthetics of Thomas Aquinas*, trans. H. Bredin, Cambridge, MA: Harvard University Press.

— (1989) *The Aesthetics of Chaosmos: The Middle Ages of Joyce*, trans. E. Esrock, Cambridge, MA: Harvard University Press.

Edwards, P. (1967) *The Encyclopedia of Philosophy*, New York: Macmillan.

Eliott, R. K. (1968) 'The Unity of Kant's Critique of Aesthetic Judgement', in *British Journal of Aesthetics*, 8, no. 3, pp. 244–259.

Emminghaus, J. H. (1988) *The Eucharist: Essence, Form, and Celebration*, trans. M. O'Connell, Minnesota: Liturgical Press.

Evdokimov, P. (1959) *L'Orthodoxie*, Paris: Delachaux et Niestlé.

— (1990) *The Art of the Icon: A Theology of Beauty*, trans. Fr S. Bigham, Oakwood, CA: Oakwood Publications.

Fabro, C. (1961) *Participation et Causalité selon S. Thomas d'Aquin*, Louvain: Publications Universitaires.

— (1968) *God in Exile: Modern Atheism*, trans. A. Gibson, New York: Newman Press.

— (1970) 'Platonism, Neoplatonism and Thomism, Convergence and Divergence', in *New Scholasticism*, 44: pp. 69–100.

— (1974) 'The Intensive Hermeneutics of Thomistic Philosophy: The Notion of Participation', in *Review of Metaphysics*, 27: pp. 449–491.

— (1982) 'The Overcoming of the Neoplatonic Triad of Being, Life, and Intellect by Saint Thomas Aquinas', in *Neoplatonism and Christian Thought*, ed. D. J. O'Meara, Albany: SUNY Press, pp. 97–108 and 250–255.

Fackenheim, E. (1967) *The Religious Dimension of Hegel's Thought*, Bloomington and London: Indiana University Press.

Fang, J. (1976) *The Illusory Infinite: A Theology of Mathematics*, Memphis, TN: Paideia.

Fay, T. (1973) 'Participation: The Transformation of Platonic and Neoplatonic Thought in the Metaphysics of Thomas Aquinas', in *Divus Thomas*, 76: pp. 50–64.

Felstiner, J. (1995) *Paul Celan, Poet, Survivor, Jew*, New Haven and London: Yale University Press.

Findlay, J. N. (1958) *Hegel: A Re-examination*, London: Allen and Unwin.

— (1975) 'Introduction to Hegel's Logic', in G. W. F. Hegel, *The Logic*, trans. W. Wallace, Oxford: Oxford University Press.

Finney, P. C. (1994) *The Invisible God: The Earliest Christians on Art*, Oxford: Oxford University Press.

Fioretos, A., ed. (1994) *Word Traces: Readings of Paul Celan*, Baltimore and London: Johns Hopkins University Press.

Foucault, M. (1971) *The Order of Things: An Archaeology of the Human Sciences*, New York: Pantheon.

— (1973) *Birth of the Clinic: An Archaeology of Medical Perception*, trans. A. M. Sheridan Smith, New York: Pantheon.

Frank, R. M. (1956) 'Origin of the Arabic Philosophical Term *anniyya*', in Musée Lavigerie: Cahiers de Byrsa, VI: pp. 181–201.

Frankland, W. B. (1902) *The Early Eucharist*, London: C. J. Clay and Sons.

Fuchs, O. (1952) *The Psychology of Habit According to William of Ockham*, New York and Louvain: St Bonaventure.

Funkenstein, A. (1975a) 'Descartes, Eternal Truths, and the Divine Omnipotence', in *Studies in History and Philosophy of Science*, 6.3: pp. 185–199.

— (1975b) 'The Dialectical Preparation for Scientific Revolutions', in *The Copernican Achievement*, ed. R. Westman, Berkeley, CA: University of California Press, pp. 163–203.

— (1986) *Theology and the Scientific Imagination*, Princeton: Princeton University Press.

— (1994) 'A Comment on R. Popkin's Paper', in *The Books of Nature and Scripture*, eds J. E. Force and R. H. Popkin, Dordrecht: Kluwer.

Gadamer, H.-G. (1975) *Truth and Method*, trans. W. Glen-Dopel, London: Sheed and Ward.

— (1986a) *The Relevance of the Beautiful and Other Essays*, trans. N. Walker, Cambridge: Cambridge University Press.

— (1986b) *The Idea of the Good in Platonic-Aristotelian Philosophy*, trans. P. Christopher Smith, New Haven: Yale University Press.

— (1997) *Who Am I, Who Are You, and Other Essays*, trans. and eds R. Heinemann and B. Knajewski, Albany: SUNY Press.

Garcia-Rivera, A. (1999) *The Community of the Beautiful*, Minnesota: Liturgical Press.

Gamow, G. (1954) 'Possible Relation between Deoxyribonucleic Acid and Protein Structures', in *Nature*, 173.

Gardet (1951) *La Pensée réligieuse d'Avicenne*, Paris: Vrin.

Garrigou-Lagrange, R. (1944) *Christian Contemplation and Perfection*, trans. M. Timothea Doyle, London: B. Herder Book Company.

— (1950) *Reality: A Synthesis of Thomistic Thought*, trans. P. Cummins, London: B. Herder Book Company.

Geiger, L.-B. (1953) *La Participation dans la philosophie de St Thomas d'Aquin*, Paris: Vrin.

Gelber, H. G. (1990) 'Review of M. M. Adams' book: *William of Ockham*', in *Faith and Philosophy*, 7: pp. 246–252.

Gerson, L. P. (1994) *Plotinus*, London: Routledge.

Gill, E. (1933) *Beauty Looks after Herself*, New York: Sheed and Ward.

Gillespie, M. (1995) *Nihilism before Nietzsche*, Chicago: University of Chicago Press.

Gilson, É. (1927) 'Avic et le point de départ de Duns Scotus', in *Archives d'Histoire doctrinale et littéraire du moyen âge*, pp. 89–149.

— (1929–1930) 'Les sources grèco-arabes de l'Augustinianisme avicennisant', in *Archives d'Histoire doctrinale et littéraire du moyen âge*, pp. 1–107.

— (1937) *Unity of Philosophical Experience*, New York: C. Scribner's Sons.

— (1952a) *Being and Some Philosophers*, Toronto: Pontifical Institute of Mediaeval Studies.

— (1952b) *Jean Duns Scotus: Introduction à ses positions fondamentales*, Paris: Vrin.

— (1955a) *History of Christian Philosophy*, New York: Sheed and Ward.
— (1955b) 'Cajetan et l'humanisme théologique', in *Archives d'Histoire Doctrinale et Littéraire du Moyen Âge*, pp. 113–136.
— (1959) *Painting and Reality*, Cleveland and New York: The World Publishing Co.
— (1965) *The Arts of the Beautiful*, New York: C. Scribner's Sons.
— (1966) *Forms and Substances*, New York: C. Scribner's Sons.
— (1978) *Elements of Christian Philosophy*, Westport, CT: Greenwood Press.
— (1991) *Spirit of Mediaeval Philosophy*, trans. A. H. C. Downes, Notre Dame, IN: University of Notre Dame Press.
— (1994) *The Christian Philosophy of St Thomas Aquinas*, Notre Dame, IN: University of Notre Dame Press.
Giovanni, George di (1989) 'From Jacobi's Philosophical Novel to Fichte's Idealism, Some Comments on the 1798–99 Atheism Dispute', in *Journal of the History of Philosophy*, 27: pp. 75–100.
— (1992) 'The First Twenty Years of the Critiques: The Spinoza Connection', in *The Cambridge Companion to Kant*, Cambridge: Cambridge University Press, pp. 417–48.
— (1994) 'Introduction: The Unfinished Philosophy of Friedrich Heinrich Jacobi', in F. H. Jacobi, *The Main Philosophical Writings and the Novel 'Allwill'*, Montreal and Kingston: McGill–Queens University Press.
Goichon, A. M. (1948) 'La Logique d'Avicenne', in *Archives d'Histoire doctrinale et littéraire du moyen âge*, pp. 58–90.
— (1956) 'The Philosopher of Being', in *Avicenna Commemorative Volume*, Calcutta: Iran Society.
— (1969) *The Philosophy of Avicenna*, trans. M. S. Kahn, Delhi: Delhi Motil al Banarsidass.
Goodchild, P. (2001) 'Why is Philosophy so Compromised by God?', in *Deleuze and Religion*, London: Routledge, pp. 156–166.
Goris, Harm J. M. J. (1996) *Free Creatures of an Eternal God*, Utrecht: Thomas Instituut; Leuven: Peeters.
Grajewski, M. J. (1944) *The Formal Distinction of Duns Scotus: A Study in Metaphysics*, Washington, DC: Catholic University of America Press.
Grant, E. (1979) 'The Condemnation of 1277, God's Absolute Power, and Physical Thought in the Late Middle Ages', in *Viator*, 10: pp. 211–244.
— (1982) 'The Condemnation of 1277', in *Cambridge History of Later Medieval Philosophy*, eds N. Kretzmann, A. Kenny and J. Pinborg, Cambridge: Cambridge University Press, pp. 537–539.
— (1985) 'Issues in Natural Philosophy at Paris in the Late Thirteenth Century', in *Medievalia et Humanistica*, 13: pp. 75–94.
Guénon, R. (1946) *Les Principes du calcul infinitésimal*, Paris: Gallimard.
— (1953) *'The Reign of Quantity' and 'The Signs of the Times'*, trans. Lord Northbourne, London: Luzac and Company.
— (1963) *The Crisis of the Modern World*, trans. M. Pallis and R. Nicholson, London: Luzac and Company.
— (2002) *The Metaphysical Principles of Infinitesimal Calculus*, Chicago: Kazi Publications.
Gutas, D. (1988) *Avicenna and the Aristotelian Tradition*, Leiden: E. J. Brill.

Guyer, P. (1979) *Kant and the Claims of Taste*, Cambridge, MA: Harvard University Press.

Hallett, M. (1984) *Cantorian Set Theory and Limitation of Size*, Oxford: Clarendon Press.

Hamacher, W. (1997) *Premises: Essays on Philosophy and Literature from Kant to Celan*, Cambridge, MA: Harvard University Press.

Harland, R. (1991) *Superstructuralism*, London: Routledge.

Harris, C. R. S. (1927) *Duns Scotus*, 2 vols, Oxford: Oxford University Press.

Harris, H. S. (1983) 'The Hegel Renaissance in the Anglo-Saxon World since 1945', in *The Owl of Minerva*, 15, Fall, pp. 77–106.

Harries, R. (1993) *Art and the Beauty of God*, London: Mowbray.

Harrison, C. (1992) *Beauty and Revelation in the Thought of St Augustine*, Oxford: Clarendon Press.

Hart, C. (1952) 'Participation and the Thomistic Five Ways', in *New Scholasticism*, 26: pp. 267–282.

Harvey, A. (1964) *A Handbook of Theological Terms*, New York: Macmillan Company.

Hegel, G. W. F. (1942) *The Philosophy of Right*, trans. T. M. Knox, Oxford: Clarendon.

— (1955) *Lectures in the History of Philosophy*, trans. E. S. Haldane and F. H. Simson, London: Routledge & Kegan Paul.

— (1959) *Geschichte der Philosophie*, ed. P. Marheineke, Berlin (1840), reprinted as vols 17–18 of the Jubilumsausgabe of Hegel's *Sämtliche Werke*, Stuttgart.

— (1962) *Lectures on the Philosophy of Religion*, trans. E. Speirs and J. Sanderson, 3 vols, New York; Routledge and Kegan Paul.

— (1967) *The Phenomenology of Spirit*, trans. J. B. Baillie, New York: Harper Colophon Books.

— (1975) *The Logic: Part One of the Encyclopaedia of the Philosophical Sciences*, trans. W. Wallace, Oxford: Oxford University Press.

— (1977a) *The Phenomenology of Spirit*, trans. A. V. Miller, Oxford: Oxford University Press.

— (1977b) *Faith and Knowledge*, trans. W. Cerf, Albany: SUNY Press.

— (1988) *Lectures on the Philosophy of Religion*, 1-vol. edition, ed. P. Hodgson, Berkeley: University of California Press.

Heidegger, M. (1962) *Being and Time*, trans. J. Macquarrie and E. Robinson, Oxford: Blackwell.

— (1970) *Traité des catégories et de la signification chez Duns Scot*, Paris: Gallimard.

— (1972) *On Time and Being*, trans. J. Stambaugh, New York: Harper and Row.

— (1978) *Basic Writings*, ed. D. Krell, London: Routledge.

— (1984) *Nietzsche*, II: *The Eternal Recurrence of the Same*, ed. and trans. D. F. Krell, New York: Harper and Row.

— (1996) *Principle of Reason*, trans. R. Lilly, Bloomington and London: Indiana University Press.

— (1998) *Pathmarks*, ed. W. McNeill, Cambridge: Cambridge University Press.

Henle, R. J. (1956) *St Thomas and Platonism: A Study of the 'Plato' and the 'Platonici' Texts in the Writings of Saint Thomas*, The Hague: Martinus Nijhoff.

Henrich, D. (1982) 'The Proof Structure of Kant's Transcendental Deduction', in *Kant on Pure Reason*, ed. R. Walker, Oxford: Oxford University Press.

— (1989) 'The Identity of the Kantian Subject in the Transcendental Deduction', in *Reading Kant: New Perspectives on Transcendental Arguments and Critical Philosophy*, eds E. Schaper and W. Vossenkuhl, Oxford: Blackwell.

— (1994) 'Identity and Objectivity: an Inquiry into Kant's Transcendental Deduction', trans. J. Edwards, in *The Unity of Reason: Essays on Kant's Philosophy*, Cambridge, MA: Harvard University Press.

Henry, M. (1973) *The Essence of Manifestation*, trans. G. Etzkorn, The Hague: Martinus Nijhoff.

Hesiod (1993) *Theogony*, trans. S. Lombardo, Indianapolis: Hackett Publishing Company.

Hintikka, J. (1973) *Time and Necessity: Studies in Aristotle's Theory of Modality*, Oxford: Clarendon Press.

— (1981) 'Gaps in the Great Chain of Being: An Exercise in the Methodology of the History of Ideas', in *Reforging the Great Chain of Being*, ed. S. Knuuttila, Dordrecht: Reidel.

Hissette, R. (1977) *Enquête sur les 219 articles condamnés à Paris le 7 Mars 1277*, Louvain: Publications Universitaires de Louvain.

Hoeres, W. (1965) 'Francis Suarez and the Teaching of John Duns Scotus on *Univocatio Entis*', in *Studies in Philosophy and the History of Philosophy: John Duns Scotus*, eds J. K. Ryan and B. Bonansea, Washington, DC: Catholic University of America Press, pp. 263–291.

Hogrebe, W. (1989) *Prädikation und Genesis: Metaphysik als Fundamentalheuristik im Ausgang von Schellings 'Die Weltalter'*, Frankfurt: Suhrkamp.

Hölderlin, F. (1998) *Selected Poems and Fragments*, trans. M. Hamburger, London: Penguin.

Hyman, A. and Walsh, J., eds (1983) *Philosophy in the Middle Ages*, Indianapolis: Hackett.

Jacob, F. (1973) *The Logic of Life: A History of Heredity*, trans. B. Spillmann, New York: Pantheon.

Jacobi, F. H. (1988) *The Spinoza Conversations Between Lessing and Jacobi*, trans. G. Valle, J. B. Lawson and C. G. Chapple, Lanham, MD: University Press of America.

— (1994) *The Main Philosophical Writings and the Novel 'Allwill'*, trans. George Di Giovanni, Montreal and Kingston: McGill-Queens University Press.

Jacobi, K. (1983) 'Statements about Events Modal and Tense Analysis in Medieval Logic', in *Vivarium*, 21: pp. 85–107.

Jaeschke, W. (1990) *Reason in Religion: The Foundations of Hegel's Philosophy of Religion*, Berkeley: University of California Press.

— (1992) 'Philosophical Thinking and Philosophy of Religion', in *New Perspectives on Hegel's Philosophy of Religion*, ed. D. Kolb, Albany: SUNY Press.

Jastrow (1900), *Fact and Fable*, Boston: Houghton Mifflin Co.

Jordan, M. (1980) 'The Grammar of Esse: Re-Reading Thomas on the Transcendentals', in *Thomist*, 40: pp. 1–26.

— (1984) 'The Intelligibility of the World and the Divine Ideas in Aquinas', in *Review of Metaphysics*, 37: pp. 17–32.

— (1989) 'The Evidence of the Transcendentals and the Place of Beauty in Thomas Aquinas', in *International Philosophical Quarterly*, 29: pp. 393–407.

— (1993) 'Theology and Philosophy', in *Cambridge Companion to Aquinas*, eds N. Kretzman and E. Stumpe, Cambridge: Cambridge University Press.

Kafka, F. (1996) *Stories 1904–1924*, trans. J. Underwood, with a foreword by Jorge Luis Borges, London: Abacus Books.

Kant, I. (1952) *Critique of Judgement*, trans. J. Meredith, Oxford: Clarendon Press.

— (1964) *Critique of Pure Reason*, trans. N. Kemp Smith, London: Macmillan.

— (1981) *Grounding for the Metaphysics of Morals*, trans. J. Ellington, Indianapolis: Hackett.

— (1991) *The Metaphysics of Morals*, trans. M. Gregor, Cambridge: Cambridge University Press.

— (1993a) *The Critique of Practical Reason*, trans. L. W. Beck, The Library of Liberal Arts, NJ: Prentice Hall.

— (1993b) *Opus Postumum*, trans. E. Forster and M. Rosen, Cambridge: Cambridge University Press.

— (1997) *Prolegomena to any Future Metaphysics*, trans. G. Hatfield, Cambridge: Cambridge University Press.

Kaplan, R. (1999) *The Nothing That Is*, London: Allen Lane, Penguin.

Karger, E. (1980) 'Would Ockham Have Shaved Wyman's Beard?', in *Franciscan Studies*, 40: pp. 244–264.

— (1999) 'Ockham's Misunderstood Theory of Intuitive and Abstractive Cognition', in *Cambridge Companion to Ockham*, ed. P. V. Spade, Cambridge: Cambridge University Press, pp. 204–226.

Kearney, R. (1984) *Dialogues with Contemporary Continental Thinkers: The Phenomenological Heritage*, Manchester: Manchester University Press.

Keats, J. (1957) *Keats: Poetry and Prose*. With essays by Charles Lamb, Leigh Hunt, Robert Bridges and others, Oxford: Clarendon Press.

Kennedy, L. (1983) 'Philosophical Scepticism in England in the Mid-fourteenth Century', in *Vivarium*, 21: pp. 35–57.

— (1985) 'Late Fourteenth-century Philosophical Scepticism at Oxford', in *Vivarium*, 23: pp. 163–178;

— (1988) 'Two Augustinians and Nominalism', in *Augustiana*, 38: pp. 142–164.

— (1989) 'The Fifteenth Century and Divine Absolute Power', in *Vivarium*, 27: pp. 125–152.

Kierkegaard, S. (1980) *The Sickness unto Death*, trans. H. V. Hong and E. H. Hong, Princeton: Princeton University Press.

— (1983) *Repetition: An Essay in Experimenting Psychology by Constantin Constantius*, trans. H. V. Hong, and E. H. Hong, Princeton: Princeton University Press.

Klein, J. (1968) *Greek Mathematical Thought and the Origin of Algebra*, trans. E. Brann, Cambridge, MA: MIT Press.

Klocker, H. (1992) *William of Ockham and the Divine Freedom*, Milwaukee: Marquette University Press.

Klubertanz, G. (1957) 'The Problem of the Analogy of Being', in *Review of Metaphysics*, 10: pp. 553–579.

— (1960) *St Thomas Aquinas on Analogy: A Textual Analysis and Systematic Synthesis*, Chicago: Chicago University Press.

Knuuttilla, S. (1978) 'The Statistical Interpretation of Modality in Averroes and Thomas Aquinas', in *Ajatus*, 37: pp. 79–98.

— (1981a) 'Time and Modality in Scholasticism', in *Reforging the Great Chain of Being: Studies of the History of Modal Theories*, ed. S. Knuuttilla, Synthese Historical Library, vol. 20, Dordrecht, pp. 163–257.

— (1981b) 'Duns Scotus' Criticism of the Statistical Interpretation of Modality', in *Miscellanea Mediaevalia* 13/1, *Sprache und Erkenntnis im Mittelalter*, ed. J. Beckmann, pp. 441–450.

— (1982) 'Modal Logic', in *Cambridge History of Later Medieval Philosophy*, eds N. Kretzmann, A. Kenny and J. Pinborg, Cambridge: Cambridge University Press.

— (1986) 'Being qua Being in Thomas Aquinas and John Duns Scotus', in *The Logic of Being*, eds S. Knuuttilla and J. Hintikka, Dordrecht: Kluwer, pp. 201–222.

— (1993) *Modalities in Medieval Philosophy*, London and New York: Routledge.

— (1995) 'Interpreting Scotus' Theory of Modality', in *Antonianum*, pp. 295–303.

— (1996) 'Duns Scotus and the Foundations of Logical Modalities', in *John Duns Scotus: Metaphysics and Ethics*, eds L. Honnefelder, R. Wood and M. Dreyer, Leiden: E. J. Brill, pp. 127–145.

Knuuttilla, S. and Alanen, L. (1988) 'The Foundations of Modality and Conceivability in Descartes and His Predecessors', in *Modern Modalities*, Dordrecht: Kluwer.

Kojève, A. (1947) *Introduction à la lecture de Hegel*, Paris: Gallimard.

— (1969) *Introduction to the Reading of Hegel*, ed. A. Bloom, trans. J. Nichols, New York: Basic Books.

Kolakowski, L. (1985) *Bergson*, Oxford: Oxford University Press.

Korner, S. (1955) *Kant*, London: Penguin.

Kovach, F. J. (1963) 'The Transcendentality of Beauty in Thomas Aquinas', in *Die Metaphysik im Mittelalter (Miscellanea Mediaevalia, II)*, ed. P. Wilpert, Berlin: de Gruyter, pp. 386–392.

— (1967) 'Beauty as a Transcendental', in *New Catholic Encyclopedia*, II, New York: McGraw-Hill, pp. 205–207.

— (1968) 'Esthetic Disinterestedness in Thomas Aquinas', in *Actes du Cinquieme Congrès Internationale d'Esthétique*, Amsterdam 1964, ed. J. Aler, Paris: Mouton, pp. 768–773.

— (1971) 'The Empirical Foundations of Thomas Aquinas' Philosophy of Beauty', in *Southwestern Journal of Philosophy*, II, 3: pp. 93–102.

— (1972) 'Divine and Human Beauty in Duns Scotus' Philosophy and Theology', in *Deus et Homo ad mentem*, I, *Duns Scot*, Rome: Societas Internationalis Scotistica, pp. 445–459.

— (1974) *The Philosophy of Beauty*, Norman: University of Oklahoma Press.

— (1987) *Scholastic Challenges*, Stillwater, OK: Western Publications.

Koyré, A. (1949) 'Le Vide et l'espace infini au XIVe siècle', *Archives d'Histoire doctrinale et littéraire du moyen âge*, 24: pp. 45–91.

— (1956) 'Review of Duhem's *Le Système du Monde*', *Archives Internationales d'Histoire des Sciences*, 35.

— (1957) *From the Closed World to the Infinite Universe*, Baltimore: Johns Hopkins University Press.

Kristeller, P. (1990) *Renaissance Thought and the Arts*, Princeton: Princeton University Press.

Lacan, J. (1966) *Écrits*, Paris: Seuil.

— (1988) *The Seminar of Jacques Lacan: Bk II. The Ego in Freud's Theory and in the Technique of Psychoanalysis, 1954–1955*, trans. S. Tomaselli, New York: Norton.

— (1989) *Écrits*, trans. A. Sheridan, London: Routledge.

— (1992) *The Ethics of Psychoanalysis, Bk VII, 1959–1960*, trans. D. Porter, London: Routledge.

— (1993) *The Psychoses, Bk III, 1955–1956*, trans. R. Grigg, London: Routledge.

— (1998) *The Four Fundamental Concepts of Psycho-analysis*, trans. A. Sheridan, London: Vintage.

Lacoue-Labarthe, P. (1993) 'Sublime Truth', in *Of the Sublime: Presence in Question*, trans. J. Librett, Albany: SUNY Press, pp. 71–108.

— (1999) *Poetry as Experience*, trans. A. Tarnowski, Stanford, CA: Stanford University Press.

Lacroix, J. (1968) *Maurice Blondel*, trans. J. Guinness, London: Sheed and Ward.

Lagerlund, H. (2000) *Modal Syllogistics in the Middle Ages*, Leiden: E. J. Brill.

Langston, D. C. (1986) *God's Willing Knowledge: The Influence of Scotus' Analysis of Omniscience*, Philadelphia and London: Penn State University Press.

Lauer, Q. (1979) 'Hegel's Pantheism', in *Thought: A Review of Culture and Idea*, 54, no. 212: pp. 5–23.

— (1982) *Hegel's Concept of God*, Albany: SUNY Press.

Lecercle, J.-J. (1999) 'Cantor, Lacan, Mao, Beckett, même combat: The Philosophy of Alain Badiou', in *Radical Philosophy*, 93: pp. 6–13.

van der Lecq, R. (1998) 'Duns Scotus on the Reality of Possible Worlds', in *John Duns Scotus, 1265/6–1308. Renewal in Philosophy*, ed. E. P. Bos, Amsterdam: Rodopi, pp. 89–100.

van der Leeuw, G. (1963) *Sacred and Profane Beauty: The Holy in Art*, trans. D. Green, New York: Holt, Reinhart and Winston.

Leff, G. (1975) *William of Ockham: The Metamorphosis of Scholastic Discourse*, Manchester: Manchester University Press.

— (1976) *Dissolution of the Medieval Outlook*, New York: Harper and Row.

Lermond, L. (1988) *The Form of Man: Human Essence in Spinoza's Ethics*, Leiden: E. J. Brill.

Levinas, E. (1991) *Otherwise than Being or Beyond Essence*, trans. A. Lingis, Dordrecht: Kluwer.

— (1996) *Emmanuel Levinas: Basic Philosophical Writings*, eds S. Critchley and A. Peperzak, Bloomington and London: Indiana University Press.

Lloyd, G. (1994) *Part of Nature: Self-Knowledge in Spinoza's Ethics*, Ithaca: Cornell University Press.

Lossky, V. (1957) *The Mystical Theology of the Eastern Church*, Cambridge, MA and London: Harvard University Press.

Lovejoy, A. (1960) *The Great Chain of Being*, New York: Harper and Row.

Lubac, Henri de (1946) *Surnaturel*, Paris: Aubier.

— (1949) *Corpus Mysticum*, 2nd edn, Paris: Aubier.

— (1956) *The Splendour of the Church*, trans. Rosemary Sheed, London: Sheed and Ward.

— (1986) *The Christian Faith*, trans. Brother Richard Arnandez, San Francisco: Ignatius.

— (1988) *Catholicism: Christ and the Common Destiny of Man*, trans. L. Shepherd, San Francisco: Ignatius.

— (1991) *Augustinianism and Modern Theology*, London: Chapman.

— (1996) *Discovery of God*, trans. Alexander Dru, Edinburgh: T. and T. Clark.

— (1999) *Medieval Exegesis: The Four Senses of Scripture*, vol. 1, trans. M. Sebanc, Edinburgh: T. and T. Clark.

— (2000a) *Medieval Exegesis: The Four Senses of Scripture*, vol. 2, trans. M. Macierowski, Edinburgh: T. and T. Clark.

— (2000b) *Scripture in Tradition*, trans. L. O'Neill, New York: Herder and Herder.

Ludlow, M. (2000) *Universal Salvation: Eschatology in the Thought of Gregory of Nyssa and Karl Rahner*, Oxford: Oxford University Press.

Lyttkens, H. (1952) *The Analogy between God and the World*, Uppsala: Almquist and Wiksells Boktwyckeri.

McColley, G. (1936) 'The Seventeenth Century Doctrine of a Plurality of Worlds', in *Annals of Science*, 1: pp. 390–412.

McGinn, C. (1999) *The Mysterious Flame*, New York: Basic Books.

McGrade, A. S. (1985) 'Plenty of Nothing: Ockham's Commitment to Real Possibles', in *Franciscan Studies*, 45: pp. 145–156.

McInerny, R. (1961) *Logic of Analogy*, The Hague: Martinus Nijhoff.

— (1968) *Studies in Analogy*, The Hague: Martinus Nijhoff.

— (1988) *Art and Prudence: Studies in the Thought of Jacques Maritain*, Notre Dame, IN: University of Notre Dame Press.

— (1996) *Aquinas and Analogy*, Washington, DC: Catholic University of America Press.

McPartlan, P. (1995) *Sacrament of Salvation*, Edinburgh: T. and T. Clark.

Macierowski, E. (1988) 'Does God Have Quiddity According to Avicenna?', in *Thomist*, 52: pp. 79–85.

Mallarmé, S. (1914) *Un coup de dés jamais n'abolira le hasard*, Paris: Librairie Gallimard.

Marion, J.-L. (1981) *Sur la théologie blanche de Descartes: analogie, création des véritiés éternelles et fondement. Philosophie d'aujourd'hui*, Paris: Presses Universitaires de France.

— (1991) *God Without Being*, trans. T. A. Carlson, Chicago: University of Chicago Press

— (1995) 'Saint Thomas d'Aquin et l'onto-théo-logico', in *Revue Thomiste*, TXCv, no. 1, pp. 31–66.

— (1998) 'Descartes and Ontotheology', in *Post-Secular Philosophy*, ed. P. Blond, London: Routledge, pp. 67–106.

— (1999) *Cartesian Questions*, ed. D. Garber, Chicago: University of Chicago Press.

— (2000) 'The Saturated Phenomenon', in *Phenomenology and the 'Theological Turn'*, trans. Thomas A. Carlson, New York: Fordham University Press.

Maritain, J. (1930) *Art and Scholasticism*, trans. J. F. Scanlan, London: Sheed and Ward.

— (1953) *Creative Intuition in Art and Poetry*, Princeton: Princeton University Press.

Marrone, S. (1983) 'The Nature of Univocity in Duns Scotus' Early Works', in *Franciscan Studies* 43, pp. 347–395.

— (1985) *Truth and Scientific Knowledge in the Thought of Henry of Ghent*, Cambridge, MA: Harvard University Press.
— (1988) 'Henry of Ghent and Duns Scotus on the Knowledge of Being', in *Speculum*, 63: pp. 22–57.
— (1996) 'Revisiting Duns Scotus and Henry of Ghent on Modality', in *Metaphysik und Ethik bei Johannes Duns Scotus: Neue Forschungsperspektiven*, eds M. Deyer and R. Wood, Leiden: E. J. Brill.
— (2001) *The Light of Thy Countenance: Science and Knowledge of God in the Thirteenth Century*, 2 vols. Leiden: E. J. Brill.
Martin, J. A. (1990) *Beauty and Holiness: The Dialogue betweeen Aesthetics and Religion*, Princeton: Princeton University Press.
Mascall, E. L. (1949) *Existence and Analogy*, New York: Longmans Green and Company.
Mason, R. (1997) *The God of Spinoza*, Cambridge: Cambridge University Press.
Mauralt, A. (1975) 'Kant le dernier occamien. Une nouvelle définiton de la philosophie moderne', in *Revue de Metaphysique et de Morale*, 1: pp. 230–251.
Maurer, A. (1962) *Medieval Philosophy*, New York: Random House.
— (1970) 'St Thomas and the Eternal Truths', in *Mediaeval Studies*, 32: pp 91–107.
— (1983) *About Beauty, A Thomistic Interpretation*, Houston: University of St Thomas.
— (1990) *Being and Knowing*, Toronto: Pontifical Institute of Mediaeval Studies.
— (1999) *The Philosophy of William of Ockham*, Toronto: Pontifical Institute of Mediaeval Studies.
Meagher, R. E. (1970) 'Thomas Aquinas – Analogy: A Textual Analysis', in *Thomist*, 34: pp. 230–253.
Melnick, A. (1973) *Kant's Analogies of Experience*, Chicago: University of Chicago Press.
Merklinger, P. (1993) *Philosophy, Theology and Hegel's Berlin Philosophy of Religion*, Albany: SUNY Press.
Merleau-Ponty, M. (1963) *The Structure of Behavior*, trans. A. L. Fisher, Boston: Beacon.
Mersch, E. (1938) *The Whole Christ: The Historical Development of the Doctrine of the Mystical Body in Scripture and Tradition*, trans. John R. Kelly, Milwaukee: Bruce Publishing Company.
— (1939) *Morality and the Mystical Body*, New York: D. F. Ryan, P. J. Kennedy and Sons.
— (1951) *The Theology of the Mystical Body*, trans. C. Vollert, London: B. Herder Book Company.
Milbank, J. (1986) 'The Second Difference: For a Trinitarianism without Reserve', in *Modern Theology*, 2, no. 3: pp. 213–234.
— (1990) *Theology and Social Theory: Beyond Secular Reason*, Oxford: Blackwell.
— (1991) 'Postmodern Critical Augustinianism: A Short Summa in Forty-Two Responses to Unasked Questions', in *Modern Theology*, 7, no. 3: pp. 225–237.
— (1995) 'Can a Gift be Given?: Prolegomenon to a Future Trinitarian Metaphysics', in *Modern Theology*, 2, no. 1, pp. 119–161.
— (1997) *The Word Made Strange*, Oxford: Blackwell.
— and Pickstock, C. (2001) *Truth in Aquinas,* London: Routledge.

Monahan, M. (1959) *St Thomas on the Sacraments*, 2 vols, London: Ebenezer Baylis and Son Limited, Trinity Press.

Mondin, B. (1963) *The Principle of Analogy in Protestant and Catholic Theology*, The Hague: Nijhoff.

Moody, E. (1935) *Logic of William of Ockham*, New York: Sheed and Ward.

— (1975) 'The Medieval contribution to Logic', in *Studies in Medieval Philosophy, Science and Politics*, Berkeley, CA: University of California Press, pp. 371–392.

Moonan, L. (1994) *Divine Power: The Medieval Power Distinction and its Adoption by Albert, Bonaventure, and Aquinas*, Oxford: Clarendon Press.

Morrell, J. (1978) *Analogy and Talking about God: a Critique of the Thomist Approach*, Washington, DC: University Press of America.

Murdoch, J. E. (1974) 'Philosophy and the Enterprise of Science in the Later Middle Ages', in *The Interaction between Science and Philosophy*, ed. Y. Elkana, Atlantic Highlands, NJ: Humanities Press.

Mulhall, S. (1990) *On Being in the World: Wittgenstein and Heidegger on Seeing Aspects*, London: Routledge.

Murphy, F. A. (1995) *Christ the Form of Beauty*, Edinburgh: T. and T. Clark.

Mullarkey, J. (1999) *Bergson and Philosophy*, Edinburgh: University of Edinburgh Press.

Navone, J. (1989) *Self-Giving and Sharing: The Trinity and Human Fulfillment*, Minnesota: Liturgical Press.

— (1996) *Toward a Theology of Beauty*, Minnesota: Liturgical Press.

— (1999) *Enjoying God's Beauty*, Minnesota: Liturgical Press.

Nichols, A. (1980) *Art of the God Incarnate*, New York: Paulist Press.

— (1988) *The Word Has Been Abroad*, Edinburgh: T. and T. Clark.

Nielsen, K. (1976) 'Talk of God and the Doctrine of Analogy', in *Thomist*, 40: pp. 32–60.

Nietzsche, F. (1969) *Thus Spake Zarathustra*, trans. R. J. Hollingdale, London: Penguin.

— (1974) *Gay Science*, Preface to the second edition, 1887, New York: Vintage.

— (1995) *On the Genealogy of Morality*, trans. C. Deithe, Cambridge: Cambridge University Press.

Nishitani, J. (1982) *Religion and Nothingness*, trans. J. Van Bragt, Berkeley: University of California Press.

Normore, C. (1996) 'Scotus, Modality, Instants of Nature and the Contingency of the Present', in *John Duns Scotus: Metaphysics and Ethics*, eds L. Honnefelder, R. Wood and M. Dreyer, Leiden: E. J. Brill, pp. 161–174.

Nyssa, Gregory of (1978) *The Life of Moses*, trans. A. J. Malherbe and E. Ferguson, New York: Paulist Press.

— (1979) *Selected Works*, vol. V, Grand Rapids, MI: Erdmanns.

Oakley, F. (1961) 'Medieval Theories of Natural Law. Ockham and the Significance of the Voluntarist Tradition', in *Natural Law Forum*, VI: pp. 65–83.

— (1963) 'Pierre d'Aily and the Absolute Power of God: Another Note on the Theology of Nominalism', in *Harvard Theological Review*, 56: pp. 59–73.

— (1968) 'Jacobean Political Theology. The Absolute and Ordinary Powers of the King', in *Journal of the History of Ideas*, 29: pp. 323–346.

— (1979) *The Western Church in the Later Middle Ages*, Ithaca: Cornell University Press.

— (1984) *Omnipotence, Covenant and Order: An Excursion in the History of Ideas from Abelard to Leibniz*, Ithaca: Cornell University Press.

Ockham, W. (1967–) *Opera philosophica et theologica*, eds J. L. Alor, S. Brown, G. Gal, A. Gambatese and M. Meilach, New York: Franciscan Institute.

— (1974) *Summa Logicae*, pt. 1. *Ockham's Theory of Terms*, trans. J. Loux, Notre Dame, IN: University of Notre Dame Press.

— (1980) *Summa Logicae*, pt. 2. *Ockham's Theory of Propositions*, trans. A. Freddoso and H. Schuurman, Notre Dame, IN: University of Notre Dame Press.

— (1990) *Philosophical Writings*, trans. P. Boehner, revised by S. F. Brown, Indianapolis: Hackett Publishing Company.

— (1991) *Quodlibetal Questions*, trans. A. Freddoso and F. Kelley, New Haven and London: Yale University Press.

— (1994) *Five Texts on the Mediaeval Problem of Universals: Porphry, Boethius, Abelard, Duns Scotus and William of Ockham*, trans. P. Spade, Indianapolis: Hackett Publishing Company.

O'Flaherty, J. C. (1979) *Johann Georg Hamann*, Boston: Twayne Publishers.

O'Neill, O. (1989) *Constructions of Reason*, Cambridge: Cambridge University Press.

O'Rourke, F. (1992) *Pseudo-Dionysius and the Metaphysics of Aquinas*, Leiden: E. J. Brill.

O'Shaughnessy, T. (1960) 'St Thomas and Avicenna on the Nature of the One', in *Gregorianum*, 41: pp. 665–679.

Otto, R. (1925) *The Idea of the Holy*, trans. J. Harvey, Oxford: Oxford University Press.

Owens, J. (1962) 'Analogy as a Thomistic Approach to Being', in *Mediaeval Studies*, 24: pp. 302–332.

— (1970) 'Common Nature: a Point of Comparison between Thomistic and Scotistic Metaphysics', in *Mediaeval Studies*, 19: pp. 1–14.

— (1992) 'The Relevance of Avicennian Neoplatonism', in P. Morewedge, ed., *Neoplatonism and Islamic Thought*, Albany: SUNY Press, pp. 41–50.

Ozment, S. (1980) *The Age of Reform 1250–1550: An Intellectual and Religious History of Late Medieval and Reformation Europe*, New Haven: Yale University Press.

Paliyenko, A. (1997) *Mis-reading the Creative Impulse*, Evanston: Southern Illinois University Press.

Palmer, H. (1973) *Analogy: A Study of Qualification and Argument in Theology*, London: Macmillan.

Pasnau, R. (1997) *Theories of Cognition in the Later Middle Ages*, Cambridge: Cambridge University Press.

Paton, H. J. (1936) *Kant's Metaphysics of Experience: A Commentary on the First Half of the 'Kritik der reinen Vernunft'*, London: Allen & Unwin.

Paulus, J. (1938) *Henri de Gand. Essai sur les tendances de sa métaphysique*, Paris: Vrin.

Pegis, A. (1937) Review of E. Moody's *Logic of William of Ockham*, in *Speculum*, 12: pp. 274–277.

— (1942) 'Dilemma of Being and Unity', in *Essays in Thomism*, ed. R. Brennan, New York: Sheed and Ward, pp. 151–183.

— (1944) 'Concerning William of Ockham', in *Traditio*, 2: pp. 465–480.

— (1948) 'On some Recent Interpretations of William of Ockham', in *Speculum*, 23: pp. 458–463.

— (1968) 'Toward a New Way to God: Henry of Ghent (I)' in *Mediaeval Studies*, 30: pp. 226–247.

— (1969) 'A New Way to God: Henry of Ghent (II)', in *Mediaeval Studies*, 31: pp. 93–116.

— (1971) 'Henry of Ghent and the New Way to God (III)', in *Mediaeval Studies*, 33: pp. 158–179.

Péguy, C. (1956) *The Mystery of the Holy Innocents and Other Poems*, trans. P. Pakenham, London: Harvill Press.

— (1958) 'Notre Jeunesse' and 'Clio 1' in *Temporal and Eternal*, trans. Alexander Dru, London: Harvill Press.

— (1965) *Basic Verities*, trans. A. and J. Green, Chicago: Henry Regnery Company.

— (1992) 'Dialogue de l'histoire et de l'âme charnelle' (Clio 1) and 'Dialogue de l'histoire et de l'âme païenne' (Clio 2), in *Oeuvres en prose complètes*, ed. R. Buran, vol. 3, pp. 594–783; 997–1214, Paris: Gallimard.

— (1998) *Portal of the Mystery of Hope*, trans. D. L. Shindler, Edinburgh: T. and T. Clark.

Pelikan, J. (1962) *The Light of the World: A Basic Image in Early Christian Thought*, New York: Harper and Brothers.

— (1984) *The Vindication of Tradition*, New Haven and London: Yale University Press.

Penrose, R. (1989) *The Emperor's New Mind: Concerning Computers, Minds and the Laws of Physics*, Oxford: Oxford University Press.

Pernoud, M. (1970) 'Innovation in Ockham's references to the *Potentia Dei*', in *Antonianum*, 45: pp. 65–97.

— (1972) 'The Theory of the *Potentia Dei* according to Aquinas, Scotus and Ockham', in *Antonianum*, 47: pp. 69–95.

Peter, C. (1964) *Participated Eternity in the Vision of God*, Rome: Gregorian University Press.

Phelan, G. (1967) 'St Thomas on Analogy', in *Selected Papers*, Toronto: Pontifical Institute of Mediaeval Studies, pp. 95–122.

Pickstock, C. (1998) *After Writing: On the Liturgical Consummation of Philosophy*, Oxford: Blackwell.

— (1999) 'Soul, City and Cosmos after Augustine', in *Radical Orthodoxy: A New Theology*, eds J. Milbank, C. Pickstock and G. Ward, London: Routledge, pp. 243–277.

Pieper, J. (1957) *The Silence of St Thomas: Three Essays*, trans. J. Murray and D. O'Connor, New York: Pantheon.

— (1966) *The Four Cardinal Virtues*, Notre Dame, IN: University of Notre Dame Press.

— (1974) *About Love*, trans. R. and C. Winston, Chicago: Franciscan Herald Press.

— (1985) *Problems of Modern Faith*, trans. J. van Heurck, Chicago: Franciscan Herald Press.

— (1987) *What is a Feast?*, London, Ontario: North Waterloo Academic Press.

— (1989) *Joseph Pieper: An Anthology*, San Francisco: Ignatius.

— (1989) *Living the Truth*, trans. L. Krauth, San Francisco: Ignatius.

— (1990) *Only the Lover Sings*, trans. L. Krauth, San Francisco: Ignatius.

— (1995) *Divine Madness: Plato's Case against Secular Humanism*, trans. L. Krauth, San Francisco: Ignatius.

Plato (1974) *The Republic*, trans. D. Lee, London: Penguin Books.

— (1993) *Sophist*, trans. N. P. White, Indianapolis and London: Hackett Publishing Company.

— (1995) *Phaedrus*, trans. A. Nehmas and P. Woodruff, Indianapolis and London: Hackett Publishing Company.

Plotinus (1991) *Enneads*, trans. S. Mackenna, London: Penguin Books.

Polanyi, M. (1967) *The Tacit Dimension*, London: Routledge & Kegan Paul.

Pomerleau, W. (1977) 'The Accession and Dismissal of an Upstart Handmaid', in *Monist*, 60, no. 2: pp. 213–227.

Portmann, A. (1967) *Animal Forms and Patterns: A Study of the Appearance of Animals*, trans. H. Czech, New York: Schocken.

— (1990) *Essays in Philosophical Zoology: the Living Form and the Seeing Eye*, trans. E. B. Carter, Lampeter: The Edwin Mellen Press.

Priest, G. (1995) *Beyond the Limits of Thought*, Cambridge: Cambridge University Press.

Randi, E. (1986) 'Ockham, John XXII and the Absolute Power of God', in *Franciscan Studies*, 46: pp. 205–216.

— (1987) 'A Scotist Way of Distinguishing between God's Absolute Power and Ordained Powers', in *From Ockham to Wycliff*, eds A. Hudson and M. Wilks, Oxford: Oxford University Press, pp. 43–50.

Reardon, B. (1977) *Hegel's Philosophy of Religion*, London: Macmillan.

Richards, R. (1968) 'Ockham and Skepticism', in *New Scholasticism*, 42: pp. 345–363.

Ricœur, Paul (1977a) *Rule of Metaphor: Multi-disciplinary Studies of the Creation of Meaning in Language*, trans. R. Czerny, K. McLauglin and J. Costello S.J., Toronto: University of Toronto Press.

— (1977b) 'Préface à Raphael Célis; l'oeuvre et l'imaginaire. Les origines du pouvoir-être créateur', Brussels: Publications des facultés universitaires Saint Louis.

— (1982) 'The Status of Vorstellung in Hegel's Philosophy of Religion', in *Meaning, Truth and God*, Notre Dame, IN: University of Notre Dame Press.

Rocca, G. (1991) 'The Distinction between *Res Significata* and *Modus Significandi* in Aquinas's Theological Epistemology', in *Thomist*, 55: pp. 173–192.

Rocker, S. (1992) 'The Integral Relation of Religion and Philosophy', in *New Perspectives on Hegel's Philosophy of Religion*, ed. D. Kolb, Albany: SUNY Press.

Rose, G. (1981) *Hegel contra Sociology*, London: Athlone.

— (1984) *Dialectic of Nihilism*, Oxford: Blackwell.

— (1992) *The Broken Middle: Out of Our Ancient Society*, Oxford: Blackwell.

— (1993) *Judaism and Modernity*, Oxford: Blackwell.

— (1996) *Mourning Becomes the Law*, Cambridge: Cambridge University Press.

Rosemann, P. (1996) *Omne Agens Agit Sibi Simile: A Repetition of Scholastic Metaphysics*, Leuven: Leuven University Press.

— (1999) *Understanding Scholastic Thought with Foucault*, London: Macmillan.

Ross, J. F. (1980) 'Creation', in *Journal of Philosophy*, 77: pp. 614–629.

— (1981) *Portraying Analogy*, Cambridge: Cambridge University Press.

— (1983) 'Creation II', in *The Existence and Nature of God*, ed. A. Freddoso, Notre Dame, IN: University of Notre Dame Press, pp. 115–141.

— (1986) 'God, Creator of Kinds and Possibilities', in *Rationality, Religious Belief and Moral Commitment: New Essays in the Philosophy of Religion*, eds R. Audi and W. J. Wainwright, Ithaca: Cornell University Press, pp. 315–334.

— (1988) 'Eschatological Pragmatism', in *Philosophy and the Christian Faith*, ed. T. Morris, Notre Dame, IN: University of Notre Dame Press, pp. 279–300.

— (1989) 'The Crash of Modal Metaphysics', in *Review of Metaphysics*, 43: pp. 251–277.

— (1990) 'Aquinas' Exemplarism; Aquinas' Voluntarism', in *American Catholic Philosophical Quarterly*, 64: pp. 171–198.

— (1991) 'On the Divine Ideas: A Reply', in *American Catholic Philosophical Quarterly*, 65: pp. 213–220.

Rotman, B. (1987) *Signifying Nothing: The Semiotics of Zero*, London: Macmillan.

Rousselot, P. (1935) *Intellectualism of St Thomas Aquinas*, London: Sheed and Ward.

— (1990) *Eyes of Faith*, trans. J. McDermott, New York: Fordham University Press.

— (1999) *Intelligence: Sense of Being, Faculty of God*, trans. A. Tallon, Milwaukee: Marquette University Press.

Rubin, M. (1991) *Corpus Christi: The Eucharist in Late Medieval Culture*, Cambridge: Cambridge University Press.

Ruskin, J. (1934) *True and Beautiful*, Chicago: Henneberry Company.

Russell, B. (1903) *The Principles of Mathematics*, Cambridge: Cambridge University Press.

Sartre, J.-P. (1962) *Nausea*, trans. L. Alexander, London: Hamish Hamilton.

— (2000) *Being and Nothingness*, trans. H. Barnes, London: Routledge.

de Saussure, F. (1960) *Course in General Linguistics*, trans. W. Baskin, London: Fontana.

Schelling, F. (1994) *On the History of Modern Philosophy*, trans. A. Bowie, Cambridge: Cambridge University Press.

— (1997) *The Abyss of Freedom and Ages of the World* (second draft, 1813), trans. J. Norman, with an essay by S. Žižek, Ann Arbor: University of Michigan Press.

Schlitt, D. (1984) *Hegel's Trinitarian Claim: A Critical Reflection*, Leiden: E. J. Brill.

— (1990) *Divine Subjectivity*, Scranton: University of Scranton Press.

Schmidt, R. (1966) *The Domain of Logic According to Saint Thomas Aquinas*, The Hague: Martinus Nijhoff.

Schmutz, J. (1999) 'Escaping the Aristotelian Bond: The Critique of Metaphysics in Twentieth-century French Philosophy', in *Dionysius*, 27: pp. 169–200.

Schoot, H. (1993) 'Aquinas and Supposition: the Possibilities and Limitations of Logic *in divinis*', in *Vivarium*, 30: pp. 193–225.

Schopenhauer, A. (1969) *The World as Will and Representation*, 2 vols, trans. E. F. J. Payne, New York: Dover Publications.

Schrödinger, E. (1967) *What is Life? The Physical Aspect of the Living Cell, Mind and Matter*, Cambridge: Cambridge University Press.

Scott, T. K. (1969) 'Ockham on Evidence, Necessity, and Intuition', in *Journal of the History of Philosophy*, 7: pp. 45–46.

Scotus, D. (1950–) *Opera omnia*, eds C. Balic *et al.*, Vatican City: Vatican Scotistic Commission, 25 vols.

— (1966) *A Treatise on God as First Principle*, trans. A. Wolter, Chicago: Franciscan Herald Press.

— (1975) *God and Creatures*, eds and trans. F. Allintis and A. B. Wolter, Princeton: Princeton University Press.

— (1987) *Philosophical Writings*, trans. A. Wolter, Indianapolis: Hackett Publishing Company.

— (1995) *Duns Scotus Metaphysician*, eds and trans. W. A. Frank and A. B. Wolter, Indiana: Purdue University Press.

Scruton, R. (1986) *Spinoza*, Oxford: Oxford University Press.

Servais, Y. (1953) *Charles Péguy: The Pursuit of Salvation*, Cork: Cork University Press.

Shanks, A. (1991) *Hegel's Political Theology*, Cambridge: Cambridge University Press.

Sherry, P. (1992) *Spirit and Beauty: An Introduction to Theological Aesthetics*, Oxford: Clarendon Press.

Shircel, L. (1942) *The Univocity of the Concept of Being in the Philosophy of John Duns Scotus*, Washington, DC: Catholic University of America Press.

Silesius, A. (1986) *Cherubinic Wanderer*, trans. M. Shrady, New York: Paulist Press.

Silverman, K. (2000) *World Spectators*, Stanford, CA: Stanford University Press.

Small, R. (1992) 'Cantor and the Scholastics', in *American Catholic Philosophical Quarterly*, 66: pp. 407–428.

Smith, D. (2001) 'The Doctrine of Univocity: Deleuze's Ontology of Immanence', in *Deleuze and Religion*, London: Routledge, ch. 13.

Smith, G. (1943) 'Avicenna and the Possibles', in *New Scholasticism*, 17: pp. 340–357.

Smith, J. (1973) *The Analogy of Experience: An Approach to Understanding Religious Truth*, New York: Harper and Row.

Smith, J. W. (1985) *Reductionism and Cultural Being: A Philosophical Critique of Sociobiological Reductionism and Physicalist Scientific Unificationism*, The Hague: Martinus Nijhoff.

Smith, N. K. (1930) *A Commentary to Kant's 'Critique of Pure Reason'*, 2nd edn, London: Macmillan.

Sophocles (1947) *The Theban Plays*, trans. E. F. Watling, London: Penguin Books.

Spargo, E. J. (1953) *The Category of the Aesthetic in the Philosophy of Saint Bonaventure*, New York: Franciscan Institute.

Spinoza, B. (1993) *The Ethics*, trans. A. Boyle, Intro. and notes by G. Parkinson, London: Everyman.

Staten, H. (1985) *Wittgenstein and Derrida*, Lincoln: University of Nebraska Press.

Stiver, R. (1996) *Religious Language*, Oxford: Blackwell.

Stock, B. (1996) *Augustine: the Reader*, Cambridge, MA: Belknap Press of Harvard University Press.

Strawson, P. F. (1966) *Bounds of Sense: An Essay on Kant's 'Critique of Pure Reason'*, London: Methuen.

Streveler, P. (1975) 'Ockham and His Critics on Intuitive Cognition', in *Franciscan Studies*, 35: pp. 223–236.

Suarez, F. (1983) *On the Essence of Finite Being as Such, On the Existence of That Essence and Their Distinction*, trans. N. J. Wells, Milwaukee: Marquette University Press.

Sullivan, R. (1989) *Immanuel Kant's Moral Theory*, Cambridge: Cambridge University Press.

Sweeney, L. (1992) *Divine Infinity in Greek and Medieval Thought*, New York: Peter Lang.

Sylwanowicz, M. (1996) *Contingent Causality and the Foundations of Duns Scotus*, Leiden: E. J. Brill.

Tachau, K. (1988) *Vision and Certitude in the Age of Ockham: Optics, Epistemology and the Foundations of Semantics, 1250–1345*. Leiden: E. J. Brill.

Taylor, C. (1975) *Hegel*, Cambridge: Cambridge University Press.

Taylor, M. C. (1984) *Erring: A Postmodern A/Theology*, Chicago: Chicago University Press.

— (1990) *Tears*, Albany: SUNY Press.

Tholuck, F. (1826) *Die speculative Trinitätslehre des späteren Orients: Eine religionsphilosophische Monographie aus handschriftlichen Quellen der Leydener, Oxforder und Berliner Bibliothek*, Berlin.

Torchia, N. (1993) *Plotinus, Tolma, and the Descent of Being*, New York: Peter Lang.

Torrell, J.-P. (1996) *Saint Thomas Aquinas: The Person and His Work*, trans. R. Royal, Washington, DC: Catholic University of America Press.

Turner, D. (1995) *The Darkness of God: Negativity in Christian Mysticism*, Cambridge: Cambridge University Press.

Uhlmann, A. (1999) *Beckett and Poststructuralism*, Cambridge: Cambridge University Press.

Vaughan, L. (1989) *Johann Georg Hamann: Metaphysics of Language and Vision of History*, New York: Peter Lang.

Te Velde, R. A. (1995) *Participation and Substantiality in Thomas Aquinas*, Leiden: E. J. Brill.

— (1998) 'Natura In Seipsa Recurva Est: Duns Scotus and Aquinas on the Relationship between Nature and Will', in *John Duns Scotus*, ed. E. P. Bos, Amsterdam: Rodopi, pp. 155–170.

Velkley, R. (1989) *Freedom and the Ends of Reason: On the Moral Foundation of Kant's Critical Philosophy*, Chicago: University of Chicago Press.

Vignaux, P. (1948) *Nominalisme au XIVe siècle*, Montréal: Institut d'études médiévales.

— (1976) *De Saint Anselme à Luther*, Paris: PUF.

Viladesau, R. (1999) *Theological Aesthetics*, Oxford: Oxford University Press.

Virilio, P. (1991) *The Aesthetics of Disappearance*, trans. P. Beitchman, New York: Semiotext(e).

Vos, A. (1985) 'On the Philosophy of the Young Duns Scotus: Some Semantical and Logical Aspects', in *Medieval Semantics and Metaphysics: Studies Dedicated to L. M. Rijk, on the Occasion of his 60th Birthday*, ed. E. P. Bos, Nijmegen: Ingenium Publishers, pp. 195–220.

— (1998a) 'Duns Scotus and Aristotle', in *John Duns Scotus, 1265/6–1308: Renewal in Philosophy*, ed. E. P. Bos, Amsterdam: Rodopi, pp. 49–74.

— (1998b) 'Knowledge, Certainty and Contingency', in *John Duns Scotus, 1265/6–130: Renewal in Philosophy*, ed. E. P. Bos, Amsterdam: Rodopi, pp. 75–88.

Vos, A. *et al.* (1994) *John Duns Scotus: Contingency and Freedom, Lectura* 1, 39, Dordrecht: Kluwer.

Vossenkuhl, W. (1985) 'Ockham on the Cognition of Non-existents', in *Franciscan Studies*, 45: pp. 33–46.

Walker, R. (1989) *The Real and the Ideal: Berkeley's Relation to Kant*, New York: Garland.

Wainwright, G. (1981) *Eucharist and Eschatology*, New York: Oxford University Press.

Ward, G., ed. (1997) *The Postmodern God*, Oxford: Blackwell.

— (1999) 'Bodies: The Displaced Body of Jesus Christ', in J. Milbank, C. Pickstock and G. Ward, eds, *Radical Orthodoxy: A New Theology*, London: Routledge, pp. 163-181.

— (2000) *Cities of God*, London and New York: Routledge.

Webb, J. C. (1980) *Mechanism, Mentalism and Mathematics: An Essay on Finitism*, Dordrecht: D. Reidel.

Weinandy, T. (2000) *Does God Suffer?*, Edinburgh: T. and T. Clark.

Weiss, P. (1963) *Religion and Art*, Milwaukee: Marquette University Press.

Wengert, R. (1981) 'The Sources of Intuitive Cognition in William of Ockham', in *Franciscan Studies*, 27: pp. 415–447.

White, V. (1956) 'The Platonic Tradition in St Thomas', in *God the Unknown*, London: Harvill Press, pp. 62–71.

Whittemore, R. (1960) 'Hegel as Panentheist', in *Tulane Studies in Philosophy*, 9: pp. 134–164.

Williams, R. (1992) 'Hegel and the Gods of Postmodernity', in *Shadow of Spirit: Postmodernism and Religion*, eds P. Berry and A. Wernick, London: Routledge, pp. 72–80.

— (1998) 'Logic and Spirit in Hegel', in *Post-secular Philosophy*, ed. P. Blond, London: Routledge, pp. 116–130.

Williamson, R. K. (1984) *Introduction to Hegel's Philosophy of Religion*, Albany: SUNY Press.

Willms, B. (1967) *Die totale Freiheit: Fichtes politische Philosophie*, Cologne: Westdeutscher.

Wilson, N. (1963) *Charles Péguy*, London: Bowes and Bowes.

Wippel, J. (1977) 'The Condemnations of 1270 and 1277 at Paris', in *Journal of Medieval and Renaissance Studies*, 7: pp. 169–201.

— (1981) 'The Reality of Nonexisting Possibles according to Thomas Aquinas, Henry of Ghent, and Godfrey of Fontaines', in *Review of Metaphysics*, 34: pp. 729–758.

— (1984) 'Thomas Aquinas and Participation', in *Studies in Medieval Philosophy*, ed. J. F. Wippel, Washington, DC: Catholic University of America Press, pp. 117–158.

Wolter, A. (1946) *The Transcendentals and their Function in the Metaphysics of John Duns Scotus*, New York: Franciscan Institute.

— (1965) 'The Formal Distinction', in J. K. Ryan and B. M. Bonansea, eds, *John Duns Scotus, 1265–1965*, Washington, DC, Studies in Philosophy and the History of Philosophy, 3: pp. 45–60.

— (1982) 'Duns Scotus on Intuition, Memory and Our Knowledge of Individuals', in *History of Philosophy in the Makin:. A Symposium of Essays to Honour Professor James D. Collins*, ed. L. Thro, Lanham, MD: University Press of America, pp. 81–104.

Wolterstorff, N. (1980) *Art in Action: Toward a Christian Aesthetic*, Grand Rapids, MI: W. B. Erdmanns Press.

Wood, D. (1988) 'Différance and the Problem of Strategy', in *Derrida and Différance*, Evanston, IL: Northwestern University Press, pp. 63–70.

Wood, R. (1987) 'Intuitive Cognition and Divine Omnipotence: Ockham in Fourteenth-century Perspective', in *From Ockham to Wyclif*, eds A. Hudson and M. Wilks, Oxford: Oxford University Press, pp. 51–61.

Wood, R. E. (1966) 'The Self and the Other: Toward a Re-interpretation of the Transcendentals', in *Philosophy Today*, 10: pp. 48–63.

Wood, S. (1998) *Spiritual Exegesis and the Church in the Theology of Henri de Lubac*, Edinburgh: T. and T. Clark.

Woznicki, A. N. (1990) *Being and Order*, New York: Peter Lang.

Yovel, Y. (1989) *Spinoza and Other Heretics*, vol. 1, Princeton: Princeton University Press.

Zedler, B. (1948) 'Saint Thomas and Avicenna in the *De Potentia Dei*', in *Traditio*, 6: pp. 105–160.

— (1976) 'Another Look at Avicenna', in *New Scholasticism*, 50: pp. 504–521.

— (1981) 'Why are the Possibles Possible?', in *New Scholasticism*, 55: pp. 113–131.

Žižek, S. (1996) *Indivisible Remainder: An Essay on Schelling and Related Matters*, London: Verso.

— (1997) 'The Abyss of Freedom', introductory essay to F. Schelling *The Abyss of Freedom and Ages of the World*, Ann Arbor: University of Michigan Press, pp. 3–104.

— (1999) *The Ticklish Subject*, London: Verso.

— (2001) *On Belief*, London and New York: Routledge.

INDEX

exitus 4, 8, 111, 123, 125, 240, 250, 265, 273
Fabro, Cornelio 8, 33, 125, 127, 185, 203, 211, 217, 233
facticity 135
factualised 55–56
factuality 19, 50, 55–56
faith without belief 245
faith-tradition 229–232, 237; see also tradition
Fang, J. 268
Fay, T. 211
Feder-Garve review (Göttingen) 99
Felstiner, J. 131, 150, 153–154
Feuerbach, Ludwig 183
Fichte, Johann Gottlieb xii, 94, 97–98, 123, 236, 249–250
fideism 274
finality, open 187, 195–196, 222, 226, 229, 264–265
Findlay, J. N. 126
finite, the 7–8, 30–33, 102–105, 108–110, 115–121, 123–124, 161; as aspectually afforded 109, 119; as an expression of the absolute 120; as ideal 115; as the infinite 110–111; as unavailable 123; untruth of 109–110; see also particular
finitude 7–8, 109–112, 221; indefinite 173
form 21, 189–190, 194–196, 199–200, 222; as act 189; as open 199; plenitude of 260; substantial 28, 221
formal distinction 20–21, 27, 91, 93–94, 119, 124
forms, plurality of 21–23, 28, 177
Foucault, Michel xv, xviii, 176, 209
foundational circumscription 7, 156, 161, 230
fourfold interpretation 204
Fuchs, O, 57
Funkenstein, Amos 38, 68, 73

Gadamer, Hans–Georg xv, 33, 131, 150
Gamow, G. 177
Garcia-Rivera, Alejandro 214
Gardet, Louis, 10–11, 13, 35–36
Geertz, Clifford 151
Geiger, L.B. 233
Geist xiv, 100–101, 104–108, 237, 254, 263

Gelber, H.G. 38
genome xiv
Gerson, L.P. 33
Gestalt xiv, 6, 32
Ghent, Henry of xv, 3, 5, 13–17, 19, 27, 29, 36–37, 39, 41, 171, 185
Gill, Eric 194, 214
Gillespie, Michael xviii, 38, 41, 269–270
Gilson, Étienne 6, 8–11, 16–17, 25, 27–28, 33, 35, 37–39, 41–42, 50–53, 58, 93, 98, 125, 129, 194, 197, 199, 205, 210–212, 214–216
Glenn, J. 153
gnosis 222
Gnostics 4–5
God 8, 41, 47–56, 59–71, 85–86, 90–94, 97–98, 101–104, 108–110, 125–127, 149–150, 168, 170, 172, 180, 182–192, 194, 196–198, 203–204, 210–213, 219–227, 229, 236, 245, 249, 257–260, 264–266, 270; as absolute person; as absolute substance 103; as *actus purus* 189, 191, 219; act of to-be 19; as both cause and principle of creation 183; creates out of love 198; derived from the word *theaste* 192; as difference 224; as essenceless 11–123; as *ipsum esse* 219; as light 192, 197, 215; as love 192, 224–225, 265; as *non aliud* 102, 225, 264; as non-God, 260, 265; the Son of 173, 191, 196–198, 204, 206, 224, 226, 228–229; without being 245; see also Christ, omnipotence, Word
Gödel, Kurt, 274
Goethe, Johann Wolfgang von 232
Goichon, A.M. 9–10, 12, 34–36
Good, the 33, 67, 193–196; as the final cause 223; as a transcendental 193
Goodchild, Philip 31, 43
Good Friday 200, 204; displacement of 204–205
Goris, Harm 10–11, 26, 34–35, 42
Grajewski, Maurice 39
Grant, E. 39
Gregory of Nyssa 30, 217, 221–222, 232, 264–265, 272

Guénon, René 29, 173, 176, 194,
208–209, 214, 216, 234, 253, 270
Gundissalinus, Dominicus 34
Guyer, P. 97

habit (*habitus*) 45, 48
hacceity 21
hairesis 171
Hallett, M. 239
Hallward, P. 257, 271
Hamacher, Werner 154
Hamann, Johann Georg 92, 98–99,
183, 207, 224, 258–259
Harland, R. 158, 164
Harris, H.S. 126
Hart, C. 211
Harvey, A. 126
heautonomy 86–87
Hegel, Georg Wilhelm Friedrich xii,
xiv, 32, 63, 70–74, 94, 100–129,
141, 150–152, 157, 159, 172,
178–179, 183, 196, 209, 228,
236–237, 249, 251, 253–254
Heidegger, Martin xii–xiii, xvi–xvii, 3,
72, 74, 112, 125, 128, 131–142,
146–155, 164, 209, 236–237, 250,
258, 270
Heine, H. 71
Hell 173
Helsinki School 40
hen xiv, 33
henology 8, 33
Henrich, D. 96
Henry, Michel 121, 125, 221
Heraclitean-stasis 172, 215, 227–228,
230
Hebert, George 266–267
Herder, Johann Gottfired von 259
Hesiod 3–5
hic et nunc 48; loss of 23
Hilary of Poitiers 215
Hintikka, Jaakko 40
Hissette, R. 40
Hitler 208
Hoeres, W. 39
Hogrebe, Wolfran 109, 127
Hölderlin, Friedrich 147
holocaust, a 68, 73, 173–175, 249
Holocaust, the 142–145, 153
Holy Spirit 204, 224, 227, 229, 264; as
second difference 224, 226
Holy Thursday 202, 204–206

homunculus fallacy 274
Hume, David 75, 84, 99, 211, 229;
problem of eternal moments
228–229, 251
Husserl, Edmund xvii, 135, 157,
163–164
Hyman, A. 40
hymen 159

idea adaequata 61, 63–64
ideas 172; as connotative terms 18–20;
deontologised 37; divine 13–20, 37,
163, 189–192, 199, 202
imaginatio 9
imagination 80–82
immanence 4, 8, 105; discounting
245–247; mediated by
transcendence 173; plane of 250
imitability, divine 13–16, 18, 38, 173,
190–192
imperatives 85; categorical 85, 96;
hypothetical 85
Incarnation, the 193, 198, 200,
202–204, 259
incompleteness theorem, Gödel's 274
incompossibility of terms 24–25
indeterminate, the, 250, 262–263
infinite, the 6, 29–33, 42–43, 94, 105,
108–112, 115, 117–125, 250–251,
264; intensive 30–31, 43
infinity 20, 26–31, 263, 264; external
62; internal 62, 65; as negative
perfection 29; as a positive
perfection 29; as a quantitative term
29–31; as a relational property 29
insignification 238
intellect 3, 10, 44–45, 59, 219; divine
18, 24; as the faculty of the other
220
intuition 77–81, 85; a pure manifold
of 80; space and time as pure forms
of 77–83
in-visibility 194, 207, 221; as the
visible 221
ipsum esse 108, 219
irreducible reminder 258

Jacob, F. 31, 209, 246, 269
Jacobi, F. H. 71, 90, 94, 97–98, 100,
125, 169, 236, 273
Jacobi, Klaus 24, 26, 37, 40–41
Jaeschke, W. 101, 125–126